KU-591-653

Cromwell

An Honourable Enemy

The untold story of the Cromwellian invasion of Ireland

TOM REILLY

BRANDON

Published in 1999 by
Brandon
an imprint of Mount Eagle Publications Ltd.
Dingle, Co. Kerry, Ireland

10 9 8 7 6 5 4 3 2 1

Copyright © Tom Reilly, 1999

The author has asserted his moral rights

ISBN 0 86322 250 1

This book is sold subject to the condition that it shall not, by way of trade or
otherwise, be lent, resold, hired out or otherwise circulated without the publisher's
prior consent in any form of binding or cover other than that in which it is published
and without a similar condition being imposed on the subsequent purchaser.

Cover painting: Cromwell by unknown artist,
courtesy of National Portrait Gallery, London
Cover design: Public Communications Centre, Dublin
Typesetting: Red Barn Publishing, Skeagh, Skibbereen
Printed by Betaprint, Dublin

FOREWORD

The subject of this book still arouses a great deal of contention. Cromwell has long since secured his place in Irish history as a bloodthirsty maniac and a religious fanatic. His visit to Ireland has been studied in enormous detail through the centuries, but never like this. I have been frequently asked if anything new can actually be said about his Irish campaign of 1649–50. The following pages certainly tell a different story of Cromwell in Ireland.

The focus of this book is to exculpate Cromwell from the charges of wholesale and indiscriminate slaughter of the ordinary unarmed people of Ireland. The question of Cromwell's guilt preoccupied many of the last century's historians. Their verdict was a resounding cry of guilty! Cromwell is once again in the dock here, but this time the evidence of the day is assessed in the legal sense, 'without prejudice'. I first noticed numerous historical anomalies concerning the period during research for my book *Cromwell at Drogheda* in 1993. Since then I have attempted to peel away the layers of tradition to reveal the facts about Cromwell's Irish mission. It was patently evident that all was not right with many documented versions of the events. While the period is left continually unrevised, the dubious traditional viewpoint is now generally accepted as authentic. I have discovered aspects to this whole period that do not fit in with the traditional version, parts of which are completely devoid of any factual basis. I had certainly stumbled on to something. The social and economic implications of the Cromwellian campaign are largely ignored here as they are, by now, very well documented.

Three hundred and fifty years have now passed since Cromwell landed at Ringsend in August 1649. It is well past time that his Irish mission is seen in the context of his times.

To Frances and Noel

Acknowledgements

The contentious nature of my version of this subject requires that I display source reference numbers with the accompanying endnotes. My chief motivation for it was a brief encounter with Jason McElligott. Thank you Jason. Eddie Quinn's enthusiasm and constructive criticism was inspirational. My parents, Paddy and Mary Reilly gave me a great deal of support during its compilation. My wife, Noeleen, and my two children, Cathy and Eoin, all deserve medals for both their patience and toleration of my sometimes arbitrary negligence of family quality time. Dr Micheál Ó Siochrú's lecture and comments were also an (unintentional) encouragement. Rev. Jim Nelson read my first draft and advised me accordingly. In Wexford I have to thank Grainne Rafferty for her patience during my tour of Wexford in which she participated. Also Celestine Rafferty who is attached to both the Wexford Historical Society and the local library, and who gave me so much of her time and assistance. In Clonmel I must thank Mrs Margaret Rossiter for a wonderful tour of the town. I must also thank Bob Withers, who is involved with the Museum in Clonmel and whose enthusiasm was a breath of fresh air. I must not forget Mary Henry MA who clarified some of my queries concerning Clonmel. I also appreciate the help I received from Marie Boland in the library at Clonmel who was so good to me. Lillian Barraud of the Cromwell Museum, Huntingdon must also get a mention. My debates with John Dunne also helped to sustain the project, as did the support I received from Una Sheehan. Harold O'Sullivan and Fr Gerry Rice; both read this narrative when it was in its infancy and I owe them a great debt for their reassurance. Donald and Deirdre Murphy both offered me their professional opinions for which I am very grateful. I would like also to thank Ruth Illingworth, Dept of Modern History, St Patrick's College, Maynooth, for her assistance and advice. I am also indebted to Dr. Kevin McKenny, whose expert knowledge of the period and magnanimous help was also much appreciated. Finally, my project became complete when I received the approval of Prof. Ray Gillespie, also of Maynooth, and Dr. Peter Gaunt, of the History Department, Chester University, and chairman of the Cromwell Association, both of whose recognition of this work I was more than pleased to secure. None of these people are responsible for what I have written.

INTRODUCTION

F ROM HUNTINGDON HIGH Street North, it is a five minute trip
through Godmanchester to the A14 and a further thirty
minute drive south to Stansted Airport. A fifty minute flight
west to Dublin and another thirty minute drive, this time north on
the N1, lies the town of Drogheda. On the approach to the town just
under the railway bridge, 'Cromwell's Lane' is barely noticeable on
the left. A final five minute walk down this lane is 'Cromwell's
Mount', on the precipice of the glen called the Dale, directly opposite St Mary's Church of Ireland church. Travelling time – approximately two hours.

In August 1649, a native of Huntingdon, England, formerly a country squire and lately an officer in the English army, then residing in
London, made this same trip by contemporary transport. He travelled
on horseback to Bristol and Milford Haven, then via sailing ship to
Ringsend, Dublin, and finally on horseback again to that same spot on
the brink of the Dale valley at Drogheda. Travelling time – approximately two weeks.

Oliver Cromwell arrived at Drogheda on the day that would eventually be called his 'lucky day', 3 September. He was accompanied by
12,000 Roundhead troops and spent twelve days in and around the
town. When his business was done there, he returned to Dublin with
the future of his rebel Commonwealth government considerably
brighter for having recaptured that town of the Pale.

He left in his wake a scene of unprecedented carnage. The defending garrison were slaughtered almost to a man, the mortality level totalling approximately 3,000. From Drogheda he marched to Wexford where a similar scene of destruction took place. He was to spend a total of nine months in Ireland, including a winter break, and ending in the heaviest defeat of his military career at Clonmel, where as well as suffering significant losses, he was cleverly outfoxed by the crafty Irish Royalists.

However, under the regulations of contemporary warfare, his actions towards Drogheda's militia cannot be reproached. At Wexford his army killed the garrison under circumstances that were not within the parameters of regular warfare. Yet, the grim consequences were not unfamiliar in an already war-torn country.

The battles of Drogheda and Wexford could be seen as exceptionally appalling. But they are not isolated events. They were both significant military encounters in the progression of the struggle between the English Parliament and their tyrannical King, Charles I, which extended into the temporary prevention of the return of the monarchy. This was a war that would claim the lives of about a third of the population of Ireland. Famine and disease became widespread. Marauding armies were living off the land. The battles for these two Royalist garrisons had an extra incentive for Parliament, as victory would also mean widespread land acquisition. The annihilation of the military defenders of both towns was not exceptional by seventeenth century military practices.[1] Parliamentary massacres of Confederate forces, including civilians and clergy, were a well established practice in 1640s Ireland by the time Cromwell had arrived.

A significant distinction can be made between the battles in Ireland and those in England at this time. The engagements in Ireland involved much more ferocity than those in England during the Civil War there. English men fought against English men at Edgehill, Marston Moor and Naseby. In Ireland the conflict was significantly more complicated. The consequences of a religious struggle between two nations, coupled with greed for land, introduced a double dose of viciousness and immorality to the Irish wars. Human lives were much less precious than religious ideals and fertile acreage during the fierce fighting on Irish soil.

In 1649, the responsibility of the continuation of Parliamentary rule in England rested solidly on Cromwell's shoulders. Failure in Ireland would have been catastrophic for him. To be exposed by long sieges in an unfamiliar country could have signalled defeat, a scenario that he could not countenance. Indeed it would eventually transpire, with the exception of the battle of Clonmel, that 'country sickness' (dysentery) was to prove more detrimental to the New Model Army than the inadequate united forces of the Confederates.

Cromwell was not defeated at Drogheda, nor was there any real likelihood that he would be. Successive writers have suggested that at the height of the battle he was to have one decidedly uneasy moment. They declare that the entire success of the revolution hung in the balance on the 11 September 1649 after two unsuccessful attempts were made on the breached walls. Cromwell was then compelled to lead the final assault himself to carry the New Model Army menacingly into the town. The facts are that he had much heavier fire power than the defenders, and his highly trained Roundhead army were in excellent attacking positions. It was inevitable that further assaults on the broken defences would have had a similar outcome. One of the reasons for the subsequent massacre was the Royalists' inability to conduct a coherent defence once the Puritans had entered the town. However, there remains the probability that mercy was offered, but then denied, when the defenders had laid down their arms.

A full appreciation of the facts surrounding Cromwell's sieges of Drogheda and Wexford will not change the everyday lives of those towns' current inhabitants. But an improved understanding of those facts will help them to appreciate these events that are very much part of their heritage. Indeed, our late twentieth century minds are extremely ill-equipped to understand the political and religious minefield that was the seventeenth century. Yet, it remains a sad fact that the perception of the battles of Drogheda and Wexford in modern Ireland is riddled with historical inaccuracies. This is the result of the plethora of nineteenth century misconstructions of the events from the pens of bigoted writers and from the subsequently unbalanced Irish educational system of the 20th century.[2]

The monstrous ideology of compulsory land acquisition and the continual ruthless suppression of the Irish for seven centuries by the British is beyond the scope of this narrative. These frightful concepts were an accepted part of contemporary life. Powerful nations continually subdued those that were weaker throughout the world. Bitter arguments concerning the torrid historical relationship between the two countries have been illustrated by a multitude of writers, and the future will inevitably furnish us with many more. An apolitical review of Cromwell's Irish campaign is long overdue. A modern objective analysis of Cromwell's time in Ireland, from an Irish perspective, is rare. That the townspeople of Drogheda were not indiscriminately massacred can now be virtually proved (inasmuch as it can be with the passing of 350 years). That many of the inhabitants of Wexford were killed during the sack of that town is certainly true. However, the town had no military garrison prior to the battle and only allowed Ormonde's defending troops access in the days preceding the siege. Many of the defending forces that were killed were civilian volunteers in military posture. Cromwell's entire Irish mission was fought on a purely military basis, and it is to his enormous credit that he never once departed from those parameters. These facts have been in the public domain for some years. Yet, as unpalatable revisionism, they appear to be condemned to the dusty shelves of academic obscurity.

Recently, theories have been abroad (albeit inconspicuously) that Cromwell was not the monster that we had once thought. So far however, these estimations have received only a low profile. Ironically most of this speculation has actually been emanating from the Drogheda area. Local historians like Rice,[3] O'Sullivan[4] and myself[5] have argued that it appears less and less likely that Drogheda's civilians were indiscriminately massacred by Cromwell's Ironside army. Other more prominent writers have also advocated the same speculation: Jeremy Black states that no civilians were killed at Drogheda or Wexford[6], and Peter Gaunt is suspicious of the allegations of civilian deaths.[7] Conversely, Roy Foster concurs with the traditional belief,[8] and Jason McElligott is also unconvinced of Cromwell's innocence.[9] Basically the current state of research on the period is inconclusive. One cannot deny that whatever really happened at Drogheda and Wexford can never now be accurately told; but with the use of eyewitness accounts and logical evaluation of all of the contemporary evidence, a discerning appraisal can now be made. There is really no other way to arrive at a legitimate conclusion. This is the key to rejecting most of the previous interpretations of the period. Evidence that has been previously scattered is submitted here in a structured fashion and for the first time. In general then, the current perception of the period has a maniacal image of Cromwell firmly embedded in the Irish psyche today as it has been for centuries.

It is true to say that the documenting of history in seventeenth century Ireland was politicised at its very source. The written word was conceived by, and directed at, the politically motivated literate classes, which represented a relatively small portion of the population. Consequently, even contemporary records are unreliable. Conclusions must be drawn with extreme caution following meticulous investigation. Writers of the day would publish outlandish lies, without the blink of an eye, if it meant that their enemies' reputation would look worse as a result of it!

Children in Irish schools today are still subjected to unbalanced history lessons. *Focus on the Past 2* by Gerard Brockie and Raymond Walsh was published by Gill and Macmillan in 1990. Using what they describe as an account of an English army officer (presumably the anonymous British officer of Sir John Clotworthy's regiment) they declare: 'Once the Irish were defeated they were all cut down and killed and no mercy was shown to man, woman or child for twenty four hours. Not a dozen escaped out of Drogheda, townspeople or soldiers.' In 1995 a book entitled *Ireland – A Graphic History* by Michael Scott and Morgan Llywelyn was published also by Gill and Macmillan. Chapter 7 deals with Cromwell's siege of Drogheda: 'Puritan priests . . . from the pulpit . . . exhorted the invading army to kill all that were young and old, children and maidens . . . the civilians of Drogheda were also being slaughtered . . . Some apologists claim Cromwell did not actually order a massacre, but the infamous comment "Nits make Lice" used to justify the murder of infants, speaks for itself.' Both of these selective accounts are quite extreme and totally inaccurate. When they are extracted from context and recklessly directed at children, it is most unfortunate.

Understanding Oliver Cromwell the man will facilitate an understanding of his actions in Ireland. Unfortunately his enigmatic personality is not readily discovered. As the Royalists reviled Cromwell, so did the Parliamentarians revere him. It is certainly the case that after diligent research one could easily conclude that he was either a highly respected, compassionate and decent man, or else a vile, unscrupulous black-hearted tyrant!

Three hundred and fifty years on, most Irish people remember Cromwell as the latter. His association with Drogheda and Wexford has left an indelible mark, one that can evoke emotion in a country that can still be inspired by its history. The Drogheda and Wexford massacres of

1649 are largely remembered as the indiscriminate slaughter of the respective garrisons, including the bulk of the civilian populations on the direct orders of a heinous monster who detested everything Catholic and, therefore, everything Irish. While this viewpoint may not occasion surprise, there are two irrefutable observations that may be made concerning its basis. Firstly, it is the result of colourful, historical indoctrination, infiltrated by prejudice, folklore and myth. Secondly, it is an absurd perception taken completely out of the authentic context of seventeenth century politics and Cromwell's Irish campaign. The contempt with which he is regarded in Ireland today is largely a consequence of the savage plantation of 1650s Ireland, over which he presided as Lord Protector. His notoriety could easily be earned for his part in the hostile transplantation of many Irish landowners 'to Hell or to Connaught'. Yet, his image remains as the slayer of countless civilians, as he exploded like a blast from Hell on an unsuspecting native Irish population. The fact is, Cromwell had no quarrel with civilians, nor did he involve those who were unarmed in the hostilities of warfare. Indeed, his military adversaries in Ireland were essentially fighting for the return of their precious King, with whom they might negotiate their future – not exactly the most 'Irish' of causes. His disreputable image in battle, on a comparative, contemporary basis, is completely without foundation. Although the revolution in which he was involved was ultimately to fail at the restoration of the monarchy, Cromwell was in actual fact the first successful English military conqueror of Ireland as well as the unpopular killer of the King in England. It is easy to see how, after his death, his Irish campaign was torn to shreds and completely rewritten. There was no shortage of Royalist cynics in either his native country or on the island of Ireland, only too eager to reinvent his Irish exploits. With our late twentieth century eyes, he is an exceptionally easy target. In the context of the seventeenth century, however, the story takes on a different slant.

From a distance of 350 years, the perception of Cromwell that has emerged from Irish history is a profound perversion of the facts. His suppression of the Irish Royalists' threat to the ruling English government and the ruthless colonisation of Ireland were not unique ambitions in Ireland's tempestuous history. Many English commanders of like mind came before him, and many would come afterwards. The legend of his personal involvement in civilian atrocities is just that, a legend. He was, in actual fact, a most honourable enemy. This is one of those peculiar periods in history where it suited both parties involved in the conflict to exaggerate the facts.

Approximately three thousand combatants lay dead on the streets of Drogheda following his departure, most of them killed 'not resisting'. However, the theory concerning the alleged wholesale deaths of the town's inhabitants amounts to mythological bunkum. The hapless besieged had forfeited their right to live by refusing to surrender to the formidable besiegers. The contemporary dictum of battle, where a besieged fort must be prepared to die if they failed to surrender when summoned by an attacking force, should the latter succeed in gaining entry, was not seen as a senseless loss of life. Lives would be saved on both sides by the surrender of the defending garrison, but no mercy was to be expected to one that resisted. A besieging force would be exposed to the sometimes atrocious rigours of nature, and deaths from disease and exposure would be inevitable even without fighting. In 1649 and for centuries afterwards, no quarter could be expected under these circumstances. The annihilation of a belligerent defending garrison was not, therefore, seen as a useless effusion of blood. What is manifestly clear is that Cromwell is nowhere on record as having ordered an indiscriminate slaughter of noncombatants during any battle in his life.

It is also arguable that his opposition to Catholicism was largely based on political, more so than theological principles. It must be remembered that in the seventeenth century Catholicism was essentially a political movement and not just a religious belief. Those difficulties that the Puritans had with the Roman faith were deep rooted in doctrinal incompatibilities. They were also intensified by the government mechanism in the church and the abuses that had resulted in the Reformation. He himself declared, on more than one occasion that he would not 'meddle with any man's conscience'. The complexities of the prevailing political and religious conditions of the day, including the turbulent aftermath of the King's execution and the evocative memory of the brutal Irish rising of 1641–42, also stimulated the train of events in Ireland in late 1649.

The Drogheda that Cromwell encountered was effectively not an 'Irish' town. English rule was long established in the Pale. Drogheda was founded by the Anglo-Normans in the 12th century, and its inhabitants had always conformed to the English design. In common with many of the urban centres of the Pale, by 1649 many of the inhabitants were Old English Catholic. These were mostly descendants of those original Anglo-French settlers, many of whom had integrated into their new society and become 'more Irish than the Irish themselves'. In certain areas they adopted local traditions and customs and subsisted in what was fundamentally a Celtic manner. Their allegiances were generally directed towards England since it was from here that they could procure improvements to circumstances within their societies and consequently their lifestyles. Irrespective of their level of assimilation, they had also become great land and property owners since the time of the Conquest. The Irish rebel Sir Phelim O'Neill would try to capture Drogheda during the unsuccessful siege of 1641–42 as it was one of the major English enclaves that held out from the rebellious native Irish. Some 15,000–20,000 rebels blockaded the town in which there was a defensive garrison of 2,000. Despite this numerical advantage, the combination of a harsh winter and lack of heavy artillery doomed the attempt to failure. While some of the citizens shared the rebels' religion, they were not about to lose their properties or land to the recently hostile Irish. Those that were supportive of the insurrectionists either fled or were expelled from the town. The government made a clear distinction between the Old Catholic lords of the Pale and the Gaelic Irish Catholics. The majority of the population of Drogheda fiercely adhered to whatever English government held power in Ireland, whether Royalist or Parliamentarian. From 1641–47 the town was held by a garrison of Protestant Royalists under the jurisdiction of the Earl of Ormonde. From 1647 to 11 July 1649 it was under the control of Michael Jones, the Parliamentarian governor of Dublin.[10] The two main church buildings in 1649 were of Protestant British origin. Despite the fact that Catholics predominated, their religion was still a suppressed faith and imprisonment or fines were frequently inflicted on its members. Conversely, in a town of such a partisan constitution, the practice of Catholicism had a generous toleration level throughout the town. An English Protestant traveller by the name of Brerton visited Drogheda in 1634. He tells us that Drogheda was:

> . . . governed by a Mayor, Sheriffs, and twenty-four Aldermen; most of these as also the other inhabitants of the town are popishly affected, inasmuch as those that have been chosen Mayors, who for the most part have been recusants,

have hired others to discharge that office . . . and the reason why they make coy to execute that office is because they
will avoid being necessitated to go to church.[11]

It appears that priorities among the townspeople clearly lay with the
various occupants of the throne in preference to their religious ideals.
As an international trading centre within the Pale, fidelity was always
shown to whomsoever held power in London, in order for the town to
prosper. Drogheda had as its motto, *'Deus praesidium, mereatura decus'*
– 'God is our strength, merchandise our glory'.[12] Dean Nicholas
Bernard, a preacher at St Peter's Drogheda in the 1640s, writes that
the Protestants of the town were only able to muster 120–140 armed
men in that same year.[13] The town's Irish section was confined to a
small area of the town known as Irish Street, and larger numbers were
reduced to living in cabins outside the defensive walls. The English
cause had always been well represented within the walls of Drogheda.

However, the English Crown in 1649 found itself without a head on
which to rest. Charles I was beheaded by his exasperated Parliament on
30 January of that year. When the new Commonwealth turned its
attention to Ireland in order to quash the very real menace of a formidable Royalist Irish attack, Drogheda was the first town to become
embroiled in the hostilities.

Notes to Introduction

1   It is obvious that many of the commanding officers on both sides of the con-
     flict in Ireland, between 1640–1653 were much more ruthless than Cromwell.
     See Maire and Conor Cruise O'Brien, *A Concise History of Ireland* (London:
     Thames & Hudson, 1972), p. 68, who argue:'From a military point of view,
     the ferocity of Cromwell and his successors in Ireland, Ireton and Ludlow
     was not extraordinary by seventeenth century military standards. The action
     of Cromwell's which lingers in the folk memory – the sack of Drogheda – was
     hardly more ferocious or macabre than that of Cashel by Murrough O'Brien,
     Earl of Inchiquin in 1646.'

2   See Toby Barnard, "Irish Images of Cromwell", *Images of Cromwell, Essays for
     and by Roger Howell Jr.*, edited by R.C. Richardson, (Manchester: University
     Press, 1993), pp. 180–206, who states that Cromwell's fearsome reputation
     was 'apparently a nineteenth century construct'. See also Jason McElligott,
     Cromwell Our Chief of Enemies (Dundalk: Dun Dealgan Press, 1994). He
     argues that Cromwell's dreadful reputation was created by Irish nationalists
     in the nineteenth century, mainly for corrupt political reasons. He writes;
     'changing perceptions of Cromwell in nineteenth century Ireland seem to

have been based largely upon the folk memory of the illiterate classes'. The two main culprits in this regard would be the Rev. Denis Murphy, SJ, *Cromwell in Ireland, A History of Cromwell's Irish Campaign* (Dublin: M.H. Gill & Son, 1883), and John P. Prendergast, *The Cromwellian Settlement of Ireland* (Dublin: Longman Green, 1865; re-issued: London: Constable and Co., 1996).

3   Rev. Gerard Rice, "The Five Martyrs", *Riocht Na Midhe, Records of Meath Archaeological and Historical Society*, vol. ix, no. 3 (1997), pp. 102–27.

4   Harold O'Sullivan, "Cromwell, No Evidence of Drogheda Massacre", *Drogheda Independent*, Friday, 1 October 1993.

5   Tom Reilly, *Cromwell at Drogheda* (Drogheda: Broin Print Ltd, 1993), Introduction and p. 62.

6   Jeremy Black, *History of the British Isles* (Basingstoke: MacMillan, 1996), p. 131.

7   Peter Gaunt, *Oliver Cromwell* (Oxford: Blackwell, 1996), p. 117; 'Even at Drogheda, the slaughter was not complete or indiscriminate. There are few indications that women and children died, and unarmed male civilians who were not playing any active role in the defence of the town seem in general to have survived.'

8   Roy Foster, *Modern Ireland 1600–1972* (London: Penguin, 1989), p.102.

9   Jason McElligot, *Cromwell our Chief of Enemies*, pp. 42–43.

10   William F. Butler emphasises the point in "Some Episodes of the Civil War of 1641–53", *County Louth Archaeological and Historical Journal*, vol. IV, no. 4 (1919), p. 285. See also C.W. Russell and J.P. Prendergast, *The Carte Manuscripts in the Bodleian Library* (London: H.M.S.O., 1871), p. 132, who highlight the change of military occupancy: 'There was resident in Drogheda just before the siege of 1649, the Lady Tichbourne, wife of Sir Henry Tichbourne, who had been the governor of the town at the outbreak of the Irish Rebellion in October 1641, and defended it during its four month's siege by Sir Phelim O'Neill and his Ulster forces, finally routing them in the month of march 1642. Sir Henry Tichbourne, being a steadfast Royalist, was for that cause removed by the Parliament Commissioners after Ormonde's surrender of Dublin in 1647.'

11   "A Seventeenth Century Description Of Drogheda", *Journal of the Old Drogheda Society*, no. 3 (1978–79), p. 31.

12   Susan O'Connor, "Tudor Drogheda 1534–1603", *Journal of the Old Drogheda Society*, no 10 (1996), p. 91.

13   Dean Nicholas Bernard, *The whole proceedings of the siege of Drogheda in Ireland with a thankful rememberance for its wonderful delivery, printed by command of the House of Commons, 14 July 1642*, quoted in W.F. Butler, "Some Episodes of the Civil War", *County Louth Archaeological and Historical Society Journal*, vol. IV, no. 4 (1919), p. 286.

Chapter One

IRELAND

'. . . for all the world knows of their barbarism'
(Cromwell, speaking about the Irish Rebels)

OLIVER CROMWELL WAS born on the northern edge of Huntingdon High Street, at 1.30am on 25 April 1599. John Speed's 1610
map of the small town of Huntingdon depicts the house on the
outskirts of the town with a modest enclosure at the rear, as does Thomas
Jefferys' 1768 plan.[1] The original building has been demolished and on
the site is the 'Cromwell Clinic' which today functions as a private hospital. Above the doorway is a large colourful reproduction of the
Cromwell coat of arms, underneath which is written the inscription,
'OLIVER CROMWELL BORN HERE 25 APRIL 1599'. He was the
fifth child and second son of Robert and Elizabeth Cromwell. Four days
later he was baptised almost directly across the road in the church of St
John the Baptist (now a small public park). Of the ten children born to
his parents, seven survived, leaving him the only boy among six girls. A
two minute walk up the street, facing the marketplace, was the Huntingdon Grammar School where he was first educated. Today the building survives and houses the Cromwell Museum.

It was at this school that the young Cromwell met a man who was
to have a very influential impact on his life, the renowned Puritan, Dr
Thomas Beard. In 1597, Beard had published *The Theatre of God's
Judgements*, maintaining that earthly transgressions are always
punished by the Almighty, either in this world or the next. To Thomas

Beard, the Pope was the Antichrist. It was under 'the diligent hand and careful eye'[2] of this man that the impressionable Cromwell was educated. Modern historians have played down Beard's Puritan influence on Cromwell but it has always been thought that his impact on the future Protector was not inconsiderable.[3]

Thomas Cromwell, Earl of Essex, Henry VIII's suppressor of the monasteries, is often confused with Oliver as the surname gradually became synonymous with religious oppression. While they were in fact direct relations, Oliver's family stock was quite the poorer of the two. Thomas Cromwell's sister married one Morgan Williams, and their eldest son, Richard, took the name of Cromwell. Richard's son, Henry, built Hinchingbrooke House, on the outskirts of Huntingdon. (Today, the building is open to visitors at weekends.) Henry's son and heir, Oliver, inherited the mansion. Henry's second son, Robert, received a much less ostentatious estate on Huntingdon High Street North, which was worth about £300 a year. It was Robert's son, Oliver, named after his uncle, owner of Hinchingbrooke, who was to become the destroyer of the garrisons of Drogheda and Wexford and the Lord Protector of the Commonwealth.

Considering his achievement in becoming supreme ruler of England, Ireland and Scotland, and refusing the kingship on two occasions, his origins were extremely modest. He would later remark, 'I was by birth a Gentleman, living neither in any considerable height nor yet in obscurity'.[4] This small-time gentleman farmer would become the first civilian or commoner to rule the British Empire and the only one to ever hold a position of such power. Although relatively little is recorded about his formative years, we know he entered Sydney Sussex College, Cambridge ('a hotbed of Puritanism')[5] on 23 April 1616, the day Shakespeare departed this world. His later physician, Dr George Bate, would remark, that during his time at college he 'laid an unsolid foundation of learning at Cambridge where he enjoyed robust health . . . being famous for football, cricket, cudgelling and wrestling'.[6] In the following year, when his father died on 24 June 1617, he cut short his college career to assume responsibility for the family. With him as the new head of the family, an intimate family bond would develop among the Cromwells, and in particular he became very close to his mother, a woman of exceptional integrity, for whom he maintained an inordinate amount of respect. She would predecease him by only four years, at the remarkable age of 89, in 1654.

No records exist concerning his life from 1617 to 1620; however it is likely that he studied law at Lincoln's Inn like his father before him.[7] Even though he spent such a short time at college, education was not lost on Oliver Cromwell. It is apparent from his writings and speeches throughout his life that his command of the English language was extremely proficient. His eloquent words, although sometimes used to describe terrible deeds, were always expressed in a masterly and exquisite form of prose.

Royalist writers gleefully filled in the gaps in his early years with stories of intemperance and debauchery since the facts were conveniently insubstantial. Their accusations were facilitated by Cromwell's own description of his lifestyle before his 'newbirth'. In 1638, Cromwell would undergo a profound spiritual conversion after many years of depression and soul searching. In 1628 Sir Theodore de Mayerne, a doctor whose patients included the King, described him as being '*valde melancholicus*' or highly melancholic.[8] He was also said to be 'a most splenetic man and hypochondriacal' by his own doctor, John Symcotts, at Huntingdon around this time.[9] He would now emerge from this depressive state to embrace the consummate power and the will and grace of God. In future, he would interpret every thought and deed with reference to the Almighty. This 'rebirth' was by no means uncommon among Cromwell's Puritan contemporaries and does not necessarily imply religious fanaticism, despite many modern day allegations. In 1638, he would write to his cousin describing the poor condition of his former self: 'You know what my manner of life hath been? Oh, I lived in and loved darkness and hated the light; I was chief, the chief of sinners. This is true; I hated Godliness, yet God had mercy on me. Oh riches of his mercy.'[10] This intense self-portrait of one who was lost, only to be saved, is typical of Puritan religious expression and can by no means be taken as revealing evidence of a dissolute past. It merely highlights his personal comparison between a previous existence, steeped in spiritual darkness, and his joy in experiencing what for him was an overwhelming religious transformation.

Puritan theology had its source in John Calvin's 'Pure' religious theories, an extension of the doctrines of the German Protestant reformer Martin Luther. Luther could find no passage in the Bible that could justify the existence of the Pope, hence his motivation for a reformed Church. Also at the heart of the Calvinistic faith was the concept of 'Predestination'. Puritans believed that the events of their lives were already preordained by God. They were the designated portion of mankind that were touched by divine grace and personally selected for salvation. This they saw as the watchful eye and paternal hand of God in people's lives. Puritans possessed a real feeling of inner satisfaction because they were in communion with God and assured of their eternal reward. Furthermore, as Calvinists they saw it as their duty to establish what they called the Puritan 'Godly Party' in England committed to hard work and effort. They believed that the English were the chosen race. As soon as England as a whole was converted, then the reconversion of the whole world would be accomplished and Christ would come again.

This spiritual alteration in Cromwell's life, reflected in the core of Puritanism, was far from the dour perception of that faith that is implied in the modern day meaning of the word 'puritanical'. The traditional idea of Cromwell and his peers, being a sullen and sombre group was quite far from reality. Despite being a Puritan, Cromwell had, in fact, an excellent sense of humour. He was quite fond of a drink, he enjoyed music and had been known to dance late into the night at particular social events.

At the age of twenty-one he had the requisite social standing to marry the daughter of a city fur and leather magnate, Sir James Bourchier of Tower Hill, London. It is highly improbable that an affluent merchant would have allowed his daughter to marry a reprobate youth of the sort invented by his detractors. The marriage ceremony to Elizabeth Bourchier took place in the church of St Giles, Cripplegate, London, on 22 August 1620. They were to have eight children. In 1650, when Cromwell was on active service in Scotland, they would exchange letters in a mutual display of enduring affection, even after thirty years of married life. She would declare, 'my life is but half in your absence'[11] and he would reply, 'Thou art dearer to me than any other creature; let that suffice.'[12]

Eleven years and six children later the Cromwells moved to rented accommodation and farmland in the town of St Ives, about five miles from Huntingdon. He had already made his first foray on to the political stage when he became MP for Huntingdon in 1628. This would be Cromwell's lowest ever social standing, what could almost be called yeoman status. Not far away in London, Charles I was enveloped by the sumptuous trappings of richly decorated palace buildings with a plethora of servants, living in the very lap of extremely luxurious surrounds. How far away from all of this splendour was Oliver Cromwell as a mere land lessee in the sleepy town of St Ives, with the even sleepier River Ouse passing slowly by. Although the passing of twenty-odd years would see this tenant farmer replace the King and inherit the finery of royalty as the head of state, it was far from this grandeur that Oliver Cromwell was reared.

During this inauspicious period as a backwoods squire devoid of property and solid financial security, Cromwell (according to several biographers) contemplated emigration to the new Puritan world of America. However, in 1636 his fortunes were to change dramatically and put an end to his colonial ideas. His maternal uncle, Sir Thomas Steward, died leaving him an enormous inheritance of various properties and lands in and around the cathedral town of Ely. (The family house left to him still stands today and is now 'Cromwell House', a visitor centre and tourist office.) It was during his time at Ely that Cromwell would fight for the rights of the local fen people, who procured an aquatic living from the swamps and fenland that surrounded the Isle of Ely (named after the many eels in the area and called an isle, since the town was elevated above the marshy ground which flooded severely in winter). This he did, during the fen drainage dispute, which threatened the livelihoods of the local country folk, and it earned him the nickname of 'Lord of the Fens.'[13] He would prove, time and time again, that he had an 'impulsive love of justice'. Cromwell was now a member of the elite classes living in Ely and was elected the new MP for Cambridge in 1641.

Understanding Cromwell's campaign in Ireland requires a chronicle of the rebellion of the Irish in 1641 and the following eight violent years. It occurred at a time when England was on the brink of civil war. Ireland's bone of contention was English rule, as indeed was England's. Religious oppression and relentless plantations were Ireland's basis of difficulty with the throne. Unnecessary taxes and unfair Royal demand's were England's. Charles' England refused to acknowledge religious and civil liberties. Nonconformists had their ears cut off and their cheeks branded with red hot irons. Their properties were confiscated for the pleasure of the Crown and sometimes the owners were thrown into prison. England needed to be rescued from this terrible condition. The interconnection of circumstances between both conflicts at this time would eventually mature within a decade with Cromwell's arrival at Ringsend on 15 August 1649.

The civil war in Ireland began on 23 October 1641. Mary Tudor and her husband, Phillip of Spain, had encouraged English settlement in Ireland. Primarily, the war was the culmination of mounting opposition to the frequency with which Irish land was skilfully whisked away from the native Irish by new English settlers, and secondly, increasing oppression of their national religion, Catholicism, from the reign of Elizabeth in the sixteenth century. Pope Pius V did the Catholics of Ireland absolutely no favours by excommunicating Elizabeth I. In the sixteenth century Ireland became a danger spot where England's main European foe, Spain, could land forces and attack from the west. This Pope's actions helped cast Ireland's faithful Catholics into a struggle as a weaker nation against their militarily superior neighbours. James I, having ascended the throne in 1603, instigated the plantation of Ulster in 1609, bringing these new English settlers to the province.

The Flight of the Earls, O'Neill, O'Donnell and Maguire, to Europe in 1607 had left Ulster virtually undefended. The Scottish King James now encouraged both Scottish and English adventurers to settle in the fertile lands of Ulster. The six counties of Donegal, Derry, Fermanagh, Tyrone, Armagh and Cavan were to be examined for plantation purposes. According to Brehon law, ownership of the land belonged not to the ruler, but to the clan as a whole. It was English law, however, that was now to prevail. A person who claimed ownership of land must now prove that it was lawfully his, despite the fact that his ancestors had occupied the territory for centuries. And so a Commission of Inquiry was set up to examine the confiscated estates and travelled through the six counties calling before them local people to provide evidence concerning the ownership and value of 'their' lands. To the native Irish these tribunals, held in an alien manner and an alien tongue, proved disastrous since their claims, at best ambiguous, were doomed to failure. The Crown's claim to numerous Irish estates was cleverly established by the land-hungry English. Indeed it was not only the native Irish who were dispossessed at this time. Some of the Catholic Old English settlers (the original Loyalists) from previous British plantations now found themselves ruthlessly dislocated from their properties. In this way, four million acres were secured for the new colonists, and by 1618 there were 40,000 new English and Scottish settlers in Ulster.[14]

However, the impracticality of introducing a British colony into Ireland was continually obvious. The intrinsic differences between Saxon and Celt were never going to result in a peaceful environment. The countries were always too close geographically to co-exist independently of each other, yet they were worlds apart when it came to making agreements. The new settlers with their strange customs were always at the mercy of the more numerous Irish and were soon forced to arm their hired hands against the constant threat of attack. The Gaelic rulers now gone and the Elizabethan wars over, many of the Irish found themselves without an occupation and took to the woods in order to plunder the newcomers. Despite these flurries of hostile activity from the native Irish, the Ulster plantation was a relative success. Thirty reasonably peaceful years were to pass in Ireland, a fact that Cromwell would now be perfectly cognizant of as he indulged in his favourite sport of hawking, around the marshy fields of Ely.

The religious composition of the population of Ireland by the mid-seventeenth century was consequently quite an assortment of theological opinions. The links that Henry VIII and Elizabeth I (however tenuous) had with the Pope, meant that there were still many 'Old English' settlers, some of whom were Catholic, and others Protestant. The Scots who came to plant Ulster brought with them Presbyterianism. Indeed, the Protestant faith became so prominent that during an Irish Parliament held at Dublin Castle in 1613 there were 132 Protestant members compared with 100 Catholics.[15]

Religious allegiance at this period was of paramount importance. Catholic subjects of the Crown in Ireland and England had been perceived as having devotion to a foreign power, the Pope. The population of England was approximately five and a half million and of that number, about 20,000 were Catholics. James I was of the opinion that: 'As they are but half subjects, they can have but half privileges.'[16] Uniformity of religion was a Utopia much pursued by English monarchs, but never achieved. When James died in 1625 his son Charles became the first King of that name to ascend the throne. There would prove to be a marked difference between father and son when it came to the tough business of running the country.

Now as an industrious landowner and Member of Parliament for Cambridge, Cromwell kept abreast of the Irish situation through the newsbooks of the day. His idyllic views of an Ireland where the new settlers existed in perfect harmony with the natives, as beautifully picturesque as it was intensely naive, was about to be shattered. On 23 October 1641 Sir Phelim O'Neill, on behalf of the suppressed Catholic

Irish, issued a proclamation at Dungannon declaring the defence of Irish liberty. (See Appendix No. 1.1)

Earlier that month on 5 October, the Celtic leaders, Sir Phelim, Conor Maguire and Hugh Óg MacMahon, had met at Loughross, County Armagh, to plan the insurrection. A plan was designed simultaneously to capture the political nerve-centre of Dublin Castle and to retake control of Ulster. The Dublin plan was betrayed, and all the potential insurrectionists were captured and incarcerated before they had a chance to act. However, all over Ulster a series of local risings took place, and the houses and estates of the new settlers were subjected to synchronised attacks.

While England was preoccupied with the King's tyranny, the Irish Catholic rebels quickly gained ground and began to seize land countrywide. O'Neill, in his declaration, affirmed the continued loyalty of Roman Catholics to Charles I, but demanded free exercise of their religion and an immediate end to plantations. He also disclosed, on 4 November, that he possessed a document purporting to be the King's written approval for taking up arms which he duly published. Later at his trial he was to admit that the document was a forgery and that he had received no such official commission from the King. However, Charles' suspected attachment to the insurrection was magnified by Parliament in England in an effort to connect him with the abominable wickedness of Popery, making his image even more odious. So, in an effort to pacify his Puritan subjects, Charles issued a proclamation on 1 January 1642 denouncing the 'Irish rebels'.

Many terrible atrocities occurred during the Thirty Years' War, which continued till 1648. Reports of the capture of Magdeburg in Germany in 1631, for example, would have reached the Puritans of England, fuelling their hatred of Roman Catholics. The horror lasted two days. The leader of the Catholic Imperialists, Tilly, and his men were responsible for the deaths of 30,000 people. Women were exposed to the double sacrifice of virtue and life, many of them beheaded, and children were thrown on to the flames of burning buildings. Dr A.W. Ward declares that 'the nameless deeds of horror committed are only too well authenticated'.[17] Eoghan Ruadh O'Neill (Owen Roe), a grand-nephew of the former Earl of Tyrone, Hugh O'Neill, returned from Flanders in July 1642. An experienced and accomplished officer, he took over from his less respected kinsman, Sir Phelim, who now had a price on his head, as the supreme commander of the Irish forces.

Eoghan Ruadh was admired even by his enemies. His resolute qualities and ability to win men to his side made him one of the most gallant and skilful soldiers of his day. He was already one of the instigators of the uprising, working diligently behind the scenes in Europe before he even arrived in Ireland. His first act was to denounce the cruelties that had been practised by his predecessor and declared that if such barbarities were again perpetrated, he would immediately return to the Continent. He quickly initiated his own training scheme for the warrior clansmen of Ulster and soon cultivated them into a professional and competent armed force. By the end of that year, all of Ireland with the exception of Dublin and some scattered towns was back under Irish dominion.

The King's Viceroy in Ireland and head of the Royalist forces was the Earl of Ormonde, James Butler. Upon seeing a portrait of Butler, Cromwell would comment later that he looked more like a huntsman than a soldier. The earl was the head of the noble house of the Butlers of Kilkenny. Kilkenny Castle was their ancestral home. Educated in England, he was brought up in the Protestant faith and his family had always adhered to the English interest in Ireland. Consequently they were well rewarded by English rulers. Ormonde would prove to be a tenaciously loyal subject to Charles.

The discommoded new English planters were driven to seek shelter within the defensive walls of those fortresses not yet captured. Some escaped to the safety of Scotland and England, carrying tales of cruelty and suffering at the hands of the Irish. It was these descriptions of Irish Catholic savagery to Protestants that was to arouse intense anti-Irish and anti-Catholic feelings in England. Many instances are on record in the depositions of the English settlers now held in Trinity College, Dublin.[18] A large number of them were orchestrated to deepen the hostility felt in England for the Irish rebels. Streams of pamphlets poured out of Dublin (still held by the English) under such titles as: *A True and Credible Relation of the Massacre of English Protestants in Ireland – by a Gentleman who was an Eye-witness* or *More News from Ireland of the Bloody Practices and Proceedings of the Papists of that Kingdom.* Many of the culprits were graphically illustrated in these publications, wearing priestly habits while committing heinous acts. Certainly priests could circulate throughout their flocks, advocating theological justification for the rebellion.

This 'legend' of the bloody massacres of 1641 contributed enormously to Cromwell's Irish campaign. It was soon accepted as truth in England that English men, women and children were murdered in their beds, disembowelled, drowned or shot. Competitions were allegedly held to see who could hack the deepest into a living human body. Babies were supposedly ripped out of their mothers' bodies and impaled on Irish pikes. Atrocities were purported to have been committed indiscriminately, resulting in the deaths of hundreds of thousands of Protestants. The real death toll can not be accurately estimated. However, it is much more likely to have been a four figure number. Five thousand is generally the agreed figure. The irony is that the same number of Catholics lost their lives during the same period.

Naturally the Irish did not have it all their own way. Ormonde, the commander-in-chief of the Royal army, was issued with instructions to quash the rebellion with ferocious vigour. His unambiguous instructions were:

> It is resolved, that it is fit that his Lordship do endeavour
> with his majesty's forces to wound, kill, slay and destroy,
> by all the ways and means he may, all the said rebels, their
> adherents and relievers; and burn, spoil, waste, consume,
> destroy and demolish, all the places, towns and houses,
> where the said rebels are, or have been relieved and har-
> boured; and all the hay and corn there; and kill and destroy
> all the men there inhabiting capable to bear arms. Given at
> his Majesty's Castle of Dublin 23 February 1642.[19]

The English, while primarily confined to the safety of walled towns and garrisons, displayed formidable resolution. When they did venture from their enclaves they did so not without some success. Atrocities were not confined to the Irish side alone. The wanton conditions of a civil war propelled the vicious instigators of evil to the forefront of the conflict. Prior to Eoghan Ruadh's arrival, the uncontrollable Celtic Ulstermen, paying little attention to orders, became a law unto themselves. Phelim O'Neill and his savage mob were well matched in excessive cruelties by Sir Charles Coote, an officer in the Royal army, who was also responsible for cold-blooded slaughter. Coote's instructions were to wage war on the Catholic rebels, and he departed from the gates of Dublin with this in mind. He soon plunged himself into a bloody campaign, slaughtering all the Irish Catholics he could find, irrespective of sex or age, armed or unarmed.

In England, the cost of sending an army to Ireland was to be defrayed by the passing of the 'Adventurers Act' on 19 March 1642. In February of that year, a group of London merchants had suggested to Parliament a formula by which 'they may have such satisfaction out of the rebel's estates as shall be thought reasonable'.[20] Sufficiently affluent Englishmen were now invited to contribute towards the cost of conquering Ireland. In return they were guaranteed Irish estates at the end of the war. Cromwell displayed the ability to speculate in order to accumulate through this unique investment project. Now living among the prosperous properties of Ely, the changes in his fortunes were evident by the size of his subscriptions. Initially he had offered £300 for the succour of Dublin. Then the princely sum of £2,050 was paid by him in three installments, two of £600 in April and one of £850 in July.[21] He was eventually granted land in the barony of Eglish in County Offaly. Any suggestion at this time that Cromwell himself would be the one with the responsibility of procuring this land in Ireland would have been preposterous. He was as yet without military experience of any sort. It was an inconceivable notion at this point that in a little over a decade his military reputation would earn him the position of supreme leader of four nations. Later, as Lord Protector, he would supervise the implementation of this act, and later still it would be entirely credited to him and become known as the Cromwellian plantation. The facts are that when the enterprise was in its infancy, he was a very small participant, and as supreme ruler he would inherit the fulfilment of this callous mechanism. He himself can not be held solely accountable for a practice that had well matured by the time he came to power. He can, of course, assume responsibility for a large percentage of the success of the exercise. After all, he had, firstly, conquered the Irish military threat and, secondly, emphatically directed operations from Whitehall from 1653 onwards.

In 1642, an English force was raised and gradually dispatched to Ireland, the numbers of which were quite significant. It was, however, to experience total neglect from Parliament and was abysmally supplied with provisions, clothing and money. It was also fragmented around the provinces, a factor that aided the Royalists rather than Parliament. After protracted negotiations it was the Scottish Parliament who agreed to dispatch a well provisioned force of 10,000 soldiers under General Monroe. They immediately landed and captured Carrickfergus and the nearby town of Newry. While garrisoned at Carrickfergus on 9 January 1642, they were responsible for the massacre of 3,000 Irish Catholic civilians at Island Magee. The cry from the Scottish attackers in justifying the deaths of the young was, 'Nits make Lice.' This phrase was later adopted by Walter Macken to enhance his fictional story and the heroic role of his central character Dominick McMahon, in *Seek the Fair Land* first published in 1959.[22]

As Oliver Cromwell collected tithes and rents from his tenants on the green outside his black-and-white half-timbered house at No. 29, St Mary's Street, Ely (today's address), he was not unaware of the tales of Irish cruelty. However, by the time the stories had reached him, they had been much embroidered. During his dispatch to William Lenthall, the Speaker of the Parliament of England, written on 17 September 1649, detailing the battle of Drogheda, Cromwell's view of his enemies is coloured by his personal assessment of 1641. He writes, 'I am persuaded that this is a righteous judgement of God upon these barbarous wretches who have imbrued their hands in so much innocent blood.'[23]

That Cromwell seems completely unaware of the retaliation of the likes of Coote and Monroe against the Irish with their comparative form of retribution is a source of some mystery. Ultimately he would justify his later Irish campaign as a vengeful mission of retributive justice. He clearly conceived that the balance of malevolence was heavily on the side of the Irish, a conviction he developed with the aid of persuasive contemporary news literature.

In Ireland the insurgents now resolved to organise a civil government. They set up headquarters at Kilkenny (Ormonde's ancestral domain!) and called themselves the Confederate Catholics of Ireland.[24] It was an attempt to unite all Catholics in the common cause of defending their lands and religion. It was solidarity in its purest form, against 'the common enemy'. The combination of the Old English and the Irish now regarded the King's cause as the one most likely to further theirs. They adopted the motto *'Pro Deo, Pro Rege, Pro Hibernia unanimis'*.[25](United for God, King and Ireland.) Both parties had one eye on the current events in England watching the acceleration of the King's decline. Charles sealed his fate by dealing and counter-dealing, first with Parliament, then with its enemies. The death of the King would finally leave the Catholics isolated and at the mercy of the anti-Catholic Puritan Parliament.

A national Synod of the Catholic Clergy met at Kilkenny from 10–13 May 1642 and declared that the Irish war was a just and necessary resistance in self-defence. They announced that they would uphold the Royal authority and the free exercise of the Catholic religion. This body effectively became the government of Catholic Ireland during the rest of the 1640s. They were also anxious to abolish the distinctions between the Old English and the native Gaelic Irish, in preservation of their common religion. The ever-present ethnic tensions between both groups, however, would prove an insurmountable barrier between them.

The Catholic clergy would be fiercely castigated by Cromwell in his declaration from his winter quarters at Youghal in 1650. He was firmly convinced that it was the wicked priests that stirred up the Irish to revolt at the outset. His perception of the clergy's involvement in instigating and glorifying the insurrection would acquire utmost significance. He believed that, among other outrages, Catholic priests had informed their flocks that the deaths of English Protestants was a merciful act as it would save them future sufferings in purgatory. Cromwell's insular opinions on this issue would eventually lead to his unacceptable exultation in the ruthless slaying of almost all of the priests that he was to encounter in Ireland. No evidence exists that will place priests at any rebel meeting which co-ordinated military events. No doubt, as an oppressed body striving for universal acceptance, their involvement in the struggle was not inconsiderable. In actual fact, during the Synod of Kilkenny, the clergy prohibited, under pain of severe penalties, all injury and retaliation inflicted on Protestants or others adverse to their cause.[26] Cromwell's later actions against Drogheda's militia was not in breach of the regulations of war. The same, however, cannot be said about his involvement in the murders of priests, always assuming that those he murdered were not actually in arms against Parliament. Whether or not they were cannot, in fact, be proven one way or the other.

Religion was to play an enormous part in Cromwell's life. He had by now become a devout Puritan, as were many of his fellow MPs. Deeply religious and austere, his conduct, philosophy, fundamental principles and every fibre of his being had their roots in the teachings of the Bible. As an extreme Puritan he distrusted anything in the Protestant Church that resembled the customs or beliefs of the Catholic Church. At a time when religion was all consuming in everyday life, Roman Catholicism to him was repulsive. The corruption and chicanery of the Roman hierarchy had contaminated that religion beyond an acceptable level. Devotion, in his eyes, was simply personal homage to God through the medium of the scriptures. The idea of an earthly circuit to the Almighty through the mere mortal, and essentially political, Roman Pope was offensive. The ceremonial pageantry of their decorative rituals in which they seemed excessively interested was also a basis for Puritan antipathy. Herein lies the key to Cromwell's mindset during his time in Ireland. These were the issues that would determine many of his decisions while on Irish soil. These were the reasons for his intolerance of what he considered to be the bureaucratic and irreligious faith of Catholicism.

In England, the tackling of the Irish situation was held in abeyance. Charles I had raised the standard at Nottingham on a wet and windy 22 August 1642, declaring war against his own Parliament. The latter had found that Charles would make promises only to break them and grant concessions only to gain time. They were dealing with a man that no ties could bind. Later, from the scaffold, the King would defend his standpoint: 'For the people I desire their liberty and freedom as much as anybody whomsoever; but I must tell you that this liberty and freedom consists in having government – that is nothing pertaining to them. A subject and a sovereign are clear different things.'[27] It is a little known fact that the King's enemies during the Civil War were convinced that it was those around him and not the King himself that were to blame for his actions. Most of the MPs had a deep respect for the monarchy, and one of their intentions in this war was to extricate the King from his corrupt advisors. The seemingly contradictory battle cry from their soldiers at the start of the war was 'For King and Parliament'. The chief commander of the Parliamentary army was the Earl of Essex, whose orders were 'to rescue His Majesty's person and the persons of the Prince of Wales and the Duke of York, out of the hands of those desperate persons who were then about them'.[28] But Parliament had a crucial difficulty with the King's perception of the 'clear' difference between a subject and a sovereign and each's right to govern. He would never accept the fact that his audacious subjects could call into question his 'Divine Right' to rule.

The outbreak of war in England was to divide Englishmen everywhere. The populace of the city of London took different sides. Even individual families had split sympathies: fathers took opposing sides to sons and brothers fought against brothers. In Ireland it was to have a monumental effect on the state of the parties. Suddenly, Ormonde, who had been the leader of the English forces up to this point, found himself in opposition to Parliament and firmly on the King's side. He was soon compelled to treat with the Catholics who had always displayed their loyalty to the King. The opposing sides now became: Royalists versus Parliamentarians. The Catholic rebels under O'Neill had appeared to be on the brink of success. They now occupied most of the country, including some of the major towns, and they did not want for food and supplies. Why should they lay down their arms and negotiate with the enemy? However, the Old English Catholic party were to prevail during the talks and soon a treaty was agreed in September 1643 between Ormonde and the Confederates, and hostilities ceased. The Ulstermen, however, disagreed and remained autonomous. O'Neill's Ulster forces were the only regular professional army in the country. Feared and distrusted by Ormonde and the Old English, their autonomy would contribute significantly to the later success of their English counterparts, the New Model Army. The Ulster squadrons would arrive late into the conflict against Cromwell.

The 'cessation' was destined to last for one year. At this point many English officers in 'Irish service' on both sides resigned their commissions and returned to England to take up arms in their own country. Parliament's view of this compromise with 'Popery' would help eventually to seal the King's fate and prove ultimately destructive to the Confederates. Parliament immediately ordered Monroe to ignore the truce, as O'Neill in Ulster, who was now deeply hostile to the Old English and their agreement with Ormonde, did.

It was about this time that Murrough O'Brien, a nobleman from the house of O'Brien and titled Lord Inchiquin, defected from his Royal authority in Munster to side with the Parliamentarians. In order to prove his commitment to his new superiors, he immediately embarked on a bloody crusade against Popery, seizing Cork, Youghal, Kinsale and Cashel, burning, looting and slaughtering as he went.[29]

In 1645, the Archbishop of Fermo, the Nuncio of the Pope, Giovanni Battista Rinuccini, arrived in Ireland. It was in the Pope's envoy that O'Neill and the native Irish would find support. This was in contrast to their co-religionists, the Old English, who found it in Ormonde and the King. Ormonde's objective in conducting peace with the Confederates was to generate an army capable of opposing the

Parliamentary forces in England. The substance of the alliance that was to bond the parties together was decidedly flimsy, since fierce animosity existed between them. To exacerbate the issue, the staunchly Protestant Ormonde delayed going into battle with his new allies.

Rinuccini was a tenacious advocate of the Pope's power and demanded from the outset that nothing less than the legal establishment of the Catholic Church in Ireland was acceptable. Since the treaty arranged between the Confederates and Ormonde did not contain a single stipulation for the free exercise of the Catholic religion, Rinuccini refused to endorse the agreement. Eoghan Ruadh O'Neill concurred. Ormonde had stood by while Inchiquin plundered Munster, Sir Charles Coote routed Connaught, and Monroe, now aided by the recently uprooted new English settlers, prevailed in Ulster. O'Neill had had enough. On 6 June 1646 he advanced towards Armagh with 5,000 foot and 500 horse soldiers. Seven miles from the town, at Benburb, he encountered Monroe's 6,000 foot and 800 horse. O'Neill's Continental military experience would be the decisive factor. He cleverly shepherded Monroe's troops into an impossible position, and he attacked. Monroe's infantry, despite having more modern weapons than O'Neill, were routed when the smoke from their muskets blew in their faces and blinded them. O'Neill pounced with his pike men and the day was won. The Parliamentarian losses were in excess of 3,000 with the victors losing not more than seventy. It was to be the most significant Irish victory of the Civil War.

O'Neill was exultant, as was Rinuccini. Ormonde, whose procrastination had suddenly made him vulnerable, was still in charge of Dublin, with a marauding Irish army, not involved in the official treaty, at large. His resolve collapsed and he turned to a body whom he disdained for help – the English Parliament. Being short of supplies and money, Dublin could not withstand a siege. His zeal for the Protestant faith, English interest and his hatred of the Catholic religion all combined to enable him to temporarily desert the Royal cause. His choice to attach himself to either the Irish rebels in the shape of O'Neill or English rebels in the shape of Parliament was an easy one for the tenaciously Protestant aristocrat. Despite his animosity for Parliament, he had more in common with them than he had with the Confederate forces with whom he was allied. Like the Puritans he was a staunch Protestant and despised the Roman power base whose influence traversed almost the whole of Ireland. Also, both Parliament and

Ormonde believed that English dominance should prevail in that country. On 19 June 1647 he left Ireland, delivered up the keys of Dublin and other towns under his command, including Drogheda, Trim and Dundalk, to Parliamentary troops under Colonel Michael Jones, who had landed just twelve days earlier near Dublin. Michael Jones, formerly a law student, like many of his peers had changed his allegiance from the King to Parliament when Ormonde fashioned the 'cessation' with the Catholics. He would become a very close friend of Cromwell. Ormonde then absconded to join the young Prince Charles in France.

This was now the position of the rival factions: the Parliamentary forces consisted of Jones at Dublin, Coote in Connaught and Inchiquin in Munster. The Irish army was led by O'Neill and Colonel Thomas Preston. The latter had been on the Continent with O'Neill, where they were rivals. He was the brother of Lord Gormanston and had returned with O'Neill in 1642, but each was unwilling to serve under the other. There would prove to be a constant rift between these two military leaders. With this in mind and the fact that there was no centralised military structure governing the Confederate forces, a military defeat on a large scale could result in disaster.

On 8 August 1647 Jones and Preston met at the battle of Dungan's Hill near Summerhill in County Meath. Preston's forces were devastated by the victorious Jones, with few prisoners taken and the vanquished Irish (some 3,500–5,000 men) mostly slain. This defeat was devastating for the Leinster section of the Confederates. With Jones abroad and Dublin guarded with only 500 men, an opportunity was missed to capture the capital, as well as a major battle lost. Preston never seemed capable of converting his achievements at siege warfare into successes in the field. The Irish also suffered another defeat at the hands of Lord Inchiquin when he cut to pieces the Munster army of Lord Taaffe. The Confederates were rapidly losing ground after their failure to capitalise on the independent O'Neill's defeat of Monroe at Benburb.

Their repeated defeats stimulated the Catholic Supreme Council at Kilkenny into lobbying the young Prince of Wales in Paris for assistance. It came on the 29 September 1648 in the shape of the remorseful Earl of Ormonde! His renewed fidelity to the King and requisite apology had now earned him the title of the King's Lord Lieutenant in Ireland. A revitalised Ormonde was now vested with the express purpose of reestablishing Royal authority in Ireland. Rinuccini had alienated the Irish Catholics with his threats of wholesale excommunications because of their arrangements with Ormonde and the King. He had also over-stepped the mark with his exuberance in involving himself directly with the conflict and returned to Italy to be admonished by the Pope.[30]

The Supreme Council of the Confederates now had a new decision to make. Ormonde had already once betrayed them to Parliament, but now he conceded that freedom of religion should no longer be an obstacle and stipulated the repeal of the abhorrent penal laws. They were hooked. They conferred on him the chief command of their troops but with appointed Commissioners of Trust to control his public operations.

Four armies were now contesting the war on Irish soil: two of them Royalist and two Parliamentarian;

The King
1. The Protestant/Royalist forces of Ormonde, including the Confederation of Old English Catholic Loyalists and native Irish.
2. The Ulster Gaelic Irish Catholics under O'Neill.

Parliament
3. The Scottish army of Monroe in Ulster.
4. The English Parliamentarians whose forces were spread around the island, their leaders being Coote, Inchiquin and Jones.

The situation was always liable to change. Ormonde was now back in league with the Catholics but still without the support of that loose cannon, O'Neill. Soon the disreputable Inchiquin would join Ormonde. The King had been beheaded in January 1649, and as a result Inchiquin crossed over from the side of Parliament, having per-petrated terrible cruelties on their behalf upon the side he was now joining. Together they made a bizarre union, but they now gained sub-stantial ground against the inadequately supplied Parliamentary forces in Ireland. Ormonde had previously surrendered Dublin into Parlia-ment's hands without so much as a single shot being fired, and so the city remained under their control. Now he must endeavour to regain it by force. Together the combined forces of the Confederate Catholics and Protestant Royalists now succeeded in capturing Drogheda, Dun-dalk, Newry, Carlingford and Trim.

O'Neill was at the head of 7,000 men in Ulster and he found him-self consistently out on a limb. His ally Rinuccini was gone and his relationship with the Kilkenny Confederacy was dismal. The leader of the Parliamentarian forces in Ulster was now General George Monck. Ormonde's inconsistency in military affairs and indifference to O'Neill's deep religious views made an alliance between the two improbable. O'Neill then entered into a truce with Monck on 8 May 1649, for a period of three months, agreeing that should Ormonde attack either side, the other would come to its defence.[31] This alliance has since cast a shadow on O'Neill's career, since he was now temporarily in league with the Puritans.

Ormonde was garrisoned at Finglas, three miles north of Dublin. Having joined with Inchiquin and others, his army now consisted of approximately 20,000 men. His overtures to O'Neill to entreat with him to attach his forces to his own, for the Royal cause, were ignored by the Celtic leader. Ormonde now diverted his attention towards the capital. He advanced to the south side of the Liffey and encamped at Rathmines, resolving to strike vigorously and retrieve Dublin for the King's purpose. However, Ormonde's persistent inability to perceive the moment of decisive action would prove his downfall. On 2 August, while he lay asleep in his tent and as his troops prepared for battle, Colonel Michael Jones seized the element of surprise, turning a speculative sally from the city gates into a victorious attack. Ormonde's troops were scattered and decisively beaten. The beleaguered Jones, though miserably supplied within the walls of Dublin, was quick to see his chance and motivate his 5,000 troops to a successful triumph. Strange as it may seem, there would not be another battle fought in the capital until Easter 1916.

Just off Milford Haven, not far from Bristol, on board *The John*, Oliver Cromwell would receive the news of Jones' victory describing it as 'an astonishinge mercie, so great and seasonable, as indeed we are like to them that dreamed'.[32] And so it was, that this was the state of the Emerald Isle that Cromwell was about to enter. Much blood had been spilled on (and ultimately for) its fertile hills and glens. The Parliamentarian massacres of Island Magee (Monroe), Dungan's Hill (Jones), Youghal and Cashel (Inchiquin) had yielded a death toll of tens of thousands of soldiers as well as thousands of unarmed men, women, children and clergy – deaths that might have been avoided were it not for the blood lust of the respective battle leaders. Many of these deaths were clearly committed well outside the articles of war.

It was the summer of 1649. Ormonde was now short of money and supplies. He had just suffered a comprehensive military defeat. O'Neill was still isolated from the Confederate forces, having never ratified the peace between the latter and the earl. By this time O'Neill was suffering from 'defluxion of the knees'.[33] His personal mobility was severely hampered and his army was also badly in need of provisions. Desertions among all of the parties had been rife over the previous years. Allegiances were constantly shifting due to the complexities of the war. For the common soldiers, 'the enemy' was always liable to change in such an environment, and this led to much unrest among regiments. The animosity between the English and Irish Catholics was bitter. Both of these groups comprised the bulk of Ormonde's forces. His continued inability to properly conduct the war confirmed Cromwell's assertion that Ormonde was more suited to hunting. The Confederate army that now awaited Cromwell's arrival, although large, was fraught with dissension, discord and mistrust. Now after Rathmines, disillusionment had set in. In Ulster, Eoghan Ruadh O'Neill's demise had begun, his life ebbing away as his gangrenous legs steadily worsened.

The chief character of the play would now enter the stage against this backdrop of disarray. He would be accompanied by a 12,000-strong, highly skilled, well-equipped and efficiently provisioned army. These fiercely motivated men, fresh from victory in the English wars, were happy to lay down their lives for their awesome leader if they deemed that God agreed. They brought with them extensive siege artillery, the likes of which was never before seen in Ireland. In stark contrast to the position of the poorly maintained Parliamentary force sent to Ireland in 1642, the odds were already stacked heavily in Cromwell's favour before he would even disembark from *The John*.

It was at the age of forty-one that Cromwell was to emerge from the placid obscurity of the contemplative fields of Ely to the turbulent and violent world of the English Civil War. Seven days after the raising of the King's standard, Cromwell took his first military steps. The Falcon Inn, Huntingdon, stands on the opposite side of the marketplace to the Huntingdon Grammar School. Both buildings still exist practically unaltered with time. It was to his home town, and presumably his former local ale house, that Cromwell now returned to muster a volunteer force of about a hundred men under his command as captain.

When the architect of the Ulster plantation, James I, died in 1625, his son, the twenty-four-year-old Charles Stewart, ascended the English throne. Until the death of James' predecessor, Elizabeth, English monarchs had almost been allowed to rule absolutely. The evolutionary trend, with a monarch's discontentment with Parliament and vice versa, was gradually coming to a head. The inevitable propensity towards a civil administration meant that in recent years Parliament had displayed an aversion to automatically agreeing to a Sovereign's demands. Following his coronation, Charles I would alienate many of his Protestant subjects by marrying the French Catholic Princess Henrietta Maria. Soon the cost of his foreign policy, including an existing war with Spain, would result in his calling sporadic Parliaments to seek financial assistance. His devious nature and persistent manipulation of his 'Divine Right' as monarch would drive a wedge firmly between him and his Parliament. It was abundantly clear that the Catholic-friendly King and the increasing number of Parliamentary members who were supporters of the Puritan line would differ drastically on political, financial and religious issues; in other words, the fundamental essence of constitutional policy.

Cromwell was the father of eight children: four boys and four girls. In 1639 his eldest son, Robert, died of an unknown fever at the age of seventeen. Some twenty years later, as he himself was close to death, he would describe the tragic loss of his first-born child: ". . . when my eldest son died . . . which went as a dagger to my heart".[34] Throughout his life he displayed much affection to his own children and, in particular, his daughter Elizabeth (Bettie). In the spring of 1644, his eldest surviving son, Oliver, would die of smallpox at the age of twenty-one. He would be posthumously described as 'a civil young man and the joy of his father'.[35] After the battle of Marston Moor and while breaking the news of the death of his brother-in-law Sir Valentine Walton's son, Cromwell would write: 'Sir you know my trials this way . . . there is your precious child, full of glory to know sin nor sorrow no more.'[36] John Maidstone, who would be his steward and cofferer when he was Protector, gives us the following description:

> His body was wel compact and strong, his stature under 6 foote (I believe about two inches), his head so shaped as you might see it a storehouse and shop both of a vast treasury of natural parts. His temper exceeding fyery, as I have known,

but the flame of it kept downe, for the most part, or soon allayed with thos moral endowments he had. He was naturally compassionate towards objects in distresse, even to an effeminate measure; though God had made him a heart, wherein was left little roume for any fear, but what was due to himself, of which there was a large proportion, yet did he exceed in tendernesse towards sufferers. A larger soul, I think, hath seldom dwelt in a house of clay. [37]

Despite contrary views, compassion was most definitely known to Oliver Cromwell.

In November 1640 he began to make an impact upon the new assembly in the House of Commons, during a Parliament that would later to become known as the 'Long' or 'Rump' Parliament. It appears that the MPs were a mixture of well–dressed gentlemen and those whose attention to attire was not high on their list of priorities for a working day in the Parliament of England. Cromwell was a member of the latter group. Nonetheless, he had the full attention of the gathering, according to Sir Phillip Warwick, MP for Radnor, who witnessed the emergence of Cromwell the politician:

> The first time I ever took notice of Mr. Cromwell was in the very beginning of the Parliament held in November 1640; when I vainly thought myself a courtly young gentleman, for we Courtiers valued ourselves much upon our good clothes! I came into the house one morning well clad; and perceived a gentleman speaking, whom I knew not, very ordinarily apparelled; for it was a plain cloth suit, which seemed to have been made by an ill country tailor; his linen was plain and not very clean, and I remember a speck or two of blood upon his little band, which was not much larger than his collar. His hat was without a hatband. His stature was of good size; his sword stuck close to his side; his countenance swollen and reddish, his voice sharp and untuneable, and his eloquence full of fervour. For the subject matter would not bear much of reason it being on behalf of a servant of Mr. Prynnes (John Lilburne) who had dispersed Libels. I sincerely profess, it lessened much my reverence unto that Great Council for this gentleman was much harkened unto. [38]

Cromwell witnessed his first major battle on 23 October 1642 at Edgehill in Warwickshire. There had not been a battle in England in 150 years, since James IV of Scotland invaded England and was killed in action at Flodden in 1513.[39] Both sides, Royalists and Parliament, claimed victory following the inconclusive Battle of Edgehill. (The latter were to become known as 'Roundheads' as they mostly wore their hair closely cropped at the start of the war and the former as 'Cavaliers' from the Spanish 'caballeros').[40] The two sides fought until twilight on that short October day and, as if by mutual consent, hostilities gradually ceased with the onset of darkness. Although he himself was to arrive some time after the engagement had already begun, Cromwell beheld a sufficient amount of the encounter to begin to develop his own personal philosophy for expedient military engagement.

As well as the conventional method of choosing officers of rank by measure of their affluence and social standing, Cromwell was not averse to recruiting officer material from the ranks of 'plain' men. He was deeply convinced that Godly men, irrespective of background, who displayed a flair for leadership, would do as good a job as their social superiors. Sometimes he felt that many of his peers did not have the enthusiasm or the bottle for the war. He argued:

> I beseech you be careful what captains of horse you choose, what men be mounted; a few honest men are better than numbers . . . If you choose Godly honest men to be captains of horse, honest men will follow them, and they will be careful to mount such . . . I had rather have a plain russet-coated captain that knows what he fights for, and loves what he knows, than that which you call a gentleman and is nothing else. I honour a gentleman that is so indeed.[41]

Soon Cromwell's troop consisted of about 1,400 God-fearing men. They were to become a part of the Eastern Association, which in turn would become a significant part of the 'New Model Army' since they were newly formed and specially trained. Cromwell would soon become known as 'Old Ironsides', when his reputation in battle would evolve – a name that would eventually transfer to his troops. It could be said that Cromwell was the creator and founder of the British army, since no comparable force had existed prior to the Civil War.

By May 1643 Cromwell's troop of horse had swelled to 2,000 men. He had by this time become a colonel in the army. His reputation for discipline among his regiments was already starting to develop according to a newspaper of the period:

> As for Colonel Cromwell, he hath 2,000 brave men, well disciplined; no man swears but he pays his twelve pence; if he be drunk, he is set in the stocks, or worse; if one calls the other Roundhead, he is cashiered; insomuch that the counties where they come leap for joy of them, and come in and join with them. Happy were it if all the forces were thus disciplined.[42]

This control that Cromwell had over his troops would create a force that, ten years later, would effectively win the war for Parliament. It would also help to place him in a unique position of authority when Parliament would struggle to maintain power. If there was a secret to Cromwell's successful career, then it would have to be the influence he maintained over his men and the bond that his leadership qualities would help develop between him and them. Nowhere would this be more apparent than during the battles in Ireland.

It was at Marston Moor in July 1644, when the Cavaliers would confront the Roundheads again, that Oliver Cromwell would discover his latent talent for active combat. He cast off his innocuous background of lack of distinction to become an expert military strategist. The Royalist forces, under Charles' nephew Prince Rupert of the Rhine, fresh from Continental battlefields, totalling 18,000 men, now faced the 22,000-strong Parliamentary army across the moor between Tockwith and Long Marston in Yorkshire.

Cromwell's cavalry regiment formed the left wing of the battle line directly opposite Rupert's own regiment. When the battle commenced, Cromwell's company acted as a close unit, never separating, adhering strictly to their leader's orders, and thus struck the telling blow that was to secure a Parliamentary victory, despite the Royalist pretension that the battle was over and won by them prior to Cromwell's final charge.

The next major battle of the Civil War in England was to occur at Naseby on 14 June 1645. The Royalist army, while camped at Market Harborough in Leicestershire, realised that the menacing Parliamentarian army was only eight miles away. Their sole objective was to force the King to fight. Cromwell was now elevated to the position of Lieutenant-General of the Commonwealth horse soldiers. As at Marston

Moor, he would display his military genius during the battle of Naseby. Active combat in the seventeenth century depended largely on an officer's ability to remain in touch with his regiment. The lines of communication must be kept open in order to charge and retreat or rally and charge again successfully. Cromwell had mastered this exercise. Again on the fields of Broadmoor, Naseby, his troops were to ensure a Parliamentary triumph. Although numerically superior, the New Model Army was not guaranteed victory. Cohesion, timing and penetrative assaults were the key to success. It was becoming very obvious that Oliver Cromwell performed these applications proficiently in his new role as a military tactician. Following Marston Moor, Naseby and all of the other successful engagements in which Cromwell was involved, he would always attribute his accomplishments to the Almighty. After Naseby he wrote to the Speaker of Parliament: 'Sir, this is none other than the hand of God and to Him alone belongs the glory, wherein none are to share with Him . . . He that ventures his life for the liberty of his country, I wish he trust God for the liberty of his conscience.'[43] He also wrote: 'When I saw the enemy draw up and march in gallant order towards us, and we a company of poor ignorant men . . . I could not, riding alone about my business, but smile out to God in praise, in assurance of victory, because God would, by things that are not, bring to naught things that are. Of which I had great assurance, and God did it.'[44]

Immediately after the battle, some Parliamentarian foot soldiers encountered a group of women around the Royalist baggage train whom they perceived to be Irish. It was a commonly held belief that there was a constant threat from Royalist Irish forces to Parliament during the Civil War, and many Irish Royalists had already engaged in the battles on English soil. The language that the women spoke was incoherent to the troops, and so they believed they were confronting those that represented the perpetrators of monstrous crimes on decent English folk in 1641. They began to slaughter the women and some they slashed on the face, leaving the ignominious mark of a common prostitute as their calling card. It would transpire that the incomprehensible dialect was more likely to have been Welsh and that they were the wives of some of the King's men.[45] It is worth noting that Cromwell's horse troops were not involved in this non-military activity.

Naseby was the last major battle of the first Civil War in England, and with it came the temporary dissolution of the King's military resistance. The siege of Basing House, just outside Basingstoke on the main road from London to the west in October 1645, in which Cromwell was involved, deserves a mention, as a comparison to his later Irish campaign. The ostentatious Catholic Lord Winchester was a devout Royal subject and had managed to retain his elaborately decorated fortress of Basing House during the years of the war. It had become such a place of refuge for the King's followers, and even priests that it was called 'the onlie rendezvous for the Cavaliers and Papists thereabouts'.[46] Cromwell laid siege to the stronghold, and his heavy artillery soon made assailable breaches in the wall for his troops to pour into the grounds. Many noblemen, six priests, one woman and a quarter of the garrison were all put to the sword since they represented the double evil of 'Popery' and the King.

On 5 May 1646 the despondent Charles finally surrendered, but not to his English adversaries. By his own choice he favoured what he perceived to be a more hospitable incarceration by his fellow Scots, and it was into their hands that he delivered himself, only to be handed over to Parliament later. For the next two years Charles would negotiate and counter-negotiate with Parliament. All the while he was hopeful of an Irish Royalist army emerging from across the sea under the control of his Protestant general in Ireland, Ormonde, or even a Scottish Royalist force from the north, to eradicate these Parliamentarian rebels. No compromise was acceptable to him; it was a word that he just did not understand. Charles Stewart's twistings and turnings finally made Parliament resolve not to treat with him further since, in their view, it was transparently futile to do so.

With no resolution in sight, their King now captive and at the mercy of the enemy, by early 1648 the English Royalist army began to stir again. In various pockets around the country they started to seize certain Parliamentarian enclaves in minor uprisings. Thus began the second Civil War, and in July, August and October 1648 at Pembroke, Preston and Edinburgh respectively, Cromwell would again excel in battle. Also at this time began the trial of 'that man of blood',[47] Charles I, by his ambitious Parliament. While many observers now called for his head, even as late as December 1648 Cromwell was far from convinced that the King should die. During a speech to Parliament, he told them, 'there was no policy in taking away his life'.[48]

Before the actual hearing a strange incident occurred. A lady by the name of Elizabeth Poole, who claimed to have psychic powers, was subjected to a detailed cross examination by Parliament regarding a vision she had had concerning the King's fate. She insisted that in her vision the King would be finally judged by his maker: 'You may bind his hands and hold him fast under . . . but . . . vengeance is mine, saith the Lord, I will repay.'[49] In a time when superstitions, witchcraft and colourful ghost stories were taken extremely earnestly, even the Parliament of England was inclined to investigate such matters. However, in this instance Mistress Poole's visionary experience was ultimately to be disregarded.

As the trial got closer Cromwell finally changed his mind on the issue of the King's execution and now became convinced that he should die. The reasons for his change of attitude are not clear, but he now embraced this new conviction with his usual vigour. Charles I was brought to Westminster Hall on 20 January 1649 to be tried as 'a tyrant, traitor, murderer and a public enemy of the Commonwealth of England'.[50] Although the isolated King refused to acknowledge the authority by which he was brought to trial, his death warrant was soon signed and personally sealed (albeit reluctantly by some) by fifty-nine Members of Parliament. The third signatory in line was Oliver Cromwell's. Colonel Ewer, one of Cromwell's officers, would later tell a story about his superior officer and a fellow regicide, Henry Marten, foolishly splattering each other with ink after signing the warrant.[51] At about two o'clock on the afternoon of Tuesday, 30 January 1649, Charles Stewart was beheaded outside the banqueting hall at Whitehall and was thus elevated to eternal martyrdom by his subjects.[52]

Charles left behind four children: Charles, Prince of Wales now nineteen; James, Duke of York, aged seventeen; Princess Elizabeth, aged thirteen; and the ten-year-old Duke of Gloucester. (The then adolescent James would eventually find himself two miles from Drogheda at the Boyne in a battle with William, Prince of Orange, over the Crown in July 1690.) While his two eldest sons were elsewhere at this time, his youngest children were taken to see him on the day prior to his execution. Later the Princess would reveal the parting words of her father that would support his aspirations for an eternal legacy:

> He wished me not to grieve or torment myself for him, for that would be a glorious death he should die, it being for the laws and liberties of this land, and for maintaining the true Protestant religion . . . He told me he had forgiven all his enemies and hoped God would forgive them also, and

commanded us and all the rest of my brothers and sisters
to forgive them. He bid us tell my mother that his thoughts
had never strayed from her and that his love should be the
same to the last.[53]

Tradition has it that Cromwell came to pay his last respects to the
dead monarch as the body lay in its coffin in Whitehall on that same
Tuesday night. Although allegedly heavily disguised, the watchers over
the corpse recognised him and heard the words 'cruel necessity'[54] as he
gazed at the sight for some time, shaking his head.

The Second Civil War ended with the capitulation of Pontefract Castle on 21 March to Parliament. It was only now that the new Commonwealth could address the prospect of an attack from Ormonde's forces in
Ireland. Immediately before the King's death, Parliament had abolished
the monarchy and formed the Commonwealth, lest they be confronted
by the young Prince Charles' harbouring delusions of occupying the
vacant throne. The Prince of Wales' best opportunity appeared now to
rest with Ormonde's Royalist/Confederate army. There were many
other incentives to take the offensive against Parliament's Irish neighbours. A large Commonwealth army was now in existence. Many soldiers
were still owed money for services rendered. The suppression of Ireland
would both continue to occupy them in battle and provide land for dis-
tribution to them as a form of remuneration. The 'Adventurers' investments in property also needed to be secured, in order for their dividends
to mature. Then there was the small matter of the grossly exaggerated
rumours of hundreds of thousands of Protestant settlers' deaths in 1641
to be avenged. But who should be vested with the responsibility of sup-
pressing this potential Irish menace? Their choice was obvious. Around
20 March 1649 the House of Commons offered the appointment of
Commander-in-Chief of the Irish expeditionary forces to their most successful military general, Oliver Cromwell.

He stalled slightly before consenting. Ireland had proved to be the
downfall of many an English military career in the past. On 23 March
during an address to the General Council of the army at Whitehall, he
explained the delay in accepting his new commission and he conveyed
his personal views of this new challenge:

> The Council of State hath by these gentlemen returned
> this answer, which in effect was to represent me as
> commander-in-chief. I told them although my will could

not but be subject to those that were over me, barely considered as matter of will; yet inasmuch as this business is of
so great importance as it is, it was fit for me in the first
place to consider how God would incline my heart to it,
how I might by seeking of Him, receive satisfaction in my
own spirit as to my own particular . . . You see they have
declared the Prince of Wales their King . . . and to seek the
ruin and destruction of those that God hath ordained to be
instrumental for their good . . . Now if we do not depart
from God, and disunite by that departure and fall into disunion among ourselves, I am confident, we doing our duty
and waiting upon the Lord we shall find he will be as a wall
of brass around us . . . In the next place we are to consider
Ireland. All the Papists and the King's party – I cannot say
all the Papists, but the greater party of them – are in a very
strong combination against you . . . And truly this is
believed: if we do not endeavour to make good our interest
there, and that timely, we shall not only have (as I have said
before) our interest rooted out there, but they will in a very
short time be able to land forces in England, and put us to
trouble here. I confess I have had these thoughts with
myself that may be carnal and foolish. I had rather be overrun with a Cavalierish interest than a Scotch interest; I had
rather be overrun with a Scotch interest than an Irish interest; and I think all of this is most dangerous. If they shall
be able to carry on their work, they will make this the most
miserable people in the earth, for all the world knows of
their barbarism – not of any religion, almost any of them,
but in a manner as bad as Papists and you can see how considerable they are therein at this time . . . This being so, I
would not have this army so much to look at considerations
that are personal – whether or no we shall go if such a commander go, or such a commander; and make that part of
our measure or foundation – but let us go if God go.[55]

And go they did. On 30 March the Commonwealth's new ruling
mechanism, the Council of State, approved Cromwell's appointment as
Commander-in-Chief of the army destined for Ireland. However, in
May during preparations for the Irish expedition, the badly paid New

Model Army were influenced by a militant political group, the Levellers, who caused a mutiny among its ranks. The inactivity of the aftermath of the war had resulted in a large body of men debating over the conditions of their employment, since no battle appeared imminent in their view. Cromwell's relationship with the army deemed that it was his responsibility to suppress the insubordination of this mutinous group. This he convincingly achieved, along with his colleague Colonel Thomas Fairfax, through decisive and sensitive negotiation. He insisted to the army that he was 'resolved to live and die with them'.[56] He arrived at the soldiers' camp at Burford on Sunday, 13 May, having covered forty-five miles with lightning speed in order to quash the mutiny. This he did, although not without some controversy, since three of the ringleaders were shot to death on his instructions. His reputation was not tarnished among the military, as the vast majority of the troops supported their superiors with a fervent religious zeal.

The regiments to be chosen to go to Ireland were put in a hat and drawn out by a child. Cromwell's own brigade, that of Colonels Venables and Phayre, had already been designated, and the child was to draw the horse regiments of Ireton (Cromwell's son-in-law), Lambert, Scrope and Horton, and the foot of Colonels Ewer, Cook, Hewson and Deane.[57] Also chosen were five troops of dragoons, of Major Abbot and Captains Mercer, Garland, Fulcher and Bolton. In total, the force numbered 8,000 foot, 3,000 horse and 1,200 dragoons.

Ormonde, who was at this time about to besiege Dublin at Rathmines, was unconvinced that Cromwell would ever leave England. His aristocratic connections on the Continent concurred. Even in the city of London, in a manner more suited to the twentieth century, odds were being offered at twenty to one that Cromwell would still not go to Ireland. On 20 June Cromwell was formally constituted as Lord Lieutenant of Ireland, and it was during these last months of the summer of 1649 that he involved himself directly with the pending expedition.

He insisted that the army was to be effectively provisioned with food, clothing, ammunition and supplies, but principally money. His expeditionary forces could not to be found wanting if the Irish campaign were to succeed. He delayed his departure until he had secured sufficient finance to justify the mobilisation of 12,000 men to a conflict that was, after all, on foreign soil. Provisions might not be readily available during the operation from an unpredictable rural Irish population.

On 5 July the train of artillery and ammunition was shipped to Dublin ahead of the army.

At this time in Ireland some of the officers of Inchiquin's army had deserted now to the side of Parliament and others covertly proclaimed their intention to do so when the time was right, with Cromwell's personal approval. On 11 July at five in the evening and still without a complete purse for the trip, he left London for Bristol. *The Moderate Intelligencer*, a government publication, announced his departure thus:

> This evening, about five of the clock, the Lord Lieutenant of Ireland began his journey by way of Windsor and so to Bristol. He went forth in that state and equipage as the like hath hardly been seen, himself in a coach with six gallant Flanders mares whitish grey; divers coaches accompanying him, and very many great officers of the army; his lifeguard consisting of eighty gallant men, the meanest whereof was a commander or Esquire in stately habit, with trumpets sounding almost to the shaking of Charing Cross, had it been now standing. Of his lifeguard are many Colonels; and, believe me, its such a guard as is hardly to be parallelled in the world. And now have at you, my Lord Ormonde! You will have men of gallantry to encounter, whom to overcome will be honour sufficient and to be beaten by them will be no great blemish to your reputation. If you say 'Caesar or nothing' they say 'a republic or nothing'. The Lord Lieutenant's colours are white.[58]

Above Cromwell's head was a milk-white standard symbolising his aspirations to return with peace from amid the evils of war. He travelled west, via Brentford and Reading, stopping at a manor near Ramsbury in Wiltshire to be entertained on the 12th, and finally arriving at Bristol on 14 July. Before embarking for Ireland he waited patiently for another three weeks for money to arrive to ensure the success of the venture. It eventually came from London in the shape of £70,000 with a further £30,000 promised to come later.

Two significant events occurred in Ireland, with contrasting impacts on Cromwell's arrangements as he waited to transport his army, now at Milford Haven. On the Commonwealth's debit side, General George Monck's truce with Eoghan Ruadh O'Neill now became an issue of some concern. Monck's movements had been severely curtailed within the walls of Dundalk, and as Inchiquin was at large, having just secured Drogheda, he sent to O'Neill for assistance in return for gunpowder, which O'Neill was badly in need of. When O'Neill's men arrived to collect the powder, they spent much of their time around the hostelries of Dundalk sampling the local *uisce beatha*. Consequently, as they emerged from the gates, their reflexes were not quite what they should have been. Inchiquin pounced, routed the drunks and relieved them of their store. He then opened an attack on the town. Since Monck's men could not bear the idea of being in alliance with the rebels who were responsible for the brutalities of 1641, many of them now declared for Inchiquin. Cromwell disowned Monck for entering into an illegal cessation with O'Neill, as did the Council of State, and Monck honourably took full responsibility for his actions.

On the Commonwealth's credit side came the news from Jones that he had defeated Ormonde at Rathmines. Cromwell received the news on 13 August and immediately wrote to his new in-law, Richard Mayor, whose daughter had just been married to his eldest son Richard:

> The Marquis of Ormonde besieged Dublin with nineteen thousand men or thereabouts . . . Jones issued out of Dublin with four thousand foot and twelve hundred horse; hath routed his whole army; killed about four thousand upon the place and taken 2,517 prisoners, above three hundred officers, some of great quality. This is an astonishing mercy; so great and seasonable as indeed we are like them that dreamed. What can we say? . . . These things seem to strengthen our faith and love against more difficult times. Sir, pray for me, that I may walk worthy of the Lord in all that he hath called me unto.[59]

Rathmines cleared the way for Cromwell to sail to Dublin. A reversal of that battle's result would have meant his attempting a landing in Munster. On 13 and 14 August 1649, a total of 130 sailing ships packed with 12,000 menacing Roundheads converged on Ireland's east coast to enter into a war, the outcome of which was never in doubt.

Notes to Chapter One

1   Town Plan of Huntingdon, performed by John Speed, 1610, available at Huntington Library. Plan of the town of Huntingdon, detail from map of county of Huntingdon by Thomas Jefferys, 1768, in County Record Office, Huntingdon.

2   Michael Byrd, "Oliver Cromwell, A Personal Biography", *Cromwelliana, Journal of The Cromwell Association*, (1997), p. 17.

3   See John Morrill, (ed.), "The Making of Oliver Cromwell", *Oliver Cromwell and the English Revolution* (London: Longman, 1990), pp. 19–48. See also David L. Smith, *Oliver Cromwell, Politics and Religion in the English Revolution, 1640–1658* (Cambridge: Cambridge University Press, 1991), pp. 49–50.

4   Cromwell's speech to Parliament, 12 September, 1654, quoted in, Sir Richard Tangye, *The Two Protectors, Oliver and Richard Cromwell* (London: S.W. Partridge, 1899), p. 27.

5   Ibid., p. 31.

6   C.H. Davidson, "The Diagnosis of Oliver Cromwell's Fatal Illness", *Cromwelliana, Journal of The Cromwell Association*, (1993), p. 27.

7   Christopher Hill, *God's Englishman, Oliver Cromwell and the English Revolution* (London: Penguin, 1972), p. 39. See also Antonia Fraser, *Cromwell Our Chief of Men* (London: Mandarin edition, 1994), p. 24. Morrill, however, emphasises the point that 'No record of his presence at any of the Inns of Court has been found . . . It is generally agreed that he attended Lincoln's Inn; but the records (and especially the accounts) of Lincoln's Inn are very full, and he is not likely to have been a non-fee-payer or to have slipped through the accounts. The case for his being at Gray's Inn is based on the loss of its records and the presence of some cousins there.' See Morrill, "The Making of Oliver Cromwell", p. 24.

8   See Davidson, "The Diagnosis of Oliver Cromwell's Fatal Illness", p. 28.

9   Ibid., p. 27. See also Hill, *God's Englishman*, p. 44.

10 Oliver Cromwell to his cousin, Mrs Oliver St. John, 13 October 1638, quoted in John Broome, *Oliver Cromwell, A Vindication* (Leicester: The Gospel Standard Baptist Trust, 1969), p. 1.

11 Elizabeth Cromwell to her husband in 1650, quoted in Byrd, "Oliver Cromwell, A Personal Biography", p. 18.

12 Oliver Cromwell to Elizabeth Cromwell, Ibid., p. 18.

13 The name was first used as a term of derision in the Royalist *Mercurius Aulicus* in November 1643 and is quoted in Fraser, *Cromwell Our Chief of Men*, p. 55.

14 The figure varies from 30,000–40,000 from source to source. It is important to realise this when it would come to the exaggerated accounts of the Protestant Massacres of 1641. The Jesuit Cornelius O'Mahony, writing in 1645, says that over 150,000 'heretics' had been killed. See R.H. Murray, "Cromwell at Drogheda – A Reply to J.B. Williams", *The Nineteenth Century*, (December 1912) LXXII p. 1226.

15   M.E.Collins, *Conquest and Colonisation, A History of Ireland*, edited by Margaret MacCurtain (Dublin: Gill & Macmillan, 1969), p. 87.

16   Ibid., p. 86.

17   Extract from Murray, "Cromwell at Drogheda – A reply to J.B. Williams", p. 1228 quoted from Schiller, *History of the Thirty Years War*, pp. 143–44.

18   There are thirty-two volumes of manuscripts of Protestant depositions from those who were persecuted during the Rebellion. The following is an excerpt from the deposition of Elizabeth Price of Portadown: 'But as to this deponent's five children [she witnesses], and about forty more, these were sent away with passes from the said Phelim O'Neill together with about three-score and fifteen more Protestants . . . who were all promised they would be safely conveyed and sent over to their friends in England; their commander or conductor for that purpose . . . being by name Captain Manus O'Cane; and his soldiers having brought, or rather driven like sheep or beasts to a market place, those poor prisoners, being about one hundred and fifteen to the bridge of Portadown, the said captain and rebels then and there forced and drove all those prisoners and amongst them, this deponents five children, by name Adam, John, Anne, Mary and Jane Price, off the bridge into the water, and then and there instantly and most barbarously drowned the most of them. And those who could swim and came to the shore, they knocked on the head, and so after drowned them, or else shot them to death in the water. And one of them was a Scottish Minister, swimming below the bridge, to or near the land of Mr. Blackett, the rebels pursued so far, and then and there shot him to death. And as for this deponent, and many others that were stayed behind, divers tortures were used upon them, to make them confess their hidden monies and means, and many were murdered after they had confessed all their means left to them, and this deponent and others were often affrighted with a block and a hatchet, which put to them more in fear, was always left near them as engines of death; and this deponent for her own part was thrice hanged up to confess to money, and afterwards let down, and had the soles of her feet fried and burnt at the fire, and was often scourged and whipped; and she and the most of the rest of the prisoners so pined and hunger starved that some of them died, and lay a week unburied, and as this deponent and others that survived were forced to eat grass and weeds, and when they asked for liberty to go out and gather their sustenance, it was denied, so that hunger forced them to burst open the window in their prison chamber, and to scrape and rake the weeds, moss or anything that they could possibly take from the walls. And in that or the like and worse distress they continued, and were tossed and haled from place to place, in the most miserable manner, for fourteen or fifteen months together.' Quoted in Murray, "Cromwell at Drogheda – A Reply to J.B. Williams", pp. 1225–26. See also Edward, Earl of Clarendon, 'A Collection of the Several Massacres and Murders Committed by the Irish', *Clarendon's History of the Rebellion in Seven Volumes*, with notes by Bishop Warburton (Oxford: Clarendon Press, 1849), vol. VII, appendix. Clarendon's words make gruesome reading indeed. He recounts stories of children being buried alive, wives being forced

to hang their husbands, or being made watch while their husbands' skin is peeled away from their bodies before they are slowly cut to pieces.

19   Quoted in Samuel Smiles, *History of Ireland and the Irish People* (London: Wm. Strange, 1844), p. 88.

20   See Fraser, *Cromwell, Our Chief of Men*, p. 80.

21   Ibid.

22   Walter Macken, *Seek the Fair Land* (London: Pan Books, 1988 edition), first published in 1959. McElligott has shown that Prendergast's prejudicial *Cromwellian Settlement of Ireland* contributed to Macken's point of view: 'Prendergast's influence on popular images of Oliver Cromwell in twentieth century Ireland is largely due to the fact that Walter Macken took the theses embedded in Prendergast's book and used them in his best selling novel 'Seek the Fair Land'. See McElligot, *Cromwell Our Chief of Enemies*, p. 17.

23   Oliver Cromwell to Speaker Lenthall, from Dublin, 17 September 1649, quoted in W.C. Abbott, *The Writings and Speeches of Oliver Cromwell*, reprint edition of 4 vols (Clarendon Press, 1988), p. 127.

24   See Collins, *Conquest and Colonisation*, p. 96.

25   Ibid., p. 96.

26   See Smiles, *History of Ireland*, p. 95.

27   Quoted in David Scott Daniell, *Battles and Battlefields* (London: Hamlyn, 1961), p. 119.

28   Ibid., p. 109.

29   Colonel Patrick F. Dineen, "The Siege of Clonmel", *Tercentenary of the Siege of Clonmel* (Clonmel: Clonmel Tercentenary Committee, 1950), p. 8. Inchiquin acquired the title of Murrough na gCath Teine, or Murrough an Totain – Murrough of the Burnings. For a short account of his life see Murphy, *Cromwell in Ireland*, appendix, p. 368. For detailed account of his sacking of Cashel, see Ibid., pp. 388–92.

30   See Smiles, *History of Ireland*, p. 115. Smiles recounts the following inauspicious end to the Nuncio's career: 'The Clergy now almost entirely abandoned him and he was urged to leave Ireland. At the same time he was summoned to Rome, in order to answer for his imprudence, intemperance and disobedience to his instructions. He shortly afterwards left Ireland, to the great joy of many and instead of being honoured with a Cardinal's hat, as he had expected would be the result of his important mission to Ireland, he was severely censured by the Pope and banished to his Bishoprick and principality of Fermo, where worn out with ennui and disappointed hopes, he soon after died of grief.'

31   Harold O'Sullivan, "Military Operations in County Louth in the Run-up to Cromwell's Storming of Drogheda", *County Louth Archaeological and Historical Society Journal*, vol. XXII, no. 2 (1990), p. 193. For further details of the truce between Monck and O'Neill see, Harold O Sullivan, *The Trevors of Rostrevor*, unpublished thesis in Louth County Library, Dundalk, reference section.

32   Cromwell to Richard Mayor Esquire, 13 August 1649, from aboard *The John*; in Abbott, *Writings and Speeches*, pp. 102–03.

33   See Smiles, *History of Ireland*, p. 125.

34   Quoted in Fraser, *Cromwell Our Chief of Men*, p. 60.

35   Ibid.,p. 117.

36   Cromwell to Colonel Valentine Walton, 1644; reprinted in Broome, *Oliver Cromwell, A Vindication*, p. 4.

37   From T Birch, (ed), *A Collection of State Papers of John Thurloe Esquire*, 7 vols, (London: 1742); quoted in Peter Gaunt, *Oliver Cromwell*, (Oxford; Blackwell, 1996), pp. 211–12.

38   Quoted in Tangye, *The Two Protectors*, p. 49.

39   Daniell, *Battles and Battlefields*, p. 107.

40   Fraser, *Cromwell Our Chief of Men*, p. 86.

41   Cromwell in August 1643, partly quoted in Fraser, *Cromwell our Chief of Men*, p. 91. Taken from Gaunt, *Oliver Cromwell*, p. 49, who says that Cromwell 'found that in practice he could not recruit exclusively from the upper echelons of society and during 1643, as he cast his net wider, so he shifted his argument. If regrettably, insufficient gentlemen came forward to serve as officers, Cromwell was quite prepared to recruit socially less elevated men.'

42   Quoted in Tangye, *The Two Protectors*, p. 68.

43   Ibid., p. 100.

44   Cromwell before the Battle of Naseby, quoted Fraser, *Cromwell our Chief of Men*, p. 150.

45   The point is made ibid., p. 161.

46   Ibid., p. 170.

47   In 1648 at Windsor, the Parliamentarian army held a large scale meeting and came to the resolution 'that it was our duty, if ever the Lord brought us back again in peace, to call Charles Stuart, that man of blood, to account for the blood he has shed, and mischief he has done to his utmost against the Lord's cause and people in these poor nations'. Quoted in Tangye, *The Two Protectors*, p. 130.

48   Cromwell to Parliament, December 1649, in *Mercurius Melancholicus*; quoted in Fraser, *Cromwell Our Chief of Men*, p. 274.

49   Quoted ibid., p. 277.

50   On 24 January, the fourth day of the trial of King Charles I, the day of sentencing, the President, John Bradshaw ordered the Clerk of the Court to read the following capital sentence: '. . . that whereas the Commons of England in Parliament had appointed them an High Court of justice for the trying of Charles Stuart, King of England; before whom he had been three times covenanted, and at the first time a charge of High Treason and other crimes and misdemeanours was read in the behalf of the Kingdom of England for all treasons and crimes this Court doth adjudge, that he, the said Charles Stuart, as a Tyrant, Traitor, Murtherer, and a public enemy, shall be put to death by the severing of his head from his body'. Quoted in Tangye, *The Two Protectors*, p. 146.

51   Fraser, *Cromwell, Our Chief of Men*, p. 287.

52   In Tangye's *The Two Protectors*, pp. 147–48, the author describes how during the first day of the trial of the King 'Considerable sensation was caused,

during the reading of the Charge, by the falling off of the head of the King's staff, which, no one offering to take up, he stooped for it himself'. Tangye continues with a description of the events on the scaffold on the day of the execution: 'Then going up the stairs into the gallery, and so into the Cabinet Chamber where he used to lie, he went to his devotions, refusing to dine (having before taken the Sacrament). About an hour before he came forth, he drank a glass of claret and ate a piece of bread. From whence he was accompanied by Dr. Juxon through the Banqueting House to the scaffold, which was covered with black velvet. The axe and block had been set in the middle of the scaffold. The ground was kept by foot and horse soldiers and the multitude of spectators was very great. The King being come upon the scaffold, looked earnestly at the block and asked "if there were no higher block?". He then delivered a speech in which he asserted his innocence of the crimes laid to his charge. Turning to Colonel Hacker, the King said "Take care that they do not put me to pain". Just then a gentleman coming near the axe, the King said, "Take heed of the axe, pray take heed of the axe". Then turning to Dr. Juxon he said, "I have a good cause and a gracious God on my side . . . I go from a corruptible to an incorruptible crown, where no disturbance can be, no disturbance in the world". The King then said to his executioner, "Is my hair well?" then he took off his cloak and his George medal giving the latter to Dr. Juxon, saying "Remember". Then the King put off his doublet and being in his waistcoat, put his cloak on again, then looking upon the block, said to his executioner, "You must set it fast". "It is fast Sir" replied the executioner. The King said to him, "When I put my hands, this way (stretching them out) then —". After that having said two or three words to himself with hands and eyes lift up, immediately stooping down, laid his neck upon the block; and then the executioner again putting his hair under his cap, the King said "Stay for the sign". The executioner replied "Yes I will, and it please your Majesty". And after a very little pause the King stretched forth his hands – the executioner, at one blow, severed his head from his body'.

53   Quoted in Daniell, *Battles and Battlefields*, p. 127.

54   Fraser, *Cromwell Our Chief of Men*, p. 293.

55   Extract from Cromwell's speech to General Council at Whitehall on 23 March 1649; quoted in full in Abbott, *Writings and Speeches*, vol. II, pp. 36–39.

56   Cromwell's speech to the army at Andover in May 1649; quoted in Fraser, *Cromwell Our Chief of Men*, p. 315.

57   Fraser, *ibid.*, p. 311.

58   Extract from *The Moderate Intelligencer* of 10 July, 1649, quoted in Rev. Denis Murphy, SJ, *Cromwell in Ireland, A History of Cromwell's Irish Campaign* (Dublin: M. H. Gill and Son, 1883), p. 70.

59   Oliver Cromwell to Richard Mayor Esq.; quoted in Abbott, *Writings and Speeches*, vol. II, pp. 102–03.

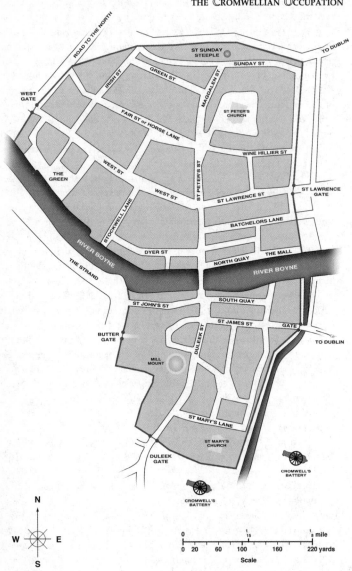

THE TOWN OF DROGHEDA
AS IT WAS DURING
THE CROMWELLIAN OCCUPATION

ROAD TO THE NORTH

TO DUBLIN

ST SUNDAY STEEPLE

SUNDAY ST

IRISH ST

GREEN ST

MAGDALEN ST

WEST GATE

ST PETER'S CHURCH

FAIR ST or HORSE LANE

WINE HILLIER ST

WEST ST

THE GREEN

WEST ST

ST PETER'S ST

ST LAWRENCE ST

ST LAWRENCE GATE

STOCKWELL LANE

BATCHELORS LANE

RIVER BOYNE

DYER ST

NORTH QUAY

THE MALL

THE STRAND

RIVER BOYNE

SOUTH QUAY

ST JOHN'S ST

ST JAMES ST

GATE

BUTTER GATE

DULEEK ST

TO DUBLIN

MILL MOUNT

ST MARY'S LANE

DULEEK GATE

ST MARY'S CHURCH

CROMWELL'S BATTERY

CROMWELL'S BATTERY

N

W   E

S

Scale

0   ⅟₁₅   ⅛ mile

0   20   60   100   160   220 yards

Scale

Chapter Two
DROGHEDA

'. . . *those barbarous wretches*'
(Cromwell, describing the defenders of Drogheda)

THE CONSEQUENCES OF plantations are essentially the reasons why the island of Ireland is divided in two. The six counties of Northern Ireland have, up until recently, been under the direct rule of the British government. At the time of writing, the Good Friday agreement, which includes representation from north and south of the country in a new system of administration, has provided Northern Ireland with the long overdue but highly delicate opportunity of enjoying sustained political stability.

In terms of religion, Ireland's national Church is today, arguably, at the weakest point of its history. The root of the decline is endemic and is not, ironically, because of religious oppression from a foreign country, despite centuries of persecution. Generally speaking, there is very little semblance of seventeenth century philosophy remaining in today's technological age. Communication methods such as 'word of mouth' and restricted politicised pamphlets have been replaced by the information super highway and computerised media technology. Imaginative superstitions and naïve wholesale gullibility, concerning both supernatural and divine matters, have been replaced by scientific solutions and informed cynicism respectively. Today, there is a growing feeling of distinct indifference to Catholicism, the religion of the majority. The Church's flock is now a much more discerning and questioning community, reluctant to accept many of the fairy story style answers to rational theological questions. The number of vocations to the clerical life is reduced to a trickle. Church congregations are at their lowest for years. Organised religion is gradually playing less and less of a part in Irish people's lives today. The Church's case is not helped by the successive sex scandals of recent years, in which many of their members have been officially indicted through the Irish courts. In Ulster, where incidentally, Cromwell never set foot, sectarianism is still at the source of the strife of twentieth century Northern Ireland.

The beauty of the Irish countryside, its cultural heritage and traditions today attract tourists from all over the world. It was to within sight of the resplendent Wicklow mountains and valleys to the south and those of the famous Mourne to the north that Oliver Cromwell now approached with his fleet of invading ships, in the summer of 1649. On his approach to the harbour at Ringsend, he would have seen the grey stone-walled city of Dublin dominating the landscape on his right. Directly ahead inland was the small village and castle of Baggatrath (Beggar's Bush today) nestling amongst the trees, not far from the Rathmines battlefield and commanding a view of the sea. Now in August, the surrounding countryside must have been a blaze of natural colour, with the foliage of the fully dressed oaks, beeches and chestnuts splashing into the air and swaying in the summer breeze. The splendour of the wild yellow furze bushes on beds of green meadows was most likely discernible across the plains of south County Dublin, to the foot of the Wicklow hills. The serenity of the countryside was shattered with the roar of cannon fire as the capital acknowledged Cromwell's arrival.

Hugh Peters, Cromwell's chaplain, tells us that the latter was 'as sea-sick as ever I saw a man in my life',[1] on the otherwise uneventful short voyage. Michael Jones had sent a carriage for him, and upon his arrival at College Green the *Perfect Diurnall* reports that he stood upright in the coach and with his hat in his hand, he declared:

> That as God had brought him thither in safety, so he
> doubted not but, by His divine providence, to restore them
> all to their liberty and property; and that all those whose
> hearts affections were real for the carrying on of the great
> work of the barbarous and bloodthirsty Irish, and the rest of
> their inherents and confederates, for the propagating of the

Gospel of Christ, the establishing of truth and peace and restoring that bleeding nation to its former happiness and tranquillity, should find favour and protection from the Parliament of England and receive such endowments and gratuities, as should be answerable to their merits.[2]

Cromwell would continue to labour the point concerning 'the barbarous and bloodthirsty Irish', most especially after Drogheda, to defend his actions against the military defenders there. Now in the land where the alleged 1641 atrocities had actually taken place, his incriminating words, mixed with his religious exhortations, are shown to be a foreboding notice of his frame of mind.

According to tradition, Cromwell's lodgings in Dublin were at a house which stood at the corner of Castle Street and Werburgh Street. (The house was demolished in 1812 by order of the Commissioners of Wide Streets).[3] It was from here that he now began his Irish campaign in earnest. The first blow he struck was with words. After issuing a declaration against 'the frequent practice of swearing, cursing and drunkenness',[4] he issued a second statement, that was as subtle as it was incisive and particularly damaging to his enemies. This was a war zone. Cromwell was by now very familiar with war zones. He also knew a little bit about human nature. He issued a proclamation to the Irish country folk offering to buy their provisions for his huge army. The frightened civilian Irish had been, up to now, used to both the Confederate and Parliamentary armies pillaging their crops, fruit and vegetables etc. in the previous years of the war. This new English army were actually willing to pay for their commodities. This not only helped to alienate his adversaries from the people they claimed to represent, but more importantly, it provided imperative sustenance for his hungry troops. (See Appendix No. 2.1).

Cromwell had no intentions of including 'Country People' or civilians, in the rigours of war. He confirms his totally non-threatening attitude to them in the declaration: *'I do hereby warn . . . all Officers, Soldiers and others under my command not to do any wrong or violence toward Country People or persons whatsoever, unless they be actually in arms or office with the enemy . . . as they shall answer to the contrary at their utmost perils . . .'*

This proclamation was to be printed and published countrywide and was issued immediately before his military campaign commenced.

Its orders were to determine the mood for the subsequent conflict. Its content depicts a commander who would hold upright the rules of contemporary warfare and one who had no desire to contravene the laws of human decency by indulging in the senseless slaughter of innocent civilians.

At the end of August, Cromwell decided that he would advance on Drogheda or 'Tredagh'. His choice was made easy. The town, now occupied by Royalists, not only had an excellent strategic position as the gateway to Ulster, but it was also considered to be a military stronghold of major consequence. On 11 July, under Ormonde's instructions, Inchiquin had besieged the town, and after a seven-day siege, terms were agreed and the garrison surrendered to him. Most of the defending soldiers then crossed over to the Royalist side. Ormonde himself arrived in the town on 17 August and installed Sir Arthur Aston as governor, at the expense of Lord Moore, whom Inchiquin had appointed.

Despite Parliament's efforts to build on Monck's unofficial truce with Eoghan Ruadh O'Neill, no terms could be agreed between the Celtic leader and the administrative body in London, even with the addition of Cromwell's negotiatory skills. O'Neill's primary objective was the liberation of both his religion and his country. He now perceived an alliance with Ormonde as being the most pragmatic course of action he could take. The latter's defeat at Rathmines, in O'Neill's view, had left the country vulnerable to Cromwell's Herculean spirit and his renowned New Model Army, now preparing for extensive military engagement prior to their march from Dublin. Plantations and religious suppression would both flourish if the Puritans were victorious. He declared to his officers, 'Gentlemen, to demonstrate to the world that I value the service of my King and the interest of my nation as I always did, I now forgive the Supreme Council and my enemies their ill practices and wrongs they did me. I will now embrace that peace which I formerly rejected out of good intent.'[5] O'Neill would have been considered to be the most 'Irish' of the leaders in the conflict (a member of the great O'Neill clan, from Tyrone), yet like his predecessor Sir Phelim at the start of the insurrection, he pledged his loyalty to the King of England. This is an indication of how intricate the contemporary political situation was. The composition of Cromwell's opponents in Ireland was now complete. With O'Neill finally on board, Ormonde was now at the head of an army that comprised the Old English, native Irish Catholics, Protestant Royalists, and all other forces hostile to the English Parliament. The 'forces of the Crown' are renowned as having been a notorious source of Ireland's woes through the centuries. Ironically, Cromwell's Parliamentarian army would encounter those very forces of the Crown on Irish soil, defending Irish cities and towns. The combination of all of Cromwell's enemies in Ireland, therefore, represented the throne, in one form or another. However, O'Neill would be dead in three months. After Rathmines, Ormonde would never take to the field again.

The beleaguered Confederate army was now scattered and Ormonde himself was camped at the house of Sir Luke Fitzgerald in Tecroghan, five miles north of Trim in the south-western corner of Meath. The way was clear for the New Model's ominous advance up the coastline, through the pastures of north County Dublin and east Meath to Drogheda. On 31 August they assembled in the field of Lord Barnwell three miles north of Dublin (probably at Turvey Castle) to check their ammunition. Twelve regiments of 'stout and resolute men' had been chosen for the Drogheda assault. They camped that night on Barnwell's estate. On 23 August a council of war had been held by the Royalists at Drogheda. Present were the Earls of Castlehaven and Westmeath, the Lords Moore and Montgomery, Sir Arthur Aston, Sir Ffoulk Hunckes, Sir Thomas Armstrong, Sir Robert Stewart, Sir Robert Byron, Colonels Mark Trevor, William Warren, Garret Wall and Michael Byrne.[6] It was resolved that the town would be maintained. 'It was then plain,' wrote Ormonde:

> We were to be on the defensive part of the war, and that he [Cromwell] would draw forth suddenly, to recover those places we had gained, and first, we were assured, he purposed to attempt Drogheda. We therefore applied our utmost industry, to supply that place with what it wanted, placed in it Sir Arthur Aston, as expert and gallant a governor as we could wish for, gave him the same men, and the same number of men, horse and foot that he desired and furnished him with the full proportion of ammunition, and other provisions that he demanded, judging that if Cromwell could be there foiled, or kept before it but for a time, it would much advantage us that had so lately received so great a blow, as required time to recover, and the rebels, in the neck of it, having received so great a

> countenance and strength as Cromwell brought with him,
> being the best of the rebels' old army in England.[7]

The decision that was taken that day to defend the town was made by the cream of the Irish Royalist leaders. It was their calculated resolution that the gamble was worth it. By reducing Cromwell's forces at Drogheda, there was always the chance that if enough time were gained, a full scale engagement in the field could be considered. However, by refusing to surrender when summoned to do so, the defenders ran the very real risk that the entire garrison could expect no quarter and legitimately lose their lives according to the laws of war.

Before leaving Dublin, Cromwell had organised the train of artillery to be transported to Drogheda by sea. The countryside was unpredictable and the march would be made easier this way. The route that the Puritans took to the town can be easily marked out. The turnpike road that linked Drogheda with Dublin was not built until 1731. The first Irish road book, *A Guide for Strangers in the Kingdom of Ireland*,[8] was published in 1647. The circuit is described thus:

> Dublin to Swords – six miles
> Swords to Balrudderie – six miles
> Balrudderie to Drogheda – eight miles.

While the distances are marked in Irish miles, they are clearly inaccurate. The most direct path would have been from Swords through the villages of Ballyboghill and the Naul, and so past Bellewstown and Beamore to Drogheda. However, to avoid the higher gradients further inland and to possibly keep within both eyesight and communicative distance of their ships, they most likely took the same route along the coastal plains as did Captain John Stevens, who fought with James II at the Boyne and described the road from Swords to Drogheda forty-one years later, in 1690 as follows:

> Tuesday ye 20th about 5 of the clock in the morning I
> returned to the Regiment and found them ready to march.
> It was ordered that neither officer nor souldier should quit
> the ranks, which was no small fatigue the weather being hot
> and the road excessive dusty, to that degree that we were
> also stifled and blinded, and so covered with dust that we
> scarce knew ourselves, all of which fell most grievously

upon such as marched afoot, whereof I was one. From Swords to Bellagh is 4 miles, thence to Ballruddre 2 both of them poor villages, these last 2 miles of the longest I have seen. Hence to Gormanston 3 miles, not worthy the name of a town, but at best only a tolerable village, most remarkable for giving title to a Lord, who has a good house in the place, but poorly provided at that time, as some of our Officers by experience, who went to it only to get any sort of a drink, there being then none to be had for mony. Here we made a halt for about 2 hours, but found no refreshment, but what we brought with us unless the coole air and grass. Hence we marched 2 miles farther to Innistown bridge where we drew up in a large field in order to pitch our tents but before the ground was marked out orders came to march to Drogheda three miles from this place and we were quartered in the City . . . All the country between this citie and Dublin is very pleasant, and a good soile, having great store of corn some good pasture. The road in summer very good but in winter extreme deep unless helped by an old broken causeway, full of holes.[9]

The prevailing blustery weather conditions ruined Cromwell's plan to make the arrival of the army coincide with that of their big guns at the walls of Drogheda. The ships were to be delayed for almost a week. There is a story that when passing Gormanston, Cromwell attempted to seize the infant heir to the Preston estate, but was foiled by the local parish priest who fled with him to France. The journey to Gormanston had been without incident. With the New Model's artillery at sea and themselves exposed on the lowlands to a possible attack from the hills on the west, it has been suggested that this was a missed opportunity for Ormonde. The truth, however, is that with his disjointed troops, Ormonde was totally incapable of facing an army of such force and repute in the field, irrespective of the fact that their cannons were on shipboard. Small bands of Royal forces that were abroad in the interior parts of Meath did attempt to obstruct the passage of the New Model machine, but could only retreat hastily towards Drogheda. Ormonde's only hope was to expose them to a long siege outside the fortifications of Drogheda where a badly supplied army would suffer from both sickness and hunger. This Parliamentarian army was, however, neither

inadequately supplied, nor were they planning any lengthy sieges outside any garrison walls.

Somewhere along the journey, it is not clear exactly where, two
Roundheads decided to ignore the Lieutenant-general's pledge to protect the local common people. Instead of using money that must have
been available to them, they decided to relieve a local woman of some
hens with no recompense whatsoever. When the news was communicated to Cromwell, he had no hesitation in hanging both of the thieves
as an example to the rest.[10]

Drogheda today is a thriving port town with a population of about
25,000 people, situated approximately thirty miles north of the capital,
on the main Dublin-Belfast road. The town's urban landscape nestles
upon the banks of the famous River Boyne, the north and south
prospects both elevated above its current as it meanders eastwards to
the sea. Today, the town sprawls far from its medieval wall boundaries
as it progressively consumes the hinterland, in the shape of the rolling
hills of Louth and Meath. It is home to many modern industries,
including, the European headquarters of Coca-Cola Atlantic Ltd. It also
houses a modern commercial establishment that is representative of
international twentieth century cuisine: a McDonalds fast food outlet.

As Cromwell descended on the town at the head of the 12,000-
strong army, through the sloping fields of Bryanstown immediately
south of the town walls, he would have had a perfect opportunity to
survey the garrison and appraise the lie of the land surrounding it. It
was not the most suitable place for siege warfare. Built by the Normans
in the twelfth century, the town was split in half by the river and was
connected by a wooden drawbridge. Both halves were totally encircled
by defensive walls that were at least twenty-two feet high. These stone
fortifications were in reasonable repair, varied in thickness from six feet
to two feet, and were supported on the inside by arcading stone but-
tresses on top of which was a wall walk. The mound known as Millmount was elevated high above the walls in the south-west corner and
was complemented by the distinguished spire of St Mary's Church
that rose higher still, overlooking the terrain outside. The southern
part of the town that Cromwell now faced was the smaller of the two
halves and was protected by a deep ravine on three sides with the river
making up the fourth. With only one main gate in the walls, the massive tumulus of Millmount and the dominating church walls, it was
also the best defended. The medieval streets and lanes of the town

within were divided by neat hedgerows and gardens. Conifers were dispersed throughout the town at various points, their greenery rising above the brown thatched and grey slate rooftops on both banks of the river. Beyond the Boyne, nestling among the houses on the hills of the north side, could be seen the prominent tower of the Tholsel 'the municipal headquarters', and further up the hill the great spire of St Peter's Church of Ireland. The Puritan army moved to within musket shot of the town, separated only from the huge fortifications by the picturesque Dale valley. (Then called the 'Dove', from the Irish 'dubh' meaning black.)[11] At the foot of the glen, the Dove stream meandered, bubbling and spilling its way towards the Boyne and from there out to sea. On the crest of the Dale opposite, just below the lofty stone edifice, was the friars' orchard, accessible from the churchyard via a small 'blind' gate. Rows of apple and pear trees stretched in perfect symmetry to the precipice of the ravine. The honey-coloured Dublin Hill (Cromwell's Mount) was audaciously engulfed by hundreds of canvas tents on that serene evening of 3 September, as the New Model hordes set up their hostile encampment on the scenic landscape. In this peaceful place, cannon fire was about to explode, the steel of pikes and swords would fiercely clash, horses would shriek and men would be sliced open, screaming and dying. It is likely that when night fell, the sombre darkness was lit up by a hundred watch fires.

Aston, into whose hands the defence of Drogheda was now entrusted, was an experienced professional soldier of international repute. One of the few Catholic commanders in the King's army, he apparently received his commission with the assistance of Queen Henrietta Maria.[12] A staunch Royalist, he had served in Russia under the Swedish King Gustavus Adolphus and had distinguished himself in the army of Sigismund, King of Poland, for valour and excellent conduct. The Thirty Years War in Europe, which had ended the year before, had offered the opportunity for military experience to many English and Irish men alike. So, like Eoghan Ruadh O'Neill, Aston had not wasted his time during his active service in continental Europe. On his return to England, he fought for the King at Edgehill and he had occupied the positions of governor of Reading and Oxford in 1643 and 1644 respectively. Due to a riding accident, he had lost a leg and now wore a wooden substitute. Unlike his agility, his proficiency for military instruction was not impaired by this handicap. Edward Hyde, the Earl of Clarendon and henchman of Charles I, would later write of Aston,

' . . . there was not in the King's army a man of greater reputation or one of whom the enemy had greater dread.'[13] Aston industriously orchestrated the plans for the defence of the town. Entrenchments were dug both inside and outside the walls at the southern end of the town to make assaults on the walls even more difficult. Aston had been in communication with Ormonde on a daily basis and they were confident that they could withstand a lengthy siege.[14] To appreciate the number of the attacking army is to realise that it was about half the number of the present population of Drogheda.

Cromwell studied the layout of the town from his southern vantage point. Since it was split by an unfordable river, he immediately concentrated on the south side as the only feasible point of attack. There was no merit in splitting his troops up and sending half of them to besiege the north side. Communication between both sides would have been impossible. Besides, the nearest bridge was eight miles away at Slane. (The river could have been crossed at 'Pass-if-you-can' or just 'Pass' about a mile from the town, where William would cross in 1690, but only at low tide.) This course of action was therefore not an option. St Mary's churchyard was in the south-eastern corner of the town. It had as its outer boundary on two sides the massive town walls and on the other two inner sides formidable churchyard walls. The area formed a perfect square. Cromwell decided to centre his attention on this section of the town, as he quickly realised that if he could take control of the yard with his infantry, then he could easily maintain it and allow his horse access to complete the invasion.

The 4 September dawned, and with it came confirmation that the train of artillery was delayed. Without it, Cromwell would not make a move. Heavy cannons were essential for the success of siege warfare. In 1641 when Sir Phelim O'Neill had attempted to take Drogheda, his weaponry had comprised of muskets, pikes and swords. Although O'Neill's objective had been to isolate the town from supplies and bring it to its knees for the want of sustenance, these weapons were useless when it came to taking the offensive against a garrison enclosed within high stone walls. Seventeenth century combat methods were broadly divided into two types: field warfare and siege warfare. Siege artillery, during the English Civil War, had proved to be most cumbersome when speed was required during a march. However its effect was devastating when called into play. Cannons were well in use in Ireland by that time. The first guns to be used in an attack on, and in defence of, an Irish town was in 1495 when Waterford was cannonaded by Perkin Warbeck's ships and the town returned cannon fire.[15] However the size and power of Cromwell's guns were awesome compared to earlier artillery fire. It is this force that would be totally underestimated by the defending army.

To fully appreciate the type of encounter that was about to unfold, a brief analysis of contemporary weaponry is constructive. Many myths and legends concerning military manoeuvres have grown up around this period of history. The word 'cavalier' has emanated from the seventeenth century, and its modern day meaning best describes the methods employed by some of the Royalists during the English Civil War. Prince Rupert in particular epitomised this sometimes carefree approach to fierce hand-to-hand combat. Alexander Dumas, who created the famous and mythical Three Musketeers, and Hollywood have glamorised musketeers as heros renowned for their swashbuckling sword skills. Genuine musketeers of the Civil War were much less glamorous. They, along with pikemen, made up the infantry section of a seventeenth century army. Musketeers generally outnumbered the pikemen by about two to one. They carried their bullets in a pouch, but in battle they held them in their mouths for easy loading. Gunpowder was carried in little tin tubes which were hung around the neck on leather belts called bandoleers. Their muskets were either matchlock or flintlock style, and the barrels were four feet long. An expert musketeer could dispatch three rounds in a minute. During the reloading procedure, the line in the immediate rear would step forward, fire and reload, and so on. Bayonets had not yet been invented. Pikes varied in size from fifteen feet to eighteen feet, but usually the accepted length was sixteen feet. There was much more honour among troops in carrying a pike, as it was considered an older, more respected weapon compared to pistols or muskets. Also because of its size and the armour that accompanied it, it usually took a soldier of considerable bulk to handle this cumbersome weapon.[16]

The cavalry was also divided into two types: the cuirassier and the harquebusier. The armour of the former was much heavier than that of the latter, and if one dismounted he was hard pushed to remount without assistance. Buff coats which were made from extremely thick leather were usually worn under the armour for extra protection. The sword was the principal weapon of the cavalry. Various types of swords were in use, including mortuary swords, basket-hilted swords and rapiers. The mortuary sword that Cromwell used at Drogheda still exists and is under the supervision of the Royal Armouries.[17] Cavalry also carried firearms that would vary, depending on availability and necessity. Generally a mounted Parliamentarian soldier carried two pistols in a holster hanging on each side at the front of his saddle. Pistol barrel lengths were about fourteen to fifteen inches.

Artillery in use in 1649 comprised mainly of cannons and mortars. Large sized artillery such as whole cannons, demi-cannons and culverins were preferred for siege warfare. The largest in use at the time was the 63pdr (pounder) cannon royal followed by the 47pdr whole cannon and the 27pdr demi-cannon. At Basing House, Cromwell had employed two demi-cannon and one whole cannon. Aging medieval walls, held together by antiquated bonding methods, were no match for the heavy shot that would be despatched from these large siege pieces. Mortars were pieces with very short barrels and very wide bores which were designed to fire with very high trajectory. The shells were effectively flung from their barrels to land from above and would explode on impact. The shell itself was a hollow iron sphere, filled with gunpowder and a slow burning fuse which would detonate as it landed. A very crude form of hand grenade called a 'grenadoe' was also employed at Drogheda.[18]

During hand-to-hand contests with these basic weapons, an individual encounter would normally be very brief. Once the telling blow was struck there was usually no possibility of a rebuttal. In such a confrontation it was quite often the case that the victim would take some time to die. The victor usually moved on to his next target as soon as the immediate one was felled, though not necessarily killed. It was not easy to kill a man outright under these circumstances, and frequently blows were aimed at the head for optimum effect. Cromwell would often use the phrase 'effusion of blood' as a euphemism, and it is easy to appreciate from where he derives the analogy, since he was a witness to so much bloodshed.

Despite Ormonde's assurances that Aston would receive every possible assistance, a week before Cromwell arrived at the town, Aston would sound the alarm bells by writing:

> Yesternight theer came heether from Dundalke 10 barrels
> of pouther, but very little match and that is a thinge moste
> wanting heer; and for round shote, not any at all. I beseech
> your Excellency bee pleased to give speedy orders for sum,

as also for the sudden coming of men and monies. Belly foode I perceive, will prove scarce amongst us, but my endeavours shall never be sparing to approve myself.[19]

Ormonde only had with him at Tecroghan a small force of 3,000 men. He would write later to Charles II:

> . . . after the defeat before Dublin, almost all those of the army that had homes of their own or their friends to go to, were retired to them, and could by no industry be gotten together . . . so the force I had with me, in the whole about 3,000 horse and foot . . . And of these our numbers daily diminished by the revolt of some officers and many private soldiers, the rest showing much dejection of courage, and upon all occasions of want, which are very frequent with us, venting their discontent in such dangerous words, that it was held unsafe to bring them within that distance of the enemy . . .[20]

At this stage he was depending largely on detachments from Munster and Connaught to arrive, but his main objective was to convince Eoghan Ruadh that his assistance was required to strengthen the defences at Drogheda. Ormonde detached the latter's nephew, Daniel O'Neill, northwards to encourage Eoghan Ruadh to mobilise. His forces consisted of about 5,000 foot and 300 horse, but he would have had no difficulty in increasing his army to 10,000 foot and 2,000 horse.[21] Daniel O'Neill wrote to Ormonde on 5 September that he had found Eoghan Ruadh at Ballykelly, twelve miles east of Derry in rapidly declining health:

> This day [added Daniel] he has a litter made for him; if tomorrow he has any manner of ease he intends to march. Whether it be his sickness or that he intends to oblige your Excellency the more, he has not talked anything as yet of his conditions. All his officers to a very few, and those of least consideration, are as passionate for submission to his Majesty's service as Sir Luke Fitzgerald would have them. The number of foot he hopes to bring your Excellency will be near 6,000 and about 500 horse, truly not so contemptible for their number as some persuaded me they were, they are well horsed and armed to a very few.[22]

Had the roles been reversed and had Ormonde been at the head of O'Neill's competent force and O'Neill in his poor personal condition commanding Ormonde's reduced army, things might well have been different. However, the Irish Royalists were continually to be at the adverse end of prevailing circumstances. Numbers they had, but cohesion they totally lacked.

Despite this, confidence was very high on the part of the Royalists that Drogheda could not be taken. Ormonde in a letter to O'Neill on 8 September indicated that he was hopeful of the timely intervention of 'Colonel Hunger and Major Sickness'[23] to infiltrate the Parliamentarian ranks outside the walls of Drogheda. Winter was approaching and his hopelessly optimistic objective was that 'if frustrated by their designs upon that important garrison [Drogheda] . . . they may . . . in a short time be reduced to a very mean and distressed condition'.[24] Within the walls of the town, Aston was at the head of a 3,000 strong garrison. Although heavily outnumbered, he was convinced that the huge walls and the topographical defensive features of the fortress meant that it was virtually impenetrable.

During that week, Aston ordered infrequent surprise sallies from the main gates. Despite Aston's determination, no real success was gained from this activity. On the contrary, during one of the forays, Sir Thomas Armstrong, who led one of these attacks from the town, had the humiliating experience of having all of his 200 men captured and only managed to escape himself due to the 'goodness of his horse'. From this inglorious charge on the enemy, Aston lost about 7 percent of his defending forces. Undeterred, he continued to dispatch much needed troops outside the walls on short sharp assault missions. His objectives in despatching sallies were no doubt to hinder the preparations of the Parliamentarians for the inevitable assault, but Aston was always up against it. He knew that the geography of the immediate area was not conducive to these ventures when he declared, 'But indeed I have not been in a place worse situated for sallies than this town is.'[25] So he invited Ormonde to join the hostilities outside the walls by asking him 'to attempt an assault on the greater camp speedily, and [he will, if he] have notice, beat up those upon St. John's Hill'.[26] He was using four barrels of gunpowder a day for his musketeers as they engaged in a futile effort to discommode the Roundhead masses.

Sir Edmund Verney, a member of a famous English noble family with proclaimed fidelity to the Crown, was one of the officers of substance who was ensconced within the fort of Drogheda. On 9 September, Verney, in a letter to Ormonde, emphasised the determined mood in the Royalist camp declaring that he had:

> great hopes and expectations that the service that I am present engaged in will receive a happy issue and the chief ground of this confidence is the unity, right and understanding and indeed friendship between ourselves. Warren and Wall are my most intimate comrades, and indeed I have not in my life known more of diligence and circumspection than in these two Gentlemen. Their men are all in heart and courage, having still had good success in our sallies, and we do little fear what the enemy can presently do against us. We ordinarily meet once a day to discourse of our condition and what is fit to be done.[27]

However despite his defiant words, unlike Aston, Verney was not convinced that the titanic Puritan army would simply succumb to the elements of an Irish autumn. He added an ominous, yet perfectly pragmatic, plea for assistance that would be ignored by the exasperatingly unheroic Ormonde:

> We are informed that your Excellency hath a considerable army, and our humble opinions are that you might advance and lodge at Slane Bridge with safety, and that the enemy could no way force you to fight unless to their infinite disadvantage and certainly they could much less maintain their siege; their camp is much subject to wants, they bringing their supplies by sea.[28]

Meanwhile, on the attacker's side of the walls, the train of artillery and supplies had arrived under the supervision of Sir George Ascough. The latter had also successfully blockaded the entrance to the harbour, thus cutting off a possibly vital supply line. Since there are no records of the mouth of the Boyne at Mornington having been fortified, it has to be assumed that the fleet sailed right up to the town unhindered. Cromwell had despatched a troop of soldiers to evaluate any activity on the northern side of the town on the riverbanks opposite. Preparations were almost ready on both sides. The Parliamentarian whole cannons, demi-cannons, culverins and mortar pieces were hauled and dragged on their gun carriages to the hill overlooking St Mary's Church that now goes by the name of Cromwell's Mount. The largest whole cannons were two cannon of eight inch bore and two of seven inch bore.[29] Aston indicated that there were 'at least eight pieces of battery, the least whereof shot twelve pounds, and one of them a thirty pounds bullet'.[30] (A whole cannon ball recently extricated from the soil near St Mary's Church weighed precisely two stone, confirming Aston's estimation.) The Roundhead gunners were some of the most experienced siege warfare personnel in Europe.

It was 8.00am on Monday, 10 September. A note in the handwriting of the Lord Lieutenant of Ireland and chief commanding officer of the Puritan army was delivered to the governor of the town. It read:

> Sir, having brought the army belonging to the Parliament
> of England before this place, to reduce it to obedience, to
> the end effusion of blood may be prevented, I thought fit
> to summon you to deliver the same into my hands to their
> use. If this be refused, you will have no cause to blame me.
> I expect your answer and rest your servant,
>
> O. Cromwell [31]

The fact that he had waited until his field pieces were in position to open negotiations illustrates that Cromwell knew only too well the kind of answer he might expect. Furthermore, should there have been any ambiguity concerning the articles of war then pertaining, he warned, 'If this be refused, you will have no cause to blame me.' Negotiations, however, ended there. They would resume later that week, under much less cordial circumstances. In his note Cromwell had displayed all the pertinent elements that would have been expected under the circumstances: a notice of identification, a summons to surrender, an explanation for this command, a direct threat, an option to avoid bloodshed and lastly, a curious politeness, all delivered in a respectful and cultured fashion. The decision that was reached during the council of war in Drogheda on 23 August, in which Aston himself had participated, now came into play. He refused to surrender.

Cromwell's Mount is today occupied by housing estates, some of which date back to the last century. The erratic geography of the area has determined that the ground has not been extensively developed. The deep glen of the Dale, where the Dubh stream is now piped underground, has only a handful of modern dwellings and is dominated by the tall spire of the present day St Mary's Church. It is a remarkable fact that a tangible historic atmosphere presently surrounds this entire location. One might very easily stand on the Mount and recreate in one's mind the booming sound of the cannons, the singing of the psalms, and the clatter of the musket shot reverberating around the valley.

Aston's predictable response to Cromwell's request, 'to the which I received no satisfactory answer',[32] resulted in his raising his red flag and issuing the order to open fire. So it began. The morning, afternoon and evening of the 10th was spent by the New Model gunners firing at the church steeple and at the corner tower. Cromwell wrote: 'I proceeded that day to beat down the steeple of the church on the south side of the town and to beat down the tower not far from the same place.'[33] No doubt Aston and some of his subordinates had experience of large siege pieces from their Continental escapades. However, the magnitude of this artillery power had not yet been seen in Ireland. Those members of the garrison who had not participated in the wars in England must have been seeing this awesome new explosive force for the first time. Aston was extremely ill-equipped to deal with this menace, as his counter battery pieces were almost non existent. He was virtually without cannon and the total of his artillery staff was a meagre six men: one master gunner, two gunners and three gunner's mates.[34] The medieval tower at the south-eastern corner of the town that was beaten down that day had stood for hundreds of years. The cold reality of contemporary modern warfare was gradually unfolding. The clouds of gunpowder smoke that hung on the attacker's side of the valley were matched by those of limestone dust that hung on the defender's side as the huge walls were slowly being scattered to rubble.

The siege of Drogheda of 1641–42 by Sir Phelim O'Neill, the Catholic rebel, must have been the type of encounter that the Royalists had now been expecting from the Puritans. On 21 November 1641, O'Neill had besieged the town with his partisan rebel troops, eventually capitulating and lifting their blockade on 5 March 1642.[35] Colonel Hunger and Major Disease and indeed Lieutenant Freeze, had all played a part in O'Neill's lack of success. The winter had been particularly bad, to the point that the Boyne had actually frozen over. When O'Neill would hear of Cromwell's success at Drogheda he would ruefully declare, 'He who could take Drogheda could take hell.'[36] It appears that Ormonde and his officers had made a gross underestimation of Cromwell's firepower capacity and resolve.

That evening Aston wrote his last words to Ormonde: 'The soldiers say well, I pray God, do well. I will assure your Excellency speedy help is much desired. I refer all things to your Excellency's provident care. Living I am, and dying will end, my Lord, your Excellency's most faithful and most obliged humble servant, Arthur Aston.'[37] Ormonde had assured Aston that Colonel Trevor's arrival from Dundalk with supplies was imminent. Aston's despondent postscript reads, 'I hear nothing, nor have not done, of Colonel Trevor. My ammunition decays apace and I cannot help it.'[38] Throughout the night, the garrison busied themselves repairing the damage that had been done to the walls. Two small breaches had been made in the southern wall, one near the east corner and a more considerable one further west nearer Duleek Gate. The following day they built a triple line of earthworks surrounding the church to make access difficult for the hostile besiegers. The Puritans renewed their battery. With every explosion, another piece of the wall crumbled. The bombardment continued for most of the day.

Meanwhile, the Protestant population of the town were represented by Aston's grandmother Lady Wilmot who expressed her desire to surrender the town to Cromwell.[39] (See Appendix 2.3). Aston promptly had her expelled to Mellifont, two miles north of Drogheda, where she and her accomplices could do no harm.[40] The number of Catholics within the town had been recently swelled by the Confederate forces who primarily consisted of members of that faith. The Catholic priests within the walls took advantage of the preoccupied Protestants. They celebrated mass, no doubt for the many soldiers who were strong believers, in the Protestant church of St Peter's, a fact that would not be concealed from Cromwell. His abhorrence of Catholic ceremonies would never waver. His Puritan beliefs led him to believe that the emphasis of Roman Catholicism on and their embracing of ritualistic formalities was totally misplaced.

At about five in the evening of the 11th, Cromwell considered the breaches to be assaultable. The three regiments of Colonels Ewer, Hewson and Castle were despatched across the glen to assail the walls. The front line regiments during field warfare in the Civil War were given the name 'Forlorn Hope'. It was these troops that now formed the head of the attacking forces. From behind the trenches within the walls, the resilient besieged drove the Roundheads out. The commander of the Forlorn Hope, Colonel Castle, was shot in the head by an accurate Royalist musketeer and died on the spot. (Colonel James

Castle was one of the few officers of the Parliamentarian army to lose his life at Drogheda. On the 8 April 1652, it was resolved by Parliament '. . . that it be referred to the commissioners of Parliament now in Ireland, to take present care of the good education and maintenance of the two children of Colonel Castle deceased'.) [41]

They retreated, rallied and attacked again. A second attack was repulsed by the sheer belligerence of the stout Royalist hearts that occupied the churchyard. Cromwell, who until now had been an exasperated spectator, called on the reserves and ran to the breach himself in a supreme effort to overcome the defenders with sheer numbers. He carried hundreds of Roundheads with him through the walls. On this occasion the Royalist officer commanding the defence of the breach, Colonel William Wall, was cut down and killed, leaving his troops without a leader and presenting Cromwell with an opportunity that he was not going to miss. Colonel Warren also lost his life at the walls.[42] The breach was now in Cromwell's hands and with it the entrenchments within, consequently the church-yard and ultimately the town.

Meanwhile, further along the wall at a tenalia (a defensive tower detached from the wall, that may possibly have been a temporary fixture since no trace remains today),[43] the invaders were attempting to overpower those Royalists that were defending that part of the wall. Cromwell furnishes us with the details of this:

> There was a tenalia to flanker the south wall of the town, between Duleek gate and the corner tower before mentioned, which our men entered, wherein they found some forty or fifty of the enemy, which they put to the sword. And this (tenalia) they held, but it being without the wall, and the sally port through the wall into that tenalia being choked up with some of the enemy that were killed in it, it proved of no use for our entrance into the town that way. [44]

Today there is a sally port in the remaining section of the wall precisely in this area, that is now filled in.

Tradition has it that the breach through which entry was gained was positioned on the eastern wall overlooking the precipitous Dale valley. A plaque presently displayed on the wall of St Mary's Church indicates this. However, it appears to be a highly improbable theory when one considers the terrain surrounding the area. Despite Cromwell's detailed account of the battle, as well as many other contemporary narratives, it is by no means clear precisely where the Roundheads actually forced their way through the walls. The town walls, both east and south are still standing in this area today. Numerous observers have expressed surprise that Cromwell should order an assault on a wall positioned on the precipice of such a steep slope. It would have been difficult for his men to climb directly upwards in a straight line and absolutely impossible for his horse to do so, such was the gradient. The odds would have been heavily in favour of the defenders.[45] (Although with the numerical advantage that the Parliamentary forces enjoyed it would not have been impossible.) It is much more likely that the successful assault occurred on the south wall, where the ground was level immediately outside the walls. Cromwell himself mentions two breaches on the east and south wall and that they were both stormed. It is most unlikely that he would have been successful where the ground was far from conducive to such activity. The position of the siege guns facing the south wall was low. Those that were directed at the east wall were at the same level of the walls opposite. This may account for the fact that the successful assault was made at the breach that was high up in the wall, which would be the case if it was fired at from a lower trajectory. It is estimated that somewhere in the region of five hundred cannon balls were despatched at the walls by Cromwell, some of which are still being unearthed today.

While the position is not obvious, it is still possible today to speculate upon the point where that breach was made. Bulstrode Whitelocke gives more details of the breaches when he declares:

> . . . that the breaches, not being made low enough, the horse could not go in with the foot, but the foot alone stormed and entered the town, but by reason of the numerousness and stoutness of the enemy, who maintained the breach as gallantly as ever men did, and by the death of Colonel Castle, whose regiment was one of those that stormed (and he was slain at the storm), our men were disheartened and retreated, which my Lord Lieutenant seeing, went himself to the breach and after a little time a fresh reserve of Colonel Ewer's men fell on with the rest very courageously, and God abated the courage of the enemy; they fled before us till we gained the town and they all agreed in the not giving of quarter.[46]

Edmund Ludlow, one of Cromwell's fellow republicans, gives us a useful account of the activity at the breach:

> The enemy defended the breach against ours from behind an earth-work which they had cast up within, and where they had drawn up two or three troops of horse which they had within the town, for the encouragement and support of their foot. The fort [Millmount] was not unserviceable to them in the defence of the breach. The Lieutenant General, well knowing the importance of this action, resolved to put all upon it; and having commanded some guns to be loaded with bullets of half a pound and fired upon the enemy's horse . . . himself with a reserve of foot marched up to the breach, which giving fresh courage to our men, they made a second attack with more vigour than before. Whereupon the enemy's foot being abandoned by their horse, whom our shot had forced to retire, began to break and shift for themselves.[47]

The testimonies of Whitelocke and Ludlow are typical of seventeenth century narrative. While the researcher is grateful for the details illustrated in their accounts, one must exercise extreme caution when quoting their words. Like many other reporters of the day, neither Whitelocke nor Ludlow were even in Ireland, never mind Drogheda, when the above events took place. Whitelocke died in 1675 and his diaries were transcribed in 1682 entitled *Memorials of the English Affairs from the beginning of the Reign of Charles I to the happy Restoration of Charles II*. Like Ludlow, during Cromwell's time in Ireland he was a member of the Council of State. In Ludlow's case he transcribed his memoirs after the Restoration while in exile in Berne, Switzerland: *Memoirs of Edmund Ludlow Esq. Lieutenant General of the Horse, Commander-in-Chief of the forces in Ireland, One of the Council of State and a member of Parliament which began on November 3 1640*.

It was at this point that the laws of contemporary warfare acquired paramount significance. The invaders had succeeded in making their entrance into a fortress, the defenders of which had refused to surrender. No mercy could have been expected. The Parliamentarians were in a highly animated state since the pitched battle at the breaches was so intense, and the regiment of Colonel Castle now had an immediate and legitimate opportunity for vengeance. Furthermore, this was the first Irish town that Cromwell had ever encountered. In the attackers eyes, these defenders (at least in theory, certainly not in practice) were some of those 'barbarous wretches' who had engaged in heinous atrocities against their fellow Englishmen in 1641. Then there was the religious element. That odious and corrupt Roman faith was also represented within the walls of Drogheda on the evening of the 11 September 1649.

It was the ineptitude of the Royalist garrison that would now cement Cromwell's grip on the town.[48] No contemporary account furnishes us with a clear understanding as to why the drawbridge was not lifted. This apparently simple manoeuvre was not sufficiently provided for. Its effect would have been highly detrimental to Cromwell's initial success at the breaches, as raising the drawbridge would have completely isolated the smaller, southern half of the town from the main part. Cromwell rode his luck and secured the entire town in one swift and decisive move. His men poured in through the holes in the walls. Cromwell's own version of events best describes the circumstances as they unfolded. As a primary eyewitness his words written only days after the events are extremely detailed. But there are precautionary measures to be taken when interpreting the words of the English commander, as there are times when he portrays circumstances to be more favourable than they actually were. This is in an attempt to paint a more appealing picture of the action for his superiors. Fundamentally, however, Cromwell's facts are correct; he was no liar. He does, however, declare that there was only one repulsed attack prior to the successful onslaught, contrary to other eye-witnesses who state that two failed advances were made. He writes:

> Although our men that stormed the breaches were forced to recoil, as before is expressed, yet, being encouraged to recover their loss, they made a second attempt, wherein God was pleased [so] to animate them that they got ground of the enemy, and by the goodness of God, forced him to quit his entrenchments. And after a very hot dispute, the enemy having both horse and foot and we only foot within the wall, they gave ground, and our men became masters both of their retrenchments and the church; which indeed, although they made our entrance the more difficult, yet they proved of excellent use to us so that the enemy could

not annoy us with their horse, but thereby we had advantage to make good the ground, that so we might let in our own horse, which accordingly was done, though with much difficulty. The enemy retreated, divers of them, into the Millmount: a place very strong and of difficult access, being exceedingly high, having a good graft and strongly palisadoed. The Governor, Sir Arthur Ashton, and divers considerable Officers being there, our men getting up to them were ordered by me to put them all to the sword. And indeed being in the heat of the action, I forbade them to spare any that were in arms in the town, and, I think that night they put to the sword about two thousand men.[49]

The controversial question concerning the wholesale denial of quarter is not entirely obvious. Cromwell himself explicitly refused it. It is reported from other sources that some of the Commonwealth officers and soldiers did offer their lives to sections of the garrison. To offer quarter to a garrison was essentially to offer mercy, in other words to spare lives. Warfare was not completely reckless at the time and general rules did apply. At all times these guidelines included the leniency of offering quarter in every circumstance where the upper hand was obvious. Sir Lewis Dyves, a loyal subject of the King, would write in his account of Irish history from September 1648 to June 1650 that Aston,

> . . . doubted not of finding Cromwell play awhile (until Ormonde come to his relief) as certainly he had done, had not Colonel Wall's regiment, after the enemy had been twice bravely repulsed, upon the unfortunate loss of their Colonel in the third assault, been so unhappily dismayed as to listen, before they had need, unto the enemy offering quarter, and admitted them in upon these terms, thereby betraying both themselves and all their fellow soldiers to the slaughter, for Cromwell being master of the town, and told by Jones that he had now in his hand the flower of the Irish Army, gave order to have all that were in arms put to the sword.[50]

Ormonde, writing to Lord Byron at the time suggested that quarter was offered also when he says that Cromwell carried the breach on the third assault:

. . . all his officers and soldiers promising quarter to such as would lay down their arms and performing it as long as any place held out, which encouraged others to yield; but when they had once all in their power and feared that no hurt could be done to them, the word "No Quarter" went round and the soldiers were forced many of them against their wills to kill their prisoners.[51]

From these reports the story has emanated that some soldiers in the Commonwealth army tried to save Royalist lives and that Cromwell insisted that they all be killed, thus ignoring his more compassionate officers. What is more likely is that quarter was offered by some Roundheads in order to save any more losses on their side, but the intention must always have been to wipe the garrison out, as was their right. Inchiquin, writing to Ormonde on 15 September, stated that 'no quarter was given there with Cromwell's leave . . . the governor was killed after quarter given by the officer that took him'.[52]

The events at Millmount are in contention concerning this issue. Aston, with some of his immediate subordinates and their troops, a total of about 200–250 men, secured themselves at the top of the great mound immediately after the breach was lost. Cromwell's interpretation of the acquisition of this huge fort was simplistic in the extreme. He had conceded that it was 'a place very strong and of difficult access'[53] It was also fortified with palisades and was certainly a formidable obstacle. (To fully appreciate the magnitude of this tumulus, it is necessary to have stood at its base.) Having had such difficulty in gaining access into the town, Cromwell was extremely loath to renew his siege, albeit on a smaller scale. His report of 'our men getting up to them' conceals the explanation of how this was achieved. This is in stark contrast to the details on a plaque currently affixed to the Martello Tower that presently occupies the summit of Millmount, that says that Millmount 'offered the stiffest opposition to Cromwell during his attack on the town in 1649'.[54] Neither of these statements are fundamentally accurate. From the top of the mount, Aston expounded continued defiance, no doubt declaring his undying loyalty to the King and questioning the legality of this regicide Commonwealth government. After all, despite having been involved in the wars in England these last years, he and the government's most successful general had never before met in battle.

Newsbooks of the day also give details concerning Millmount. In the *Perfect Diurnall*, printed for Parliament on 8 October by Samuel Peckes, there is an anonymous letter that tells the circumstances surrounding the taking of Millmount:

> The mount was very strong of itself and manned with 250 of their principal men, Sir Arthur Aston being in it, who was governor of the town; which when they saw their men retreat, were so downcast and disheartened, that they thought it vain to make any further resistance, which if they had, they could have killed some hundreds of our men before they could have taken it. Lieutenant Colonel Axtell of Colonel Hewson's regiment with some twelve of his men went up to the top of the mount and demanded the governor the surrender of it, who was very stubborn, speaking very bigge words, but at length was persuaded to go into the windmill on top of the mount, and as many more as the chiefest of them as it would contain, where they were all disarmed and afterwards all slain.[55]

Ludlow also heard of the events at Millmount, and gives us a hint as to why the drawbridge was not lifted. He writes, that the Commonwealth soldiers:

> . . . followed them so close that they overtook them at the bridge that lay across the river, and separated that part where the action was from the principal part of the town, and preventing them from drawing up the bridge, entered pell-mell with them into the Place where they put all they met to the sword, having positive orders from the Lieutenant General to give no quarter to any souldier. Their works and fort were also stormed and taken and those that defended them put to the sword also, and amongst them Sir Arthur Aston, Governour of the Place. A great dispute there was amongst the souldiers for his artificial leg, which was reported to be of gold, but it proved to be of wood, his girdle being found to be the better booty, wherein two hundred pieces of gold were found quilted.[56]

No doubt, Aston had a most undignified death. Thomas Wood, a soldier in the Commonwealth army who has become notorious for his colourful stories surrounding these entire events says that Aston 'was believed to have hid away his gold for security in his wooden leg. This they seized upon as a prize when he fell, but finding nothing in it, they knocked out his brains with it and hacked his body to pieces'.[57] He says nothing of the gold in Aston's belt, but in true character highlights his gruesome death.

One cannot imagine that such tenacious Cavaliers as Aston and his officers would have marched into the windmill, handed over their weapons and offered their bodies for mutilation. The fortitude and valiant words that these gallant officers had proclaimed in their letters to Ormonde as the walls were being battered fly in the face of this idea. It is a ludicrous suggestion. No doubt they were promised their lives, but then the promise was ruthlessly withdrawn when they were in no position to negotiate. There is also reason to believe that these fallacious methods were employed throughout the town as the defending soldiers retreated from the hordes of Roundheads exacting their revenge on those 'barbarous wretches'. This can be gleaned from the smallness of the losses on the attackers side (allegedly sixty-four men in total) compared to the 3,000 Royalist deaths. These numbers do not suggest that there was any hand-to-hand combat within the walls of the town, just plain butchery. Throughout the narrow streets, the Roundheads swarmed, killing all of the military defenders that they encountered. It is difficult to conclude that there was any resistance at all from the Royalists at this stage. Those that didn't escape must have been promised quarter and then denied it.[58] No contemporary account whatsoever describes any actual fighting that took place within the walls of the town. If resistance had been sustained, Royalist writers would naturally have wanted to emphasise the courage of the garrison as they fought to the bitter end. They did not fight to the bitter end. The only courage that is reported to have been displayed was shown at the breaches. The flower of Ormonde's army that stood between Cromwell and the end of all resistance appear to have been fatally deceived into losing their lives. Cromwell, in his despatch to Parliament declares, 'that night they put to the sword about 2,000 men'.[59] His own words do not offer any details as to how this was achieved. The cream of the Irish Royalist army was therefore barbarically 'put to the sword'. In this case however, no explanation is necessary, as to put them to the sword is to simply slaughter unresisting soldiers in cold blood.

The steep Pillory Street (or Peter Street) on the north side of the town had been the scene of many public spectacles. A gallows had stood at its foot in the centre of the town for years, and it also contained stocks for the embarrassment of petty criminals. Not before or since has that street witnessed scenes of such turmoil. St Peter's Church, which had one of the highest spires in the world (it was blown down by a storm in 1548),[60] on the hilltop, was the location of the next major incident. Cromwell writes:

> . . . divers of the officers and soldiers being fled over the bridge into the other part of the town, where about one hundred of them possessed St. Peter's church steeple, some of the West Gate and others a strong tower next the gate called St. Sundays. These being summoned to yield to mercy, refused, whereupon I ordered the steeple of St. Peters church to be fired where one of them was heard to say in the midst of the flames, "God damn me, God confound me I burn, I burn.[61]

Cromwell uses the frightful final words of a burning Royalist soldier to demonstrate to Parliament that these men displayed unGodly irreverence even as they died, with the use of blasphemous language.

The Dean of the church, Nicholas Bernard, whose allegiance was firmly to the King, gives us a more elaborate version of events:

> Not long afterwards came Colonel Hewson and told the Doctor he had orders to blow up the steeple (which stood between the choir and the body of the church), where about threescore men were run up for refuge, but the three barrels of powder which he had caused to be put under it for that end blew up only the body of the church. The same night, Hewson caused the seats of the church to be broken up, and made a great pile of them under the steeple, which, firing it, took the lofts wherein five great bells hung, and from thence it flamed up to the top, and so at once men and bells and roof came all down together, the most hideous sight and terrible cry that ever he was a witness of at once.[62]

In the newsbook *Perfect Occurrences* that was printed on 5 October, Hewson's own letter is published, and he tells us that:

The rest fled over the bridge where they were closely pursued and most of them slain. Some got in to two towers on the wall and some into the steeple, but, they refusing to come down, the steeple was fired and then fifty of them got out at the top of the church, but the enraged soldiers put them all to the sword, and thirty of them were burnt in the fire, some of them cursing and crying out 'God Damn them' and cursed their souls as they were burning. [63]

There are no heroic tales of courageous resistance in the Royalist ranks. All we have are reports that the remainder of the garrison left alive that night and the next day fled to any available hiding place and cowered. This is not in keeping with the carefree Cavalier approach to combat that was prominent during the Civil War in England. The point is that during those battles on English soil, there was always a chance for a Cavalier to succeed. Here now at Drogheda, there was no prospect at all in giving battle. Those remaining unfortunate Confederate Catholic forces must have seen terrible sights as their comrades met atrocious deaths at the points of Puritan swords and pikes. There are other related incidents regarding the deaths of Royalist officers that occurred in the days following the 11th. The death of Sir Edmund Verney is described in a letter written on 18 November 1649 by a Mr James Buck from Caen and addressed to Sir Edmund's brother, Ralph:

Your brother and my dear friend Sir Edmund Verney – who behaved himself with the greatest gallantry that could be – he was slain at Drogheda three days after quarter was given him as he was walking with Cromwell by way of protection. One Ropier, who is brother to Lord Ropier, called him aside in a pretence to speak with him, being formerly of acquaintance, and instead of some friendly office which Sir Edmund might expect from him, he barbarously ran him through with a tuck; but I am confident to see this act highly revenged. The next day after, one Lieutenant Colonel Boyle, who had quarter likewise given him, as he was at dinner with my Lady More, sister to the Earl of Sunderland, in the same town, one of Cromwell's soldiers came and whispered him in the ear to tell him that he must presently be put to death, who rising from the table, the lady asked whither he was going. He answered, 'Madam to

die' who no sooner stepped out of the room but he was shot
to death. These are cruelties of those traitors who, no doubt
will find the like mercy when they stand in need of it.[64]

Mr Buck does not confirm that he actually saw these incidents. As he
was obviously a Royalist, had he witnessed them, it is unlikely that he
would have lived to recount the details. His account of the deaths of the
two officers contrast drastically with the frenzied attack on the town.
While some officers' deaths most certainly occurred on the days subsequent to the 11th, this hardly credible disclosure suggests an attempt to
both glorify Verney and Boyle's deaths and to further indict Cromwell
and his men. It is more plausible to presume that the officers found alive
the next day were subjected to court martials and were found guilty of
bearing arms against Parliament. This would mean that they would have
been immediately put to death. These particular acts were fuel for the
fire for those who wished to blacken the deeds of the Parliamentarians
and their commander. On this basis, it was easy to protest that Royalists
were struck down in cold blood after the hostilities had ceased.[65]

The slaughter continued all through the night of the 11th. Having
learned that mass had been celebrated for the soldiers in St Peter's
Church, Cromwell thought that it was 'remarkable that these people at
first set up the mass in some places in the town that had been monasteries, but afterwards grew so insolent, that the last Lord's day before
the storm, the Protestants were thrust out of the great church called
St. Peters and they had public mass there'.[66] He adds a chilling confirmation that the area in and around the church was consumed with
Puritanical rage as 'in this very place near one thousand of them were
put to the sword fleeing thither for safety'.[67]

The next day it was discovered that some of the Confederates had
taken refuge in two of the towers attached to the great walls. Cromwell
writes that some of the enemy had possessed 'West gate, and others a
strong round tower next the gate called St. Sundays'[68] West Gate was
positioned at the west end of Narrow West Street. There is a 300 foot
section of the town wall still standing today that runs from that position down to the river. The tower that was next to St Sundays is long
demolished. In that area today, Magdalene Tower, the remains of a
medieval Dominican priory, is also still remaining and would have
stood 'next the gate called St. Sundays'. It is not however a round
tower. The tower that Cromwell mentions may well have been the

'Tooting Tower' that occupied the modern day junction of King Street with Magdalene Street and Scarlet Street. Of these military survivors, Cromwell tells us:

> The next day, the other two towers were summoned, in one of which was about six or seven score; but they refused to yield themselves and we knowing that hunger must compel them, set only good guards to secure them from running away until their stomachs were come down. From one of the said towers, notwithstanding their condition, they killed and wounded some of our men. When they submitted, their officers were knocked on the head and every tenth man of the soldiers killed, and the rest shipped for the Barbadoes. The soldiers in the other tower were all spared as to their lives only and shipped likewise for the Barbardoes.[69]

Colonel John Hewson confirms this:

> Those in the towers being about 200, did yield to the Generals mercy, where most of them have their lives and be sent to the Barbadoes. In this slaughter there was by my observation, at least 3,000 dead bodies lay in the fort and the streets, whereof there could not be 150 of them of our army, for I lost more than any other regiment and there was not sixty killed outright of my men.[70]

There are many vital conclusions to be drawn from this incident of the soldiers that barricaded themselves in the towers. Firstly, this activity furnishes us with the only piece of scant resistance that was made within the walls of Drogheda. It is not, however, a tale of illustrious Cavalier bravery. Secondly, it is noticeable that by the day following the storm, Puritan tempers had very much abated. Quite a number of these lives were spared. The occupants of one of the towers, probably Tooting Tower, paid for their audacity in firing at their guards by being literally decimated, with every tenth soldier and all of the officers killed. The occupants of the other tower were all spared. This is in stark contrast to the horrendous commotion of the previous night. The orders from the top had been to kill all that were in arms. The vast majority of these soldiers, some 250 men, were not slaughtered. Then there is the question as to why they surrendered at all. Cromwell indicated that hunger would eventually compel them to succumb. He hardly expects us to believe that after only a day in hiding (or even five days which was the amount of time that Cromwell spent in the town) they suddenly all got hungry and surrendered themselves to an army that would have had no hesitation in cutting them down as soon as they were disarmed. Strangely, this did not happen. Mercy was indeed shown in the wake of the wholesale slaughter of only a few hours earlier. Since Cromwell himself recounts these details, it is highly probable the he was personally involved in the incidents. It is also likely that it was Cromwell himself who negotiated the submissions, as Hewson implies. Since the offers of quarter had been withdrawn consistently throughout the night, these survivors must have been persuaded by an officer of high rank for them to emerge from their hiding places and put their trust in the negotiator. Their decision to capitulate was justified. When it comes to the analysis of the indiscriminate massacre of the town's civilian inhabitants, this point will be paramount. Following the heat of action and the hostile treatment of the military the previous night, mercy was subsequently shown to members of that very garrison the next day. Some writers would have us believe that even though he spared the lives of these soldiers (lives he had every right to take), Cromwell ordered every civilian man, woman and child to be extricated from their homes and killed, with the exception of a mere handful.

Cromwell's perception of the Catholic clergy is by now well documented. Not only did he view them as legitimate targets, he also gives them special attention when reporting the deaths of those found in Drogheda to Parliament:

> I believe all their Friars were knocked on the head promiscuously but two; the one of which was Father Peter Taaff (brother to the Lord Taaff) whom the soldiers took the next day and made an end of; the other was taken in the round tower under the repute of a lieutenant, and when he understood that the officers in that tower had no quarter, he confessed he was a friar; but that did not save him.[71]

There were five Catholic priests massacred by Cromwell's troops at Drogheda: Fathers Peter Taaffe, his brother John Taaffe, Robert Netterville, Dominick Dillon, and Richard Overton.[72] Even the Catholic governor Aston was uncertain of the motives of priests at

Drogheda when he advised Ormonde on 1 September that two friars 'who intended no good' had arrived at Drogheda.[73]

The following contemporary missive is written by a cleric and quoted in the Jesuit Father Denis Murphy's *Cromwell in Ireland*, first published in 1883. Murphy's publication is a tremendously detailed and exhaustively researched work. However, as the work of a Jesuit priest, it is also the source of many sweeping statements concerning Cromwell's Irish campaign and has been responsible for inciting bigotry among nineteenth century Irishmen against the English. In the following extract, the use of emotive language and lack of first hand evidence is unfortunate, in the context:

When the city was captured by the heritics, the blood of the Catholics was mercilessly shed in the streets, in the dwelling houses and in the open fields; to none was mercy shown; not to the women nor to the aged, nor to the young. The property of the citizens became the prey of Parliamentary troops. Everything in our residence was plundered; the library, the sacred chalices, of which there were many of great value, as well as all the furniture, sacred and profane were destroyed. On the following day when the soldiers were searching through the ruins of the city, they discovered one of our fathers, named John Bathe [Taaffe], with his brother a secular Priest. Suspecting that they were religious, they examined them and finding that they were Priests, and one of them moreover a Jesuit, they led them off in triumph, and, accompanied by a tumultuous crowd, conducted them to the marketplace and there, as if they were at length extinguishing the Catholic religion and our society, they tied them both to stakes in the ground and pierced their bodies with shots till they expired. Father Robert Netterville, far advanced in years, was confined to bed by his infirmities; he was dragged thence by the soldiers, and trailed along the ground, being violently knocked against each obstacle that presented itself along the way; he was then beaten with clubs and when many of his bones were broken, he was cast out on the highway. Some good Catholics came during the night, bore him away and hid him somewhere. Four days later, having fought the good fight, he departed this life, to receive, as we hope the martyr's crown.[74]

It is impractical to take to task the detail that is outlined concerning the priests' deaths in this account. It is perfectly legitimate, however, to take issue with the writer regarding his assertions that no mercy was shown to the women, the aged or the young. The contrast of details is sufficient to make the case. None whatsoever are offered concerning the deaths of civilians. Nor is the author an eyewitness. The unfortunate clerics at Drogheda may have taken up arms in defence of their religion. It is quite likely that their deaths were ordered by Cromwell to quench the insatiable desire of his men to exact revenge on these 'men of blood' who, in their opinion, had incited the Irish rebels to murder innocent Protestants in 1641.

It is obvious that some of the Confederates made good their escape. Richard Talbot, the future Lord Tyrconnell, who was only a teenager at the time, was one of those who succeeded in eluding the Roundhead.[75]

On 12 October 1649, *Perfect Occurrences* published a letter that is simply signed R.L. It gives a short account of events and confirms the small losses on the side of the Parliamentarian forces:

> Colonel Cassell's regiment led on the forlorn hope, himself slain, our men beaten a little back, but the Lord General led them up again with courage and resolution, though they met with hot dispute. When we were entered into that part of the towne where the breach was made, our men came on to a great mill hill mount, wherein they had a hundred men, put them all to the sword; here our horse and foot followed them so fast over the bridge which goes over a broad river, it being very long and houses on both sides, yet they had not time to pull up the drawbridge. There our men fell violently in upon them, and I believe there was above 2,000 put to the sword. We had about twenty or thirty men slain and some forty wounded. Their governor was killed in the first onset.[76]

Almost without exception the phrase 'put to the sword' is used by both sides when describing the annihilation of the Drogheda garrison.

There can be no doubt that a massacre of huge proportions took place within the walls of Drogheda. There can be no doubt either that Cromwell's ruthlessness there shocked many observers, both Royalist and Parliamentarian.[77] The Battle of Drogheda was, in truth, not a battle at all. Once the breach was won, what took place was nothing short of the systematic execution of its defenders. Despite Aston's pleas to Ormonde, no help had arrived to attack the main camp, and Cromwell then took them all by surprise by gaining the town before they had time to conduct a conventional siege. The propaganda surrounding the events began almost immediately, making an analysis from a distance of 350 years somewhat precarious. Yet without the words of one Thomas Wood, whose account will be scrutinised in the next chapter, none of the eyewitnesses so far quoted have used terminology that could be described as anything other than military when describing those that were killed and the manner in which they died. Contemporary writers knew well that there was no indiscriminate slaughter of the civilian population.

It is at this point that one must remember the other Parliamentarian massacres by Monroe at Island Magee, Jones at Dungan's Hill, Inchiquin (before he changed sides) at Cashel and the arbitrary behaviour of Coote the elder.[78] Three thousand Catholics, the majority of whom were civilians, were massacred by Monroe, thousands more by Inchiquin, and Jones was responsible for the slaughter of some 3,500–5,000 Royalists at Dungan's Hill. Coote's brutality was also well known in the early years of the war until his death on 7 May 1642. Parliamentary massacres of Irish Royalist forces were already in vogue in 1640s Ireland. So why was it that Cromwell was the one to acquire unwavering notoriety among the Irish for centuries? It is perfectly legitimate to assume that the shock factor among Cromwell's contemporaries was compounded by the fact that he himself did not have a reputation for this type of barbarity before Drogheda. It is also the case that neither Monroe, Jones, Inchiquin nor Coote went on to totally reduce the Irish resistance as Cromwell did. Nor did they rise to a subsequent political position where they would oversee the successful, but vicious, planting of many English Protestants throughout that country as Cromwell also did.

The day after the storm, aside from negotiating with the soldiers in the towers, Cromwell had a busy day. He found time, however, to write a letter to the commander of Dundalk. He wasted no time in utilising the fear of the massacre as a threat to others. Colonel Chidley Coote, with two regiments of horse and one of foot bore the menacing note to Dundalk, which read:

> For the Chief Officer commanding in Dundalk: These;
> Sir, I offered mercy to the garrison at Tredagh, in sending the governor a summons before I attempted the taking of it, which being refused, brought their evil upon them.
>   If you, being warned thereby, shall surrender your garrison to the use of the Parliament of England, which by this I summon you to do, you may thereby prevent effusion of blood. If, upon refusing this offer that which you like not befalls you, you will know whom to blame.
>   O. Cromwell. Sept. 12 1649.[79]

Cromwell's theory of instilling fear into others was an immediate success. Not only did the garrison surrender, they fled the place, ignoring Ormonde's orders to burn it to render it useless for its next occupants. Two days later Cromwell displayed clemency to some of Drogheda's inhabitants:

> To Henry Parker
> Ordering the protection of Christopher St. Laurence and certain of the inhabitants of Drogheda and the peaceful behaviour of the troops.
> At the Camp, before Drogheda, this 14th of Sept. 1649.[80]

This does not indicate that five days of slaughtering took place, as Ormonde would suggest. He would declare that 'Cromwell exceeded himself and anything that he had ever heard of in the breach of faith and bloody inhumanity; and that the cruelties exercised there for five days after the town was taken . . .'[81]

At Trim the garrison also fled and left behind their artillery. Cromwell was back in the capital on the 16th, and as his military position dictated, he proceeded to document a complete disclosure of his work to date for the administrative body in London. (See Appendix No. 2.2).

On the 27th, Cromwell, still in Dublin, was about to join with the army that had already marched south and was at this time in Arklow. In another letter to Lenthall, in which he details the taking of Carlingford and Newry by Colonel Venables, there is a postscript giving more details about the slain at the taking of Drogheda:

P.S. I desire the supplies moved for may be hastened. I am verily persuaded, though the burden be great, yet it is for your service. If the garrisons we take swallow up your men, how shall we be able to keep the field? Who knows but the Lord may pity England's sufferings, and make a short work of this. It is in his hand to do it, and therein only your servants rejoice. I humbly present the petition of Captain George Jenkins his widow. He died presently after Tredah storm. His widow is in great want.

A list of the officers and soldiers slain at the storming of Tredah: Sir Arthur Aston, Governor; Sir Edmund Verney, Lieutenant Colonel to Ormond's regiment; Colonel Fleming, Lieutenant Colonel Finglass, Major Fitzgerald, with eight captains, eight lieutenants, and eight cornets, all of horse; Colonel Warren, Wall and Byrn, of foot, with the lieutenants, majors etc; the lord Taaff's brother, an Augustine friar; forty-four captains, and all their lieutenants, ensigns etc; 220 reformadoes and troopers, 2,500 foot soldiers, besides staff officers, surgeons, etc and many inhabitants.[82]

The point can not be over-laboured that Cromwell's rigid enforcement of the rules of war was rarely, if ever, implemented during the Civil War in England. The justification for such action could easily be explained away by the articles of seventeenth century warfare, but Cromwell had many ulterior motives for cutting the Drogheda garrison down where they stood. Not the least of which was that it would speed up his Irish campaign by encouraging others to surrender. Both sides were therefore perfectly happy to have rumours spread throughout Ireland and England that the majority of the living souls in the town were wiped out enmasse. Parliament could not afford a long siege. Resistance to their army in Ireland had to be minimal. If wild exaggerations of civilian deaths assisted their cause and helped to reduce defiance from the Royalists, then so be it. The cost of a bad press that might influence public opinion and stain their image was as inconsequential as it was routine. Royalist views on the matter were that these stories would help to paint a disreputable picture of Cromwell. This suited their cause perfectly too, in a war where loyalties constantly wavered. Even though, so far as we have seen, during the war in Ireland he had adhered strictly to the letter of the law and, in effect, did not step outside the military domain.

On the 18 September, the Council of State, before hearing of the fall of Drogheda, expressed their financial concerns regarding their expeditionary forces, in a letter to Cromwell: 'Every support must be made to make Ireland bear this charge, which is no longer supportable by England. You know what a large sum the last expedition has cost and that "the tree which bear this treasure hath no roots"...' The country can not bear the expense of this war any longer.[83] Some writers have suggested that it was a lack of money that caused the slaughter at Drogheda.[84] There are numerous reasons why it happened, and it was on the basis of it that Cromwell was just beginning to earn his reputation as the butcher of innocent Irish civilians. Many have asserted that Drogheda was a Royalist town and hence his inspiration for a holocaust, but the Royalist garrison had only occupied the town for the previous three months. It had been held by Parliament under the control of Jones from 19 June 1647, when Ormonde deserted Ireland, right up to July 1649, when Inchiquin captured it for the Royalists. So far we have no solid proof that any unarmed civilians had died at Cromwell's hands. Indeed, to date, not one man had died in the cause of Irish Nationalism. There was of course no shortage of those who had died giving their lives for the defence of the English monarchy.

Notes to Chapter Two

1   Letter from Hugh Peters of 16 August, 1649, printed in *Perfect Diurnall*, 23 August 1649 and quoted in W. C. Abbott, *The Writings and Speeches of Oliver Cromwell*, reprint edition, 4 vols. (Oxford: Clarendon Press, 1988), p. 107.

2   *Perfect Diurnall*, 23 August 1649, ibid.

3   See Abbott, *Writings and Speeches*, vol. II, p. 108, using Thomas Cromwell, *Excursions through Ireland* (1820), vol. II, p. 81. Thomas Cromwell was a direct descendant of Oliver's. The last of the male heirs was also an Oliver who died in 1821. Today the descendants are mainly from the female lineage and are alive and well under the name of Cromwell-Bush.

4   Declaration to the City of Dublin; printed in *Perfect Diurnall*, 29 August 1649, ibid., pp. 110-11. This act appears to have been made to inflict his discipline on those Parliamentarian soldiers already in Dublin over whom he had just acquired control.

5   The Rev Denis Murphy, SJ, *Cromwell in Ireland, A History of Cromwell's Irish Campaign* (Dublin: M.H. Gill & Son, 1883), p. 134.

6   From The Carte Manuscripts' Collection in the Bodliean Library, vol. XXV, p. 214; in John T. Gilbert, *A Contemporary History of Affairs in Ireland from 1641 to 1652,* 3 vols (Dublin: Irish Archaeological and Celtic Society, 1879), vol. II, p. 230. Also in Harold O'Sullivan, "Military Operations in County Louth in the Run-up to Cromwell's Storming of Drogheda", *County Louth Archaeological and Historical Journal*, vol XXII, no. 2 (1990), p. 197.

7   Quoted in John D'Alton, *History of Drogheda*, 2 vols. (Dublin: M.H. Gill & Son, 1844; reissued Drogheda: Buvinda, 1997), pp. 266–67.

8   David Broderick, *An Early Toll Road, The Dublin-Dunleer Turnpike, 1731–1855* (Dublin: Irish Academic Press, 1996), p. 11.

9   Ibid., pp 11–12.

10   J. G. Simms, "Cromwell at Drogheda 1649", *The Irish Sword* (1974), p. 214

11   Tom Reilly, *Cromwell at Drogheda* (Drogheda: Broin Print, 1993), p. 37.

12   Gilbert, *Contemporary History*, p. xviii. See also p. 232 where Gilbert quotes from Anthony Wood's *Athenae Oxonienses* concerning Aston: 'This person (who was the son of Sir Arthur Aston of Fulham in Middlesex, and he was the second son of Sir Thomas Aston in Bucklow hund. in Cheshire who was of an ancient family in that country), was a great traveller, had spent most of his time in wars in several countries beyond the seas. His majesty, having a great opinion of his valour and conduct made him governour of the garrison of Reading in Berkshire, where he beat the Earl of Essex, general of the Parl. forces, thrice from that place, til having received a dangerous wound he was forced, as tis said to devolve his command . . . he was lately made governour of the garrison of Oxford and afterwards expressed himself very cruel and imperious while he executed that office . . . being discharged from his office, to the great rejoicing of the soldiers and others in Oxon (Oxford) . . . Sir Arthur Aston had, at that time, his broken leg cut off to save his life, and in its place had one of wood put; so that being recovered and in a posture to do His Majesty further service, he went with the flower of the English veterans into Ireland, where he became governour of Drogheda commonly called Tredagh, about which time he laid an excellent plot to tire and break the English army.'

     See also Christopher Hibbert, *Cavaliers and Roundheads, The English at War, 1642–1649* (London: Harper Collins, 1993), p. 153. Hibbert also states that while governor of Oxford, Aston had quite a reputation for being cruel. He too quotes from Anthony Wood's post-Restoration work which in English was called, *History and Antiquities of Oxford*: 'Aston walked the streets of the city at his peril and one night was "wounded in the dark by a scuffle in the street".' Anthony Wood described him as 'a testy, forward, imperious, and tirannical person, hated in Oxon and elsewhere by God and man who, kerverting on horseback in Bullington Green before certaine ladies, his horse flung him and broke his legge, so that it being cut off and thereupon rendered useless for employment. One Colonel William Legge succeeded him. Soon after, the country people comming to the market, would be ever and anon asking the sentinell "who was the governor of Oxon?" They answered "One Legge". Then, replied they "A pox upon him, is he governor still?".'

13   From Edward, Earl of Clarendon, *Clarendon's History of the Rebellion and Civil Wars in England*, 7 vols. (Oxford: Clarendon Press, 1849), vol. II, p. 231, also printed in D'Alton, *History of Drogheda*, p. 269.

14   Aston's correspondence with Ormonde from Drogheda is in The Carte Manuscripts' Collection in the Bodleian Library, Oxford. Following his letters regarding the female conspiracy (see *Appendix 2.3*).

15   G.A. Hayes-McCoy, "The Significance of the Siege of Clonmel", *Tercentenary of the Siege of Clonmel* (Clonmel: Clonmel Tercentenary Committee, 1950), p. 34.

16   For military descriptions of contemporary weaponry see C.H. Firth, *Cromwell's Army* (London: Methuen & Co., 1967); David Blackmore, *Arms and Armour of the English Civil Wars* (London: The Trustees of the Royal Armouries, 1990).

17   Royal Armouries reference no. IX 1096. See Blackmore, *Arms and Armour of the English Civil War*, Cromwell's Mortuary Sword, Fig. 31, p. 25; also full colour illustration, Plate 6, p. 58.

18   See Firth, *Cromwell's Army*, and Blackmore, *Arms and Armour of the English Civil War*.

19   Aston to Ormonde, 27 August 1649. From The Carte Manuscripts' Collection, vol. XXV, p. 233; reproduced in Gilbert, *Contemporary History*, p. 236, the full text of which reads: 'May it pleas your Excellency, Beeing by an expres, I returned your Excellency an answer of the resaite of your letter yesternight. I kept your messinger untill this morninge, and have in obediens to your Excellency's orders, sent 60 hors in severall parties abraude for to drive in cattle; (as for corne), I can only threatten, but beeing eather the most of it is in stacks, or growing, it will bee very difficulte to get any conciderable proportion heether in time. Your excellency sent mee orders to deliver sum cattle unto won O'Brian, but your seconde commaundes will put a prevention to any further proseedings theerin, then only to gather them togeather for the present. This morning a gentleman, a neer neighbour heer, tells mee that Jones having summoned all his forses, or of divers adiasent quarters, with whot Cromwell broughte with him, and all he had before, the Munster amounted unto 8000 foote and 4000 horse, and that it is generally beeleeved that thay intend theer march eather tomorrow or at the furthest uppon Tuesday. It is reported thay intend to devide theer armey, parte to martch towards Kilkenny and the rest to cleare (as they call it) theas quarters. In the meane time, I wish I were well cleared of theas femall spies that are heere, the which I beeseetch your Excellency expres order, for if the ould elady were not so neer in relation unto mee as she is, I should have been very sparing of any serrimonyous proseedings with her. Yester night theer came from Dundalke 10 barrels of pouther, but very little match, ad that is a thinge most

wanting heer, and for rounde shot not any at all. I beseetch your Excellency be pleased to give speedy orders for sum, as also for the sudden coming of men and moneys; belly foode I perceave will prove scaers amongst us, but my endevours shall never bee sparing to approve myselfe.

'My Lord your most faithfull, humble servant, Arth. Aston. Trogodagh, this 27 August, 1649.

'Just now my wife is arrived and just now I wish she weare at Athlone. For his Excellency the Lord Lutennant: Theas humbly. Endorsed: Sir Ar. Aston 27 Aug., 1649, Cromwell's army consists of 8000 foote and 4000 horse, etc.'

Also partly quoted in Murphy, *Cromwell in Ireland*, p. 86.

20   From The Carte Manuscripts' Collection, vol II, p. 396, reproduced in O'Sullivan, "Military operations in Co. Louth in the Run-up to Cromwell's Storming of Drogheda", *Co. Louth Archaeological and Historical Society Journal*, p. 199. Also in Murphy, *Cromwell in Ireland*, p. 114.

21   Bishop of Raphoe to Ormonde, 1 September 1649 printed in Gilbert, *Contemporary History;* also in Samuel Rawson Gardiner, *The History of the Commonwealth and the Protectorate*, vol. I, 1649–1650 (Stroud: The Windrush Press, 1988 edition), p. 111.

22   Daniel O'Neill to Ormonde, 5 September 1649; in Gilbert, *Contemporary History*; reproduced in Gardiner, *History of Commonwealth and Protectorate*, p. 112.

23   Ormonde to Eoghan Ruadh O'Neill, 8 September 1649; in Gilbert, *Contemporary History*, p. 254; reprinted in O'Sullivan, "Military Operations in Co. Louth in the Run Up to Cromwell's Storming of Drogheda," p. 198.

24   Ibid.

25   Aston to Ormonde, 8 September 1649 quoted in Simms, 'Cromwell at Drogheda 1649', p. 216.

26   Aston to Ormonde, 9 September 1649, in *Aphorismical Discovery*, vol II, preface p. xxii, in The Carte Manuscripts' Collection, vol. XXV, p. 317; quoted in Simms 'Cromwell at Drogheda 1649', p. 216; also, Murphy, *Cromwell in Ireland*, p. 92.

27   Edmund Verney to Ormonde in The Carte Manuscripts' Collection, vol. XXV, p. 312; reproduced in Gardiner, *History of the Commonwealth and the Protectorate*, pp. 114–15.

28   Ibid.

29   See Simms, "Cromwell at Drogheda 1649", p. 217.

30   Letter to Ormonde in *Aphorismical Discovery*, vol. II, appendix LXI, p. 259; quoted in Murphy, *Cromwell in Ireland*, p. 93.

31   Oliver Cromwell to Aston, 10 September 1649, from The Carte Manuscripts' Collection; reproduced in Abbott, *Writings and Speeches*, vol. II, p. 118. Also in Murphy, *Cromwell in Ireland*, p. 92.

32   Extract from Cromwell to Lenthall, 17 September 1649; reproduced in full in Abbott, *Writings and Speeches*, vol. II, pp. 125–28.

33   Oliver Cromwell to Lenthall, 17 September 1649, quoted in Abbott, *Writings and Speeches*, vol. II, p. 125.

34   From *Aphorismical Discovery*, vol. II, preface, pp.18–19; quoted in Murphy, *Cromwell in Ireland*, p. 87.

35   For detailed description of the siege of Drogheda, 1641–42, see D'Alton, *History of Drogheda*, pp. 221–56.

36   In *Exact History of Several Changes*, p. 45, quoted in Abbott, *Writings and Speeches*, vol. II, p. 122. Abbott says, 'Sir Phelim O'Neill, hearing that Cromwell had taken Drogheda "burst out in a passion, swearing that if Cromwell had taken Drogheda by storm, if he should storm Hell, he would take it".'

37   See Gilbert, *Contemporary History*, pp. 259–60; also quoted in Simms, "Cromwell at Drogheda, 1649", p. 217.

38   Ibid.

39   The Lady Wilmot affair is related in the letters that passed between Aston and Ormonde during the last days of August. (see *Appendix 2.3*.)

40   Gilbert, ibid., vol II, p.xix, says that *'Aston was much embarrassed by the movements of Lady Wilmot, Lord Blayney's daughters, and other ladies, his near relatives, then in Drogheda, whom he discovered to be in communication with Colonel Michael Jones and officers of the Parliamentary Army at Dublin.'* Gilbert proceeds to give a family background to Aston's grandmother: *'Lady Mary Wilmot, daughter of Sir Henry Colley of Castle Carberry, Co. Kildare. Her first husband was Sir Garret Moore of Mellifont, Co. Louth, who died in 1627, leaving, by her seven sons and five daughters. She re-married with sir Charles Wilmot, Viscount Wilmot of Athlone and died in 1654. Francis Moore referred to by Aston, was her sixth son. Her second son, Sir James Moore of Ardee, married Lord Blayney's daughter, Jane. One of the above mentioned Henry Wilmot, the second Viscount of Athlone, was the father of John Wilmot, the noted Earl of Rochester who died in 1680.'*

41   MSS in the Library of the Royal Irish Academy, quoted from Murphy, *Cromwell in Ireland*, p. 95.

42   See Simms, "Cromwell at Drogheda, 1649", p. 220, quoting from *County Louth Archaeological and Historical Society Journal*, no. IV, (1916). Simms writes 'the story of Colonel Warren's fate is horrific; it is that in the defence of the breach both his feet were blown off by a cannon ball, but he continued to fight on his stumps till he was overpowered. Another story is that his horse escaped and galloped riderless to his stable at Warrenstown.'

43   Murphy, *Cromwell in Ireland*, p. 95: 'Tenalia, now called Tenaille by engineers, a kind of advanced defensive work, which gets its name from its resemblance to the lips of a pair of pincers. It stood in the orchard which now occupies the ground from the south-east angle of the wall to Duleek Street . . . These Tenalia were small towers, originally placed at regular distances round the town wall. Only one now remains at the rear of Millmount.' This 'Tenalia' that Murphy refers to still stands today, although it is now known as the Butter Gate.

44   Cromwell to Lenthall, 17 September 1649; quoted in Abbott, *Writings and Speeches*, p.126.

45   The east wall has fallen down in many areas over the years, and it is difficult to say how much of the existing wall is medieval. The south wall that still stands is much older in appearance, and it is easy to discern where a breach might have been made.

46   Bulstrode Whitelocke, *Memorials of the English Affairs from the Beginning of the Reign of King Charles I to the Happy Restoration of Charles II*, (London; 1682: reprint Oxford: 1842); quoted from Murphy, *Cromwell in Ireland*, p. 96.

47   Edmund Ludlow, *Memoirs of Edmund Ludlow Esq. Lieutenant General of the Horse, Commander-in-Chief of the Forces in Ireland, One of the Council of State and a member of Parliament which began on November 3 1640* (Canton of Bern: 1698; reprint Oxford: C.H. Firth, 1894), vol. I, p. 302.

48   Harold O'Sullivan, 'Military Operations in Co. Louth in the Run Up to Cromwell's Storming of Drogheda', pp. 187–208, argues that the garrison at Drogheda was an ineffective fighting force put there to decoy Cromwell northwards while Ormonde re-grouped in the south after the devastating battle of Rathmines.

49   Cromwell to Lenthall, 17 September 1649; in Abbott, *Writings and Speeches*, vol. II, p. 126.

50   A Letter from Sir Lewis Dyves, quoted from Gardiner, *History of the Commonwealth and the Protectorate*, p. 117.

51   Ormonde to Byron in The Carte Manuscripts' Collection, vol. III, p. 412; Carte MSS, *The Life of James, Duke of Ormonde*, 3 vols. (London: 1735), vol. II, p. 84; quoted from Murphy, *Cromwell in Ireland*, p. 97.

52   From *The Calender of Clarendon State Papers*, commencing 1621, R Scrope and T Monkhouse, eds., 3 vols. (Oxford: 1767–86), vol. II, p 22; also in Simms, "Cromwell at Drogheda 1649", p. 220.

53   Cromwell to Lenthall, 17 September 1649, in Abbott, *Writings and Speeches*, vol. II, p. 126.

54   Now a Martello Tower, in Cromwell's day there was a windmill on its summit. Hugh De Lacy the founder of the town had his castle positioned here. The panoramic view of the town and hinterland from this spot has determined that it has always been a focus of military engagement throughout Drogheda's history. The plaque is positioned immediately inside the gate on the approach to the tower itself. At the time of writing, the Millmount Tower is being completely restored to its original Martello Style, having been shelled in 1922.

55   From *Perfect Diurnall*, 8 October 1649; quoted in J.B. Williams, "Fresh Light on Cromwell at Drogheda", *The Nineteenth Century*, LXXII (September 1912), p. 485.

56   Ludlow, *Memoirs*, vol. I, pp. 302–03.

57   From 'Life of Anthony Wood', prefixed to, *Athena Oxonienses*, 2 vols. (Oxford: 1791–96); quoted from Murphy, *Cromwell in Ireland*, p. 99.

58   The testimony of Inchiquin seems to substantiate this: '. . . the governor was killed in the Mill Mount after quarter given by the officer that first came there'. From Gilbert *Contemporary History*, vol. II, pp. xxvii; quoted in Williams, 'Fresh Light on Cromwell at Drogheda', p. 484.

59   Cromwell to Lenthall, 17 September 1649; Abbott, *Writings and Speeches*, vol. II, p. 126.

60   See Murphy, *Cromwell in Ireland*, p. 101, see also D'Alton, *History of Drogheda*, vol. I, p. 9. The present church dates from 1753 and is built on the site of the one that Cromwell burned in 1649.

61   Cromwell to Lenthall, 17 September 1649; in Abbott, *Writings and Speeches*, vol. II, p. 126.

62   From *A Brief Relation of that Bloody storm at Drogheda in Ireland and the Doctor's* (Dean Bernard) *Sufferings by Oliver Cromwell in it, and after it with his Preservation;* quoted in Murray, 'Cromwell at Drogheda – A Reply to J.B. Williams', p. 1234. (See *Appendix 6.2*).

63   *Perfect Occurrences*, 5 October 1649; reproduced in Williams, J.B., 'Fresh Light on Cromwell at Drogheda', *The Nineteenth Century*, p. 483.

64   James Buck to Sir Ralph Verney of Claydon, Buckinghamshire, printed in Lady Verney, *Memorials of the Verney family during the Civil War* (London, 1892), vol. II; reproduced in Williams, 'Fresh Light on Cromwell at Drogheda,' p. 486.

65   Abbott, in *Writings and Speeches,* vol. II, p. 122, has said that biographer J. Buchan in his *Oliver Cromwell* (London: 1934) finds the story 'Frankly incredible.'

66   Cromwell to Lenthall, 17 September 1649; in Abbott, *Writings and Speeches*, vol. II, p. 128.

67   Ibid.

68   Ibid., p. 126.

69   Ibid., p. 127.

70   *Perfect Occurrences*, 5 October 1649; reproduced in Williams, 'Fresh Light on Cromwell at Drogheda', p. 483.

71   Cromwell to Lenthall, 17 September 1649; Abbott, *Writings and Speeches*, vol. II, p. 128.

72   For details of the ecclesiastics killed by Cromwell at Drogheda, see Rev. Gerard Rice, 'The Five Martyrs of Drogheda', *Riocht Na Midhe, Records of Meath Archaeological and Historical Society*, vol. IX, no. 3 (1997). In an extensively researched work the author has come to the conclusion that there was no indiscriminate slaughter of the civilians of Drogheda.

73   Aston to Ormonde, 1 September 1649; in Gilbert, *Contemporary History*, p. 246. (See *Appendix 2.3*).

74   From MSS in the Arundel Library, Stonyhurst; quoted in Murphy, *Cromwell in Ireland*, p. 107.

75   Simms, 'Cromwell at Drogheda, 1649', p. 220. He would eventually succeed Ormonde as James II's Viceroy in Ireland, the major difference between the two was that Tyrconnell was a Catholic.

76   From *Perfect Occurrences*, 12 October 1649; reproduced in Williams, 'Fresh Light on Cromwell at Drogheda', p. 485.

77   See David L. Smith, *Oliver Cromwell – Politics and Religion in the English Revolution, 1640–1658* (Cambridge: Cambridge University Press, 1991), p. 7, who states 'Cromwell's virulent anti-Catholicism was most notoriously

displayed during the conquest of Ireland in 1649–50. While always remaining technically within the rules of seventeenth century warfare, he nevertheless showed a brutality not seen elsewhere in his career.'

78   Sir Charles Coote senior was killed 'whether by the enemy or by one of his own troopers was variously reported' on May 7 1642. His son, also Sir Charles, immediately took over the command of his father and became President of Connaught for the parliamentary cause. Peter Berrisford-Ellis, *Hell or Connaught* (Belfast: Blackstaff Press, 1988), p. 19.

79   Cromwell to the Chief Officer commanding in Dundalk, 12 September 1649; reprinted in Abbott, *Writings and Speeches*, vol. II, p. 122.

80   See Abbott, *Writings and Speeches*, vol. II, p. 122. This indicates that Cromwell may have stayed in his tent during his time at Drogheda and contradicts the tradition that he stayed in a principle building on the main street, West Street.

81   From Ormonde's letter to Lord Byron in the The Carte Manuscripts' Collection, vol. II, p. 412; quoted in Murphy, *Cromwell in Ireland*, p. 109. Murray in 'Cromwell at Drogheda – A Reply to J.B. Williams', has given the official table of events from *'A History or Brief Chronicle of the Chief Matters of the Irish Wars, With a Perfect Table or List of all the Victories Obtained by the Lord General Cromwell, Governor of Ireland, and the Parliament's forces under his Command there'*: From Wednesday last the 1st of August, 1649, to the 26th of the present July 1650. Henry Scobel, Cleric: Parliament;
On September 11th Drogheda was taken by storm.
On the 12th of September his Excellency reduced the garrison of Trim. He also took Dundalk.
In the interim Colonel Venables took Carlingford, in the north of Ireland.
The Lord Lieutenant in this month of September took Killingbericke.
Took Arklow Passage, Esmond House, Castle of Ferns, Fort at Slane Passage, Castle of Enniscorthy.
October 1 marched to Wexford.
October 11 his Excellency took Wexford.
October 18 he reduced Ross.

82   From *Letters from Ireland, the Lord Lieutenants letters, from the original edition printed by John Field for Edward Husband, printer to the Parliament of England, and published by their order.* Reproduced from *The Old Parliament History*, vol. XIX, p. 207–09; reprinted in Abbott, *Writings and Speeches*, p. 131.

83   Council of State to Cromwell, 18 September 1649; quoted from Williams, 'Fresh Light on Cromwell at Drogheda', p. 488.

84   Ibid.

Chapter Three

DROGHEDA – AN ANALYSIS

'. . . and many inhabitants'
(The alleged words of Cromwell after the battle of Drogheda)

THE POPULATION of Drogheda in September 1649 is a source of some speculation. The thriving medieval town had trade links with Flanders, Gasgony, Bordeaux and even Iceland.[1] Agricultural produce, hides, corn and victuals were some of the primary commodities that were exported from this busy commercial centre.[2] Naturally, an urban development on this scale was inhabited by a mixture of citizens who formed the necessary economic base for this level of international trade. Businessmen that represented numerous trades were operating within the walls of the town. In a census carried out in 1659 the number can be calculated to be approximately 3,000.[3] If the civilian inhabitants had been practically wiped out, it is very unlikely that within a ten year period the town's population would have replenished itself. The minute book of the Drogheda Corporation from 1649 still exists.[4] Within its pages is ample evidence that the town did not lose thousands or even hundreds of its citizens. This was a period when the Cromwellian settlement was in full swing in other parts of the country. Landed gentry of high ranking military positions who had pledged their allegiance to the King during the Irish wars were being transplanted from their lands and moved to Connaught.[5] Occupants of estates in and around the town of Drogheda were virtually untouched by this activity,[6] unlike those of Wexford. Here Cromwell makes no mention of preferential holdings available for plantation within the borough of the town to his superiors.[7] He was aware that English gentlemen (albeit mostly Old English Catholics) already occupied this strategic urban centre. His objective was to leave a garrison of his troops in the town that would ensure Parliamentary dominance in both military and municipal operations.

No Corporation records exist prior to 1649. The traditional viewpoint is that the previous Corporation records were burned in the storm. While no eyewitness gives us details of fires being set *throughout* the town, there is substantial indirect evidence that at least some of the town was plundered and burned.[8] Proof exists that the Corporators did not have a meeting in their own chambers between 6 April 1649 and 29 July 1656.[9] Since the town had been in Royalist hands, some of the principal buildings may have been destroyed by either them or the Parliamentarians. An entry in the records six years after the battle confirms the fact that the Corporation headquarters at the Tholsel had been left in some disarray by the marauding soldiers. During an assembly 'Heald at Tredath, the 8th day of May 1655 . . . At which time and place it was then, by the whole consent of the towne agreed upon, that the Tholsell of the said towne bee, with all competent speede built, and repaired . . .'[10] From the records that do survive, it is clear that a red book and a white book, both of which contained ancient laws and customs, were not destroyed.[11] However, they have been lost in the intervening period. By October 1649, the short Royalist occupancy of the town had abruptly ended and Parliamentary administration in the shape of the local Corporation would now govern regional affairs. The Corporators of Drogheda settled down to a period of little unrest, while the conquered Royalist hierarchy, both Protestant and Catholic aristocrats throughout the country, lost their lands to the new English Adventurers and Commonwealth soldiers.

Prior to the storm, the allegiance of some of the Protestant municipal authorities appear to have been in favour of the King. During a sermon to his flock, Dean Bernard expressed the view that their lives may well have been in danger as well as their goods.[12] He may have felt that as supporters of the King they could have been exposed to the wrath of the Parliamentary troops. He confirms that his congregation survived the siege safely. To suggest that as Protestants they could expect no hostility from Cromwell is naive. *The dividing line in this war was between Royalist and Parliamentarian, not Protestant and Catholic.* One of the many complications of the conflict was that the two beliefs of Protestantism and its sister religion, Puritanism, were thoroughly English in essence. Conversely, Catholicism in this context was essentially Irish. Those Protestants in league with Irish Catholics had little in common except their opposition to the rebel English government and their absolute contempt for each other. It can also be said that religion often created the boundary for many of the participants. Cromwell sometimes thought less of fellow Protestants who were allied to Catholics than the Catholics themselves. He had many opportunities to vent these feelings as the Royalist ranks were a theological mix of both religions.

Cromwell's admission of guilt concerning the deaths of civilians, on the face of it, appears confirmed in those last three words at the foot of the official version of his despatch to the Speaker, Lenthall, on 27 September.[13] In his defence, at best, the point could be made that he means *armed* inhabitants. At worst it could be argued that he refers to a large scale massacre of Drogheda's unarmed innocents. Neither statement is correct. Firstly, aside from pure conjecture, there is no evidence whatsoever that will put a sword or a pike into the hands of a citizen of Drogheda in September 1649. Secondly, without the absurd statements of one individual (which will be scrutinised in this chapter), no details exist concerning deaths of persons not in arms.[14]

These three small words need to be examined carefully. On the face of it, Cromwell freely admits that 'many inhabitants' were slain. If the assumption were to be made that they were unarmed and that this was his way of telling the world of his treacherous deeds, then this seems like an enormous turnabout from the Commander-in-Chief of the Commonwealth forces. This same man, a month earlier, had issued explicit orders to the entire Parliamentarian forces 'not to do any wrong or violence towards Country People or persons whatsoever unless they be actually in arms . . .[15] These instructions were decidedly conclusive and did not differentiate on theological grounds. All persons whatsoever, not in arms, either Catholics or Protestants, were to be excluded from Puritan wrath. Immediately prior to the sacking of the town he had hanged two of his soldiers who had disobeyed this order. Is it likely that he could now casually justify the deaths of hundreds, if not thousands of innocent civilians, even as the unfortunate but necessary result of collateral damage, or as the intentional consequence of enraged Puritan behaviour? This massacre he would have had to have carried out by discriminating in the tumult of a storm between which of the inhabitants had Royalist sympathies and which had Parliamentarian leanings – this would seem like a most preposterous notion.

Yet these three words are exceptionally incriminating, and a case could possibly be made for a commander in a fit of rage and an army out of control to have slain many defenceless inhabitants, irrespective of political persuasions, as Cromwell himself seems to have alleged. But did he? Do these words actually come from the pen of the future Protector? The short answer is no, it is most likely that they did not. The actual letter that Cromwell wrote to the Speaker with quill and ink on vellum paper, in Dublin Castle on 27 September 1649, has not survived. The manner in which the text of the despatch has come down to us is through licensed government printers of the day. Cromwell's letter is published in the following newsbook: *Letters from Ireland, relating to the several great successes it hath pleased God to give unto the Parliament forces there, in the taking of Drogheda, Trym, Dundalk, Carlingford and the Nury. Together with a list of the chief commanders, and the number of the officers and soldiers slain in Drogheda. Die Martis, 2 Octobr. 1649. Ordered by the Commons assembled in Parliament, that the several letters from the Lord-Lieutenant of Ireland, together with so much of Colonel Venables letter as concerns the successes in Ireland, be forthwith printed and published. Hen. Scobell, Cleric. Parliament London, printed by John Field for Edward Husband, printer to the Parliament of England and published by their order, 3rd October 1649.*[16] This letter was reproduced in the *Old Parliament History*.[17]

Thomas Carlyle and Charles Firth, both biographers of Cromwell, have cast aspersions on the three words at the end of Cromwell's reproduced letter.[18] This publication, including the full transcript of Cromwell's dispatch, was in actual fact the official version of events, issued on the instructions of Parliament. Carlyle was incensed with the editor of the *Old Parliamentary History*, whom he suggested had added the words independently.[19] Firth has alleged that the entire list given at the end of the postscript was added by the printer John Field, perhaps in compliance with the orders of Parliament.[20] The latter version would appear to be the more credible as Cromwell had already furnished us with his list of those killed in his letter of the 17th.[21] Whichever story is true, it can certainly be concluded that it is quite likely that Cromwell himself did *not* write that they had slaughtered 'many inhabitants'. Unless they were in arms, it would have been completely contrary to his proclamation at Dublin and the entire manner in which he contested the war. It is worth bearing in mind that Cromwell himself said that the slaughter was necessary 'to prevent the further effusion of blood' and that his actions otherwise 'cannot work but remorse and regret'. His conscience was obviously stirred in the cold light of day after the storm, yet he was reporting to men who would have applauded him if he had slain 100,000 Irish Royalists. Furthermore, there is no proof whatsoever to suggest that these inhabitants (if killed at all) were unarmed.[22]

But Cromwell's vindication from crimes of outrageous inhumanity will not emerge from either the existence or absence of three words at the end of a postscript. Many people witnessed the events at Drogheda. The difficulty is that only a handful of observers actually transcribed their versions of events. The various accounts that have survived can be broken down into two primary categories: eyewitnesses and non-eyewitnesses. It is also necessary to remember that the world was a much bigger place in 1649. If an English pamphlet or newsbook were to assert that the civilian population of Drogheda was wiped out, people were not about to travel to Drogheda to see for themselves. Ireland might as well have been on the other side of the world as far as most English people were concerned. Since we don't have the benefit of reports from war corespondents (an occupation of the future), there are four main contemporaneous areas from which we can glean details of the battle of Drogheda:

1. Cromwell's own account which is the most detailed that has come down to us.[23]
2. Documented military communications between Ormonde and Inchiquin, written in the days afterwards.[24]
3. Newsbooks of the day that carried eyewitness accounts and that were published the following month, when they had reached the London printers.[25]
4. The memoirs and books of various eminent persons such as Whitelocke,[26] Ludlow,[27] Clarendon,[28] Bernard,[29] Bate[30] and the officer in the regiment of Sir John Clotworthy,[31] all of which were written years afterwards and are important. It stands to reason, however, that these accounts were probably influenced by a multitude of factors in the intervening period. Of these, Bernard is the only eyewitness and therefore his testimony must be treated as such.

There is no real merit in using accounts written centuries after the events to prove Cromwell's guilt or innocence in this matter. A lot of the narratives of these events that were published in the eighteenth and nineteenth centuries were written for dishonest political reasons. By and large those writers who could be perceived as English generally looked upon the barbarity of the slaughter of the military personnel at Drogheda as Cromwell's only iniquity. From the pens of Irish writers, however, the story of the wholesale massacre of the town's inhabitants is usually given unequivocal credibility. In the nineteenth century, Victorian writers such as Carlyle,[32] Firth[33] and Gardiner[34] all refuted these grave charges against Cromwell. These writers' contributions are invariably dismissed in Ireland. Both Gardiner and Firth's infraction was their British nationality, which immediately suggested prejudicial motives. Although Carlyle was Scottish, his obvious admiration of Cromwell was enough to render his statements suspect.

The chief contemporary accounts of the taking of Drogheda can be summarised as the following:

Eyewitnesses	Non-eyewitnesses
Cromwell himself	Edmund Ludlow (his memoirs)
Colonel John Hewson	The Earl of Ormonde
Dean Nicholas Bernard (Preacher at St Peter's)	Dr George Bate (physician to Cromwell, and both Charles I and Charles II)
Anonymous letter in *Perfect Diurnall*	Lord Inchiquin
Anonymous letter signed R.L. in *Perfect Occurrences*	Anthony Wood (whose brother Thomas was present)
Hugh Peters (Cromwell's chaplain)	The Earl of Clarendon (who wrote a history of the war in England and Ireland)
	Officer in the regiment of Sir John Clotworthy in *Perfect Occurrences* (who also wrote his account of the Irish wars)

There are other contemporary non-eyewitness chronicles of the taking of Drogheda including various pamphlets and newsbooks, which are significant, but they do not either improve or disprove the central thesis of this debate.[35]

To take the non-eyewitnesses first, James Butler, Lord Ormonde, was Cromwell's chief adversary in Ireland as supreme commander of the Confederate/Royalist forces. His evidence concerning this issue is enormously significant. Writing to Inchiquin in the immediate aftermath he says; 'The cruelties expressed in Drogheda for five days after the town was taken would make as many pictures of inhumanity as are to be found in the book of Martyrs or in the relation of Amboyna'.[36] Here Ormonde refers to 'relations' that had a huge effect on English public opinion at the time. They were, respectively, John Foxe's famous book of Protestant martyrs and the pamphlet describing the atrocities of the Dutch against the English settlers in the East Indies in 1623. During the nine months of Cromwell's time in Ireland, Ormonde must have written hundreds of letters concerning the exploits of his adversary. The above quotation does not specify civilian deaths at Drogheda, nor do any other letters that he wrote at the time, or indeed afterwards. While the two publications that he mentions refer to civilian deaths, he clearly makes no attempt to exploit the fact. His comparisons could be understood to underline his shock at the extent of the loss of life. Despite the potential that he had to blacken Cromwell's name further, had non-combatants been killed, on this most contentious issue, Ormonde is silent. Surely if whole communities were obliterated on the scale that is suggested by some, Ormonde would have had something to say about it.[37]

That soldier of fortune Inchiquin, who performed his duties with ruthless expedience, does not mention the deaths of civilians either. He writes that:

> Many men and some officers have made their escape out of Drogheda, amongst them Garret Dungan is one and is now at Tecraghan and Lieutenant/Colonel Cavanagh. Some of every regiment are come unto me. All conclude that No quarter was given there with Cromwell's leave but many were privately saved by officers and soldiers; the governor was killed after quarter was given by the officer that first came there, that some of the towers were defended until yesterday, quarter being denied them, and that yesterday

morning the towers within they were blown up. That
Varney, Finglass, Warren and some other officers were alive
in the hands of some of Cromwell's officers twenty-four
hours after the business was done, but whether their lives
were obtained at Cromwell's hands or that they are yet
living, they cannot tell.[38]

As Inchiquin received many of the survivors, it seems logical that
had these escapees declared stories of civilian deaths, Inchiquin would
have mentioned it somewhere. He does not. In fact he tells us that
many of the garrison were actually spared. He also adds weight to the
treachery theory concerning the offer of quarter and the withdrawal of
it as soon as the defenders were disarmed.

We now come to the non-eyewitness accounts that were written
years after the events. We have already discovered that Edmund Ludlow was not in Ireland when the storm of Drogheda occurred. His evidence is contained in his memoirs published in 1698, with the title
*Memoirs of Edmund Ludlow Esq. Lieutenant General of the Horse, Com-
mander in chief of the forces in Ireland, One of the Council of State, and
a member of the Parliament which began on November 3rd 1640.* Ludlow
arrived in Ireland in 1651 to become deputy Commander-in-Chief of
Ireland to Henry Ireton, Cromwell's son-in-law. Aside from detailing
the activity at the breach, Millmount and the drawbridge, his most
significant comments about Drogheda are contained in the sentence,
'The slaughter was continued all that day and the next; which extraordinary severity, I presume was used, to discourage others from making opposition.'[39] Ludlow's words do not imply that any of the
inhabitants were killed. His use of the words 'extraordinary severity'
could imply that as a fellow MP and, at that time, a friend of
Cromwell's, he was shocked to see that the garrison were all slain as
the rules of war were ruthlessly employed.

The obscure narrative of Doctor George Bate, whose only claim to
relating an account of Drogheda is that he was Cromwell's doctor for
a period, should be seen in context.[40] He never visited Ireland in his
life. In 1685 his *Elenchus Motuum Nuperorum in Anglia* or *Historical
account of the rise and progress of the late troubles in England*, was published. Bate was also medical adviser to Charles I and as such was sufficiently qualified to be Cromwell's physician. When the monarchy was
restored, he became doctor to Charles II.[41] Naturally in his capacity as

a Royalist and in the wake of the failure of the Commonwealth and the restoration of the Crown, his words concerning the rebel Parliamentary forces are not complimentary. After asserting that 4,000 were killed at Drogheda (1,000 more than the official version), he continues:

> . . .neither the gown nor the dwelling house offered any protection, nor was there any great respect had to either sex. The soldiers continued for three days in cruelly slaying the townspeople that had carried arms, whom they dragged out of their lurking holes nay, and those who after the third day came creeping out of their hiding places were most inhumanely put to death.

Anthony Wood was a historian at Oxford University in the seventeenth century. His brother Thomas was a Parliamentarian officer and was present at Drogheda. Anthony would transcribe some of his brother's adventures during the war. It was not until 1663 that he would publish Thomas Wood's testimony about Drogheda, which is the most controversial account that has come down to us. By this time, the English throne was quite warm again, since Charles II had restored a Royal seat upon it. This was a period when Cromwell's fellow republicans and regicides were in hiding for their lives following the failure of their revolution. Cromwell's body had already been exhumed, hanged, decapitated and buried again. Publications that would discredit that recent *Usurper* Cromwell, in the light of the Restoration, were circulating at a rapid rate throughout England. Individuals from every walk of life clamoured to display their loyalty to the new monarch.[42] Scurrilous profiles of Cromwell abounded in such a climate. The kingship had returned, and it was ultimately at the behest of Parliament that it would do so. In a way, common sense was to prevail and the English people rejoiced at the thoughts of renewed monarchial stability. This was the atmosphere into which Wood's descriptions of the battle of Drogheda would emerge. His is the *only* narrative that details the deaths of innocent women and children. His is the only report that discloses colourful descriptions of individual deaths during the slaughter. Basically, his is easily the testimony that we can describe as the least trustworthy.

Anthony's words concerning his brother are as follows:

> About a yeare before that time viz in 1650, he returned for a time to Oxon., to take up his arrears at Ch. Church, and to settle his other affaires at which time being often with his

mother and brethren, he would tell them of the most terrible assaulting and storming of Tredagh [Drogheda], wherein he himself had been engaged. He told them that 3,000 at least, besides some women and children were, after the assailants had taken part, and afterwards all the town put to the sword on the 11 and 12 Sept. 1649; at which time Sir Arthur Aston, the governor had his brains beat out, and his body hack'd and chop'd to pieces.

He told them, that when they were to make their way up to the lofts and galleries in the church and up to the tower where the enemy had fled, each of the assailants would take up a child and use it as a buckler of defence, when they ascended the steps, to keep themselves from being shot or brain'd. After they had killed all in the church, they went into the vaults underneath where all the flower and choicest of the women had hid themselves.

One of these a most handsome virgin and arrayed in costly and gorgeous apparel, kneeled down to Thomas Wood with tears and prayers to save her life; and being strucken with a profound pity, took her under his arm, went with her out of the church, with intention to put her over the works and to let her shift for herself; but then a soldier perceiving his intentions, ran his sword through her belly or fundament; whereupon Mr Wood seeing her gasping, took away her money, jewels &c., and flung her down over the works.[43]

Anthony paints a quaint picture of Thomas, on one of his return trips back home in England (he settled in Drogheda, died and was buried there), around the fireside of an evening with his family and friends. He would be describing the terrible deeds that his comrades got up to at Drogheda, while, of course, he himself, courageously attempted to save lives. His bravery was however to be foiled by the other bloodthirsty soldiers. But then he remembered himself and stole the girl's jewels and money and threw her over the town walls. This story, obviously full of inconsistences, has a very contrived ring about it. Yet, in Ireland over the years, it appears to be the only account that has taken on the authority of the Holy Writ! This is the picture of Drogheda in 1649 that has been committed to memory through the

Irish educational system of the last hundred years. The irony is that it was done in the name of Irish Republicanism.

Thomas Wood had served as a Royalist in the early stages of the Civil War in England. Having made a name for himself as a prominent follower of Charles I, he fled to Ireland because Parliament was in the ascendancy in his own country. In true mercenary fashion, he ended up on the side of Parliament as an officer in the regiment of Colonel Henry Ingloldsby at Drogheda.[44] Ingoldsby appeared to be quite fond of the ebullient Thomas, of whom he would remark, 'that he was a good soldier, stout and venturous, and, having an art of merriment called buffooning'.[45] His brother's depiction of Thomas holding an audience captive with his absorbing tales seems to correspond with Ingoldsby's judgement of the attention-seeking buffoon. The dubious character of Thomas Wood, in this instance, is merely the icing on the cake as far as ridiculing his evidence is concerned. His spurious words themselves speak volumes against the authenticity of his story.

How likely is it that mothers would let their children loose while they were concealed in cellars below ground? Is it normal for a lady to reveal to an attacking soldier the intimate fact that her virtue was still intact, during their brief and stormy encounter? Is it credible that this same lady would dress in her finest apparel, decorate herself with jewellery and carry sums of money on her person, at a time when the town in which she lived is being stormed? How plausible is it that Wood would scale a twenty foot wall to drop a corpse over it when bodies must have been already randomly scattered throughout the streets at the time? Answers to these rhetorical questions are useless. Just as Wood's complete deposition is impracticable. Aston's bloody demise, horrible descriptions of the use of children, the sexual reference as to how the virgin was killed and the fact that she was 'most handsome', all serve only to highlight Wood's proficiency for graphic fiction.

The farcical detail contained in the words of Anthony Wood is the only evidence that will convict Cromwell of indiscriminate genocide at Drogheda. He was not an eyewitness, although his disreputable brother saw what happened and obviously invented the rest at a time when such a thing was perfectly acceptable. The Wood brothers were by no means fans of the late Protector and Anthony describes Cromwell as being a 'debauchee and a boisterous and rude fellow'.[46] Take away Wood's missive and the case against Cromwell and a civilian massacre is decidedly weak, if extant at all.

Edward Hyde, the first Earl of Clarendon,[47] was an ardent servant to the throne and was personal advisor to Charles I during his turbulent reign. At the Restoration, Hyde would also commit to paper his version of *The History of the Rebellion and Civil Wars in England*. Like so many other Royalist authors writing years after the events, Hyde had no real credentials to describe what happened at Drogheda. He had, of course, a sizeable axe to grind with Cromwell. His account is also second hand and well matured by the time he came to write it. Royalists like Hyde disdained the actions of the Commonwealth, and with this in mind his contribution to this debate is almost predictable. In his chronology of events, Drogheda gets a passing mention and naturally he adds fuel to the 'civilian massacre' theory:

> A panic fear possessed the soldiers that they threw down their arms, upon a general offer of quarter; so that the enemy entered the works without resistance, and put every man, governor, officer and soldier to the sword; and the whole army being entered the town they executed all manner of cruelty and put every man that related to the garrison, and all the citizens who were Irish to the sword.[48]

Having ignored the fierce hostility at the breaches due to either imperfect recollection or plain misinformation, Hyde goes on to tell us that the soldiers carried out a massacre of the Irish population only. His lack of understanding of the Pale town of Drogheda obviously meant that he thought all Irish were Catholic and all English were Protestant. He therefore expects us to believe that this massacre was carried out with meticulous theological discrimination.

Finally, the testimony of the officer in the regiment of Sir John Clotworthy (quoted in the Introduction as an excerpt from *Focus on the Past 2* by Brockie and Walsh, which is currently on the school curriculum) is frequently used to confirm the civilian massacre theory. Independent of an analysis of this sort, the anonymous officer's words are, on the surface, harrowing: 'But [the Irish] being overpowered, were all hewed down in their ranks and no quarter given for twenty-four hours to man woman and child, so's that not a dozen escaped out of the town of townspeople or soldiers.'[49] Brockie and Walsh state that this was the testimony of an English army officer, presumably the implication being that he was one of those of the attacking army at Drogheda. The regiment of Sir John Clotworthy was not in action at

Drogheda.[50] The officer concerned was one of those many opportunists who fought for both sides in the war. He described Ulstermen as his 'countrymen' which has lead to the conclusion that he was from the north of Ireland.[51] His *History of the Warr in Ireland from 1641 to 1653* was written about 1685.[52] It lay dormant until it was discovered and transcribed *circa* 1750 by Rev. F. Betagh S.J. During the copying process Father Betagh left many blank spaces where the original was imperfect. Edmund Hogan reproduced and published the account in 1873 and admitted to filling in many of the blanks. Yet again we have a nineteenth century influence on an account of Cromwell at Drogheda. It is obvious that the officer concerned was not present at Drogheda when one realises that this author advances the ridiculous idea that from the total numbers of civilians plus those of the military, a mere dozen people were left alive. By the time this man came to write his account, he had turned Royalist. As a Parliamentarian, he fought under Clotworthy in 1641, Hewson in 1642, Monroe in 1644, Monck in 1647 and Jones in 1649. By 1650 he was fighting for the King. His only involvement in military activity in 1649 appears to be when he and a Major Dunbar, in command of 100 horse, were sent by Jones to watch the movement of Ormonde's army before Rathmines. Again, this Royalist testimony is both hearsay and sweeping, with no details of civilian deaths offered to substantiate its inordinate claim. It may be virtually dismissed on the basis that its writer is so foolish as to allege that a mere handful of people survived the storm. Indeed, this writer also exaggerates Cromwell's forces as having consisted of 25,000 men. When it comes to Wexford, it will be seen that this anonymous officer has an extremely dubious ability for recollection. Wild rumours that had spread through the rank-and-file of the Royalist army and later recorded for posterity by a literate soldier have now come to represent the undisputed truth.

When it comes to actual eyewitnesses, we find that the deductions could be precisely the same. Cromwell is the chief eyewitness to Drogheda in 1649.[53] Unless the reader has a prejudicial motive, there is no reason whatever to doubt the veracity of the words contained in his two detailed despatches regarding Drogheda. Throughout both letters there are no references to civilian deaths, aside from those of the priests. If we assume (and we have every reason to do so), that the list of those slain appended to his reproduced letter of the 27th to Lenthall were not the words of Cromwell, then the case in his favour is strengthened. Some may, of course, as a matter of some speculation, conclude that there were small numbers of private individuals who took up arms and eventually gave the ultimate sacrifice in defence of their town. There is, however, not one shred of proof to substantiate this conjecture.

In the last century, due to the publication of Johnston's *History of Drogheda* in 1826, a story that the occupants of St Peter's steeple were 'the most respectable of the inhabitants of the town' was circulated.[54] The fact is, all of the contemporary documents refer to those persons in military terms. Cromwell himself says that 'divers of the officers and men being fled over the bridge, into the other part of the town, where about one hundred of them possessed St. Peter's church steeple'.[55] The evidence of John Hewson concurs:

> The rest fled over the bridge, where they were closely pur-
> sued, and most of them slain. Some got into the towers on
> the wall and some into the steeple, but they, refusing to
> come down, the steeple was fired; and fifty of them got out
> at the top of the church, but the enraged soldiers put them
> all to the sword and thirty of them were burned in the fire,
> some of them cursing and crying out "God damn them"
> and cursed their souls as they were burning. Those in the
> towers, being about 200, did yield to the General's mercy,
> where most of them have their lives and be sent to the Bar-
> badoes. In this slaughter there was by my observation, at
> least 3,000 dead bodies lay in the fort and the streets,
> whereof there could not be 150 of them of our army, for I
> lost more than any other regiment and there was not sixty
> killed outright of my men.[56]

Dean Nicholas Bernard was the Protestant preacher at St Peter's, Drogheda, in 1649. He lived near by, in the church grounds. He was questioned by Cromwell after the storm because he was a loyal subject of the King and survived to tell the tale. In a sermon appended to the third edition of *The Penitent Death of a Woeful Sinner* preached in 1649, he speaks of the storming of the town, '. . . when not only your goods – according to the custom of war – were made a spoil of, but your lives were in the like danger, and were in equal hazard, but by a special prov-idence of God were preserved'. Although Bernard would have been preaching to the Protestant minority in the town, he never mentions a

single death of any of the inhabitants of any religious persuasion.[57]
Indeed Bernard is actually documented as having sent his wife and
children out of the town, which was likely to have been the practice of
the day.[58]

On 28 September, Captain Samuel Porter arrived in London carrying a sealed package containing two of Cromwell's despatches on the
fall of Drogheda to be delivered to the Speaker of the House. He was
also the bearer of a short private letter from Hugh Peters, a chaplain in
the Commonwealth army, dated 15 September and addressed to Henry
Walker, preacher at Somerset House and sometimes known as 'Luke
Harruney', writer of the newsbook *Perfect Occurrences*.[59] At this stage
the taking of the town had not been officially confirmed in London and
Peters' telegram style note was the first to be read and published. It
read:

> Sir, the truth is, Tredagh is taken, three thousand, five hun-
> dred fifty and two of the enemy slain and sixty four of ours.
> Colonel Castles and Captain Simmons of note, Aston, the
> governor killed, none spared. We also have Trim and Dun-
> dalk and are marching to Kilkenny. I came now from giv-
> ing thanks in the great Church, we have all our army well
> landed. I am yours, Hugh Peters Dublin September 15,
> 1649.[60]

Peters tells us that none of 'the enemy' were spared. As a contemporary account of the events, even this short note addressed to Walker,
which Peters obviously expected him to publish, does not include a reference to dead townsfolk, however brief. It is also obvious that his report
is somewhat misleading as we know with some certainty that the occupants of the two towers were definitely spared. Cromwell was still in
Drogheda on the 15th. Peters wrote his note from Dublin, so either he
had left Drogheda early or had remained in the capital during the battle.

By October, pamphlets began to emerge in London confirming the
capture of Drogheda. John Dillingham, who at one time had been the
leader of the Parliamentary Press, published his *Moderate Intelligencer*,
which gives a full account of Drogheda in which he suggests justification
for Aston's death: 'In which slaughter there fell Sir Arthur Aston, a
papist, as were most of the garrison, the reason given of his death is said
to be the rage of Colonel Castle's soldiers for the death of their Colonel
and also for that Aston gave not a civil answer when summoned.'[61] While

Dillingham himself was not an eyewitness, his source does acknowledge the impunity afforded to civilians when he reports, 'Where their horse were, we know not, probably they went as common men.' The implication being that as common men they were absolved of military responsibility and would not be included in the slaughter.

Perfect Diurnall was a newsbook written by Samuel Peckes. In the edition of the 8 October, it contains a letter from an anonymous eyewitness. It is a unique source as it tells us that before the town was taken the north side was beset by a number of Parliamentarian soldiers: 'We sent over the water to the other side (north) of the town to hinder relief from coming to them and to prevent them from running away, 2,000 horse and foot.'[62] It does seem quite rational that Cromwell would have ordered this manoeuvre, although he omits it from his own dispatch. If 12,000 men surrounded the tiny south side of the town, he could easily have afforded to dispatch 2,000 across the river for the purposes mentioned by the anonymous soldier. Needless to say, throughout his text, this soldier does not make a mention of a civilian massacre on any scale. The other eyewitness account, signed simply R.L., that appeared in the 8 October edition of *Perfect Occurrences* also refers only to the deaths of the garrison.[63]

The earliest unofficial document that exists that confirms the seizure of Drogheda is a private letter dated 14 September 1649 and sent from Liverpool to London.[64] Subsequently printed by Robert Ibbitson in a London newsbook, it reads:

> There is come hither a vessel from Dublin, the master of which had just been with Coll. Birch, our governor and saith that just before he came away, there was news come of the certain taking of Drogheda. On Wednesday 12th September 1649 the Lord Lieutenant stormed the garrison of Drogheda where he found much opposition, yet through the glorious power of God (which was wonderfully seen there) they made entry into the town near the Mount by the Church where they found resistance, quarter was offered but it would not be accepted of, so they were forced to fight their way into the town which they did with great resolution and courage and killed of the enemy near three thousand. Amongst which Sir Arthur Aston (their Governor) and divers other considerable men, putting all to the

sword that were in the streets and in the posture of soldiers. But many that they found in houses and in a quiet and orderly posture they gave quarter to.[65]

All of the foregoing are the dissertations of those people who were actually at Drogheda in September 1649 and others who were not involved in the conflict at all and were elsewhere when it occurred. The common thread is that all of these individuals chose to record the events they had either seen or heard about, and it is this contemporary documentation that is the basis of our knowledge of events. With the unlikely exception of the emergence of other contemporary accounts that have since remained untouched in the deep recesses of academic and governmental institutions or indeed in private collections, these narratives alone furnish us with the details of the taking of Drogheda. Therefore, the sum total of detailed evidence against Cromwell and the slaughter of innocent unarmed civilians is contained within the colourful fireside stories of a notorious buffoon. It is therefore alarming to realise that despite the traditional viewpoint which is still offered as historical fact in Irish schools today, it is manifestly obvious that the proof of an indiscriminate massacre of the town's civilian population is conspicuous by its absence. Indeed the contrary is actually the case. We know that Cromwell forbade his men to indulge in the murders of 'persons whatsoever not in arms'. There is the strong suspicion that the priests who lost their lives did so while bearing arms in defence of their faith. We also know from Aston that certain priests had recently arrived in the town to cause trouble. Why otherwise would a priest end up in a tower sheltering for his life with a section of the garrison? Surely he had been on the streets in the posture of a soldier. He would certainly not have been out for a casual stroll. No doubt he was involved in the fracas and fled with those soldiers for whom he had previously said mass to the temporary sanctuary of the tower. It would appear that Cromwell would not differentiate between priests in arms or otherwise. If found, their fate was death regardless. A Catholic priest to a Puritan soldier in seventeenth century Ireland was a common outlaw and nothing more.

However, the wholesale dismissal here of the evidence of Royalists like Clarendon and Bate may appear to some observers like a convenient sidestep in order to affirm the case in support of Cromwell. Little credence is given here to these writers since there is every reason to believe that their reports were politically motivated. Then of course there is the folk tradition. The historian that ignores tradition is carrying a dangerous torch. But unless traditions can be shown to have existed before they appeared in print, then there is no basis to them. Local tradition or *beal oideachas* is usually a strong contender to contain at least some elements of truth. In the case of Drogheda, however, local tradition cannot offer any proof, solid or otherwise, that the townspeople were subjected to an indiscriminate massacre. The 'tradition' concerning 1649 has, as its source, contemporary propaganda literature, and over the centuries it is this colourful imagery that has come to represent impressions of the events.

There are many eminent modern writers who still adhere to the folk tradition of wholesale slaughter. Roy Foster,[66] P.J Corish[67] and Peter Berrisford Ellis[68] all suggest that the townsfolk of Drogheda were indiscriminately massacred. In the event of all of the above conclusions being treated as selective revisionism, why not let the civilians of Drogheda speak for themselves.

A General Assembly was held by the Drogheda Corporation on 6 April 1649, before Inchiquin would capture the town for the Royalists.[69] At the meeting, as was their custom, they arranged to meet again at the mid-summer Assembly. However, it is recorded that due to the hostility that was experienced when Inchiquin attempted to take the town, 'The midsommer assembly followinge was adiorned until Michaelmas followinge, in regard of the then troubles.'[70]

At a Corporation meeting on 7 October 1658 (a month after Cromwell's death), there is an entry that suggests that the municipal authorities were well out of harm's way at the time of the storm. Jonas Ellwood, who was an alderman and perhaps a brother of the mayor in September 1649, William Ellwood, was granted a lease of 'the lowe seller under the Tholsell: for sixty and one yeares at the rent of twenty shillings per Ann. Provided that in case of Warrs or Rebellion the Corporacon if required may make use thereof for that present occasion.'[71] It may be surmised that like all of the townspeople, they knew only too well to be off the streets during the time of an assault on the town. Naturally, as the town fathers, they had their choice of secure hideaways.

When the Corporation reconvened at Michaelmas, all of its members were in a state of perfect health. It is obvious from the handwriting that the minutes of the April Assembly were written in October after Cromwell had left. At the General Assembly of 5 October (the venue is not given), the names are the same as those that attended the April meeting, which took place at the Tholsel, still intact at the time.[72] Contained in the Corporation minute book are the name of hundreds of civilians who went about their normal daily business in the days, weeks and months following the storm. It is useless to suggest that these were new English planters, because the time frame makes it impossible, and in any case, no proof exists to substantiate it. If the whole community had been obliterated in mid–September, how likely is it that it would be completely replenished by 5 October with the full mechanism of local government completely restored! Only three days earlier Samuel Porter had arrived in London carrying the packages containing Cromwell's letters to the ruling body in London announcing the official news that Drogheda had fallen. At that time in Drogheda, life was as normal as it could have been under the circumstances. Free members were admitted to the Corporation, leases were granted, gate customs were collected, and petitions were granted and refused.

This was a military encounter between two essentially English factions in the struggle for power over the dominions of Ireland, England, Scotland and Wales. The townspeople of Drogheda were not standing in anybody's way in this struggle.[73] It is vital to remember that for two solid years the town of Drogheda had been under the control of the Parliamentarian army of Michael Jones. During this time, there was not a peep out of the townspeople concerning the military occupants who were of Cromwell's party. In fact the only evidence we have concerning some of the inhabitants' direct displeasure with a military garrison is when it was under the Royalist command of Aston.[74]

Not only did the Catholic inhabitants of Drogheda survive the storm, but in an amazing twist of fate, a local Catholic civilian merchant actually *acquired* some land during the subsequent plantation. George Pippard, a member of a local prosperous family, was granted confiscated land at Beaulieu near Drogheda when it was realised that he had contributed the sum of £1,000 to help keep the town supplied during the siege of 1641-42. This he achieved in the face of a request for him to be transplanted.[75]

There is a local tradition which asserts that Aston, during his short time in the town, lodged at the house of a famous Drogheda family in Patrickswell Lane (now demolished) called the Elcocks. There is also a tradition that two of the Elcock family were killed by the Roundheads.[76] The name Elcock is first mentioned on a gravestone in St Peter's

Church of Ireland that dates from 13 April 1571. Their association with the town was always strong, with many of the males having occupied the position of mayor. Luke J. Elcock was the last of the family to hold that position in 1927. He died in 1938.[77] It is alleged that at the time of the storm there were four Elcock brothers living in the town, two of whom were killed and two who escaped. This reference is the only local source we have that suggests that particular civilian individuals were killed. It does not give us any detail as to whether or not they were armed. In fact, one of the main difficulties concerning the tradition is that it can only be traced back as far as 1873.[78]

On 16 December 1653, Oliver Cromwell was installed as Protector, the supreme figurehead that would effectively take the place of the abolished monarchy. Since the King had been executed in January 1649, no one individual leader had existed in London. The members of Parliament that had represented the Commonwealth were now guided by Cromwell as their dictator. On 8 May 1655, the Corporation of Drogheda swore oaths to that ruling body:

> By order from the Commrs. of Parliament,
> THE OATH ADMINISTERED TO THE MAIOR OF DROGHEDA:
> You shall sweere that you shall be faythfull and true to the Commonwealth of England, as is now established, without a King or house of Lords, you shall well and truly execute the office of a Mayor within the Towne of Drogheda, and Liberties thereof, to the best of your knowledge and power, so helpe you God.[79]

During the assault of Drogheda and amid the passion of the battle, Cromwell had ordered Colonel John Hewson to set fire to the Protestant church of St Peter's. Up to a hundred men had climbed its steeple only to be burned alive or killed at the point of a sword as they fled to the roof. Eight years later, by 1657, the church was still in the state in which Hewson had left it. In an extraordinary irony, the Corporation petitioned the man who actually gave the orders to burn it for financial assistance to rebuild it. At a General Assembly held on 9 October of that year they:

> Agreed upon &c, that the Mayor and Aldermen are to take the best advice they can gett (for and in ye name of this Corporacon) to frame a peticon to his Highnesse the Lord

Protector or the lord Deputy and Council of Ireland for ye rebuilding and repairinge of Peeter's Church and that they be Impowered to nominate and appoynt a fitt person or persons to prosecute ye businesse and to be payd what they generally agree upon for his or theire paynes and labour out of the Towne Treasury.[80]

Further verification of Cromwell's innocence concerning non-combatants at Drogheda is contained in the mathematical impossibility of wholesale indiscriminate slaughter. It would be difficult not to conclude, considering the combined testimonies of all of the witnesses on both sides, that 3,000–3,500 defenders were slain. It is possible that the total number of human beings within the walls was somewhere in the region of 6,000, i.e. 3,000 soldiers and 3,000 inhabitants. It is also possible that most of the noncombatants had evacuated the town. Only Bate suggests that the number killed was in excess of 3,500, and he was not qualified to guess.[81] He was, however, highly qualified to exaggerate: 6,000 people were not killed. There is no room in the official (or any credible unofficial estimate) number of dead for thousands or even hundreds of civilian deaths. This point, while easily made, says an enormous amount about Cromwell at Drogheda.

From contemporary muster rolls and the 'official list of the principal officers slain at Drogheda', the number of military personnel behind the walls of the town can be reasonably ascertained.[82] The muster roll from 30 August 1649 shows that the total number of soldiers was 2,552. This figure was made up of ten troops of horse, the commanders of which were Colonel Fleming (69 men), Lieutenant-Colonel Finglas (57), Captain Plunkett (29), Lieutenant-Colonel Dungan (29), Major Butler (36), Captain Fitzgerald (?), Captain Harpall (29), Lord Dempsey's son (?), Sir James Preston (41) and Sir John Dungan (30). There were six regiments of foot soldiers, a total of 2,500, and a group of 220 'reformadoes' (renegade Royalist troops that were not part of any regiment and found themselves in the Drogheda garrison). The rank-and-file of the foot were commanded by Colonels Garret Wall (495), Michael Byrne (480), and William Warren (637). Ormonde's own regiment was led by Sir Edmund Verney (539). There was also Lord Westmeath's regiment (200) and that of Sir James Dillon (200). From 30 August to the day of the storm, Ormonde furnished the garrison with small numbers of reinforcements which would have increased the number beyond 3,000.[83]

This number corresponds almost exactly to the official list of deaths issued by Parliament on 3 October 1649.[84] It also accords with almost all of the other contemporary accounts. It may be concluded that there was no physical body count since this was not a practice of contemporary warfare. Therefore it is impossible to determine the actual figure. The conclusions that can be drawn from the muster rolls of those present on 30 August merely gives us a basis from which to work. It does not allow for the fact that 200 soldiers were spared of their lives after surrendering from the two towers. It does not compensate for the fact that Inchiquin tells us that, 'Many men and some officers have made their escape out of Drogheda.'[85] It can be surmised that since all of the writers, both official and unofficial, imply that almost all of the military defenders were wiped out, the number of deaths has been determined by the information that they had concerning the constitution of the garrison. No account allows for the survival of significant numbers of soldiers, perhaps 200–500. Yet, we can now say that the number of surviving military must have been at least 300. Any suggestions that this number could be replaced with civilian fatalities to top up the figure to 3,500 can be dismissed for lack of evidence. Therefore, based on the numerical evidence alone,[86] the deaths of the inhabitants of Drogheda by Cromwell cannot be accounted for.

Since religious persuasion took such an active part during the war in Ireland and as the mainly Puritan Parliamentarian army were using the memory of 1641 to justify their cruelty, it is interesting to ruminate on the theological structure of the Drogheda garrison. *The Moderate Intelligencer* of the 19 September states that, 'Sir Arthur Aston chose rather to have Irish than English for his garrison.'[87] Aston himself was English, although he was a Catholic. Sir Edmund Verney was also English and came from a prominent Protestant aristocratic family. These men that defended Drogheda were a mixture of Irish and English, Protestants and Catholics, and as Royalists they provided suitable fodder to the anti-King and Pope-hating Commonwealth army. Despite Cromwell's claims that he was exacting revenge on the rebels of '41 and their alleged atrocities on his fellow Protestants, it can be stated with some certainty that none of the Drogheda garrison had been involved in these crimes. The native Ulster Irish, to whom these crimes can be attributed, were not represented within the walls of Drogheda. It is an indictment of Cromwell's lack of understanding of Ireland that he chose to believe that the enemy at Drogheda were responsible for those actions of eight years earlier. When Drogheda was being stormed the Gaelic Ulster squadrons which comprised O'Neill's and the Earl of Clanricarde's regiments were hundreds of miles from Drogheda, at Derry and Galway respectively.

Despite the fact that 3,000 men lay on the streets of Drogheda after the departure of the Roundheads, few traces of these bodies have ever been located. Anne Hughes in her *History of Drogheda* of 1893 gives us an idea where some of the skeletons may still lie. Houses that would be eventually given the name of St Mary's Cottages were being built on the site of Cromwell's eastern battery at that time:

> On Saturday 31st of October 1891 the workmen employed by F. Gogarty, the contractor of the houses, designed by the late P. J. Dodd, in the course of excavating, discovered a lot of human skeletons, supposed to be the remains of Cromwellian soldiers shot down after scaling the walls. There were five complete skeletons with the skulls, of which the teeth were in a perfect state of preservation. Some musket balls and buttons were also discovered. One skull was found remarkably well preserved and complete in all its bones, except in one region where its wall had been driven in. On examination, out of it dropped a conical bullet, which presumably carried with it that soldier's death warrant. The skeletons appeared to be those of men of about five feet eight inches to five feet nine inches in height. When the small tumulous, known as Cromwell's mount, was being disturbed in the course of excavations half a century since, it was found to be choke full of mortal remains of the Cromwellian soldiery 'in one red burial blent'. The quality of human remains turned up from time to time in and around this historic locality testifies as to how stoutly the walls were defended during the two days siege, and the deadly execution of the small arms of the brave defenders. [88]

More recently, in 1976, during building being carried out at No. 18 St Mary's Cottages, a complete skeleton was discovered. It was reputedly in a sitting position and was extricated from its unofficial grave by local residents. A musket ball that had been flattened on one side was found in its skull. [89] This area is the one that Hughes describes and is the site of the batteries and the assaults on the walls. Due to its irregular elevation, little development has occurred there in the intervening centuries. Perhaps some day more questions will be answered in the event of further discoveries being made in this area. It is highly unlikely, however, that all of the bodies that had been killed throughout the town were brought here for burial. It is more likely that funeral pyres were set and the slain disposed of through the medium of fire.

The 'small tumulous' that Hughes refers to is believed locally to have been the actual position of the eastern battery. It is located adjoining Cromwell's Lane and comprises an elevated knoll which is about thirty feet in diameter. It has been suggested that the mound itself is an earlier passage grave that at one time overlooked the river.[90] Aside from local tradition, there is no real evidence to suggest that Cromwell's big guns were sited on this small hill.[91] The likelihood is that they were positioned much closer to the walls, precisely where St Mary's Cottages are situated and directly opposite the churchyard. Cromwell had no fear of Aston's counter battery capability, as Aston did not have sufficient artillery for such activity. Besides, the position of the hill is too far away from its target to have had the effect for which Cromwell's cannons and culverins were responsible.

In Murphy's 1883 book, *Cromwell in Ireland*, he carries a version of the tradition of Drogheda's presently named Scarlet Street. 'The street leading to St. Peter's church retained even within the memory of the present generation the name of Bloody Street; it is the tradition of the place that the blood of those slain in the church formed a regular torrent in this street.'[92] The street that Murphy refers to leading to St Peter's would be Peter Street, which from this remote distance could easily have been commonly called Bloody Street, although there are no records of it ever having been. Local research has repudiated the involvement of today's Scarlet Street in the tradition since it did not exist in 1649. Anyway, the location would have been outside the town walls and well away from the fighting, making its involvement in the myth pure supposition.[93] However, there was a lane that was commonly called Scarlet Lane in the 1650s that may have been the source of this folklore, since it was in the immediate area of the breached walls.[94] The tradition may simply have moved geographically from the former Scarlet Lane to the current Scarlet Street and still exists even today.

To summarise this evaluation of the events at Drogheda, it seems that not only was there no outright slaughter of the defenceless inhabitants, but we now find that there is absolutely no evidence to substantiate the stories of the massacre of even one unarmed person on the streets of Drogheda. It is the words of the actual participants that we have used and not those transcribed years later which Nationalist historians have so far relied upon. Cromwell may well have had no moral right to take the lives of the defending garrison of Drogheda, but he certainly had the law firmly on his side.

Notes to Chapter Three

1   John Bradley, *Drogheda, Its Topography and Medieval Layout* (Drogheda: The Old Drogheda Society Publications Committee, 1997), p. 26; reprinted from *County Louth Archaeological and Historical Society Journal*, vol. XIX, no. 2 (1978). 'The Topography and Layout of Medieval Drogheda.'

2   Ibid., p. 27.

3   Moira Corcoran, 'The Streets and Lanes of Drogheda – Part 2', *Journal of the Old Drogheda Society*, no. 3 (1978–79), p. 22.

4   Rev. Thomas Gogarty, CM (Ed.) *Council Book of the Corporation of Drogheda, vol. I, From the year 1649 to 1734* (Drogheda: 1915; reissued Dundalk: County Louth Archaeological and Historical Society, 1988).

5   See John P. Prendergast, *The Cromwellian, Settlement of Ireland* (London: Constable & Co., 1996), p. 28. The author finds it difficult to justify the transplantation of land owners whom he assumed had nothing to do with the blood spilling of the early 1640s: 'But for blood, death, not banishment was the punishment; and the class most likely to be guilty of blood – the ploughmen, labourers, and others of the lower order of poor people – were excepted from transplantation.'

6   Rev Gerard Rice, 'The Five Martyrs of Drogheda', *Riocht na Midhe, Records of the Meath Archaeological and Historical Society*, vol. IX, no. 3 (1997), p. 118. He writes, 'Very few of the Catholics seem to have been transplanted from Drogheda. By 1649 two leading Catholic merchants, Ignatius and Thomas Peppard, were in partnership with a prominent newcomer and Protestant, Thomas Leigh in chartering a ship between them *The Thomas of Drogheda* . . . it is as if the great events of the 11 and 12 September 1649 washed over the town, leaving little permanent effect on its landscape or its citizens.' John D'Alton, *History of Drogheda*, 2 vols. (Dublin: M.H. Gill, 1844; reissued Drogheda: Buvinda, 1997), pp. 280–81, writes 'One native alone is recorded to have received a gratuity of land from Cromwell; that individual of the name of Delahoyde, was proprietor of the mill which gave name to the Mill-mount, and his having supplied Cromwell's army with meal, during their sojurn here, is assigned as the motive for this grant, the benefit of which some of his descendants are said still to enjoy.'

7   Cromwell to Lenthall, 14 October 1649; reproduced in W.C. Abbott, *The Writings and Speeches of Oliver Cromwell*, reprint edition, 4 vols. (Oxford:

Clarendon Press, 1988), p. 143. After the acquisition of Wexford, Cromwell would encourage new English planters to the area: 'And it were to be wished, that an honest people would come and plant here, where are very good houses, and other accommodations fitted to their hands.' In *Calander of State papers Domestic (1649–50)*, p. 369, the Council of State were ordered by Parliament to consider transplanting families into Wexford; quoted in Abbott, vol. II, p.143, who continues 'Cromwell apparently, at this or a later time, wrote to settlers in Connecticut (his old associates) urging them to come to Ireland.'

8   See Gogarty, *Council Book of the Corporation of Drogheda*, p. 46. At a General Assembly, 9 April 1657, there is an entry that suggests some commotion took place: 'The peticon of the Master of Wardens and Fraternity of Taylors praieing to have a coppy of their charter wch. was casually lost at ye storme of ye towne.' It is to be noted, that while the charter may have been lost, the fraternity of tailors were still alive and well and seeking to continue their business.

9   Ibid., p. 24–36. Despite the Tholsel being the meeting place of the Corporation, no meeting was held there during this period.

10   Ibid., p. 31.

11   Ibid., Introduction.

12   Samuel Rawson Gardiner, *History of the Commonwealth and the Protectorate, vol. I, 1649–1650*, 4 vols. (Stroud: The Windrush Press, 1988 edition), p. 123, quotes from a sermon preached by Bernard in 1649, appended to the third edition of *The Penitent Death of a Woeful Sinner*, p. 310 (1121, b. 19) 'when he speaks of the storming of the town "when not only your goods – according to the custom of war – were made a spoil of, but your lives were in the like danger, and were in an equal hazard, but by a special providence of God were preserved". Gardiner adds, 'This is hardly language which would have been used if more than very few of the inhabitants had been killed . . .'

13   Cromwell to Lenthall, 27 September 1649; Abbott, *Writings and Speeches*, vol. II, p. 131.

14   Anthony A. Wood, *History and Antiquities of Oxford*, first published 1663, quoted in James Carty, *Ireland From the Flight of the Earls to Gratton's Parliament (1607–1782)* (Dublin: Fallon, 1949), p. 69–70. The evidence of Thomas Wood as told by his brother who described himself as a well known Oxford historian.

15   Declaration of Cromwell to the Irish People, 24 August 1649; in *Perfect Diurnall*, 14 September 1649; quoted in Abbott, *Writings and Speeches*, vol. II, p. 113.

16   J.T. Gilbert *A Contemporary History of Affairs in Ireland from 1641–1652, vol. II*, 3 vols (Dublin: Irish Archaeological and Celtic Society, 1879), p. 263; also Abbott, *Writings and Speeches*, vol. II, footnotes, p. 131.

17   Ibid.

18   Gardiner, *History of the Commonwealth and the Protectorate*, p. 122. Also Abbott, *Writings and Speeches*, vol. II, p. 131.

19   Thomas Carlyle, *The Letters and Speeches of Oliver Cromwell, With Elucidations*, supplemented and enlarged index by S.C. Lomas, with an introduction by C.H. Firth, 3 vols. (London: Methuen & Co., 1904), vol. I, p. 475. Carlyle writes, 'Parliamentary History (xix. 207–9) has copied this letter from the old Pamphlet (as usual giving no reference); and after the concluding "Surgeons, &c.," has taken the liberty of adding these words "and many inhabitants", of which there is no whisper in the old Pamphlets; a very considerable liberty indeed.'

20   Gardiner, *History of the Commonwealth and the Protectorate*, p. 122; also Abbott, *Writings and Speeches*, vol. II, p. 131.

21   Cromwell to Lenthall, 17 September 1649; quoted from 'Letters from Ireland' in *Severall Proceedings*, 2 October 1649; also in Abbott, *Writings and Speeches*, vol. II, p. 128.

22   See Rice, 'The Five Martyrs of Drogheda': 'Contemporaries knew well that there was no general massacre at Drogheda. There were about 3500 killed after the fall of the town which, not by coincidence, was the number that made up the garrison . . . The legend of the fall of Drogheda is that there was a general massacre of inhabitants . . . the evidence surviving indicates that only two clearly defined groups of people were executed methodically after the fall of Drogheda, the soldiers of the garrison and the Priests taken in the town.' See also Harold O'Sullivan, "Cromwell, No Evidence of Drogheda Massacre", *Drogheda Independent*, Friday 1 October 1993; O'Sullivan declares 'no general massacre took place in the course of the storming of the town.'

23   Cromwell to Lenthall, 17 September 1649; Abbott, *Writings and Speeches*, vol. II, pp. 125–28.

24   See The Carte Manuscripts' Collection in the Bodleian Library Oxford; also Gilbert, *Contemporary History*.

25   See various contemporary pamphlets, some of which are quoted in this chapter, *The Moderate Intelligencer*, 11 and 13 September, 4 October 1649. *Perfect Occurrences*, 14 September, 21–28 September, 5 October, 12 October 1649. *Perfect Diurnall*, 8 October. *Kingdom's Faithfull and Impartiall Scout*, 14 September, 5 October 1649. *The Perfect Summary*, 27 October 1649. *Kingdomes Weekly Intelligencer*, 28 September 1649. *A Brief Relation of Some Affaires and Transactions, Civill and Military, Forraign and Domestique*, October 1649. *Man-in-the-Moon*, 17–24 October 1649.

26   Bulstrode Whitelocke, *Memorials of the English Affairs from the beginning of the Reign of Charles I to the Happy Restoration of Charles II*, 1682, 4 vols. (republished: Oxford: 1842).

27   Edmund Ludlow *Memoirs of Edmund Ludlow Esq. Lieutenant General of the Horse, Commander-in-Chief of the Forces in Ireland, One of the Council of State and a Member of Parliament which began on November 3rd 1640* (Canton of Berne; 1698; republished: Oxford: C.H. Firth 1894).

28   Edward Earl of Clarendon, *The History of the Rebellion and Civil Wars in England*, edited by Dunn Macray, 6 vols. (Oxford: Clarendon Press, 1888).

29   *A Brief Relation of That Bloody storm at Drogheda in Ireland, and the Doctor's* (Dean Bernard) *Sufferings by Oliver Cromwell in it, and after it with his*

Preservation. Secondary sources who quote from this contemporary document include, Gardiner, *History of the Commonwealth and the Protectorate;* Murray, 'Cromwell at Drogheda', *The Nineteenth Century*, LXXII. (December 1912), p. 1234.

30   Dr. George Bate, *Elenchus Motuum Nuperorum in Anglia* (Historical account of the Rise and Progress of the Late Troubles in England), 2 vols. (London 1685). Bate displayed his loyalty for the throne and his disgust for the Puritan Revolution when in 1661 he published *The Lives, Action and Execution of the Prime Actors and Principall Contrivers of that Horrid Murder of Our Late Pious and Sacred Soverign.*

31   Edmund Hogan (ed.), *History of the Warr in Ireland from 1641–1653, by an Officer in the Regiment of Sir John Clotworthy* (Dublin: McGlasahan & Gill, 1873). Original author unknown, c. 1685.

32   See Carlyle, *The Letters and Speeches of Oliver Cromwell.* For details of Carlyle's views of Cromwell, see Ivan Roots, 'Carlyle's Cromwell', *Images of Oliver Cromwell, Essays for and by Roger Howell Jr.*, edited by R.H. Richardson (Manchester: Manchester University Press, 1993), p. 74–95.

33   C.H. Firth, *Cromwell's Army*, with an introduction by P.H. Hardacre (London: Methuen & Co., 1967).

34   Gardiner, *History of the Commonwealth and the Protectorate.*

35   For instance, *Mercurius Pragmaticus* of 17 September 1649, quoted in D'Alton, *History Of Drogheda*, p. 282 as follows: 'Lord Noll had turned his nose towards Tredagh thinking to fire the town but the sea had formerly so cooled it, that it looked as if he had wrapped it in an indigo bag, to keep it from firing the gun room . . . More certain news that Cromwell hath now his Ironsides banged to purpose, and is, as one letter speaks, beat back into Dublin with a very great loss, at least 4,000 slain and 600 taken, himself wounded but not mortal; the junto; [i.e. The Parliament] have caused proclamation to be made at all seaports for letters that this news should not be divulged; but as secret as they carry it, it is sufficiently known for truth. The King is said to be landed in Ireland, which adds new life and valour in the commanders and common soldiers, that by the next year you will go near to hear of Dublin being besieged, if not stormed, all their forces now drawing that way. There is good store of money in the castle which will make the soldiers storm lustily'. Also in Murphy, *Cromwell in Ireland*, p. 113.

Also the *Irish Monthly Mercury* December 1649, from Cork, which was then occupied by Parliament, reports the following despatch: '. . . not long after the sally at Dublin, which the enemy out of modesty, call the battle of Rathmines, the Lord Lieutenant landed at Dublin, with an army so nourished in victory, that they never saw any defeat but those they gave their enemies. The first design we undertook was the gaining of Tredagh, in which Ormonde had placed above 3,000 of his select men, and Sir Arthur Aston for commander, one as unable to stand to it as to run away and it may be that's the reason he fell in the service, doubtless he was better for a retreat, since every step he would make a halt. In a word, if the rule be true, of judging Hercules by his foot, one may conclude this a wooden governor, yet he had made so good earthen fortifications, that by trusting to his works he showed what religion he was of. Their first retrenchment against us was the church, out of which they were soon dislodged, and I dare say it was the first time they ever went from church unwillingly, this being done too by some ordinances of Parliament, tis not unlikely the grave Presbyterians (if ever the drowsy assembly come into play again) may question their proceeding, and aver we have a mind our enemies should still continue Papists, by so pregnantly evincing there was no salvation for them in our church. At length the breach being found assaultable (more from the vent than the largeness of it), our army were so little courtiers, as to enter the town without so much knocking at the gate, where all lost their lives but those that saved them. Of the first qualification there were about 3,000, of the latter, 30, be it more or less.' D'Alton, *History Of Drogheda*, pp 278–279; Murphy, *Cromwell in Ireland*, pp. 112–13.

Also relevant is the account of Frost, Parliament's Secretary and Bookkeeper, which was published on 2 October 1649: 'The newes we long expected is come at last from Ireland. What we formerly heard is, for the general, confirmed by letters, whereof take the substance. That the Towne of Drogheda having been summoned and refusing to yield, it was after battery stormed, upon Wednesday the twelfth instant. There was in it a very strong garrison, for the enemy, not daring to abide our forces in the field, had put into that towne (whereof Sir Arthur Aston was governor) the chiefest of all their men, being above three thousand Horse and foot in seven or eight regiments, whereof Ormonde's owne was one, which was commanded by Sir Edmund Verney. Hoping to break our force upon this siege, they made stout resistance, and we, having entered near a thousand men, they fell on again and entered it, beating the enemies from their defences which they had made by three retrenchments in the right and left; which they were forced to quit. The whole garrison was put to the sword; it is believed not twenty escaped, except above seven or eight score, which were taken in two towers afterwards, to whom their lives were given, but are reserved in safe custody to be sent to the Barbadoes. It is not known that any one officer escaped but one lieutenant, who, going to the enemy, reports that he was the only man that escaped out of all that garrison.' In Williams, 'Fresh Light on Cromwell at Drogheda', *The Nineteenth Century*, LXXII, (September 1912), pp. 478–9.

In the *Moderate Intelligencer*, 4 October, the following appears: 'Behold a victory remarkable, first discovered by a letter of Mr. Peters, the contents whereof might be omitted, having been divulged in a whole sheet (separate pamphlet), but in regard the numbers slain on both sides are so strong viz, that more were slain of the besieged than of the besiegers in the taking of Tredah, viz, 3,000 of the rebels and sixty of the besiegers it is probable the loss was equal during the enemies standing and that the rest were killed not resisting.' Quoted in Williams 'Fresh Light On Cromwell at Drogheda', p. 481.

All of the above are essentially contemporary accounts, although none are eyewitnesses. Even so, the deaths they refer to can all be seen to have been the members of the military garrison only.

36   Ormonde to Lord Byron in The Carte Manuscripts' Collection, vol. II, p. 412; quoted in Murphy, *Cromwell in Ireland*, p. 109.

37   Ormonde's letters to Charles II and Lord Byron concerning Drogheda are in The Carte Manuscripts' Collection and are both reproduced in Gilbert, *Contemporary History*, pp. 269–71.

38   Inchiquin to Ormonde, 15 September 1649, The Carte Manuscripts' Collection reprinted in Williams, 'Fresh Light on Cromwell at Drogheda', p. 484.

39   Ludlow, *Memoirs*, vol. I, p. 303.

40   Bate's account of Drogheda is reproduced in Gilbert, *Contemporary History*, pp. 274–75. The relevant extract is as follows: 'In this town the Lord-lieutenant had put the flower of his veterane souldiers, most English under the command of Sir Arthur Aston, a gentleman renowned in the wars, both at home and abroad, but for the most part unfortunate. And here Cromwell resolved to make his first essay of the war. Aston, on the contrary, laid his design to tire out and break the enemy, insolent through victory, by the badness of the weather, watching and hunger; then expose them to be harrassed and alarmed by the Lord-lieutenant's horse, and the foot that were shortly to be recruited, until the Royalists being reassured, and encreased in force, might have the courage to provoke the Cromwellians, and fight them in a pitched battel.

'But he flatters himself in vain, for Cromwell attacks not the place by opening of trenches, slow approaches and the other acts of a siege; but having forthwith caused a battery to be raised on the north side of the town, and planted with guns, he so plied the place with continual shooting, that he quickly made two breaches in the wall, and immediately commands an assault to be made, that with courage and resolution they might force their entry into the place. But this having been twice unsuccessfully attempted, he himself, with Ireton, commanding the attack, with indignation and courage, redoubled by the former repulses, they make the way which they found not into the town, and put to the sword all they meet, without favour or compassion. The governour, with some of the souldiers, fled instantly to the castle, a place strong by art and nature, but the Cromwellians entering pell-mell with them (some of whom clambered up the walls, not without the help of the soldiers of the garrison), they were all put to the sword. Some flying into the church were killed as sacrifices at the Divine altars; not a few poor wretches having got up to the church roof, were forced to tumble down by the smoke of kindled hay and gunpowder. There was but one single person that saved his life by despair, who for fear of the flames, throwing himself headlong down from the top of the church, fell amongst the enemies, without any other hurt but that he broke his leg; whom, for the extraordinariness of the thing, they spared and kept alive. The rest fleeing to the ramparts begg'd quarter, but in vain. All were knocked down wheresoever they are found, neither the gown nor the dwelling house afforded any protection, nor was there any great respect had to either sex. The souldiers continued three days in cruelly slaying the townspeople that had carried arms, whom they dragged out of their lurking holes, and in pillaging and plundering the town: nay, and those also after the fifth day came creeping out of their hiding holes, were most inhumanely put to death.

'About four thousand men died in that butchery, rather than fight. So within the short space of one week was that city undone, which for whole three years together had resisted all the rage and attempts of the Irish Rebels. This town being thus taken and plundered, the royal cause was quite extinguished in Ireland; for all the other garrisons were terrified into so great a consternation, that they trembled at the very name of Cromwell'.

41   C.H. Davidson, 'The Diagnosis of Oliver Cromwell's Fatal Illness', *Cromwelliana, Journal of The Cromwell Association* (1993), p. 27. Also Antonia Fraser, *Cromwell Our Chief of Men* (London: Mandarin 1994), p. 672. Of Bate's view of his former patient the Lord Protector at the Restoration, Fraser says, 'Cromwell's sudden collapse at the end even led to accusations of poison. Dr. Bate (turned Royalist) was even supposed to have boasted in later years of having administered the poison himself.'

42   See Roger Howell Jnr. 'That Imp of Satan, the restoration image of Cromwell', *Images of Oliver Cromwell,* pp. 33–47.

43   From Anthony Wood, *Athenae Oxonienses* (first published Oxford: 1663; republished: London: Bliss, 1815). Gilbert's *Contemporary History* pp. 275–76, relates the full tract: 'Thom. Wood, eldest brother to A[thony] W[ood], died of the flux at Drogheda commonly called Tredagh, in the month of Decemb. He was borne at Tetsworth, neare to Thame in Oxfordshire, where his father then had a farme, educated mostly in the free school at Thame under his kinsman Mr. W. Burt, was made student of Ch. Church in 1638, as I have before told you, and afterwards was the first, or one of the first yong scholars in Oxon. That threw off his gowne and ran to Edgehill battle. See more under the year 1642. At his returne thence, he was actually created bach. Of arts among soldiers that had done service at the said battle: and then his father, seeing that he could not persuade him from being a soldier, he bought a horse, armes, cloaths, &c., set him up for a troper, and got him a place to ride in the troop of captaine Tho. Gardiner of Cudeson neare Oxon. Afterwards he became a stout and desperate soldier, was in several battles, and besieged in divers garrisons, particularly, if I am not mistaken at basing in Hampshire, and was made a lievtenant of horse. When the warr was terminated, and the King's cause utterlie vanquished, he returned to his college, was actually created Mr. of arts, an. 1647, but in the next yeare [1648], he, to avoid being taken and hanged for it, fled to Ireland, where finding out his quondam school-fellow at Thame, called col. Hen. Ingoldesbie, he became a lievtenant in his regiment, afterwards a captaine, and, as I have heard, had a commission, a little before his death, to be a major. About a yeare before that time viz in 1650, he returned for a time to Oxon., to take up his arrears at Ch. Church, and to settle his other affaires at which time being often with his mother and brethren, he would tell them

of the most terrible assaulting and storming of Tredagh [Drogheda], wherein he himself had been engaged. He told them that 3,000 at least, besides some women and children were, after the assailants had taken part, and afterwards all the town put to the sword on the 11 and 12 Sept. 1649; at which time Sir Arthur Aston, the governor had his brains beat out, and his body hack'd and chop'd to pieces.

'He told them, that when they were to make their way up to the lofts and galleries in the church and up to the tower where the enemy had fled, each of the assailants would take up a child and use it as a buckler of defence, when they ascended the steps, to keep themselves from being shot or brain'd. After they had killed all in the church, they went into the vaults underneath where all the flower and choicest of the women had hid themselves.

'One of these a most handsome virgin and arrayed in costly and gorgeous apparel, kneeled down to Thomas Wood with tears and prayers to save her life; and being strucken with a profound pity, took her under his arm, went with her out of the church, with intention to put her over the works and to let her shift for herself; but then a soldier perceiving his intentions, ran his sword through her belly or fundament; whereupon Mr Wood seeing her gasping, took away her money, jewels &c., and flung her down over the works.

'In the latter end of 1680 when the Parliament sate at Oxon. A. Wood was walking with Sir Hen. St. Georg Clarentius, king of armes, in the school-quadrangle. Sir Hen. Then meeting with col. Hen. Ingoldesbie before mentioned and telling him who A.W. was A.W. thereupon did discourse with him concerning his brother Thomas, and among several things that the colonel told him, was that Thomas was a good soldier, stout and ventrous, and having an art of merriment called buffooning, his company was desired and loved by the officers of his regiment. He told him then, he buried [him] in a church at Tredagh, answerable to his qualitie, but could not tell him when he died. This Thos. Wood was a tall, proper and robust man, like his father, but black and swarthy, unlike in that to any of his brethren, or father.' Also in James Carty, *Ireland from the Flight of the Earls to Gratton's Parliament* (Dublin: Fallon, 1949), pp. 69–70, also in Murphy, *Cromwell in Ireland*, pp. 104–05; also in Murray, 'Cromwell at Drogheda – A Reply to J.B. Williams', p. 1236; also in Gardiner, *History of the Commonwealth and the Protectorate*, pp. 120–21.

44   S.R. Gardiner, *History of the Commonwealth and the Protectorate*, p. 121. Gardiner puts no trust in Wood's account when he says, 'It will be seen that I have made no use of the story told by Thomas Wood . . . just the sort of man, in short, to invent a story to shock his mother and his steady, antiquarian brother.' Robert H. Murray says of Wood's words, 'Such a letter immediately strikes the trained investigator as suspicious and when he asks a few questions, he sees its worthlessness.' Murray, 'Cromwell at Drogheda – A Reply to J.B. Williams', p. 1237.

45   Gardiner, *History of the Commonwealth and the Protectorate*, p. 121.

46 Michael Byrd, 'Oliver Cromwell, A Personal Biography', *Cromwelliana*, *Journal of The Cromwell Association* (1997), p. 17.

47 See Fraser, *Cromwell Our Chief of Men*, p. 49.

48 Edward, Earl of Clarendon, *The History of the Rebellion and the Civil Wars in England*, quoted in W.F. Butler, 'Some Episodes of the Civil War of 1641–53', *County Louth Archaeological and Historical Journal*, vol. IV, no. 4 (1919). D'Alton, *History of Drogheda*, pp. 272–73, also quotes from Clarendon; 'The Clergy mingled with the soldiery, as they fled before the ferocious conqueror, perished indiscriminately with them, "so that" says Lord Clarendon, "except some few, who, during the time of the assault, escaped at the other end of the town, and others, who, by mingling with the rebels as their own men, so disguised themselves that they were not discovered, there was not an officer, soldier, or religious person belonging to that garrison left alive, and all this within the space of nine days after the enemy appeared before the walls . . . This indeed was a much greater blow than at Rathmines, and totally destroyed and massacred a body of above 2,000 men with which, in respect of the experience and courage of the officers, and the goodness and fidelity of the common men, the Marquess would have been glad to have found himself engaged in the field with the enemy, though upon some disadvantages."

49 Gerard Brockie and Raymond Walsh, *Focus on the Past 2*, (Dublin: Gill and MacMillan, 1990), pp. 132–33. The text is carelessly altered and is taken from Edmund Hogan (ed.), *The History of the Warr in Ireland from 1641–1653 by a British officer in the Regiment of Sir John Clotworthy*, pp. 86–87. His full tract concerning Drogheda is as follows: ' . . . and so we will leave them awhile and see what Crumwell has been doing since he landed. Which was that after he mustered his army on Oxmantown Green, as foresaid, he marched to Drogheda, wherein was a strong garrison from the Lord Lieutenant, (that is to say) one Collonel Wall, one Collonel Warren, one Collonel Fleming, the first two of foot, and the last of horse, and one Major Finglass of horse likewise, and all of them very gallant men at Armes. The forces they had to resist were about twenty-five thousand Foot and two-hundred and fifty Horse. As soon as Crumwell came before it, [he] sent his Trumpet to bid those within surrender the place unto him, but was returned with a resolute answer, that, till they lost their Lives, they would not yield the King's Garrison put into their trust, unto him that was a notorious enemy to his Majesty. On which Crumwell fell to his Batteries with Six pieces of Canon, and within a few days Battered the Walls, and made a long level breach on the South side of the Town and the River, where the Mount is that Commands the whole Town, and stormed twice very courageously, but were very manfully beaten back with great loss; at which Crumwell stormed to see his men knocked down, and of his chief Collonels one Castleton, and then stormed the third time, and himself in the head of them, till he went to their Breach, and then stepped by under the Wall to see his men entered, which after hard fight they did thick and three fold, and were again fought with in the streets very

smartly. But [the Irish] being overpowered, were all hewed down in their Ranks, and no quarters given for twenty-four hours to Man, Woman, or Child: so that not a dozen escaped out of the Town of Towns people or soldiers and the governor of it, one Sir Arthur Austin, an old Soldier with a wooden leg, was knocked on the head at the Mount, and got no quarters. He was in the Warrs of England Governor of Oxford for King Charles the First.'

50   Muster Rolls taken of the Royalist forces on 30 August 1649 did not include Clotworthy's regiment. See Harold O'Sullivan, 'Military Operations in County Louth in the Run-up to Cromwell's Storming of Drogheda,' *Co. Louth Archaeological and Historical Society Journal*, vol. XXII, no. 2 (1990), pp 199–204. See also Gilbert, *Contemporary History*, vol. II, p. 496.

51   Hogan (ed.), *The History of the War in Ireland from 1641–1653 by a British Officer in the Regiment of Sir John Clotworthy*, p. 4. Incidently, Christopher Hibbert, *Cavaliers and Roundheads, The English at War 1642–49* (London: Harper Collins, 1993), p.297, tells us that Clotworthy himself 'was accused of embezzling funds and of making trouble between Parliament and the Army. He was Arrested and imprisoned in 1651. Released, he returned to Ireland where he served the King so well that he was created Viscount Massereene in November 1660. He died five years later.'

52   Hogan, ibid., see reference no. 49. See also Phillip O'Connell, 'The Defenders of Clonmel, Contemporary Accounts of the Siege of Clonmel,' *Tercentenary of the Siege of Clonmel* (Clonmel: Clonmel Tercentenary Committee, 1950), p. 30.

53   Cromwell to Lenthall, 17 and 27 September 1649; Cromwell to Bradshaw, 16 September 1649; in Abbott, *Writings and Speeches*, vol. II, pp. 124, 125–28, 131.

54   L.C. Johnston, *History of Drogheda From the Earliest Period to the Present Time*, (Drogheda: Kelly Prntrs., 1826), p. 61. D'Alton: *History of Drogheda*, p. 274, repeats Johnston's account almost verbatim.

55   Cromwell to Lenthall, 17 September 1649; Abbott, in *Writings and Speeches*, vol. II, p. 126.

56   *Perfect Occurrences*, Friday, 5 October, 1649, Letter of John Hewson; reprinted in Williams, 'Fresh Light on Cromwell at Drogheda', *The Nineteenth Century*, vol. LXXII, September 1912, p. 483.

57   Gardiner in his *History of the Commonwealth and the Protectorate*, quotes at length from Bernard's contemporary tract, unaware of its title, *A Brief Relation of that Bloody Storm at Drogheda in Ireland and the Doctors Sufferings by Oliver Cromwell in it, and after it, with his Preservation*. Bernard was a Royalist and was therefore a potential target for Cromwellian troops in this complicated war. Gardiner says 'Not only does Bernard say nothing of Wood's horrors, but he implicitly denies their existence when he writes that "when the town was stormed and all that bare arms in it put to the sword". Bernard was a strong Royalist having taken a prominent part in proclaiming Charles II at Drogheda. He had been threatened by death by Cromwell and he had

no reason to spare him, especially after his tract was published after the Restoration'. *(See Appendix 3.1.)*

58   See, Bernard's tract at *Appendix 3.1.*

59   Williams, 'Fresh Light on Cromwell at Drogheda', p. 476.

60   In Gilbert, *Contemporary History,* p. 262; also quoted in Rice, 'The Five Martyrs of Drogheda', p. 117.

61   *The Moderate Intelligencer,* 4 October 1649, reproduced in Williams, 'Fresh Light on Cromwell at Drogheda', pp. 481–82. The full tract reads, 'On the 11 September about four in the afternoon the assault began. The violence of the enemy made our men give back, so fierce was the opposition, which the Lord Lieutenant seeing, ran on foot to the soldiers and encouraged them, which occasioned the renewing of the charge, and it was done with such resolution that they immediately carried the town putting to the sword as fast as they could. In which slaughter there fell Sir Arthur Aston, a Papist, as were most of the garrison, the reason given of his death is said to be the rage of Colonel Castle's soldiers for the death of their Colonel, also for that Aston gave not a civill answer when summoned. Sir Edmund Varney also was slain, who had the charge of the mount, also Colonel Fleming, Lieutenant Colonel Finglass, Major Gerald, Sir Robert Hartpool, Captains, Lieutenants and Cornets of horse, eighty – where their horse were we know not, probably they went as common men. Of foot Colonel William Waller, Colonel Warren, Colonel Burne, the Lord Taaf's brother, an Augustine Frier, of Captains and inferior officers of foot, 44, 220 reformadoes, 2000 within the town were put to the sword, the rest that had that kind of execution leapt over the wall, who are about 500, which makes in all about 2,900; being all Papists no doubt, and many of them of that party called Toryes, who used to rob and kill without mercy and no doubt were of that wretched party that killed so many Protestants at the beginning of the rebellion, and so God, the Avenger of murder (which is to kill contrary to his rule of direction) hath met with them and sooner or later will with all such bloody minded men.'

62   *Perfect Diurnall,* 8 October 1649, reproduced ibid., p. 485. The account reads, 'We sent over the water to the other [north] side of the town to hinder relief from coming to them and to prevent their running away, 2,000 horse and foot ... The mount was very strong of itself and manned with 250 of their principal men, Sir Arthur Aston being in it, who was governor of the town; which, when they saw their men retreat, were so cast down, and disheartened that they thought it vain to make any further resistance, which if they had, they could have killed some hundreds of our men, before they could have taken it. Lieutenant-Colonel Axtell of Colonel Huson's regiment, with some twelve of his men, went up to the top of the mount, and demended the governor the surrender of it, who was very stubborn, speaking very bigge words, but at length was persuaded to go into the windmill at the top of the mount, and as many more of the chiefest of them as it would contain, where they were all disarmed and afterwards all slain.'

63   *Perfect Occurrences*, 12 October, 1649, reproduced in Williams, "Fresh Light on Cromwell at Drogheda", *The Nineteenth Century*, p. 485. Williams suggests that the writer, R.L., was one of Cromwell's horse soldiers. The extract is as follows: 'Colonel Cassell's regiment led on the forlorn hope, himself slain, our men beaten a little back, but the Lord General led them up again with courage and resolution, though they met with hot dispute. When we were entered into that part of the towne where the breach was made, our men came on to a great mill hill mount, wherein they had a hundred men, put them all to the sword; here our horse and foot followed them so fast over the bridge which goes over a broad river, it being very long and houses on both sides*, yet they had not time to pull up the drawbridge. There our men fell violently in upon them, and I believe there was above 2,000 put to the sword. We had about twenty or thirty men slain and some forty wounded. Their governor was killed in the first onset.'* This is the one of the few pieces of evidence that exists that suggests there was once a bridge over the Boyne at Drogheda that had houses on both sides. See also Gogarty, *Council Book of the Corporation of Drogheda*, p. 113, where the Corporation minutes refer to a 'house on the east side of the bridge'.

64   Quoted in Rice, 'The Five Martyrs of Drogheda', p 117. Also in Harold O'Sullivan, 'Cromwell in Drogheda, No Evidence of Drogheda Massacre', *The Drogheda Independent*, October 1993.

65   Perfect Occurrences, 21–28 September 1649, carries a letter from the same date, and it is quoted in Williams, 'Fresh Light on Cromwell at Drogheda', p. 478: 'On the 11th came Mr. Peters with the last part of the forces from Milford to Dublin. And we heard that the Army was resolved to storm Drogheda on the next day being September 12th. On September 12th being this day, news is come hither that their guns have been heard to play hard, and it is said we have entered Tredagh, we are hourly expecting the particulars.' Williams says that 'The letter was not sent by ordinary post via Milford and reached London by way of Liverpool.'

66   Roy Foster, *Modern Ireland 1600–1972* (London: Penguin, 1989), p. 102. Foster asserts that the massacre of the townspeople of Drogheda 'is one of the few massacres in Irish history fully attested to on both sides'.

67   J.W. Moody, F.X. Martin, and F.J. Byrne (eds.), *A New History of Ireland* (Oxford: Clarendon Press, 1976). In the chapter 'The Cromwellian Conquest', by Patrick J. Corish, are the following words: 'That this justification could be advanced for the massacre of the inhabitants of a town that had never at any time been in the hands of the Confederate Catholics was a sombre indication of how far the guilt for the "innocent blood" was now presumed to extend', p. 329.

68   Peter Berrisford-Ellis, *Hell or Connaught, The Cromwellian Colonisation of Ireland 1652–1660* (Belfast: The Blackstaff Press, 1975), p. 21. The author asserts that 'Some 3,500 men, women and children had been killed' at Drogheda.

69   See Gogarty, *Council Book of the Corporation of Drogheda*, p. 24.

70   Ibid.

71   Ibid., p. 61.

72   Ibid. p. 24. For use of the original handwritten version, permission needs to be acquired from the Corporation authorities as it is held in a strongroom in their offices at Fair Street, Drogheda.

73   See O'Sullivan, 'Military Operations in County Louth in the Run-Up to Cromwell's Storming of Drogheda', *County Louth Archaeological and Historical m Society Journal*, pp. 203–04: 'The prospect of the town becoming a cockpit in the struggle between the Royalists and the Parliamentarians cannot have pleased many of the townspeople, not least the Protestant New English whose loyalty to the King had never been very strong and who must have been dismayed at the compact made between Ormonde and the Kilkenny Confederacy. The replacement of Lord Moore by Sir Arthur Aston and the changes subsequently made in the composition of the garrison would have been a breaking point for many of them. Throughout the years of the insurrection of 1641 Drogheda had maintained a constant good affection towards the English interest, Catholic and Old English and Protestant New English alike contributing substantial sums of money in the defence of the town and the maintenance of the garrison. They were not less loyal to the Parliamentarians than they were to the King.' The author's footnote reads, 'This is evident from the substantial number of Catholic merchants who proved their "constant good affection" to the English interest and were not transplanted during the period of the English Commonwealth, see T.C.D. MS, The Transplantation Proceedings of the Revenue Commissioners of the Precinct of Trim; The Peppard Papers N.L.I. and T. Gogarty (ed.), Council Book of the Corporation of Drogheda.'

74   The Lady Wilmot affair.

75   Rice, 'The Five Martyrs of Drogheda', p. 108.

76   John McCullen, 'The Elcocks of Drogheda', *Journal of the Old Drogheda Society*, no. 4 (1983), p. 37. This source can be traced to *The Drogheda Argus*, 22 February 1873, where an article appeared on the family name, which had previously appeared in *The Boston Pilot* earlier that year. The writer says, 'I discovered an inscribed stone, which lay over an arched vault. The stone was embedded in the earth about eight feet. Some fifteen years ago I had it raised to the surface. At the time, I entered the vault with a lighted candle, descending by a stone staircase, and took a look at the black dust which formed the chief contents of the sepulchre. Between A.D. 1571 and the time of the invasion of Cromwell in August 1649, there were at least two mayors of Drogheda, of the name as the town records will show. When Drogheda was assaulted and captured by Cromwell's forces, of a family of four brothers of the name, two fell by the sword and two escaped out of the town.' Unfortunately, the writer asserts this incidently, and does not point to any contemporary record of the deaths of two Elcocks by the sword. If the story were to be taken literally, to die *by the sword* could easily imply that they were actually in arms. Yet without any contemporary proof, the story must be added to the many colourful traditions associated with Cromwell in Ireland.

77   Ibid., p. 39.

78 *Drogheda Argus*, 22 February 1873.

79 Gogarty (ed.), *Council Book of the Corporation of Drogheda*, p. 35.

80 Ibid., p. 49.

81 Gilbert, *Contemporary History*, vol. II, p. 273. See also Fraser in *Cromwell Our Chief of Men*, who says that Bate asserts that 4,000 were killed at Drogheda, p. 338. Cromwell himself actually says *'they having in the town the number specified in this enclosed, but some say near four thousand'*. The difference is that Cromwell does not suggest that he killed 4,000 men, he merely suggests that it was rumoured that the garrison may have been that numerous.

82 The muster rolls are taken from Gilbert, *Contemporary History*, vol. II, p. 496., and used along with other contemporary documents by O'Sullivan, in 'Military Operations in County Louth in the Run-Up to Cromwell's Storming of Drogheda', pp. 199–204, to identify the composition of the Drogheda garrison.

83 O'Sullivan, ibid., pp. 119–204.

84 In *Letters from Ireland . . . Old Parliament History*; reproduced in Abbott, *Writings and Speeches*, vol. II, p. 131.

85 Inchiquin to Ormonde, 15 September 1649; reprinted in Williams, 'Fresh Light on Cromwell at Drogheda', p. 484.

86 Rice in 'The Five Martyrs of Drogheda', p. 103, says, 'There were about 3,500 killed after the fall of the town which, not by coincidence, was the number that made up the garrison.'

87 *The Moderate Intelligencer* 11 September 1649 declares, 'Sir Arthur Aston is governor of Drogheda, He hath 2,000 with him in it most of them are Irish.' In *The Moderate Intelligencer*, 13 September 1649, it states, 'In this town are two thousand Irish foot and two hundred horse, Sir Arthur Aston chose to have Irish rather than English for his garrison'; in Williams, "Fresh Light on Cromwell at Drogheda", p. 474.

88 Anne Hughes, *History of Drogheda Up-to-date, Ecclesiastical Sketches* (Drogheda: A Hughes, 1893), p. 164.

89 Verbal information received from Dermot Fairtlough, during research for *Cromwell at Drogheda*, by the author in 1993.

90 Victor Buckley and P.D. Sweetman, *Archaeological Survey of County Louth* (Dublin: Stationery Office, 1991), p. 46.

91 It is now encompassed in Tuite's horse-riding field at the top of Poor House Lane, Drogheda.

92 Murphy, *Cromwell in Ireland*, p. 102.

93 Tom Reilly, *Cromwell at Drogheda* (Drogheda: Broin Print, 1993), pp. 71–72.

94 Gogarty (ed.), *Council Book of the Corporation of Drogheda*, p. 61. The entry is from a meeting that was held on 7 October 1658: 'Granted to Thomas Cockaine the Towne interest of in and to, two little garden plotts formerly belonginge to Bartholamewe ffyan adjoininge to the Town walles, and the lane commonly called by the name of the Scarlett lane for sixty and one yeares at the rent of twelve pence p. Ann.'

Chapter Four

WEXFORD

'If we got the castle, the town would easily follow.'
(Cromwell's summary of the Wexford defences)

THE TOWN OF Wexford can trace its roots back to the ninth century, thereby claiming Viking or more particularly, Norse origins.[1] Its strategic position on the estuary of the River Slaney has determined that it has also had more than its fair share of historical mischiefs through the centuries. The county town owes its name to the early Scandinavian settlers who called it 'Weisfjord' or 'the harbour of the mud flats'.[2] Unfortunately the languid flow of the Slaney has resulted in so many large deposits of silt and mud in the estuary that the channel is now practically non-negotiable.[3] When the Normans landed twenty miles away at Bannow under the leadership of Robert Fitzstephen in May 1169, they immediately captured the town for the benefit of their migrant communities.[4] As with most of the Norman towns in Ireland, the new Anglo-French occupants began to construct high stone defensive fortifications. The volatility of the times required protection of the community within from hostile forces. The stone from the local granite and sandstone quarries give it a rustic guise, in contrast to the grey limestone of Drogheda. Of the five gates that were originally built, only one, the Westgate Tower, still stands. (There is a local theory that suggests that this tower gate was actually part of the nearby Selskar Abbey and was not in fact a principal gate, since no road leads from it, nor is there a trace of one having ever existed in the immediate area.[5]) The town today still retains its medieval streetscape of wonderfully narrow, winding streets and lanes. Substantial remains of the town wall survive throughout the town, now mostly covered with ivy and peering out from back gardens. There are also significant sections that are exposed and well maintained. The preservation of the remainder, however, as at Drogheda, is totally ignored by the municipal authorities. The nucleus of the town itself is still centred behind the quays on Main Street, running parallel to the harbour walls. The modern Wexford is renowned for its opera festival. Held over seventeen days every October, the internationally acclaimed gala plays to packed houses and attracts both participants and visitors from all over the world. The unspoiled historic atmosphere and the quaint alignment of the narrow Norman street routes, coupled with the fact that there are numerous coastal resorts in the area, combine to make Wexford a most desirable tourist destination.

The threat of a French invasion of England via Ireland in 1798 by way of Wexford, among other places, resulted in the area becoming involved in the discord between the two European foes. The Irish rebels eager to maintain links with England's enemies were eventually overcome by the forces of the Crown and hostilities ceased. The 200th anniversary of these events in 1998 saw the commemoration of a conflict that was significantly more representative of Irish Republicanism than was 1649. It is this struggle that has stirred the folk memory of the local population in preference to the current topic.

With the fall of Drogheda, Cromwell had ensured that the chances of an affiliation of the forces under Ormonde with those of Eoghan Ruadh were now extremely remote. The main route from the capital to Ulster was now under the jurisdiction of the Commonwealth of England. Cromwell's intelligence personnel would have informed the Lord Lieutenant of O'Neill's declining condition. Coote, in the north, was in control of Antrim and Down. Venables had captured Belfast and Lisburn, and communications were now open with all of the Commonwealth forces in the northern half of the country.

Of all of the towns in Ireland, why did Cromwell next choose Wexford? There are in fact countless reasons for this decision. Having initially been forced by bad weather to abandon his designs on the south, that destination was now a foregone conclusion. Parts of Munster were already in Commonwealth hands, with the exception of the region's principal city, Cork, and the larger garrisons of Waterford and

Wexford. To fully appreciate his motives, however, it is necessary first to establish a background to Wexford in 1649.

From its earliest days Wexford had almost Pale status as its allegiance to the English throne was unremitting. As early as 1171, Henry II spent a six-week sojourn in the town as he delayed his departure to Wales due to adverse sea crossing conditions.[6] It is estimated that his presence there assisted in the development of the town. As the strategic harbour town grew, it gradually became a major maritime haven for passage to and from Wales, England and the Continent. Reclamation continually took place as urban pressure for property increased over the years, and the town gradually borrowed much needed land from the estuary. In the seventeenth century, the population, including the Old English, was primarily comprised of the Roman faith. At Drogheda, the inhabitants largely opposed the rebellious Catholic Confederacy, whereas Wexford had proclaimed its support for the insurrection and embraced its ideals from the very start. Following Sir Phelim O Neill's proclamation of 23 October, Wexford eagerly joined the insurgents on 21 December, only two months after the official date of the rising.[7] In the county 1,500 men were mustered and in the town the number was 800.[8] Officers were quickly appointed under the authority of the Supreme Council of the Confederate Catholics, whose seat was at Kilkenny. Colonel Nicholas Stafford was installed as governor. According to the Protestant Nicholas Rochford by his deposition of 29 July 1642:[9]

> The Gentlemen of the county [names given] had declared themselves to be in rebellion. The townsmen of Wexford joined themselves likewise into the said rebellion, and made captains among themselves to command the several inhabitants within the parishes of the said town . . . the men under the command of the Captains numbered 800.

In January 1642 an order was issued by Viscount Mountgarret and Pierce Butler of Clough that all Protestants were to vacate the town.[10] In an attempt to depart by sea, eighty Protestants had crammed into a frigate which got into difficulties in the estuary, either by accident or design, and only one survived.[11] The deposition of Nicholas Rochford continues to indict a certain local ecclesiastic and some officials of overt religious intolerance, when he advises us that they ' . . .took an oath before Sir Nicholas French, Priest, and Sir William Devereux, Vicar

General, that they shall suffer noe English or Protestants to live in this Kingdom, or beare any office here, noe not so much as a Petty Constable's place'.[12] Nicholas French, as Bishop of Ferns, would have much to say concerning Cromwell's reduction of Wexford later, in 1649. Throughout the 1640s we find that there are many stories of cruelty to the Protestants of Wexford contained in the petitions of those surviving Protestants themselves.[13] It is therefore important to consider that at the time of Cromwell's arrival before the walls of Wexford, the supreme commanding officer of the Confederate forces in Ireland, whose army would be required for the defence of Wexford, was the tenacious Protestant, James Butler, Earl of Ormonde.

In 1641, agents of the Confederacy in Flanders were requested to look for 'able and honest men'[14] who would control the Irish coastline and improve the chances of the success of the rebellion. It was considered that terrorising English vessels would seriously hamper communication between both countries and frustrate any plans that Parliament may have had for its ships to regulate these hazardous waters. As compensation for the expensive business of privateering, the participants were authorised to 'enrich themselves by the prizes taken upon our coast'.[15] They were granted approval to accost all enemies of the 'Catholic cause' in Ireland and adversaries of Charles I in England as they patrolled the waters surrounding the island. There was a remarkably enthusiastic response from mariners of Flemish, French, Irish and even English origins. As a result, by the mid-1640s, Wexford had become a notorious lair of international piracy. Now living within its walls were highly accomplished and vastly experienced pirates whose intimate knowledge of the treacherous Irish coastal seas made their profession extremely remunerative.

As Parliament tried to get to grips with the mercenary Wexford-based frigates in the Irish Sea, the local privateers simply extended their catchment area to include the western Isles of Scotland, the North Sea, the English Channel (which proved most fruitful), and the coastlines of Holland, Normandy and Brittany.[16] Sometimes, Wexford pirates could be found in Baltic and even Mediterranean waters, such was their thirst for booty. Wexford soon became a tremendously prosperous area due to the occupations of many of its seafaring inhabitants. Even though the activity was illegal, it was after all a time of war, and most of the targets were English vessels, although other foreign ships of German, Spanish, French and Turkish origin also fell foul of the

Wexford patrol frigates. In 1642 a Dublin business magnate, Daniel Hutchinson, had his ship with its £50 cargo taken by Wexford privateers.[17] In the same year the *Hopewell* of London was taken off the Saltees by Wexford corsairs.[18] In 1646 Wexford privateers took possession of the *Blessing* of Rotterdam, belonging to the burghers of Amsterdam and Rotterdam.[19] In 1647 the 200-ton Dutch *Orange Tree*, while en route from Brill to Scotland, was taken by a Wexford frigate. Many local merchants and officials had investments in individual privateering frigates. In 1643 even the mayor of the town, Nicholas Hayes, had a share in the *Patrick*, since his brother Walter was a link in the chain of command of that ship.[20] Other pillars of local society who had commercial interests in the privateering business were John Coffie, Nicholas Devereux, James Dillon, James Hay, William Keating, Patrick Lamport, Henry Roch, John Rooth, John and Michael Stafford, John Talbot and Michael Tooting.[21] Aside from the mayor, three town officials are also documented as being patrons of the trade: Alderman Alexander Roch, Richard French (collector of customs) and Patrick Rooth (bailiff).[22] The latter, Rooth, was part owner of the man-of-war called *Mary and John of Wexford*, whose captain, John Rosseter, was killed defending his ship.[23] In 1644, Rosseter, who was described as 'an Irishman of warre' had 'pilladged much goods taken away from ye English and were brought into Wexford'.[24] Symon Synnott, who was 'a Pyrat', was known to have sometimes sailed with Rosseter.[25] James Welsh, a seaman of Wexford who lived in the town, was a 'Pyrat in the ffriggot called the Ffrancis and brought in much plunder'.[26] John Rooth, a brother of Patrick and part owner of the *Mary and John*, was the beneficiary of the plunder of that vessel and would 'entertaine, harbour and relieve, in his house in Wexford, many seamen employed in the above and pyrats who robbed the English'.[27]

The illicit bonanza of goods and commodities that was acquired, apart from the enormous value of the captured vessels themselves, comprised of cargoes of: beef, pork, various grains, beans, salt, vinegar, butter, malt, wine, oil, sugar, raisins, tobacco, goat and sheepskins, wood, tiles, tar, cloth, whiskey, silver and bullion.[28] These goods, with the entrepreneurial enterprise of the inhabitants of Wexford, dissolved into the local economy for a fraction of their market worth. At a time when the rest of the country was in a destitute condition, the population of the south-eastern corner of Ireland was experiencing a period of comparative affluence. The plundering of the town by the Roundheads would serve up a most worthwhile haul as a testament to the years of illegitimate maritime expeditions. Significantly, even Cromwell himself would remark on the prizes that would ultimately fall into his soldiers' hands.[29]

The assembling at Bristol of Cromwell's expeditionary army did not go unnoticed by the inhabitants of Wexford. On 6 August 1649, the mayor, Michael Boylan, wrote to Ormonde to tell him that a Captain Bradshaw, recently arrived from England, informed him that there were '20 ships in Milford Harbour and 26 more making for Milford to carry soldiers to Ireland; there are 15,000 men, 7,000 horse and 8,000 foot at Pembroke, ready to come for Ireland and the markets of Pembroke, Hereford and Milford are kept open'.[30] No Royalist garrison was stationed in the town and the inhabitants were not keen to accept assistance from the Protestant Royalist hierarchy. On 19 September it was realised that after Drogheda, Wexford would now be Cromwell's target.[31] The Supreme Council at Kilkenny ordered a general levy of men and arms in the area. In the county, 523 men were rallied, in Wexford town only fifty and in the nearby town of Ross, only twenty-five.[32]

Cromwell nominated John Hewson as governor of Dublin and headed off with his wife to meet with his army at Arklow on 27 September. The following day, the town of Arklow, confronted by the immense Roundhead army on its doorstep, capitulated to the Parliament of England. As coincidence would have it, at this time in Arklow there lived a local man by the name of Cromwell, who was the owner of a small piece of land at the lower end of the town. A local tradition has it that upon hearing that a namesake of his resided in the area, Cromwell had the man summoned to appear before him. When he was asked what, if anything, the Lord Lieutenant could do for the man, the local replied that he wanted nothing but to remain in possession of his small plot of land. Cromwell then told the less famous Mr Cromwell that this would be the case and added 'A poor man I find you and a poor man I leave you.' This location today is still known as 'Cromwell's Plot', presumably named after the less notorious of the two Cromwells.[33]

There was still quite a distance to be covered from Arklow to Wexford, through open and mountainous countryside. The Puritan army were constantly on the alert to small-scale Royalist ambushes as their huge army gradually mobilised southwards. Legend has it that it was during one of these skirmishes that Cromwell would lose his own horse among many others to the adventurous Christopher Tuohill, who was involved in an attack under the leadership of Brian McPhelim O'Byrne. Cromwell immediately circulated word that he was offering £100 reward for the return of his favourite mount, to which the thief's father replied, 'For gold and silver he would not give him back, but preferred to keep him as a monument.'[34]

Cromwell was anxious to capture all of the fortified towns and castles that dominated the coastline along the way in order to maintain control over, and access to, the sea and the mainland beyond. He took Rosseminoge Castle, a fort at Slane Passage, the small town of Limbrick and Enniscorthy. He had a fleet of ships sail parallel to the land route within communication distance, should the occasion arise for him to suddenly desire immediate embarkation. It was the sea vessels that would reach the port of Wexford first, on Saturday, 29 September, followed soon after by an advance party of the Parliamentarian army on 1 October. The fleet, however, due to bad weather and the fact that the mouth of the harbour was well defended, could advance no closer to the town. The next day, the remainder of the army arrived and camped at the north-west corner of the town. They had passed by the right bank of the Slaney and travelled along the old road at the back of Ardcandrisk.[35] The main body was now depleted to about 9,000 men because the garrisons that they had captured always required personnel to protect their acquisitions.

As the Puritan forces had made their way southwards, Cromwell himself had taken the opportunity to seek shelter at night. Castlehaven got wind of his attempts to locate comfortable lodgings and gives us a view of the English commander that is contrary to the traditional one of a barbarian who murdered, plundered and pillaged as he passed through Ireland:

Lord Castlehaven to Lord Ormonde

My Lord – You may perceive by the enclosed how Cromwell permitts his friends to tamper with the people of the Country; he is most kinde unto them, last night he gave £5 in the house where he lay, so that if you do not presently appeare with some party to countenance your friends and punish those that goe into protection, cirtainly, all will be lost. I hear that Wexford is alreadie treating and have drawn their condicons for to become subjects of the rebells. I hope it is not trewe. I have stoped My Lord Tafe's regiment seing My Lord fuagh [Iveagh] is marching for Waxforde. I know not whether they wil gett in, yet I can not learne that the rebells have passed Scarawaltch, the only passage on the Slane, the governor of Duncannon is here which is in as bad a case as this towne which wants everything necessary for their defence.

Your humble Servant, Castlehaven. Rosse, 30 September, 11 o'clock P.M.[36]

On 3 October the Council of State had by then digested the news carried in the packages by Samuel Porter that Drogheda had fallen. The next day, the Parliamentary Speaker, Lenthall, replied to Cromwell in a letter congratulating him on his wonderful success and informing him that 30 October would be designated as a day of national thanksgiving.[37] They also bolstered his crusade with the news that they were arranging to send him a further 5,000 men to ensure further victories on Irish soil.[38] Only three weeks earlier, London had advised Cromwell, who had yet to prove himself as a competent commander of so large a force, that 'the country can not bear the expense of this war any longer'. The 'tree that bear this treasure', which had a previously barren source, had now suddenly grown roots. Previously, Ireland had proved to be the termination of many an Englishman's military career. It is obvious that the administrative body had earlier been apprehensive about this expeditionary war. However, now that Cromwell was continuing his string of successes, even in the notoriously hostile environment of Ireland, they were much relieved and became assured of further conquests.

There were marked differences between the preparations for the defences of Drogheda and Wexford. Ormonde could not afford to let such a strategic location fall into the hands of the Parliamentarian army; it was through this port that the Royalist armies would receive arms and supplies from the Continent.[39] While the citizens of Wexford may have had similar loyalties to the people of Drogheda to Charles I, they had dedicated themselves to the Pope's envoy Rinuccini during his time in Ireland. This blatant display of Roman Catholicism did not sit at all well with the diligently Protestant Ormonde. Yet it was up to him to co-ordinate the defence of the town of Wexford against the enemies of their prospective King. This, despite the fact that the townsmen were most disinclined to make a stand against the might and power of the New Model Army. Ormonde had assigned the defence of the south of Ireland to the Earl of Castlehaven. On 27 September, Castlehaven wrote to Sir Edmund Butler, the governor of the County of Wexford (who is sometimes confused with David Sinnott, the governor of the city of Wexford), noting his concern at the town's capability for defence:

> Whereas by severall wayes his Excellency, the Lord Lieutenant hath been informed that Lieut. Generall Cromwell is ready and resolved to march for the invasion of this County of Wexford and takeing in of the townes and other Holds within it, which County and Townes are not, as he understands in so good a posture of defence as they ought for the resisting of so great a power as is now coming against them.[40]

Castlehaven, in turn, on 28 September appointed Colonel David Sinnott, as governor of the town, much to the dissatisfaction of the majority of the town's inhabitants. Sinnott had served under Thomas Preston, one of the senior officers of the Confederation and antagonist of Eoghan Ruadh. Like the latter, the men of Wexford had found solace in the Papal party of the Italian emissary and had never really approved of the alliance between the Kilkenny Confederation and the Earl of Ormonde. David Sinnott or Synnott hailed from Raheen in the barony of nearby Scarawalsh and was the eldest son of Michael Sinnott of Raheen or Rahines. David Sinnott's only son, Timothy, who was an infant at the storming of the town, would be one of the defenders of Derry against James II.[41]

The documentation that exists describing the battle of Wexford contrasts conspicuously in one particular area with that which survives concerning Drogheda. At Drogheda there are no references whatever to armed townsmen having taken part in the conflict. At Wexford it is most apparent throughout the contemporary accounts that a large number of the armed defenders are described as 'inhabitants' or 'townsmen'. The Old English Drogheda Catholics had accepted the treaty that the Confederation of Kilkenny had made with Ormonde. The Catholics of Wexford, like Rinuccini, had considered Ormonde to be their archenemy until the King had been executed and Ormonde found himself in opposition to the London government. Therefore he had neither the authority nor the inclination to have a garrison stationed there in anticipation of an attack from the New Model. Besides, he had further alienated himself from them when he had surrendered Dublin to Parliament in 1647, and his association with Inchiquin, the destroyer of towns like Cashel and Youghal, did not please the people of Wexford. How could they trust one who could treat with the enemy in such a manner? Wexford was therefore a very Confederate town. When the point would be emphasised that the inhabitants of the town were massacred by Cromwell, it must be noted that those very inhabitants, who were mainly 'mariners', constituted a significant percentage of the military garrison that would conduct the defence of the town. The only thing that Drogheda and Wexford had in common, as far as Cromwell was concerned, was that they were both strategic forts that had to be reduced if Parliament were to enforce the Adventurers Act and to extinguish Irish support for the young Prince of Wales.

The Corporation of the town tried to convince Castlehaven that the appointment of Sinnot was not such a wise move. He disagreed and refused to alter his decision. The population, knowing well the events at Drogheda the previous month, were now inclined to open the gates to the attackers to avoid bloodshed. On 30 September, Sinnott wrote as follows to Ormonde:

> Lieutenant Colonel David Sinnott to the Lord Lieutenant Generall of Ireland
>
> Most Excellent Sir, – Being entrusted by the General of the Horse with the comaund and government of this towne of Wexford, I came hither Friday last to putt the same into the best posture of defence for H.M's service which I may, but it please your Excellency, I find noe resolution in the Townsmen to defend the towne, but to speak truth nakedly, I find and perceave them rather inclined to capitulate and take condicons of the Enemy, in so much as I cannot as yett, find admittance for those few assigned hither for the defence of the place, nor a muster of the townsmen to know what strength they have for the defence thereof, in which respect seing I am not able to doe H.M. any service I am resolved to leave the towne without I find their undelayed conformity, all which out of my duty, I humbly offer to your Excellency and assure your Lordship that the place will be lost to H.M. without your Excellency's interpose H.M.'s forces for the defence

thereof, which if sene by the towne will incouradge them and nothing else as I conceave such [an] impression they have of Drogheda. All of which I humbly submitt unto your Excellency more grave consideration, resting My Most Excellent Lord.

Your Excellency's humble Servant, Da. Sinnott.[42]

Cromwell had been optimistic that Wexford would be delivered up to him following his preliminary summons. There is every reason to believe that he was convinced that a repeat of Drogheda was not a serious possibility. He had ordered the massacre there in an attempt to prevent resistance elsewhere in Ireland. He certainly did not expect a similar scene so hot on the heels of 11 September. Sinnott was not an acceptable governor as far as the men of Wexford were concerned, and he was well aware of the fact, yet they found themselves in quite a predicament. The massive force of the Roundhead army was camped in the environs of the town with every intention of attempting to capture it. The recent news concerning the slaughter at Drogheda was still fresh, as were, no doubt, the blood stains on the weapons of the Puritans, who waited patiently outside the walls in the wind and rain for the orders to attack. Rumours of wholesale indiscriminate massacres were already abroad. The only source of reinforcements was from Ormonde via Sinnott. Similar to many instances in this complicated war, there was much compromising of principles for an attempt to be made to defy the mighty power of the rampant King-killing army. This was the tenuous backdrop behind which the town would be fortified. The combined forces that would command the defence of the town were united only in so far as they were both staunchly opposed to the Parliamentarian ethic. They were also, however, consumed with hostility to each other. Had Sinnott departed, as he was first inclined to do, the inhabitants would simply have surrendered their town to Cromwell, like those defenders of Arklow and other towns, and many lives would have been spared.

Castlehaven was also concerned that the inhabitants of Wexford were ready to become 'subjects of the rebells' by capitulating. Butler wrote his final letter on 30 September to Ormonde, and in it he also displays his anxiety that the town is willing to submit:

I hope the losse of Drogheda was revenged. If there has been any breach of quarter in it, it were good it were divulged, it would settle the hearts of the communaltye

whose pressure makes them – espetiall att Wexford – inter-
tayne some inclinations to be in slavery under the English
usurpation. The forte of Wexford is not fynished and the
Towne weake . . .[43]

It is alleged that in the town, a gentleman by the name of Hugh
Rochford, who was the recorder of the Corporation and 'a most influential Gentleman', began to draw up conditions of surrender. Mr
Rochford, it appears, was mindful of the prevailing influences and col-
luded with a Nicholas Loftus to design a set of settlement provisions
for the townsmen. Butler was quick to extinguish such an eventuality,
no doubt with the employment of decisive military coercion. Rochford
then departed the town and left himself open to long-standing accusations of attempting to betray the town to Cromwell. Upon hearing of
these allegations, Rochford wrote to Ormonde to seek an audience with
him in order to explain his actions, which he insisted were not born out
of duplicity.[44]

A set of military instructions, still existing today, were issued, and
they describe in some detail, plans to beset the New Model assembly
on their approach to Wexford. Today they appear to be somewhat
quaint, but even at that time they did not stand much of a chance of
succeeding. They are as follows:

Proposals for Attacking the Enemy's Leaguer at Wexford.

1. That ye Commander in Chief att Wexford be sent too
with all speed, to assure him of all reliefe and incouradge
ye towne; and that he may be ye more confident some of
ye circumstances to be declared to him. That at ye present he procure and send by his espialls what he can collect of ye enemy's condition, of ye order they ly in, what
guards they keep and where. In what part Cromwell, Ireton and their traine ly, how they dispose of their horse in
ye night; by what way they might be best attaqued; and
that these spys be such as be well acquainted with ye
country there abouts, and may serve us for guides. That
he be ready at ye hour appointed to fall on his quarter,
with our signe and words, and doe his uttermost to presse
towards that quarter of their leaguer where their traine
and ammunition lyes of which he is to convey what he can

into ye towne, and ye rest destroy, burneing ye carriages and nayleing ye canon.

2. That some that know ye country and may serve us for guides be sent from hence into ye enemy's campe to spy ye above advantages and that their intelligences may be compared.

3. That there be 1,000 horse and 2,000 foot chosen for ye designe, all of commanded men, and that ye foot consist of two part piques and one part firelocks.

4. That ye fforlorne consist of 100 horse flanked on each side by 100 foot, drawne up eight deepe, with ye firelocks in ye second and last ranks but one, that in case they be attaqued both in ye front and reere they make a good defence.

5. That there be six bodyes more drawne out, consisting of ye like number and order to second them and doe ye execution, in which no man is to alight from his horse or breake his ranke. Nor none of those bodyes to pursue any routed party above 50 paces, still keeping their firme order which they may not breake for any seeming advantage.

6. That ye reserve consist of two equall bodys of 100 horse and 250 foot apiece in ye like order, that they may with more ease succour either wing or both at once, if occasion be. I propose this order that they may better overcome all difficulties which they may incounter with, and preserve ye flankes and reare of our horse from being attaqued by ye enemy. These horse to carry every one, a pitched ffagot.

7. That three of ye first and chiefest bodys have everyone a guide (as all the rest) to conduct them readily to Cromwell, Ireton, Jones [and] ye traine ammunition and victualls. And that ye body that seizeth ye traine, guard it whilst ye garrison souldiers convey itt into the towne and what is not [so conveyed] to destroy; the rest of ye bodys still moving to keepe the enemy from rallying.

8. That 100 horse and 100 ffire locks be sent from ye body when itt approacheth neere the enemy to give the false alarme, on ye side towards our campe who must keepe

constantly shooteing, and may hang up many light matches in ye enemy's sight to frighten them, and to be ye signe to ours which way to make their retreite if occasion be. But this false alarme is not to be given till ye other be falne on.

9. That there goe along with this party 50 pioniers to make a by way when we approach neere the enemy, the better to avoyde his scouts and guards, and prevent ye alarme.

10. That ye party make their attaque by way of Dublin about two hours before day, and that the body of our army towards which they are to retreite, march along by ye river side, so as to be within three or four miles of ye enemy at ye time of the falling on, where if our party returne with ye least considerable successe, we may be bold to incampe ourselves and doubtlesse in a short time force them to abandon their siege.

Endorsed – Proposal for attaqueing the enemy's leaguer before Wexford in October, 1649.[45]

While it is admirable that an outline for a surprise attack was being proposed, it is obvious that without the realisation of many inconceivable outcomes, the plan was hopeless and would never have succeeded. That spies could so easily infiltrate the Roundhead ranks, that there was a cohesive body of troops within the town to carry out their instructions, that the ammunition train could so easily be accosted and most of it gained for the town, all appears now to have been quite improbable. This attacking army was one of the most proficient in Europe, and their expert scouts and intelligence divisions were not so easily encroached.

The October weather was taking its toll on the besieging army. Dysentery was spreading through its ranks and their temporary canvass shelters were inadequate for the persistently squally weather. For Cromwell, Wexford would be a tough nut to crack. The estuary of the Slaney separated him from the town on the opposite banks. The town, according to Cromwell, was 'strong, having a rampart of earth within the wall, near fifteen foot thick'.[46] The ships carrying the artillery train had yet to enter the estuary, the mouth of which was dominated by the Confederates ten miles away at the fort of Rosslare, which commanded the harbour. There was no easy way into the town from where the Puritans were camped, particularly since their big guns had still to arrive. However, as at Drogheda, Cromwell knew that to succeed he must have his batteries in a controlling position. So on 2 October, he despatched Jones with some dragoons to the fort of Rosslare in an effort to secure access for the fleet. Unbelievably, upon the arrival of the Roundhead detatchment, the defenders of that stronghold simply threw down their arms and jumped into the nearest boat to escape. Hugh Peters wrote to a friend in London on 3 October briefly describing this astonishing fortune that was bestowed on the Puritan invaders:

> Yesterday we tooke in the Forte here before Wexford which commanded their harbour, which is now become ours. They fled into a Frigot which lay [close] by their Fort which our ships had chased in. They also tooke the Frigot, a new vessel of the Lord of Antryms, with 14 guns in her. The fort had 7 guns. There be many other ships above at the towne, which if God give, the towne will fall in. They have put 1500 men into the towne where there were 2000 before. Here is a very good country. We want nothing but more men to possess it. I wish our soldiers in England were here to become landed men. All our soldiers are well paid – viz., a horseman 2s. 3d. a day, and the foot 4s. 10d. weekly. Many Country Gentlemen come in daily for protection. We have here a Fleet of about 20 saile before the harbour.[47]

A Colonel Richard Deane wrote to the Council of State on 5 October telling them that they 'arrived at Wexford on 29 September and my Lord [Lieutenant] came withe the whole army on the 2nd instant, the enemy having put into the town, on the 1st a governor with 1,500 foot. The castle at the mouth of the harbour was quitted at the approach of the army. The Lord Lieutenant has summoned the town and they are in treaty.'[48]

The sea and the river were now under Cromwell's control without so much as a single shot having been fired. Now he could land his guns and his men on the town side of the estuary and engage it on *his* terms. On the south side of the town, detached from the town walls, was the castle of Wexford. Behind this, further south, was a hill overlooking the town in the area known today as Maudlinstown. On that hill is a cluster of rocks, still locally known today as the Trespan

Rocks, or just 'the rocks'.[49] It was from this position that Cromwell would direct his cannons towards the indecisive defenders of Wexford. He began to make preparations to move his whole army to this position. By this time Ormonde's troops, which had been recently swelled by 1,000 foot and 300 horse from the Earl of Clanricarde, were in the vicinity, and Cromwell was becoming anxious to proceed with the negotiations. Sinnott, with his 1,500 foot soldiers had only been allowed through the gates at the intimidating prospect of the Parliamentarian ships in the harbour. Ormonde had also hoped that Butler would intervene between the townsmen and Sinnott, and it was as a result of these negotiations that the latter was finally permitted take up his command.[50] On 3 October, Cromwell despatched his usual demand for control of a town to the unpopular governor:

> For the Commander-in-chief within the town of Wexford:
>
> Before Wexford, 3rd October 1649.
>
> Sir, Having brought the army belonging to the Parliament of England before this place, to reduce it to obedience, to the end effusion of blood may be prevented and the town and country about it preserved from ruin, I thought fit to summon you to deliver the same to me, to the use of the State of England. By this offer, I hope it will clearly appear where the guilt will lie, if innocent persons should come to suffer with the nocent. I expect your speedy answer; and rest, Sir,
>
> Your Servant, O. Cromwell.[51]

While the essence of the summons is similar to that which he sent to Aston at Drogheda, there are subtle differences to be discerned between both messages. Cromwell threatens the garrison at Wexford with collateral destruction to the town and the immediate area in the event of a successful attack. It is noticeable that he did not issue a similar warning to the occupants of the County Louth town. He also makes a distinction between what he perceives as the guilty and the innocent. Again, he did not make a similar statement at Drogheda. Naturally, this forewarning that the 'innocent should come to suffer with the nocent' was ultimately interpreted as a threat to unarmed civilians when the reports of the battle would come to be written. The alternative and

more credible viewpoint is that Cromwell was referring to local property owners who would not be involved in the conflict and whose properties might be destroyed during the sack. Nor could he guarantee at
that stage, considering the reputation that the town had acquired, that
his soldiers could easily discriminate between combatants and non-
combatants. However, the orders of the New Model Army to *exclude*
non-military personnel from battle *had not altered* since Cromwell had
first issued them at Dublin. In these words to Sinnott he actually re-
enforces the idea that his campaign was being conducted strictly
according to the rules of war by acknowledging the exemption of the
innocent from warfare, i.e. 'persons whatsoever not in arms'.[52] It is also
obvious that he is clearly laying the blame at the door of the governor
should such mistakes occur. In the ensuing correspondence between
the two men, he would continue to display his desire for leniency and
his aspirations for a peaceful settlement. He was also thinking ahead,
since to lay waste to the town would not be conducive to any subsequent planting of the area when that time would come. He had also ear-
marked the town as a possible venue for his winter quarters.

Had Butler not arrived, the men of Wexford would still have delivered the town to the Puritans upon the receipt of the initial summons.
Sinnott had other ideas. It was his opinion that the town must be
defended, or at the very least, surrendered under his terms. However,
he was not at all certain of the competence of the force now within the
walls to withstand a siege from the Roundheads. He thought that he
would play for time. Where Aston refused even to answer Cromwell's
demand for control of the town (which had long been decided by the
Council of War), Sinnott immediately opened communications with
the Lord Lieutenant. If Sinnott had refused to answer, the orders to
attack would have been imminent. Since the town was in no fit state to
conduct a proper defence at that stage, he had no option but to reply
to Cromwell:

> For the Lord-General Cromwell. These: Wexford, 3rd
> October 1649
>
> Sir, I have received your letter of summons for delivery of
> this town into your hands. Which standeth not with my
> honour to do myself; neither will I take it upon me with-
> out the advice of the rest of the officers, and Mayor of this
> corporation, this town being of so great consequence to all

Ireland. Whom I will call together and confer with, and return my resolutions unto you to-morrow by twelve of the clock. In the meantime, if you be so pleased, I am content to forbear all acts of hostility, so you permit no approach to be made. Expecting your answer in that particular, I remain, My Lord

Your Lordship's servant

D. Sinnott[53]

To accentuate the divisions among the defenders, the townsmen proceeded to perform a most bizarre act of benevolence to the leader of the attacking army. They despatched a cart load of gifts addressed to Cromwell containing 'sack, strong waters and strong beer' for his pleasure while he waited outside the walls in the appalling weather conditions.[54] This attempt to placate Cromwell and his officers clearly indicates that the atmosphere surrounding the deadlock was not like that of Drogheda where such a scheme would have been totally implausible. Exactly what they sought to gain is a matter of speculation, but it is likely that they were anxious to alert Cromwell to the division in the town between the civilian defenders and Sinnott's military forces. They may have hoped that their gesture would invoke clemency towards them, their ships, their goods and their properties.

Cromwell immediately replied to Sinnott:

Sir, I have received your resolutions to return your answers by twelve of the clock to-morrow morning, which, I agree unto; but for the other part of your letter to forbear all acts of hostility, I consider that your houses are better than our tents, and so shall not consent unto that, I rest, Sir,

Your servant, O. Cromwell [55]

It was obvious as to which of the sides had the upper hand in the circumstances, and Cromwell saw no reason not to remind Sinnott of this fact. Neither would he agree to a cessation and he advised Sinnott accordingly. The weather had not abated and the camp was now reduced to a quagmire. However, in pursuit of a peaceful settlement to the dilemma then pertaining, he acquiesced to Sinnott's request for time to communicate with his colleagues. The next day the following answer was despatched to Cromwell:

For the Lord-General Cromwell

Wexford, 4th October 1649

Sir, I have advised with the Mayor and officers, as I promised; and I am content that four whom I shall employ, may
have a conference with four of yours, to see if any agreement may be begot between us. To this purpose I desire
you to send mine a safe-conduct, as I do hereby promise to
send to yours when you send me their names. And I pray
that the meeting may be had to-morrow at eight in the
forenoon, that they may have sufficient time to confer
together and determine the matter; and that the meeting
and place be agreed upon, and the safe conduct mutually
sent for the said meeting this afternoon. Expecting your
answer hereto, I rest, My Lord,

Your servant, D. Sinnott

Send me the names of your agents, their qualities and
degrees. Those I fix upon are: Major James Byrne, Major
Theobald Dillon, Alderman Nicholas Chevers, Mr William
Stafford.[56]

Sinnott's efforts to gain time were by now in full swing. It could be
surmised that his motives were totally honourable during these liaisons
and that at all times his idealistic intentions were to fashion an acceptable treaty that would exclude a hostile seizure of the town. The futil-
ity of this agenda lay in the determination of the Parliamentarian senior
ranks to acquire the town for their benefit, irrespective of the claims of
its inhabitants to their estates. Cromwell again reacquainted Sinnott
with the salient facts concerning the balance of power, when he wrote:

Sir, Having summoned you to deliver the town of Wexford
into my hands, I might well expect the delivery thereof, and
not a formal treaty; which is seldom granted but where
things stand upon a more equal foot.

If, therefore, yourself or the town have any desires to
offer, upon which you will surrender the place to me, I
shall be able to judge of the reasonableness of them when
they are made known to me. To which end, if you shall
think fit to send the persons named in your last, intrusted

by yourself and the town, by whom I may understand your
desires, I shall give you a speedy and fitting answer, and I
do hereby engage myself that they shall return in safety to
you. I expect your answer hereunto within an hour; and
rest your servant.

O. Cromwell [57]

In this letter, Cromwell displays a sarcastic aspect of his personality
by continuing to entertain Sinnott's desire to negotiate, while declaring,
that irrespective of the discussions, the result will still be the same. Wexford would ultimately be his. For the time being, however, he would
encourage a conference from which might result favourable conditions
being offered to the defenders of the town and possession of it to him.
After all, he was still of the opinion that the slaughter at Drogheda
should discourage further bloodshed. He had already laboured the point
that this was why the Drogheda garrison were massacred. His intentions
at Wexford were drastically different from those at Drogheda. This was
the motivation that he had in pursuing a peaceful settlement. It must be
remembered that the prevailing circumstances were perfectly conducive
to a non-violent resolution. The garrison were willing to discuss terms.
The townsfolk had already made a peace offering and a peaceful settlement had always been their preference. The framework of an amicable
compromise was well in place. It would, however, all go horribly wrong.

Having only had minutes to initiate his reply, Sinnott quickly
renewed the correspondence:

For the Lord-General Cromwell

Wexford, 4th October 1649

Sir, I have returned you a civil answer to the best of my
judgement; and thereby I find you undervalue me and this
place so much, that you think to have it surrendered without capitulation or honourable terms, as appears by the
hour's limitation in your last.

Sir, had I never a man in this town but the towns men and
the artillery here planted, I should conceive myself in a
very befitting condition to make honourable conditions.
And having a considerable party with them in the place, I
am resolved to die honourably, or to make such conditions

as may make my honour and life in the eyes of my own party.

To which reasonable terms if you harken not, or give me time to send my agents till eight of the clock in the forenoon to-morrow with my positions, with a further safe conduct, I leave you to your better judgement and myself to the assistance of the Almighty; and so conclude.

Your servant, D. Sinnott [58]

The conditions that Sinnott alludes to would soon be made available for Cromwell's perusal. At this time Sinnott was still negotiating with Castlehaven and Ormonde for extra troops to be deployed for his use. On 5 October, having received no reply to his last letter, Sinnott was now ready to submit his proposals to Cromwell and so he wrote to advise him of that fact:

For the Lord-General Cromwell

Wexford, 5th October 1649

Sir, My propositions being now prepared, I am ready to send my agents with them to you; and for their safe return, I pray you to send a safe conduct by the bearer to me, in the hope an honourable agreement may thereupon arise between your Lordship and, my Lord,

Your Lordship's servant, D. Sinnott [59]

Meanwhile Cromwell was busy completing his siege preparations, by now at quite an advanced stage. He was at this time expecting a delegation from the town with their conditions. These he would compare to his own demands and if there was common ground, then the town could be captured peaceably. However, still no deputation from the town had arrived. Even so, Cromwell did not see a reason to take the initiative and strike at the castle walls with his batteries. He waited, even though his patience by now must have been wearing quite thin with the procrastinating governor. The reason for the delay within the walls was obvious. Castlehaven had arrived that day at the only side of the town left open, having accompanied the Ulster regiment of Lord Iveagh, consisting of 1,500 men, to the gates of the town.[60] Sinnott, who was just about to issue his conditions to Cromwell, was now obliged to seek approval of them from Castlehaven, who was the Lord General of the Royalist horse and superceded him in the military chain of command. Sinnott explains this to his adversary outside the walls, his relationship with whom was now under some duress:

For the Lord-General Cromwell

Wexford, 6th October 1649

My Lord, Even as I was ready to send out my agents to you, the Lord General of the horse came hither with relief. Unto whom I communicated the proceedings between your Lordship and me, and delivered him the propositions I intended to despatch unto your Lordship, who hath desired a small time to consider them and to speed them unto me, which, my Lord I could not deny, he having a commanding power over me.

Pray, my Lord, believe that I do not do this to trifle out time, but for his present content; and if I find any long delay in his Lordship's returning them back unto me, I will proceed of myself according to my first intention, to which I beseech your Lordship give credit, at the request,

My Lord, of your Lordship's ready servant,

D. Sinnott [61]

On that same day Sinnott wrote another letter, but this time to Ormonde, requesting relief, therefore playing a duplicitous trick on the commander of the Parliamentarian forces:

Lieutenant Colonel David Sinnott to the Lord Lieutenant-General

May it please Your Excellency, the reliefe your Lordship sent came very seasonable, but our necessityes and wantes of all sortes of provision in and weakness of our walls debarrde us from sending of partyes for fitchinge in reliefe. The enemy hath now landed their artillery and victualls for their soldiers, they have already raysed a Battery to command the Ferry on the south syde, it be[ing] night, men may be brought over, or any other provisions, théy are hard att worke and making their preparations for the rest of there Batteryes, so as my Lord delays wilbe very preiudi-tiall. It would be extreme well ordered to face them tomor-row with horse, that preadventure will gain us some tyme, and preserve this place, and much distress them for want of forradge which is very scarce in these parts, if there weare 500 men more soe as provision weare sent a longe with them it would give us a great succor, but if your Lordship draw tymely upon them we shall with what men we have, make shift for a tyme to defend ourselves. This, my Lord, being theis present relation of this place, I most humbly take leave and rest, my Lord,

Your Excellency's faithful servant, Da. Sinnott [62]

Meanwhile, Cromwell's reply to Sinnott's first letter that day con-tained renewed resolve and a display of indifference to the excuses of a governor whom he had concluded would assume no responsibility for his own actions. It was also communicated with his usual aptitude for intimidation veiled in literate propriety:

To the Commander-in-chief of the town of Wexford
Before
Wexford, 6th October 1649

Sir, You might have spared your trouble in the account you give me of your transaction with the Lord General of your horse, and of your resolution in case he answer not your expectations in point of time. These are your own con-cernments, and it behoves you to improve them, and the relief you mention to your best advantage.

All that I have to say is, to desire you to take notice, that I do hereby revoke my safe-conduct from the persons men-tioned therein. When ye shall see cause to treat, you may send for another, I rest Sir,

Your servant,

O. Cromwell [63]

Cromwell continued to demonstrate remarkable patience towards the occupants of the town. It would soon become clear that the aspirations of the defenders contrasted drastically from those of the attackers. However, Cromwell was *still* prepared to entertain the demands of Sinnott and his comrades. Ormonde himself arrived at the Ferrybank opposite the town on 8 October and immediately opened his own written dialogue with those within, offering assistance.[64] In keeping with the communicative nature of the build up to the storm, Ormonde wrote first to Sinnott:

> Lord Ormonde to Colonel David Sinnott
>
> After,&c. The particulars of your present condition and necessities being expressed in yours of this day's date by Captain Bartlett, wee shall imploy our uttermost industry soe to provide and supply that place as to enable it to preserve itselfe from its Enemyes, now wee hope in such distresse as [that they may] not [be] able to continue their siege much longer. We doubt the men and horse you desire cannot be conveniently brought to the ferry side this night, however it shalbe endeavored and in case they may, or at any time when they shalbe, notise shalbe hastened unto you to the end the Boates may be at the ferry bank ready to receive them at the very instant of their coming thither And soe &c.,
>
> Your affectionat friend, Ormonde 9 Oct 1649, 9 a.m. [65]

Ormonde then wrote to the mayor of the town and requested the evacuation of those civilians that were not involved in the conflict. He indicates that in the light of the hostile siege conditions, sustenance for his troops and the defenders of the town in general would not be readily secured. So it was easier to reduce the number of mouths to be fed with the departure of those that no longer had any reason to be within the town walls at such a dangerous time:

> Lord Ormonde to the Mayor of Wexford
>
> After &c. Wee are come hither to countenance the maintenance and to relieve the necessities of that towne, and doe find upon examination of the conditions thereof that provision of victuals wilbe the greatest want in all probability to draw any distresse thereon, and withall finde the Country

here soe exhausted that it wilbe difficult to supply the
Towne with provision for all sortes of people there. And
therefore pray and require you after examination of each
Inhabitants provision that you send out the unnecessary
people, as ould men, women and children with that expedition that whilst wee are here wee may send them whither
they propose to [go] themselves most safely. As for the
souldier and such of the townsmen as are enturnes wee shall
take such care as they shall not want, and for the remaining
Townsmen they shall have good marketts to supply their
necessities, with fitting care of a place whereon the interest
of the Kingdom and the rebells ruine so much depends.
[We] shall expect your care of husbandinge the provisions to
the best advantage of lasting for such competent time as wee
may be hopefull on the other side if neede be to relieve you,
and that your unanimity and compliance with the Governor
and Commissioners there may be such as the service may
vigorously and without trouble goe on.

From Farralstown 9 October 1649 [66]

While Ormonde was in the locality, he offered to put a further 400
or 500 men into the town, but the men of Wexford refused them. He
soon realised that he had ventured too close to the town with his 3,000-
strong army, since it was a perilous place to be if he were not considering a field engagement, which he was not. He withdrew his troops
successfully despite being pursued by Michael Jones and 1,500 cavalry
on Cromwell's instructions. The plea from Ormonde to send out all of
the civilians that were in the town is of huge significance. These
'unnecessary people' were to be totally evacuated from the town in
anticipation of the battle.

Cromwell was being frustrated by a town whose defenders were still
divided and whose numbers were still deficient to consider an adequate
stand of defiance. There were by this time some 2,500–3,000 men under
Sinnott's command sequestered in the town. Cromwell was not going to
wait for their numbers to swell again, nor was he going to spend much
more time exposed to the elements while the insolent defenders enjoyed
the protection of their buildings. He had by now completely moved his
camp to the stony terrain still known today as 'Cromwell's Fort' on the
elevated ground to the south-eastern corner of the town.[67] The battery

of four big guns were directed firmly at the castle and ready for battle on the evening of the 10th. In the early hours of the 11th, Cromwell gave the order to fire and so the cannonade began. That night they shot over a hundred missiles at the castle and it was not long before two large breaches had appeared in the walls. To take the castle would make the town extremely vulnerable, such was its commanding position. They could then turn the big castle guns on the town, which was only yards away. The commander of the castle was a Captain James Stafford, whose part in these proceedings would eventually prove to be immense. By noon on the 11th, Sinnott demanded to reopen the dialogue. He sent his trumpeter out and insisted that Cromwell receive his delegation of four persons to discuss their proposals for surrender. Although Cromwell still maintained the upper hand, especially now that the employment of his heavy artillery had emphatically proved the point to the defenders, he was *still* willing to negotiate in order to save lives. Sinnott reminded Cromwell that he had promised a safe conduct for his four consultants if and when the time would arise:

> For the Lord General Cromwell
> Wexford, 11th October 1649
>
> My Lord, In performance of my last, I desire your Lord-
> ship to send me a safe conduct for Major Theobald Dillon,
> Major James Byrne, Alderman Nicholas Chevers and Cap-
> tain James Stafford, whom I will send to your Lordship
> instructed with my desires. And so I rest,
>
> My Lord your servant,
>
> D. Sinnott [68]

The submissions of Sinnott and the inhabitants of the town con-sisted of ten resolutions. (See Appendix No. 4.1.)

Even with the passage of 350 years, the ability that Sinnott and his co-negotiators displayed for negotiation, with these partisan overtures, appears highly questionable. In short, they were demanding free exer-cise of the Catholic religion for the inhabitants, the preservation of the possessions of the Catholic clergy and the conservation of their bish-ops authority, the safe withdrawal of the entire garrison and the armed inhabitants, the continuance of the charters and liberties of the town, the protection of the properties of all of the inhabitants, latitude for the seafaring inhabitants to trade freely in England, and finally, they desired that all of their previous crimes of piracy and smuggling be completely absolved and the individual offenders unreservedly exonerated. In the Puritan mind, the sheer audacity of the defenders of Wexford contained in these conditions of surrender must have bordered on the ludicrous. It is likely that Sinnott expected Cromwell to return with counter measures, which they could peruse and reply to, eventually reaching an amicable compromise. But Sinnott's demands were too far removed from the reality of the situation for Cromwell to even discuss them. The governor, with the approval of Castlehaven, had now wasted enough of Cromwell's time. They might well have anticipated an immediate renewal of hostilities in the shape of a direct assault on their walls, if only as a reaction to the content of their outrageous provisions. Instead, a written response was drafted by a yet tolerant Cromwell, who was obviously still hopeful that there would be no 'further effusion of blood', as he persistently strove for a non-violent resolution. His view was, that the town would be his, the exercise of the Catholic religion would not be tolerated, any clergy found would be punished for their part in the 1641 rising, and all valuable properties would be confiscated for the use of the Parliament of England. He replied to Sinnott thus:

For the Commander-in-Chief in the town of Wexford.

Before Wexford, 11th October 1649

Sir I have had the patience to peruse your propositions; to which I might have returned an answer with some disdain. But, to be short, I shall give the soldiers and non commissioned officers quarter for life and leave to go to their several habitations, with their wearing clothes; they engaging themselves to take up arms no more with the Parliament of England; and the commissioned officers for their lives, but to render themselves prisoners. And as for the inhabitants, I shall engage myself that no violence shall be offered to their goods and that I shall protect their town from plunder.

I expect your positive answer instantly; and if you will, upon these terms, surrender and quit, and in one hour

send to me four officers in the quality of field officers and
two Aldermen, for the performance thereof, I shall thereupon forbear all acts of hostility. [69]

Cromwell was totally prepared to save the lives of all of the occupants of the town, including his military adversaries. To the soldiers he
offered quarter and freedom, to the officers quarter but not freedom,
and to the inhabitants quarter, freedom and protection from plunder.
However, it appears that Sinnott never actually received Cromwell's
reply. The storming and resultant sacking of Wexford is now centred
around the bizarre events that would follow.

Captain James Stafford, governor of the castle, who was one of the
delegation of four that had gone to treat with Cromwell in his tent,
appears to have suddenly handed over control of his fort to the Puritan
army. 'Stafford' (like Synnott) is a name that is today still prominent in
Wexford, as it has been for centuries. The eighteenth century house
(now deserted) sited at Cromwellsfort was the home of the Staffords
for some years.[70] In the intervening years, Stafford has been accused of
intentional treachery. A contemporary writer has described him as a
'vain, idle young man and nothing practised in the art of military'.[71]
Other writers are convinced that Cromwell himself maliciously
deceived Stafford into surrendering the castle to him.[72] It has also been
advanced that he saw further resistance as being futile and, having a
weak will, he capitulated.[73] Whatever the reason, it is certain that it was
as much of a surprise to Cromwell as it was to anyone else. It is also definite that Cromwell had no personal part in the subsequent and immediate seizure of the castle and town. At Drogheda he had led the
successful final assault himself and was directly involved with the conflict at the breaches. At Wexford, he was still in his tent preparing his
equitable reply to the governor when all hell broke loose at the castle.
He had not given the order to storm. The army were now virtually out
of his control and pouring rapidly in on the surprised defenders, who
were still expecting a written answer to their conditions. This they
might have got, were it not for the baffling Stafford affair.

The castle was situated about thirty yards away from the town
walls and it was suddenly in enemy hands. The Roundheads redi-
rected the castle guns to face the town, and the defenders on the walls
opposite promptly deserted their posts in a fit of terror. With the
walls at that part of the town abandoned and with no resistance from

above, some of the attackers embedded their pikes in the cracks and easily scaled the walls. Scaling ladders were then thrown up by others, and soon hundreds of Parliamentarian soldiers had engulfed that end of the town. Meanwhile the unguarded gates in the immediate area were then thrown open to provide easier access to the bulk of the army, who jumped at the opportunity to enter the town unhindered. Despite Cromwell's best efforts to prevent a repeat of Drogheda, and the defenders of Wexford having particularly endeavoured to achieve clemency, they were now in a position that none of the principal negotiators on either side had really wanted. The town guardians had to defend themselves from one of the most competent and ruthless military forces in Europe as they spread through the narrow Wexford streets.

At Drogheda, two assaults had been rebuffed by the Royalists, who had initially displayed fortitude by resisting the approaches of the New Model Army at the breaches. In theory, once the town had initially refused to surrender, the attackers could legitimately kill the defenders, even after they had ceased resisting. The occupants of the town of Wexford had *not* officially refused to deliver the town into enemy hands. As far as the primary representatives of both sides were concerned, negotiations had not broken down and dialogue was ongoing. However, the rank-and-file of the Ironsides were not concerned with such niceties. It was their prerogative as the successful besiegers to engage in battle with the ill-fated besieged. Drogheda was fresh on their minds as they cut down the Royalist troops of Wexford, whose courage had disintegrated due to the strength of the attackers. The ensuing scene was by now a familiar part of 1640s Ireland. Any man in arms now on the streets of Wexford did not stand a chance, as they were outnumbered by at least three to one. As at Drogheda, no significant resistance is recorded on the part of Sinnott's men, either soldiers or armed townsmen, after the Roundheads had entered the town. The Royalist/privateer force were all hewn down where they stood. The question of quarter is one that is just as significant here as at Drogheda. If the talks had eventually broken down, if Sinnott had still refused the town to Cromwell and had Cromwell then successfully surmounted the town's defences, then a repeat of Drogheda would have been justifiable. While it might have been expected under the reasonably affable circumstances, quarter was not offered by the rampant and unruly Puritan forces. It came down to a street fight between the disorganised defenders of Wexford and the professional Roundhead army. There was always going to be only one victor.

It is not certain exactly at what point Cromwell himself entered the town, but it is quite likely that, unlike at Drogheda, he did not engage in the fighting himself and appeared when the battle was at an advanced stage. Meanwhile, the attacking cavalry were experiencing some difficulty with ropes that had been stretched across the streets in order to impede their progress.[74] Some of the garrison had withdrawn to the market place (today called the Bull Ring) where many of the armed privateers were making a stand. Here the bulk of the defenders were killed by an uncontrollable Roundhead killing machine. The illicit occupations of the inhabitants of the town who constituted the civilian defence were now being called to question. The stories of cruelties being perpetrated on both local Protestant families and harmless merchants' ships going about their regular commercial transactions were being dreadfully avenged. The Royalist representatives of the Prince of Wales under Sinnott were being given equivalent treatment. Yet, the attackers did not make any distinction between the two parties of defenders. This town was to be an acquisition of the Parliament of England by whatever means it took, and the pitiless measures that the Ironsides implemented were by now a well established practice in this harrowing conflict. The taking of Wexford was achieved within an hour from when the soldiers first fell upon the walls.

Cromwell would inform Parliament that most of the inhabitants of the town 'are run away'.[75] The River Slaney was used as a way of escape by many of the soldiers after the Puritans had entered the town. Cromwell writes, 'Two boatfuls of the enemy, attempting to escape being overprest with numbers, sank, whereby were drowned near three hundred of them.'[76] Obviously, those that didn't stand and fight simply made a run for it, and Cromwell has adjudged that this comprised the majority of the defenders. Those that managed to escape had decided that there was no merit whatever in maintaining their positions when the gates were opened and the attackers were inside the walls. Those that stayed were overcome by the sheer might of the sword-brandishing Ironsides. They were shown no mercy from an army who were by now getting used to paltry resistance from the defensive forces of Irish towns. As at Drogheda, the predatory Commonwealth soldiers ran amok among the defenders of Wexford. Priests that were found in the town were brutally struck down as a chilling Puritan statement to the Catholic Confederation that they would not tolerate their instruments of indoctrination. Sinnott, attempting to cross the river, was shot in the head. A contemporary account entitled *A narrative after the defeat of Rathmines 1649* describes Sinnott's death:

> Lieutenant Col. Wm. Butler escaped out of Wexford by swimming over ye ferry and brought ye news that ye governor was not above two hours in ye town giving orders for ye ferrying over Colonel Mayarts regiment when he was forced by ye enemy who entered ye ports by ye Treachery of one Captain Stafford who commanded ye Castle to Indeavor his safety likewise by swimming, but being shot in ye head by some of the enemy he was unfortunately drowned.[77]

There is quite a temptation to compare the death of the governor of Wexford with that of the governor of Drogheda a month earlier. Aston had made a second stand of defence on Millmount and spoke 'very bigge words' to his assailants. The conclusion that might be drawn is that he remained at his post until the bitter end, even though he had been cajoled into handing over his weapons. He was then slaughtered where he stood. On the other hand, Sinnott, having orchestrated the town's defence, proceeded to order its impetuous evacuation as soon as the enemy were over the walls. There is no record of his being involved in the stand of the defenders in the market place. If this account contains any truth, then his leadership qualities must be called into question. Despite the fact that there were cannons inside the walls, no counter battery took place, nor were there any significant measures taken to impede the attackers, save the setting up of 'cables' across some of the principal streets. However, there is the fact that the storming and massacre of Wexford was never really considered a serious possibility by either Cromwell or Sinnott until the castle had mysteriously fallen into enemy hands.

Chaos reigned throughout the town on that October day as the stampeding Roundhead army were not checked by their superior officers, nor indeed by Cromwell himself. Within an hour, resistance had ceased, further resistance being thought futile, and the town was won. Of the defenders, 1,500 were killed outright. The remainder managed to make good their escapes.

On 14 October, Cromwell, the ever diligent commanding officer, sat down to write his account of the events relating to the taking of

Wexford for the Speaker of the House. In his report he confirms the stance of the Wexford townsmen as being hostile to Parliament, suggesting that 'the town having until then been so confident of their own strength as that they would not at any time suffer a garrison to be imposed on them'. He also tells us his opinion of the conditions that Sinnott had sought and even goes so far as to submit them to Lenthall when he declares that they 'brought out the propositions enclosed, which for their abominableness, manifesting also the impudency of the men, I thought fit to present to your view . . .' In this letter he also shifts the responsibility of the massacre to a much higher level than himself as supreme commander by writing: '. . . hoping the town might be more use to you and your army, yet God would not have it so: but by an unexpected providence in His righteous justice, brought a just judgement upon them to become a prey to the soldier, who in their piracies had made preys of so many families and made with their bloods to answer the cruelties which they had exercised upon the lives of divers poor Protestants.' (See Appendix No. 4.2)

The notoriously Confederate town of Wexford, which had been continually hostile to Cromwell's developing regime in the surrounding seas and elsewhere, was now under his control. On the face of it, accountability of the massacre of the Wexford defenders seems not to have been an issue to him as the atrocity looks to have completely washed over the Puritan commander. No remorse whatsoever was displayed save the regret he expressed towards the ruining of the town's buildings and properties during the sack. It appears that he took the events completely in his stride, no doubt happy in the knowledge that he had unquestionably meted out revenge at last to what in his mind were the 'barbarous wretches' of Wexford.

Notes to Chapter Four

1   Billy Colfer, 'Medieval Wexford', *Journal of the Wexford Historical Society*, no. 13 (1990–91), p. 6.

2   Ibid.

3   For details of the difficulties associated with the harbour see Phillip Herbert Hore, *History Of the Town and County of Wexford* (London: Elliot Stock, 1906), p. 54.

4   See Colfer, 'Medieval Wexford', p. 13.

5   Ibid., p. 16. Colfer argues that the 'gate was in fact a private gate exclusive to Selsker Abbey which has borrowed the name of the adjacent West gate, formerly situated about forty metres away. . .'

6   Ibid., p. 18.

7   See Hore, *History of the Town and County of Wexford*, pp. 253–54.

8   Ibid., p. 254.

9   Ibid.

10   Ibid., p. 255.

11   Ibid., p. 255, is the deposition of Mr John Archer, who deposes 'that more than threescore passengers being on shipp board at Wexford intending to goe for England were willfully cast away by the Irish owners or seamen for their wealthes sake, and as the said passengers did swymm to shore they were thrust back into the sea againe and drowned by the saylers and rebells on shore, none escaping but the seafaring men, and one Papist woman who made her boast thereof at her returne to Wexford'.

12   Ibid.

13   For instance quoted ibid. is the following: 'John Simmes of Templeshanboe, a maltster, deposes that on 11 Nov., 1641 he was robbed of goods &c., to the value of £136. He gives the names, most of them tenants and servants of Sir Morgan Cavanagh. He says the Rebels told him "they were discontent[ed] gentlemen and were the Queenes souldyers and noe rebells and charged him and the rest not to call them rebels, and said that wee, meaning the Protestants were rather rebells than they". He says that Phillip Rogers of Clohamon, with his wife and children and their goods, flying for safety to England, were drowned and cast away with others to the number of 80, and that one of his children died in a ditch on the way from cold and want. He says he was imprisoned for 11 days, but escaped by night to Wexford, where he and divers others distressed and robbed English stayed for six weeks and some longer, but some of them were in the open streets stript of all their clothes and died in the churches through cold and nakedness.'

14   Jane H. Ohlmeyer, 'The Dunkirk of Ireland, Wexford Privateers During the 1640s', *Journal of the Wexford Historical Society*, no. 12 (1988–89), p. 23.

15   Ibid. See also J.T. Gilbert (ed.), *History of the Irish Confederation and the War in Ireland, 1641–43*, 7 vols. (Dublin, 1882–91), vol. II, pp. 125–26, 203–05 and pp. 261–63.

16   Ohlmeyer, 'The Dunkirk of Ireland', p. 27.

17   Ibid.

18   Ibid.

19   Ibid.

20   Ibid., p. 28. See also Hore, *History of the Town and County of Wexford*, p. 260, who says of the mayor, 'The Mayor of Wexford, Nicholas Hay, was a very active agent in procuring foreign seamen, in fitting out and instructing masters of Wexford frigates to capture English ships.'

21   Ohlmeyer, 'The Dunkirk of Ireland', p. 28.

22   Ibid.

23   Hore, *History of the Town and County of Wexford*, p. 261.

24   Ibid.

25   Ibid.

26   Ibid.

27   Ibid.

28   Ohlmeyer, 'The Dunkirk of Ireland', p. 28.

29   Cromwell to Lenthall, 14 October 1649 in W.C. Abbott, *The Writings and Speeches of Oliver Cromwell,* reprint edition, 4 vols. (Oxford: Clarendon Press, 1988), vol. II, p. 142.

30   Michael Boylan to Ormonde, 6 August 1649 marked: 'These for his Excellency the Lord Lieut. Generall, Haste. Haste. Post Haste.' Quoted in Hore, *The History of the Town and County of Wexford,* pp. 273–74.

31   Ibid., p. 276.

32   Ibid.

33   The story is told by Murphy in *Cromwell in Ireland, A History of Cromwell's Irish Campaign* (Dublin, M.H. Gill & Son, 1883), p. 141; also in Abbott, *Writings and Speeches,* vol. II, p. 132.

34   From *Aphorismical Discovery;* quoted in Gilbert, *A Contemporary History of Affairs in Ireland from A.D. 1641 to 1652,* 3 vols. (Dublin: Irish Archaeological and Celtic Society, 1879), vol II, p. 54; also Abbott, *Writings and Speeches,* vol. II, p. 132, adds, 'On September 9 Ormonde ordered Col. Hugh Byrne to annoy Cromwell in Wicklow when he should pass there.' See also Murphy, *Cromwell in Ireland,* p. 142.

35   Hore, *History of the Town and County of Wexford,* p. 281, writes: 'On the 1st of October Cromwell's advanced guard, passing by the right bank of the Slaney from Enniscorthy and by the old road at Muchwood and the back of Ardcandrisk arrived at the north-west point of the town . . .'.

36   In *Perfect Occurrences,* 5–12 October 1649; also in The Carte Manuscripts' Collection in the Bodleian Library, Oxford, vol. XXV, p. 395; also Hore, *History of the Town and County of Wexford,* p. 280. Also partly quoted in R.H. Murray, 'Cromwell at Drogheda – A Reply to J.B. Williams', *The Nineteenth Century,* LXXII (December 1912), p. 1240.

37   *Calander of State Papers Domestic (1649–1650),* pp. 326–27; quoted in Abbott, *Writings and Speeches,* vol. II, p. 133.

38   *Calander of State Papers Ireland,* Addenda, p. 792; quoted in Abbott, *Writings and Speeches,* vol. II, p. 133.

39   Murphy, *Cromwell in Ireland,* p. 144.

40   Lord Castlehaven to Sir Edmund Butler, 27 September 1649; extract quoted in Hore, *History of the Town and County of Wexford,* p. 278.

41   Ibid., p. 276.

42   Ibid., p. 279.

43   Extract from Butler's letter to Ormonde, 30 September 1649; quoted in Hore, *History of the Town and County of Wexford,* p. 281.

44   The Rochford affair is told in Murphy, *Cromwell in Ireland,* pp. 144–45; also Abbott, *Writings and Speeches,* vol. II, p. 135. Abbott says that 'Rochford had served in Parliament as sheriff of the county and was to continue his career with credit later'. In Hore, *History of the Town and County of Wexford,* the

author writes the following about the episode: 'There is no evidence that Rochford intended any betrayal of the town, but it is quite probable that influenced by Nicholas Loftus - whom Carte describes as "a very active instrument in engaging all the inhabitants of Wexford to be subservient to Cromwell's purposes" - He may have drawn out some proposals for surrender, more especially as he was aware of the hopeless condition of the garrison to withstand a siege and of the utter of want of cohesion, discipline and spirit of resistance which prevailed. His flight to Waterford on the advent of Cromwell's scouts, doubtless supported the notion of betrayal.' Hore adds that Rochford's 'sudden departure appears to have been caused by anxiety for the protection of his cattle on the advent of the enemy'. Rochford's letter to Ormonde is set out in full in Hore, *History of the Town and County of Wexford*, p. 282.

45   Hore, *History of the Town and County of Wexford*, pp. 282–83.

46   Cromwell to Lenthall, 14 October 1649; reproduced in Abbott, *Writings and Speeches*, vol. II, p. 143.

47   Hugh Peters to a friend in London, 3 October 1649, titled 'A letter from the siedge before Wexford', in Hore, *History of the Town and County of Wexford*, p. 285. Hore, himself had something to say about the events surrounding the fort at Rosslare: 'That the approach of a few Dragoons to summon a fort which had seven guns, was well supplied with ammunition, and supported by an armed frigate close by, should immediately cause its surrender, is one of the mysteries attending this extraordinary campaign, and can only be attributed to the amazing terror, which the approach of Cromwell inspired. It was absolutely disastrous to the town, for the fort, as the writer says, commanded the entrance to the harbour, and no effective blockade of the town could have been made so long as it was provided from the sea.'

48   Ibid., p. 286.

49   The area today is being engulfed with new houses as the growth of Wexford continues to spread its urban development to the surrounding hills.

50   Carte says, 'if Sir Edmund Butler had not come himself, they would have opposed Sinnott's entrance with his men, and delivered the town to the enemy at the first summons'. Quoted in Murphy, *Cromwell in Ireland*, pp. 145–46. Also in Thomas Carte, *The Life of James, Duke of Ormonde*, 3 vols. (London: 1735–36), vol. II, p. 90.

51   From *Tanner MSS*; reproduced in Gilbert, *Contemporary History*, vol. II, p. 283; also in Hore, *History of the Town and County of Wexford*, p. 287; also in Murphy, *Cromwell in Ireland*, p. 147; also in Abbott, *Writings and Speeches*, vol II, p. 135.

52   Cromwell's 'Declaration to the People of Ireland', printed in *Perfect Diurnall*, 29 August 1649; quoted in Gilbert, *Contemporary History*, vol. II, p. 231; also in full in Abbott, *Writings and Speeches*, vol. II, p. 111.

53   From *Tanner MSS*; quoted in Murphy, *Cromwell in Ireland*, p. 146, who uses Cary, *Memorials of the Civil War*, vol. II, p. 168; Hore, *History of the Town and County of Wexford*, p. 287.

54   From *Perfect and Particular Relation*, and *Aphorismical Discovery*, vol. II, appendix lxxxvii, p. 284; quoted in Murphy, *Cromwell in Ireland*, p. 147; Hore, *History of the Town and County of Wexford*, p. 287; Abbott, *Writings and Speeches*, vol. II, p. 135.

55   The text varies somewhat in the following sources: *Severall Proceedings, 19–26 October 1649*, in *Tanner MSS*; quoted in Gilbert, *Contemporary History*, vol. II, p. 284; Hore, *History of the Town and County of Wexford*, p. 287; Murphy, *Cromwell in Ireland*, p. 147; Abbott, *Writings and Speeches*, vol. II, p. 136.

56   Murphy, *Cromwell in Ireland*, p. 147; Hore, *History of the Town and County of Wexford*, pp. 287–88.

57   Abbott, *Writings and Speeches*, vol. II, p. 136; Murphy, *Cromwell in Ireland*, p. 148; Hore, *History of the Town and County of Wexford*, p. 288.

58   Murphy, *Cromwell in Ireland*, p. 148; Hore, *History of the Town and County of Wexford*, pp. 288–89.

59   Murphy, *Cromwell in Ireland*, p. 148–49; Hore, *History of the Town and County of Wexford*, p. 289.

60   Castlehaven's *Memoirs*, quoted in Carte, *Life of James, Duke of Ormonde*, vol. II, p. 140; Abbott, *Writings and Speeches*, vol. II, p. 137; Murphy, *Cromwell in Ireland*, p. 149; Hore, *History of the Town and County of Wexford*, p. 289.

61   Hore, *History of the Town and County of Wexford*, p. 289; Murphy, *Cromwell in Ireland*, p. 150.

62   Hore, *History of the Town and County of Wexford*, p. 290.

63   Murphy, *Cromwell in Ireland*, p. 150, in full; extract in Hore, *History of the Town and County of Wexford*, p. 290.

64   Hore, *History of the Town and County of Wexford*, p. 291.

65   Ibid., p. 292.

66   Ibid.

67   The house that occupies the site is now derelict, but for years it was the home of the Staffords. In Murphy's day it was occupied by a Mr Cormack.

68   Murphy, *Cromwell in Ireland*, p. 152.

69   Original in the Library of the Royal Irish Academy, contemporary copy in The Carte Manuscripts' Collection, XXV, p. 446; copy in Gilbert, *Contemporary History*, facing p. 288; Murphy, *Cromwell in Ireland*, p. 154; Abbott, *Writings and Speeches*, vol. II, p. 139.

70   See footnote 67. I am grateful to Celestine Rafferty of the Wexford Historical Society for this and a wealth of other information concerning Wexford.

71   *Aphorismical Discovery*, vol. II, p. 54; quoted in Murphy, *Cromwell in Ireland*, p. 157. Gilbert asserts that the author of the *Aphorismical Discovery* was 'an Irish ecclesiastic'. This would be a predictable enough summary of Stafford's character from a contemporary priest. The full name of the publication was *Aphorismical Discovery of Treasonable Faction*. Gilbert states, 'the author, it will be seen writes as an Irish Royalist, fully in sympathy with his countrymen who, devoted to Charles I, had taken arms for the defence of his prerogatives.' Gilbert, *Contemporary History*, vol. I, preface, p. ix. He also says that the work 'appears to have been written between 1652 and 1660'; vol. I, preface, p. iv.

72   *The People*, Saturday, 21 June 1913: 'Cromwell's assertion that he "fairly
     treated" the young Captain Stafford means that he deceived him.'

73   Murphy unequivocally accuses both Stafford and Cromwell of treachery:
     'It is obvious that the advantage taken of Cromwell of "treating" Stafford
     and entering the town while the terms of surrender were under discussion,
     was fraudulent and treacherous. The local tradition says that Cromwell and
     Stafford had a meeting at midnight by the riverside. Carte's words leave no
     room for doubting the governor's guilt: "the enemy entered the gates by the
     treachery of Captain Stafford." Clarendon is still more explicit: 'Stafford
     gave up the place to Cromwell, and took conditions under him, and thereby
     gave entrance to him into the town.' See Carte, *Life of James, Duke of
     Ormonde*, vol. II, 1735, p. 63. Murphy persistently quotes non-participant
     attestation to support his points. On Stafford's credit side is the work of J.B.
     Williams in 'Cromwell's Massacre at Wexford', *Irish Ecclesiastical Review*,
     series 5, vol. I, pp. 561–68. Also the work of Kathleen A. Browne, *Was
     Cromwell Betrayed to Wexford?* (Rathronan Castle: K.A. Browne, 1940).

74   Letter in *A Very Full and Particular Relation*; quoted in S.R Gardiner, *His-
     tory of the Commonwealth and the Protectorate*, reprint edition, 4 vols.
     (Stroud: The Windrush Press, 1988), p. 130. The quote reads, 'they had
     gabled all their streets'. See also Hore, who quotes at length from the letter,
     History of the Town and County of Wexford, pp. 295–96.

75   Cromwell to Lenthall, 14 October 1649; in Abbott, *Writings and Speeches*,
     vol. II, p. 143.

76   Ibid., p. 142.

77   There is some confusion as to who exactly this drowning refers to. Sir
     Edmund Butler had recently replaced Sinnott as the military governor, yet
     Hore suggests that this account refers to the latter. See Hore, *History of the
     Town and County of Wexford*, p. 294.

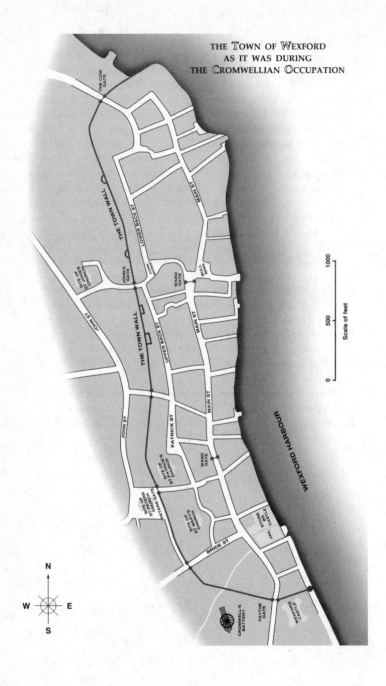

THE TOWN OF WEXFORD
AS IT WAS DURING
THE CROMWELLIAN OCCUPATION

THE COW GATE

THE TOWN WALL

LOWER BACK ST

MAIN ST

SITE OF S JOHN'S CHURCH

JOHN'S GATE

CORN MARKET

WARD GATE

BULL RING

THE TOWN WALL

UPPER BACK ST

MAIN ST

JOHN ST

JOHN ST

PATRICK ST

WARD GATE

SITE OF S PATRICK'S CHURCH

SITE OF S SELSKER'S CHURCH

PETER'S GATE

SITE OF S MARY'S CHURCH

BRIDE ST

STONE BY CASTLE

JAIL CASTLE

WEXFORD HARBOUR

1000

500

0

Scale of feet

N

W E

S

CROMWELL'S BATTERY

FAYTHE GATE

WEXFORD CASTLE

Chapter Five

WEXFORD – AN ANALYSIS

'Most of them are run away'
(Cromwell, describing the defenders of Wexford)

AND SO, MORE lives were tragically lost at Wexford amid the quicksands of inept Confederate opposition. So far, Ormonde and his army could easily have been responsible for the derivation of the phrase 'fighting a losing battle'. If the storming of that town had originated in the form of an adventure novel and not the result of historical fact, then there would have been quite a spectacular climax to this story since it had such an auspicious build up. Unfortunately, writers of the day did not furnish us with comprehensively detailed accounts of actual battles. No extensive narratives exist concerning the hand-to-hand combat on the streets of either Drogheda or Wexford. It is from the short snippets of general accounts of the war that we must draw our conclusions. So no descriptive saga can be written about the fighting on Wexford's streets. Cromwell's own letter about Wexford is probably the most detailed and authoritative that we have. Naturally, if in general the sincerity of his words is unacceptable to the reader, then the fundamental information source concerning his entire campaign would be foolishly disregarded. If, on the other hand, his reports are perceived to be dependable, then they should be seen in perspective. This particular examination of Wexford will also be seen to have excluded unarmed civilians from premeditated deaths. Most action novels contain a struggle between a hero and a villain, in order for good to eventually triumph over evil. The miscreant in this story is most certainly Cromwell. In today's vernacular (far from the eloquence of the seventeenth century) he might well acquire the title 'Cromwell the bastard'. Indeed, the appellation has been already associated with him in Irish circles for quite some time now. The problem is that this particular story lacks a hero.

To acquit Cromwell of the accusations of indiscriminate slaughter at Wexford is a more complicated task than it is for Drogheda. This may seem odd when one considers the fact that no eyewitness whatsoever provides us with details of the deliberate deaths of unarmed men, women or children in that former town. There are no additional chilling anecdotes from Thomas Wood concerning the events at Wexford. The main thrust of the suspicion against Cromwell at Wexford are the transcripts of Irish priests, who were not present in the town at that time and who later had unrivalled motivation for their written denunciations of that 'bastard', Cromwell. Throughout nineteenth and twentieth century Ireland, it was impossible to objectively compare Cromwell's post-battle descriptions with the highly evocative and consistently one-sided descriptions of the ruthlessly persecuted Catholic clergy. Upon inspection, a dispassionate analysis of the words of the ecclesiastics reveals their allegations of the murders of non-combatants to be quite unsubstantiated. Their inspiration, however, was obvious. In comparison to the scathing words of the Irish clergy, who years later would recount inhumane atrocities, is the silence of all of those people who were actually in Wexford on 11 October 1649. Yes, civilians were killed, but the evidence will show that the majority were likely to have been fully armed and engaged in the conflict. Those that weren't probably died as the result of accidental drowning. Yes, priests were killed. For this there is no apparent justification, except to reemphasise the perception in which they were held in the Puritan mind. Yes, the garrison was slaughtered in cold blood, when no regulations of battle would vindicate the culprits. However, this was not a new development in contemporary Ireland.

How then were the garrisons of both Drogheda and Wexford so easily obliterated with such minuscule losses on the side of the Roundheads? The answer is elementary. This highly trained and expertly skilled Parliamentarian army was one of the most aggressive and ambitious forces in Europe. With a total disregard for compassion they took the lives of the Drogheda defenders, which was an unpleasant prerogative that they had legitimately earned.[1] The rules of war could not impeach their actions. With sheer strength and power they easily overran those of Wexford, who mostly ran for their lives. These Parliamentarian soldiers were also highly disciplined and only feared God more than their domineering and intolerant commanding officer. Disobedience of orders would not be tolerated by Cromwell in the Parliamentarian ranks.[2] The ultimate retribution was sometimes dispensed out to endemic lawbreakers. The orders to exclude civilians from warfare had not been withdrawn from the operation. No exceptions were to be made, even in the volatile circumstances of a sack. The conseqences were there for all to be seen. The two individuals that had stolen hens from the old woman outside the walls of Drogheda had their lives taken away from them by their own superior officer as an example to the rest. So not only was there no motivation for the attacking soldiers to indulge in indiscriminate slaughter, we find that there is plenty of solid evidence to suggest that they carried out their orders to the letter.

It is the easiest thing in the world to assert that significant numbers of civilians *must* have been killed in both towns as they would have been caught up in the general mayhem of a storm. The popular perception regarding Drogheda is that this was an English army, attacking an Irish town, and innocent people were bound to have died. However, Drogheda was a town that had only recently been captured by the Royalists; it was not what could be called a Celtic Irish town. It had repulsed the attempts of the Celtic warrior, Sir Phelim O'Neill, to gain it for the Ulster rebels, whom Cromwell believed were the 'barbarous wretches'. To him, the defending Royalist army in September 1649 might as well have been O'Neill and his gang. Cromwell himself was well aware of the allegiance of its townspeople to the London government. There is no solid evidence that civilians were out and about during the battle of Drogheda. The probability is that they were either absent from the town or shut up in their houses. They were content to let the forces of the Crown battle it out with the forces of Parliament for the strategic garrison town.

It could also be effortlessly said that Cromwell's army, like every other army of the day, simply ran amok and indiscriminately killed the inhabitants of the two locations. The streets of an Irish town in 1649 during the invasion of a ferocious Roundhead army was not exactly the place to casually appear. Yet this commanding officer was no Monroe, Inchiquin or Coote. Cromwell was governing a highly disciplined force that functioned with the consistent threat of an impartial internal judicial system. The previous atrocities that had been committed by those other commanding officers in 1640s Ireland were committed under conventional contemporary circumstances and usually with very imprecise instruction to their troops. Cromwell's instructions were neither reckless, nor were they ambiguous. His devoted disciples were therefore highly effective, primarily because they did as they were told, and not because they killed everything in sight, contrary to popular belief.

The Rev. Denis Murphy SJ, by his *Cromwell in Ireland, a History of Cromwell's Irish Campaign* of 1883, has had a massive influence on Irish public opinion and is still regarded as a genuine version of events.[3] As a Jesuit priest writing in the middle of the last century, Murphy's evaluation of Cromwell's Irish mission is far from complimentary to the Member of Parliament from Huntingdon. He indulges in a systematic condemnation of the actions of the Ironsides and advances sweeping statements concerning their storming of Drogheda and Wexford. He writes: 'There is abundant testimony of contemporary writers to prove that the cruelties practised at Wexford on the clergy and people were as great as those of which Drogheda was the scene a month before.'[4] Naturally, he fully accepts the fables of Thomas Wood as bona fide, never once doubting the authenticity of those colourful words. He proceeds to draw to the attention of the world the manuscripts of seventeenth century ecclesiastics whose bigoted and fanatical accounts would indict Cromwell of appalling deeds. Murphy uses secondary sources such as Carte,[5] Clarendon[6] and Bishop Nicholas French,[7] and cleverly builds up his case, rarely using the reports of actual eye-witnesses since they do not corroborate his allegations. Carte wasn't born until 1686; Clarendon, a Royalist, was never in Ireland; and French, who was not in Wexford during the sack, had a major axe to grind as an oppressed Irish priest.

Murphy assembles his thesis with the aid of the following extracts:

> Dr. Fleming, archbishop of Dublin, writing to the secretary of the Propaganda at Rome very soon after, says that many Priests, some religious, innumerable citizens, and two thousand soldiers were massacred. Father S. Leger, S.J., in a letter to his superiors in Rome in 1655, containing an account of the events of the preceding years, states that when Wexford was taken, Cromwell exterminated the

citizens by the sword. Colonel Solomon Richards, too, says
that the town of Wexford was much depopulated in its taking by Oliver Cromwell. [8]

Murphy continues:

> Dr Nicholas French, the Bishop of Ferns, was then lying ill
> in a neighbouring town. In a letter to the Papal Nuncio,
> written from Antwerp in January 1673, he thus describes
> what took place:'On that fatal day, October 11th 1649, I lost
> everything I had. Wexford, my native town, then abounding
> in merchandise, ships and wealth was taken at the sword's
> point by that plague of England, Cromwell, and sacked by
> an infuriated soldiery. Before God's altar fell sacred victims,
> holy priests of the Lord. Of those who were seized outside
> the church, some were scourged, some thrown into chains
> and imprisoned, while others were hanged or put to death
> by cruel tortures. The blood of the noblest of our citizens
> was shed so that it inundated the streets. There was hardly
> a house that was not defiled with carnage and filled with
> wailing. In my own palace, a boy hardly sixteen years of age,
> an amiable youth, and also my gardener and sacristan were
> barbarously butchered; and my chaplain, whom I had left
> behind me at home, was pierced with six mortal wounds
> and left weltering in blood. And those abominable deeds
> were done in the open day by wicked assassins! Never since
> that day have I seen my native city, my flock, my native land,
> or my kindred and this it is that makes me the most
> wretched of men. After the destruction of the town, I lived
> for five months in the woods, every moment sought after
> that I might be put to death. There, my drink was milk and
> water, my food a little bread; on one occasion I did not taste
> food for five whole days. I slept under the open sky without
> any shelter or covering. At length the wood in which I lay
> concealed was surrounded by numerous bodies of the
> enemy, who came to seize me and send me in chains to Eng-
> land. But thanks to my guardian angel, I escaped their
> hands, owing to the speed and swiftness of my horse. [9]

Murphy uses more of French's words to bolster his argument:

There is another letter of Dr. French still extant in the library of Trinity College; it is entitled 'Apologia' and seems to be a defence of his leaving Ireland and seeking safety in a foreign land:

You say nothing about my native city Wexford, cruelly destroyed by the sword on the 11th of October 1649; nothing of my palace that was plundered, and of my domestics, impiously slain; nothing of my fellow labourers, precious victims, immolated by the impious sword of the heretic before the alter of God; nothing of the inhabitants weltering in their own blood and gore. The rumour of the direful massacre reached me whilst I was ill in a neighbouring town, suffering from a burning fever. I cried and mourned and shed bitter tears and lamented; and turning to heaven with a deep sigh, cried out in the words of the prophet Jeremias and all who were present shared in my tears. In that excessive of my soul, a thousand times I wished to be dissolved and to be with Christ, That thus I might not witness the sufferings of my country. From that time I saw neither my city nor my people, but, like an outcast, I sought refuge in the wilderness. I wandered through woods and mountains, generally taking my rest and repose, exposed to the hoar-frost, sometimes lying hid in the caves and caverns of the earth. In the woods and groves I passed more than five months, that thus I might administer some consolation to the few survivors of my flock who had escaped from the merciless massacre, and dwelt there with the herds of cattle. But neither woods nor caverns could afford me a lasting refuge; for the heretical governor of Wexford, George Cooke, well known for his barbarity, with several troops of cavalry and foot soldiers, searching everywhere anxious for my death, explored even the highest mountains and most difficult recesses; the huts and habitations adjoining the wood, in which I had sometimes offered the holy Sacrifice, he destroyed by fire; and my hiding places, which were formed of branches and trees were all thrown down. Among those who were subjected to much annoyance on my account was a nobleman, in whose houses he supposed me to be concealed. He searched the whole house with lighted tapers, accompanied by soldiers holding their naked swords in their hands to slay me the moment I should appear. But in the midst of all those perils God protected me, and mercifully delivered me from the hands of this blood thirsty man. [10]

Bishop French acknowledges the fact that he was absent from the town when it was stormed. His survival alone is testament to this. He seems to have been quite involved in local politics. His was one of the local signatories that callously dislocated local Protestants from their homes, preventing them from ever living within the Wexford walls.[11] He declares that the town was 'abounding in merchandise', but without divulging the dubious origin of the bulk of those illegally gained commodities. Like the stories of Wood concerning Drogheda, French's letters would materialise in the years after the Restoration when Cromwell was the central target of political and religious rebuke. He employs a frequently used post-Restoration label of Cromwell by calling him 'that plague of England'.[12] He even admits that he had not been in Wexford from before the storm to 1673 (he died in 1678). He offers us no details of the deaths of innocents except to bewail and despair over the decimation of his flock. This same flock that had obviously been responsible for the fact that Wexford was 'abounding in merchandise', the acquisition of which, he clearly saw as ethical. The 'wicked assassins' that 'barbarously butchered' his gardener and sacristan could very easily have been confronted by two sword-wielding defenders in hand-to-hand encounters similar to others in the town. French makes copious use of the savage suppression of his faith when describing the months that he spent on the run. No doubt the 'hiding places that were formed of branches and trees' were a far cry from the grandiose surrounds of his Wexford palace.[13]

The Murphy tract continues:

> The following account of the massacre of some Franciscan Fathers of the convent of Wexford is taken from 'A brief history of the Irish Province of the Friars Minor of the Regular Observance' by Father Francis Ward.
>
> On the 11th of October, 1649, the octave of our holy father, St. Francis, seven religious of the Order of St. Francis, all

men of great merit and natives of the town, perished by the swords of the heretics in Wexford, viz: Father Richard Synnott, professor of theology, formerly guardian of the convent; Father John Esmonde, preacher, who had singular power in relieving energumenes; F. Paulinus Synnott, who had suffered much for the faith among the Turks, and had received from Pope Urban VIII, full jurisdiction over all the Catholic captives; Father Raymond Stafford, who had been left a considerable inheritance, and despising everything for Christ, had chosen to imitate the poverty of Christ under the standard of St. Francis. Fifteen months before his death he had retired to an island, and led there an austere and mortified life, using only once each day, lenten fare. Fr. Peter Stafford too, was much devoted to prayer. During the times of persecution, in the absence of the secular clergy, he discharged for fifteen years the duties of parish priest with great credit. Brother Didacus Chevers, over seventy years of age and blind; Brother James Rochford, both men of exemplary lives, and devoted to work. Some of these were slain while kneeling before the altar, others while hearing confessions. F. Raymond Stafford, holding in his hand a crucifix, came out of the church to encourage the citizens, and even preached with great zeal to the enemy, until he was slain by them in the market place. All these were men of most exemplary life, and as they fell, the Lord deigned to show how precious their death was in his sight.

1. When they were fired at, the balls fell close to some without doing them any harm whatsoever. This I heard from a noble lady, Margaret Keating, to whom the enemy related it in presence of her children and servants.

2. Whilst they were being put to death, it happened that a little of their blood fell on the hands of one of the executioners; this he could not wash off ever after or remove by any means whatsoever. I heard this from Mr. John French of Ballolonie, who had himself seen the blood and learned the circumstances from the mouth of the wicked man after the capture of the city; he spoke of the crime with great

sorrow, saying that he bore about on his hand the token that he had slain the religious "whose blood you see" and would carry the mark with him to the grave.

3. Mrs Margaret Keating, the wife of Captain Doran and daughter of Mr William Keating an alderman of Wexford, told me she heard a soldier of the English army named Weaver say, that when the religious were mortally wounded and lay expiring in the streets, through compassion for them and wishing to put and end to their sufferings, he fired at one of them twice. Though the balls touched his cowl, they did not penetrate it, they fell gently near the cowl as if they had no force. He then shot at his body but the result was the same. Weaver was asked to fire again; he replied "have done so already as well as I could; hitherto I have slain none of the Irish, nor shall I do so in future". He left the army and became a Catholic. I was sought to reconcile him to the church, but as I was not found, I did not see him. But to a certainty, he was reconciled by the Rev. Patrick Hampton, chancellor of Ferns, of pious memory.

4. Some of the soldiers who put on the habits of the religious, died miserably. Mr William Hore of Harperstown told me that he warned in a friendly manner one of the English soldiers who had the habit on, to lay it aside, as it was not right to mock at St. Francis or the other saints. He replied "That is all nonsense and superstition". "Tell me, I beg you" said Mr. Hore, "tomorrow morning if you have had any dream." He agreed to do so. After he had gone to rest he was tortured by spectres all night, thinking mad dogs were dragging him about. He was so terrified at these sights that he took sick and died.

5. Francis Whitty, a man of noble birth, told me that he saw one of the English soldiers who had the habit on, die while uttering blasphemies.

6. It is commonly reported that a soldier fired at the crucifix which F. Raymond held in his hand and the ball turned

aside and killed the captain of the company. This I heard from Sir Thomas Esmonde and from many others.

7. The Rev. John Turner, the parish priest of Maglass, declared that on the day when the religious and others were slain at Wexford, he saw a beautiful woman ascending towards the sky. This he saw when he was five miles from Wexford, before he heard anything whatever about its capture.

8. Divers mishaps befell those who were daring enough to dwell in the convent that formerly belonged to the religious. Many of them, soon after they came to the place, died and were buried in the convent garden. Those who survived were frequently troubled during the night by spectres; they told their neighbours that they thought they had done wrong in killing the religious, and that they would remain no longer in the convent, even though they should find no other place to live in. This I heard from one of their neighbours who knew well of their death and burial, and who had heard from these persons that they were tormented in this way by spectres.

I the undersigned, declare, on the word of a priest, that I heard the above facts related by the aforesaid persons and have set them down in writing exactly as they were told.

Father Francis Stafford, Of the Conception, preacher and confessor and ex-guardian of the convent of Wexford.[14]

Mad dogs dragging people about in dreams, from which when they awoke they keeled over and died; bullets that were divinely intercepted and diverted; comely maidens floating overhead; and a plethora of psychotic evil spirits pestering English soldiers: all this and more is advocated by Murphy and the author, Stafford, as historical fact. That just about sums up the illusory and fanciful climate of the world of seventeenth century Ireland. In fact it also speaks volumes for the nineteenth century, since Murphy saw fit to reintroduce Stafford's words as being genuinely realistic accounts. As an example of contemporary thinking,

Stafford's transcript, by which he swears, is an illustration of the conditioning of the populace. The temptation to describe Stafford's narrative as absolute drivel is contradicted by the convenient fact that despite the outrageous but quaint details, he does not apply them to the deaths of defenceless civilians. That temptation is also negated by the fact that his words were meant for readers of the day whose ideals were quite different from ours today. Suffice it to say, the use of his words in *this* particular analysis is to illustrate the irrational tendencies of some contemporary characters. It will be seen by modern standards that ecclesiastics would make many madcap statements concerning Cromwell at Wexford. Stafford was, at least, in good company. Yet it should be remarked that the experiences of those who reported them to Stafford were very believable at the time. And Stafford's transcription of them was no doubt honourable. However judgmental we can be today about such stories, they were told with very genuine conviction and with a strong belief in their authenticity. This is a perfect example of Catholics believing that God was on their side in this war. Conversely, Cromwell himself had many reasons for being convinced that God was on his.

Murphy reproduces the melodramatic folklore yarn about 300 women being slaughtered in the market place; he says that they had:

> . . . flocked around the great cross which stood there, in the
> hope that Christian soldiers would be so far softened by the
> sight of that emblem of mercy as to spare the lives of unre-
> sisting women. But the victors, enraged at such supersti-
> tion, and perhaps regarding their presence there as a proof
> that they were Catholics, and therefore fit objects for their
> zeal, rushed upon them and put them all to death.[15]

He does, however, accept that it is merely a 'tradition current in Wexford', and obviously finds no contemporary grounds for its credibility. The origin of the story itself is usually attributed to McGeoghegan, chaplain to the Irish troops in the French service, who published his *Histoire de l'Irlande* in 1763.[16] Mr J.B. Williams, a fierce turn-of-the-century assailant of Cromwell's Irish campaign, has proved that the tradition has earlier origins. He states:

> The story is told in both the second and sixth editions of a
> book entitled, 'The rise and growth of Fanaticism' or 'A

view of the Principle Plots and Pernicious Practices of the Dissenters for upwards of 150 years etc.' Both were published in London in 1715, the sixth being undated . . . tells the tale as follows; Before I take a view of their [the Dissenters?] plots and practices in the reign of King Charles II, I shall beg to mention a notorious and barbarous piece of cruelty, perpetrated by that meek and spotless lamb, Oliver Cromwell. When the Usurper entered the town of Wexford, in Ireland, three hundred women of the best rank and fashion fled to the Cross. Oliver, to manifest himself a thorough pae'd bloodhound encompassed them with his merciless dragoons and having no regard to their sex or innocency, caused them all to be butchered, not one being suffered to escape. This done, the presumptuous wretch draws up his regiment and began to pray and preach, giving thanks perhaps for such a glorious and honourable victory.[17]

Mr Williams then declares that he had discovered an even earlier account of this legend: 'In a book published in 1682, a tract that is in the Grenville Library at the British Museum is entitled *"Arbitrary Government displayed to the life – in the tyrannic usurpation of a junto of men called the Rump Parliament, And more especially in that of the Tyrant and usurper Oliver Cromwell . . . London, Printed for Charles Leigh in the year 1682"*.' [18] In actual fact, this myth was first published in James Heath's *Flagellum or the Life and Death, Birth and Burial of Oliver Cromwell, the Late Usurper*, the second edition of which was published in 1663.[19] This story can be traced as far back as one might be pleased to do. But like so many other stories of the period, unless it has solid eyewitness attestation by more than one source, then it is likely to have no basis whatever. No eyewitness nor contemporary writer of any sort, even the Reverends French or Stafford, mention such an occurrence, when it would have been *such* fodder for their respective dissertations.[20] Without affording the myth much more credence, it is fairly obvious that if the town fell within an hour, and the main thrust of the defence was planned for the market place, it is totally illogical to suggest that this location was a possible place of refuge for 300 helpless women.[21]

We have a contemporary document from 1649 by Walter Frost who published two anonymous letters concerning Wexford from two military communicants who were on the side of the besiegers. It is entitled *A Very Full and Particular Relation.*[22] An extract from the first letter reads:

> All our disadvantage is we fight not with men armed with steele, but with walls lined with men, and that our Enemies doe not onely lye in ambuscadoe behind walls, but (as I may say) behind diseases, tempests, wants and difficult ways; for nothing is more obvious to sense than this, that a Lyon-like heart is inspired into our men, whilst all that is man-like is taken from our enemy.[23] (See Appendix No. 5.1)

The author of the letter, having taken an active part in the proceedings, in his final paragraph, interestingly describes the manner in which the Roundhead army vanquished their foe. As a Parliamentarian soldier who was obviously not used to siege warfare and preferred his battles to be fought in open fields, it is nonetheless, enthralling to discover his perception of Confederate battle competence. To him, this was the most obvious aspect to the war. If these were the thoughts of the majority of the attackers, then their frame of mind in battle is much easier understood. While the besiegers gained the immortal hearts of Lions, the besieged simply lost their own fallible, man-like mettle and crumbled under the pressure.

The writer also substantiates the theory that non-military personnel were being evacuated from the town before hostilities begun, writing, 'The people within could not be restrained from boating away by water ...' Ormonde had requested the departure of the likes of 'unnecessary people as ould men, women and children' when he wrote to the mayor on 9 October and the above writer was a witness to their departure.

For an excerpt from the second letter contained in Frost's *A Very Full and Particular Relation*, see Appendix No. 5.2.

From this detailed report of the sacking of Wexford it can be confirmed that the idea of an intentional general massacre of citizens is due in no small way to the spiteful prattling of contemporary clergy. This writer even tells us that there was 'more sparing of lives of the Souldiery part of the enemy here than at Drogheda'. Yet those ecclesiastic essayists would have us believe that even though large numbers of the military were spared their lives, within that fateful hour, defenceless men, women and children were systematically butchered by the attacking army.

It is easier to believe the content of these battle reports that were published in newsbooks of the day, which appeared within weeks of the events, than contributions made years later. These accounts were not influenced by the benefit of hindsight concerning the subsequent plantation, the eventual failure of the Puritan Revolution and the inevitable denunciation of Cromwell. While there are plenty of typical religious expressions contained in these documents, they tell us a great deal about the Puritan mind-set at the time. Both of these letters are written by Parliamentarian soldiers and they *appear* more factual than fabricated. The clerical authors, French, Stafford and Lynch, wrote their accounts after a period of ferocious persecution during what would become known as the Cromwellian plantation, and their judgement was immensely jaundiced by this time.

By the time Murphy came to pen his version of Cromwell's campaign in 1883, it was to emerge into an Ireland that was already overflowing with anti-English literature. Then, of course, there was the perennial antagonistic state of Anglo-Irish relations to inflame nineteenth century chauvinism and therefore Irish nationalism. The fallibility of contemporary clergy is emphasised in their wild assertions of wholesale human carnage at the hands of the only army whose explicit orders were precisely to the contrary. There is no merit in making judgements by equating the staff of today's Catholic Church with those of seventeenth century Ireland in an attempt to condone their actions. While priests have always been afforded their due respect through the centuries, clearly those of the 1600s were perfectly capable of adhering to the sometimes fallacious methods of communication of their time. This soldier also displays the Puritan attitude to a crucifix-waving cleric. Roman Catholic priests were the deceivers, and their flocks the deceived. Their idolatrous imagery of a dead Saviour in the shape of the Cross, as opposed to a Risen Christ, to a Puritan represented Catholicism in its most abhorrent form, and in the climate of a town under storm, there was no hope for those poor clergy.

In this letter is also proof that the story concerning the Protestants that were starved to death in the local church at the beginning of the war caused some consternation among the Puritan invaders. In fact Cromwell himself also mentions this incident in his letter to Lenthall and remarks also on the episode of the Protestants that were sent into the estuary in a leaking boat by the locals. Interestingly enough, Cromwell could find no similar instance at Drogheda concerning the suppression of local Protestants to recount to Parliament, save for the fact that the 'Protestants were thrust out of the great church called St. Peter's, and they [the Catholics] had public Mass there'.[24] His use of the phrase 'barbarous wretches' after Drogheda was totally misdirected, since there was no proof that the garrison there had been involved in cruelties to Protestants in the early years. When he discovered specific tales of such deeds at Wexford, he wasted no time in conveying their details to the Council of State to arouse their indignation. He also relates these particulars to offer some justification for the severity that was repeated at Wexford, even though he himself was the only one who thought such an excuse necessary.

After Drogheda he had declared that his actions there 'will prevent the effusion of blood, which otherwise cannot but work remorse and regret'.[25] The words 'remorse' and 'regret' are not usually associated with Oliver Cromwell. Yet he shows that he had an active conscience, and were it not for the desire for revenge for the Irish rebellion of 1641, he indicates that he may well have avoided the slaughter of the garrison. There is every reason to believe that this would have been the case, since this behaviour was out of character for the English Puritan.

Mercurius Elencticus, dated 29 October–5 November 1649, a Royalist pamphlet published by Sir George Wharton, launches a scathing attack on Frost's eyewitness letters that describe the sack.[26] Apparently Mr Frost printed his name on the cover of his pamphlets as Walter Frost Esquire, and Wharton generally referred to him as 'Squire'.[27] Wharton says:

> But that which fills up the remainder of the Squire's sheet is the news they have received from Ireland of the treacherous surprisal of Wexford (alias Washford) even during the time of cessation and treaty, as himself in the manner confesseth and the barbarous murther of the most part of the inhabitants and soldiers, their blood thirsty hands not distinguishing anything either of age or sex, as you will perceive by the following letter, which coming from one of their own party (though not altogether of their judgement), I thought fit to insert, that the world may see and bear witness of their cruelly, who pretend to righteousness and mercy – I will not wrong them a syllable; 'Sir the 16' of this instant we came to this town, where we received the joyful news of My Lord Lieutenant's taking of Washford by

storm on Thursday – instant, about two of the clock in the afternoon, all being put to the sword, men, women and children, except some three or four Aldermen, etc. Dublin 19 October 1649.'[28]

This letter printed in the Royalist leaflet is asserted by Wharton to have been written by a Parliamentarian who had just arrived in Dublin and heard the news. It does not, however, represent an eyewitness account, and as it emerged into the propaganda battle between both sides in 1649, it must obviously be treated with caution. In comparison to Frost's two detailed accounts of Wexford the best that can be said of it is that it was advanced by the opposition as second-hand hearsay evidence.

The writer who called himself R.L. and who described the battle of Drogheda also gives a short account of the taking of Wexford: 'In that town were 1,700 men at the least, some say 3,000 of which we have a general belief that there escaped not above four hundred at most. Many were drowned endeavouring to get over the river and two boats sunk in which is said, the governor to have been. Of ours not above one or two killed etc.[29]

The *Irish Monthly Mercury* of 6 February 1650 was printed in the nearby city of Cork, and it reads:

Washford is the Dunkirk of Ireland and a place only famous for being infamous, this also the army took by storm, but a few were spared and but a few were put to the sword for the Divine Justice manifested itself to be what it is, making those who had ruined many by the sea to be ruined in it. 'Tis a frequent rule with God to evidence the sin in the punishment, near 2,000 of these others were drowned, which was generally esteemed a misfortune only because there were no more.[30]

The unusual use of the word 'Washford' makes one suspicious that Wharton's contributor merely reported what he had read in this Parliamentarian newspaper and added what he might have heard as rumour on the streets of Cork.

Cromwell's chaplain, Hugh Peters, was a consistent correspondent to his peers in England during the war, and his brief account of Wexford is as follows:

On the 11th of October we took in Wexford, where the hand of God wonderfully appeared. We were forced to storme Wexford, where the enemy was very strong every way. Our men after battery of the Castle, yeelded by Captain Stafford, the Governor, entered upon their [i.e. the besieged's] flight over the water, and 2,000 were killed and drowned. Colonel Roe's jaw [was] broken with a bullet, who is since dead. We lost but five men every way. We have neere 80 ships and 100 boats to fish in, of which here is a fine trade. God hath spoyled the spoyler; abundance of plunder and rich. It is a fine spot for some Godly congregation, where house and land wait for inhabitants and occupiers. I wish they would come.

We are marched to Duncannon. Colonel Tuttle and Colonel Collam's Regiments of foot, and my Lords of Horse are gone tither. We hear Owen Roe O'Neale is upon his march this way.

Yours, H. Peters[31]

Colonel Richard Deane, a Parliamentarian officer, wrote to a Colonel Edward Popham on 22 October. The following is an extract from that short chronicle:

On the 11th he began his batteries, upon which they sent a trumpet[er] to desire leave for some gentlemen to come out who brought articles. Before the [Lord] Lieutenant's answer was sent in the governor of the Castle perceiving the Cannon had made a great breach in it, offered to deliver it to us, provided they might have their lives and liberties, which were granted. We therefore delayed sending my Lord's answer until they saw that we had the castle, hoping they would surrender and that we might save the town. But as soon as the enemy perceived that our men were in the castle and fired into the town, they began to run away from the walls where[up]on they on the Castle called to those by the batteries to fall on, and without orders or word they got ladders and climbed the walls, and in half an hour we had possession of the town with the loss of only 7 men. The

> Enemy lost at least 1,000 slain or drowned. On the 16th my
> Lord marched to Ross.[32]

This letter sheds quite a different light on the Stafford incident, and indeed offers a more believable version of the castle governor's agenda. Colonel Deane suggests that Stafford sought terms for himself and his men and implies that at the sight of the castle being under Roundhead control, the defenders might realise their position was then hopeless and they would capitulate. He also expresses the desire to 'save the town'. However, instead of surrendering, and before the return of the negotiators, those inside the walls panicked at the castle having fallen into enemy hands and deserted their posts. The Parliamentarian forces, by then substantially weather-beaten, did not wait for a written invitation to scale the undefended walls. It appears that the timing of the events, coupled with poor communication methods, led to the downfall of Wexford. Whatever the real truth, the involvement of Stafford at some level in the climax of the conflict is profound. His actions, whether honourable or corrupt, were the turning point. Needless to say, as an eyewitness, Deane does not corroborate the civilian massacre theory.

Following the initial fracas and when the combat was at an end, in true Civil War style, many of the defending soldiers actually declared for Parliament. Colonel Deane tells us this in his list of prisoners appended to his note to Popham: 'One Colonel, one Lieutenant Colonel, five Captaines, six Lieutenants, four Ensignes, three Serjeants, one hundred fourscore and fifteen soldiers, fourscore and fifteen whereof are taken to be pioneers in our army.'[33]

Prior to Cromwell's arrival at Wexford, a private letter was written on 22 September by Nicholas Loftus of Dublin to a private citizen called Pierce Laffan concerning Puritan treatment of ordinary civilians:

> They [i.e. the people of Wexford] need not fear any vio-
> lence of the English soldiers, unless it be those that they
> find in arms against them, for all the other must not be
> touched in their bodies nor their goods, and to this end
> there is now a proclamation put out here [i.e., Dublin] that
> on pain of death, no soldier shall take from any man what-
> soever to the value of one penny.[34]

This note endorses the policy that the Parliamentarian army had adopted under their Commander-in-Chief, who was a strict disciplinarian and whose reputation was obviously known in civilian circles. It was generally the case that most men who were capable of bearing arms in times of war did so in order to protect the principles in which they believed. Those who didn't were only involved in battle when they were forced to protect themselves from marauding forces who had no respect for civilian immunity. Before Cromwell's army entered Ireland, these occurrences had been relatively frequent and people arbitrarily lost their lives purely on religious grounds. Those who *should* have been outside military jurisdiction were males who were either infirm or elderly, and all women and children. Cromwell always took the line that he would stay within the lawful constraints of the military arena during his entire career in active service. So far, in Ireland, when the layers of propaganda from the intervening years are peeled away, we have discovered that this was precisely the case.

We now come to one of the real clues of the source of damning evidence of civilian deaths at Wexford. When the Ironsides first appeared on the streets of Wexford, there was a manic rush for boats which were docked on the estuary. Having been quickly overfilled with people, the boats sunk and the occupants mostly drowned. Today it is generally believed that large numbers of miscellaneous civilians, including women and children, were involved in this attempt to flee from the fierce invaders. It is from this single episode that writers have accused the invading army of terrible deeds. There is a different slant that can be put on this incident which is more logical under the circumstances. We already know that Ormonde had requested the evacuation of such persons that were not necessary for the defence of the town. We also know that many of the citizens availed of this belated opportunity to depart. Therefore, boats were on the quays ferrying away those persons to safety. There is a possibility that while some boats were half filled with escapees, the sudden melee in the streets encouraged armed defenders to leap on to the boats in a frenzy and sail away. Thus might civilians have possibly been caught up in the commotion and died as the result of it. The likelihood is that most of the vulnerable citizens had already vacated the town and left it to the coalition of armed townsmen and Ormonde's military contingent to conduct its defence. The number of innocents that died must have been small. What is certain is that these deaths were not premeditated, nor were they deliberately planned. It is still the case that no eyewitness gives details of either an indiscriminate slaughter or the death of even one unarmed defender.[35]

In a newsbook licensed by Rushworth, who was Cromwell's secretary to the army, called *The Perfect and Particular Relation* it is stated that Cromwell:

> . . . being willing to save the inhabitants of the town and to preserve it from plunder, condescended to let the soldiery repair, everyone to their homes, they engaging not to bear arms any more against the State of England and the officers were to have their lives, but to render themselves prisoners. Just as my Lord was ready to sign this [his undertaking handed to the four Commissioners] and sent it into the town, such a fear fell upon them that their soldiers left the wall and all, both men and women, officers and soldiers endeavoured to betake themselves to fly over the water in boats, for the safety of their lives. Our men saw this and scaled the walls to stop them in their intended flight. They did not find very much opposition, but in less than the space of an hour, the whole town was cleared and gained. There was a wonderful providence seen in it, that when they were even on the brink to have conditions it should be marvellously denied them.[36]

In Frost's *A Brief Relation* for 13-20 November 1649, the writer records that the lives of many of the fishermen, whether combatants or not, were saved: 'The fishing trade wholly managed to the advantage of the Army, the salt and casks being all our own, which was no small quantity. And the boats also, which was about 100, whereof 80 fitted well. I thought it my duty to desire of my Lord [Cromwell] the lives of all the fisher men.' The writer then describes the sights he saw regarding those pirates of Wexford whom he obviously thought were receiving their just rewards for their past crimes: 'There I saw the spoiler spoiled, the drowner drowned, they that have made naked were themselves naked; and which was strangest I saw the hogs gnaw their flesh and suck their blood, and had divers other witnesses of it; and their ill gotten goods so scattered into strange and several hands, that we know not who hath them or who will be mended by their torn condition.'[37]

Allegations of a deliberate civilian holocaust also emanate from the petition of the people of Wexford to Charles II in 1660, who boldly proposed that almost the entire population of men, women and children were killed. This document is still in existence, and it is these words that are the most incriminating to Cromwell. Bizarre as it may seem, they could be seen to totally impeach *every single* eyewitness account, even those that were written by the hands of the Confederate defenders themselves. Any study of the storming of Wexford is compounded by the expressions contained in this controversial document. This was a climate when the beleaguered population of Ireland optimistically flooded the new monarch with petitions in order to erase the memory of the devastating Cromwellian period from the country at large. The Wexford document was composed immediately after the Restoration in an effort by some locals for restitution of their properties and possessions. The first reference on it is dated 4 July and the next, a certificate, dated 21 May 1661. It probably took a year to reach the King himself. There is no recorded reply. It was generally the case with most comparable appeals of the time, that they were totally ignored by a King, who had neither the authority nor the desire to get involved in such trivialities.

They opened the petition with confirmation of their loyalty to England by reminding the King that they had promised to make ten ships for the Royal cause early in the war, and they also declared that they 'have always been a people adhering to the interest of the Crowne and ancient Collonies since the reigne of King Henry the second'. After declaring that upon Cromwell's arival before the town, they had been ready to 'expose their lives and fortunes for the defence' of their town, they continued to implore Charles II for atonement, by announcing that they 'doe most humbly beseech your Majestie to be graciously pleased to look on them as deserved objects of your favour and justice'. (See Appendix No. 5.3)

To refute the statements contained in this document could be considered audacious if not downright foolhardy and could invite contradiction. It has always been described as having been written by the surviving friends and relations of the dead innocent civilians.[38] It might appear that this document alone confirms the deaths of innocents at both Drogheda and Wexford, and for some people, there the story should end. Even the most objective of historians have treated its content with respect. The problem is that it just *does not work*.[39] The square peg of the petition of the ancient natives of Wexford does not fit into the round hole of the storming of that town eleven years earlier. If taken in the context of the period following the collapse of the Parliamentary revolution that saw the accession of Charles II to the throne (with reduced powers), the essence of the affidavit arouses suspicion.

The use of the term *Usurper* confirms the regard with which Cromwell was then held. This term was widely in use in post-Restoration England and including it on any document immediately exposed the writer's Royalist sympathies. Now that he was dead and the primary target of Restoration contempt, these casualties of war would take every opportunity to further blacken his name. Firstly, the petitioners give a figure of 1,500 dead, which (similar to Drogheda) is precisely the official number of fallen armed defenders. There is absolutely no room in the figures to account for every 'man, woman and child to a very few' having being killed.[40] It can be further discredited in the manner by which it describes the sacking of Drogheda as an indiscriminate slaughter. These scandalous stories clearly spread like wildfire among a people in whose time word of mouth flourished and incriminating rumours turned into authoritative detailed reports. Today's rational communication disciplines are a far cry from the totally derisory standards of the seventeenth century. With regard to the entire period, it is very important that one does not believe all that one reads. In the title, the authors declare to be representing the 'heires, orphanes, and widowes of such of them as are dead'. This, of course, is not in dispute as large numbers of inhabitants were killed in the battle. There is, however, no recorded instance of any of them having been totally innocuous and in a non-threatening posture. It appears that blatant untruths could be disguised as heart-rending facts by those victims of transplantation who would obviously stop at nothing to regain their houses and estates. After all, as the successful conqueror of Ireland, Cromwell's success inflicted the intervening years of mandatory colonisation and relentless persecution of their faith. It must be concluded that in an attempt to achieve satisfactory recompense, the petitioners simply complied with contemporary propaganda techniques and significantly exaggerated their case.

Roy Foster in his *Modern Ireland* [41] agrees with the intentional civilian massacre theories at both Drogheda and Wexford: 'The tone was set by his massacre of the civilian population of Drogheda – a town that was taken by Inchiquin but with no record of Confederate support. Like the later horror at Wexford, it is one of the few massacres in Irish history fully attested to on both sides; even Edmund Ludlow saw it as extraordinary severity.'[42] It is quite probable that Ludlow saw the killing of the entire garrison of Drogheda and those 1,500 of Wexford as 'extraordinary severity'.[43] Most likely he had never believed that

Cromwell would engage in such activity. To use Ludlow's words, who was not even in Ireland at the time, as proof of a general massacre in both towns is quite out of the question. Ludlow wrote these words in exile in Switzerland, long after he had declined to recognise the Protectorate regime of his former friend and well after the Restoration.

The People of 3 November 1934 reports that 'the sacking of Wexford and the massacre of its people will be associated with the name of Cromwell until the end of time'.[44] This will certainly be the case, but there must be some caution attributed to this statement. To take the traditional viewpoint and to try to fit it into the facts about Wexford on 11 October 1649 creates too many difficulties. It does not ring true. It is clear that Cromwell's orders to his troops not to harm civilians meant that as well as being a humanitarian, he did not want to be painted with the same brush as some of his predecessors. There are many more references to the deaths of women and children at Wexford than at Drogheda, and that fact is difficult to ignore.[45] Still, however, there is no concrete proof that any of them were intentionally killed. Even more difficult to ignore is the absence of detailed evidence to substantiate the general statements of those who assert a civilian bloodbath took place. If we assume that the Roundheads did cut down defenceless women and children, surely we would have at least *one* observer to tell us details of such incidents, from either side. Would it not make sense that since there was more sparing of lives of the soldiers, some eyewitness somewhere would say that he actually saw a woman or a child being killed on some street or other? The Confederate leadership of Ormonde, Castlehaven and Inchquin, all of whom were the writers of thousands of letters during the period, do not mention the butchering of any innocents at either Drogheda or Wexford.

Finally, the words of the anonymous British officer in Sir John Clotworthy's regiment about Wexford are worth a mention. As much as he overstates Cromwell's storming at Drogheda, this writer understates his actions at Wexford. His brief and erroneous account of the battle of Wexford emphasises the inconsistencies throughout his narrative:

> . . . where as soon as Crumwell came, he sent them a trumpet to offer Conditions, which was denied with great Resolution. On which he fell to his Batteries, and made great Breaches in two several places in the Wall, and then assaulted and [was] beaten off, and assaulted again with

courage and fury, and entered the Town; where again the fight was renewed, and continued till those within were hacked down, and some of them, endeavouring to escape, were lost without mercy.[46]

How wide of the mark is this? This writer seems to be quite mixed up between Drogheda and Wexford. Yet the evidence of this officer concerning Drogheda that 'not a dozen escaped out of the town, of townspeople or soldiers' is used today as a serious version of events.

Cromwell's treatment of ordinary Irish people was always honourable. This entire period would see the rise and fall of the Parliamentarian revolution, the decapitation of the King, the Protectorate government, the colonisation of Ireland, the subjugation of Catholicism, and the Restoration of the Stuarts. All of these events intervened, to cause Cromwell's military career to be viciously torn apart and reinvented by thousands of detractors. His compassionate policy towards Irish civilians totally backfired, and it is his name that is today associated with callous slaughter of the Irish and not others who deserved it so much more. One wonders if, had he simply melted back into the military framework and not gone on to achieve international distinction as Protector, his reputation would have been quite the same in Ireland. Indeed, had the Puritan revolution succeeded and had the House of Cromwell continued to rule, it is quite likely that these stories would never have been invented at all. Throughout his life he wrote thousands of letters and made hundreds of speeches. Contained in these documents, the bulk of which have come down to us, are many indications of his personality, and his sense of honesty is conspicuous. There is little evidence of deceitfulness. Conversely, many of the Royalist attacks that were made on him, in particular his Irish campaign, are widely acknowledged as pure fabrication, made with the specific purposes of his defamation. It is difficult to accept (but not impossible) that a hypocrite and a liar of the magnitude suggested by some could have acquired supreme power in England even at such a capricious time in the history of that country.

When the period is appraised, it is difficult not to pity those Catholic Irish soldiers who stood defiant for Ormonde in the name of the English throne. Those two Kings, Charles I and his son, would never be really bothered about their allegiance and only ever perceived them as a thorn in their Royal sides.

Notes to Chapter Five

1   It seems that the Drogheda garrison may have been admitted to quarter in various pockets around the town and then had it ruthlessly withdrawn. Gardiner has suggested that this action was well outside the rules of contemporary warfare: 'Those modern critics who argue that Cromwell merely put in force the law of war as exercised by Tilly and others, forget that the question is whether he did more than he himself had done in England. There, except at Basing House, he had been uniformly merciful. He now treated Irishmen worse than he treated Englishmen. This is the only thing of importance. The question of his allowing prisoners, who had been admitted to quarter, to be put to death stands apart. It was contrary to the military practice of his own day. At the siege of Limerick, Ireton cashiered an officer who had killed prisoners received to quarter by a subordinate, and made ample apologies to the commander of that place. *Severall Proceedings*, 786, 29. It has, however to be proved that Cromwell knew at the time that he gave the command that some of the enemy had been admitted to quarter.' See S.R. Gardiner, *History of the Commonwealth and the Protectorate*, reprint edition, 4 vols. (Stroud: The Windrush Press, 1988), pp. 125–26.

2   The question of a Parliamentarian army out of control and lacking in discipline at Wexford is counteracted by the fact that they were not given any orders to cease the slaughter of the garrison by their commanding officer. Therefore, Cromwell must bear the chief responsibility for not attempting to check the stampede of his army.

3   The Rev. Denis Murphy, SJ, *Cromwell in Ireland, A History of Cromwell's Irish Campaign* (Dublin: M.H. Gill & Son, 1883).

4   Ibid., p. 161.

5   The Rev. Thomas Carte was born in 1686 in Clifton, Warwickshire, and died on 2 April 1754. During his lifetime he amassed an enormous amount of documentation on 1640s Ireland and in particular, Lord Ormonde. On his death he bequeathed most of his documents to his wife, who in turn, left it to the Bodleian Library, Oxford. In 1735–36 he wrote, *The Life of James, Duke of Ormonde, Containing an account of the most material affairs of his time and particularly of Ireland under his government with an appendix and a collection of letters serving to verify the most material facts in the said history*, 3 vols. (London, 1735–36). See also The Carte Manuscripts' Collection in National Archives, Dublin and Bodleian Library, Oxford.

6   Edward, Earl of Clarendon, *The History of the Rebellion and Civil Wars in England*, Dunn Macray (ed.), 6 vols. (Oxford: Clarendon Press, 1888). See also R. Scrope and T. Monkhouse (eds.), *Calender of Clarendon State Papers, commencing 1621*, 3 vols. (Oxford: Clarendon Press, 1767–86).

7   See, Murphy, *Cromwell in Ireland*, pp. 162–64.

8   Taken from the *Kilkenny Archaeological Journal* for 1862, p. 88; quoted in Murphy, *Cromwell in Ireland*, p. 162.

9   Murphy, Cromwell in Ireland, pp. 162–63.

10   Ibid., pp. 163–64.

11   See Philip Herbert Hore, *History of the Town and County of Wexford* (London: Elliot Stock, 1906), p. 255.

12   After the return of the Stuarts to the throne in the shape of Charles II, this would become known as 'the Blessed Restoration' and Cromwell would be called 'the plague of England' or 'the late Usurper'.

13   Hore, in his *History of the Town and County of Wexford*, p. 302, states: 'Nicholas French, Bishop of Ferns, who writes a long account of his place of exile in January 1673, of terrible hangings, scourgings, and other atrocities in the town on the 11th October, not having himself been present at the siege. . .' Hore also quotes from a writer of his day: 'Mr Griffiths in his *Chronicles*, p. 120 says "Father Raymond, a Franciscan Friar preached to the infuriated enemies till he was killed." We doubt if the soldiers would pay the least attention to his preaching and adds "six Franciscan fathers, Ric. Sinnott, Fras. Stafford, Paul Sinnott, John Esmonde, D. Cheevers and Jas. Rochfort were slain in their chapel hard by the Market Place, some kneeling at the altar, and others whilst hearing confessions".' Hore adds, 'we are as sceptical of the preaching and hearing confessions as we are of the hangings and scourges of the Bishop of Ferns. There was no time for such things. The town was taken and sacked in one hour. One writer says half an hour.' p. 298.

14   Murphy, *Cromwell in Ireland*, pp. 165–66.

15   Ibid., p. 167. Murphy cites his sources as being, Jesse, *Court of England under the Stuarts*, vol. III, p. 43; Taylor, *Civil Wars* &c., vol. II, p. 24; and Lingard, *History of England*, vol. VIII, p. 136 and appendix, p. 313.

16   See R.H. Murray, 'Cromwell at Drogheda', *The Nineteenth Century*, LXXII (December 1912), p. 1239; Gardiner, *History of the Commonwealth and the Protectorate*, p. 132; Murphy, *Cromwell in Ireland*, p. 167. It is no surprise to learn that McGeoghegan was an Irish Priest. Murphy tells us that 'he was born in 1701, and was sent at an early age to France, where he entered the church'. *Cromwell in Ireland*, pp. 167–68.

17   J.B. Williams, 'Cromwell's Massacre at Wexford', *Irish Ecclesiastical Review*, series 5, vol. I (1913), p. 563. See also *The People*, Saturday, 14 June 1913, which quotes from Williams' article.

18   Ibid.

19   James Heath, *Flagellum or the Life and Death, Birth and Burial of Oliver Cromwell, the Late Usurper*, 2nd edition enlarged (London: 1663, republished 1674). Quoted in Antonia Fraser, *Cromwell Our Chief of Men* (London: Mandarin edition 1994), p. 345, who writes: 'Heath in his biography of 1663 gave a terrible picture of two hundred women, many of them of high rank, asking for mercy "with the command of their charming eyes and those melting tears" - but it was denied to them.' See Morrill, John (ed.) 'The Making of Oliver Cromwell', *Oliver Cromwell and the English Revolution* (London: Longman, 1990), p. 20, who says of Heath: 'I have made very little use of two very jaundiced restoration authorities - James Heath, *Flagellum* (1663, 1664) and Sir William Dugdale, *A Short View of the Late Troubles* (1681). To rely on them, as many biographers have, whenever they are

uncorroborated is irresponsible, since they are so unreliable whenever they can be checked.'

20 Hore, in his *History of the Town and County of Wexford*, p. 302, says the following concerning the story: 'We dismiss altogether the legend of the massacre of 300, or any other number, of defenceless females before the cross in the Market Place. There is not a particle of evidence in support of the statement, a mere tradition (but still implicitly believed in) which appears to have originated in a volume published by him in 1763 and repeated with varying additions by other writers, such as Dr. Lingard, Rev. Matthew Russell, Cardinal Moran, and of course Mr. Griffiths in his Chronicles. We have carefully examined the voluminous correspondence of the Carte Collection in the Bodleian library and can find no trace of any such statement.'

21 This legend has survived intact right down to the present day. The journalist Roy Kerridge visited Wexford recently and writes, 'In 1649 Cromwellian troops took Wexford. First of all they knocked down a tall market cross that stood where now a green rebel of '98 roars speechless defiance. Secondly they slaughtered three hundred citizens as they kneeled, praying to the Blessed Virgin for deliverance. Thirdly they sacked the town and left only four hundred people alive. No wonder the Catholics of Wexford replaced the sign of peace by a sign of war.' Roy Kerridge, *Always Ireland, An Englishman in Ireland* (Dublin: Poolbeg, 1993), p. 116.

22 See Hore, *History of the Town and County of Wexford*, pp. 286–87 (first letter), pp. 295–96 (second letter). Also quoted in Williams, 'Cromwell's Massacre at Wexford', *Irish Ecclesiastical Review*, pp. 561–78.

23 Ibid.

24 Cromwell to Lenthall, 17 September 1649; in Abbott, *Writings and Speeches*, vol. II, p. 138.

25 Ibid.

26 Williams, 'Cromwell's Massacre at Wexford, p. 571; *The People*, Saturday, 14 June 1913.

27 Ibid.

28 Ibid.

29 *The People*, Saturday, 14 June 1913.

30 Ibid.

31 Hore, *History of the Town and County of Wexford*, pp. 298–99.

32 Ibid., p. 299.

33 Ibid., Hore, suggests that *'most of these were probably the garrison of the castle who surrendered'*. p. 299.

34 Murray, 'Cromwell at Drogheda – A Reply to J.B. Williams', p. 1240.

35 Gardiner in his *History of the Commonwealth and the Protectorate*, p. 133, has the following to say on the matter: 'With respect to the slaughter of women generally, we have nothing but generalities. The author of the *Aphorismical Discovery* for instance says Cromwell "slaughtered all that came his way without exception of sex, or person, age or condition, only such as were of the conspiracy, many of the soldiers saved themselves by boats or swimming, but great mortality did accompany that fury of both soldiers and

natives, all sex and age indifferently, then perished".' Gardiner adds, 'All this looks like rhetorical exaggeration and is easily accounted for by the writer's mixing up the losses by drowning with those by massacre.'

36   *The People*, Saturday, 21 June 1913.

37   *The People*, Saturday, 14 June 1913.

38   See Williams, 'Fresh Light on Cromwell at Drogheda', *The Nineteenth Century*, LXII (September 1912), p. 489, who states, 'Surely the words of those whose relatives and friends died are worth listening to?'

39   See Hore, *History of the Town and County of Wexford*, p. 298: 'There was no GENERAL MASSACRE. Many of the soldiers surrendered and were drafted into Cromwell's army. Fifteen hundred the number here mentioned as slain exactly agrees with that given in the Petition of the Ancient Natives in 1660. If these figures are correct it is obvious that the whole population, men, women and children, cannot have been killed.'

40   Gardiner in *History of the Commonwealth and the Protectorate*, p. 131, states: 'there can be no doubt that many of the townsmen were killed. Cromwell writes that most of them are run away, and many of them killed in this service.' The evidence of the writer of the second letter [from *A Very Full and Particular Relation*] is to the same effect: 'There was more sparing of lives, of the soldiery part of the enemy here than at Drogheda; yet of their soldiers and townsmen here were about 1,500 slain and drowned in boats sunk by the multitude and weight of people pressing into them.' Gardiner continues, 'This number exactly agrees with that given in a Petition from the inhabitants of Wexford to Charles II after the Restoration. After asserting that Cromwell put "man, woman and child to a very few" to the sword, the Petitioners estimate the loss of life of "the soldiers and inhabitants" at 1,500. It is obvious that if this figure is correct, the whole population, "man, woman and child" cannot have been killed. No doubt we have sweeping statements especially from ecclesiastics.'

41   Roy Foster, *Modern Ireland, 1600–1972* (London: Penguin, 1989).

42   Ibid., p. 102.

43   Edmund Ludlow, *Memoirs, of Edmund Ludlow, Esq. Lieutenant General of the Horse, Commander-in-Chief of the Forces in Ireland, One of the Council of State and a member of the Parliament which began on Nov. 3rd, 1640*, 2 vols. (Canton of Berne, 1698; reissued Oxford: C.H. Firth, 1894), vol. I, p. 303.

44   *The People*, 4 November 1934.

45   Murphy in his *Cromwell In Ireland*, p. 170, attempts to prove the slaughter of women at Wexford by alleging: 'The murder of Irish women was nothing new to the Puritans. After the battle of Naseby one hundred females, some of them of distinguished rank, were put to the sword, under the pretext that they were Irish Catholics.'

46   Edmund Hogan (ed.), *The History of the Warr of Ireland From 1641–1653 by a British Officer in the Regiment of Sir John Clotworthy* (Dublin: McGlashan & Gill, 1873), p. 87.

Chapter Six

THE MUNSTER CAMPAIGN

*'Good now, Give us an instance, since my coming into Ireland, of one man
not in arms, massacred, destroyed or banished.'*
(Cromwell's challenge to the Irish Catholic clergy)

THE FACTS SURROUNDING Cromwell's Irish mission are that his
unambiguous objective was to subjugate the Irish, suppress
their religion and steal their houses and properties. Whatever
way one looks at it today, that is exactly the way it will seem. His plan was
ruthless and his methods vicious. Then followed the atrocious
Cromwellian plantation that would etch his name in Irish history for
evermore. He came, saw, conquered and left a tyrannical legacy in his
wake. Mandatory acquisition of land was the evil consequence of the dia-
bolic massacres of the Drogheda and Wexford garrisons. Cromwell took
a bite of Ireland, chewed it up and spat it out with no opportunity for the
Irish to redress the balance. How deplorable all of this appears today. It
is no wonder that he is remembered in Ireland as an English bastard
whose soul will be damned for all eternity. Yet, Cromwell's God is the
same God as that of the Irish Roman Catholic. It is obvious that he was
much more passionate about his religion than most of today's Catholic
Irish population. His every word, thought and deed was a profound
religious experience. Yet for his time he was no eccentric religious fanatic.
People of the seventeenth century, irrespective of their denomination or
nationality, were much more passionate about their religion than most of
us are today, as it enveloped almost every aspect of their daily lives.

How can such contrast be reconciled? So far, this current analysis has found that he was brave, compassionate, decisive, fair, honest and ruthless, but above all, he was devout. It can be said with some justification that he was a product of his time. If he were born into today's modern age, his personality and sense of morality might be no different, but his implementation of his values would contrast enormously today from the methods acceptable in the seventeenth century. Indeed, to take this a step further, if he were to see Ireland today there can be very little doubt that he would be devastated and ashamed of the results of his work. Even in that savage era, he would never have contemplated taking a defenceless civilian and putting a bullet in his head simply because of his religion.

Those living in the 1640s had no way of knowing what life would be like in the late twentieth century. Equally, our understanding of that time is severely restricted by an inability to comprehend the routine of their world. To us, these people might well have been from a different civilisation. To them, colonisation was part of everyday life, as was warfare, slaughter, destruction and religious intolerance. Cromwell was not the founder of any of these abominations. He cannot be held responsible for practices that had been part of the heritage of Ireland since the Vikings and the Normans. It was a time when the strong prevailed over the weak and the morality involved was deemed irrelevant. With this revision of his actions in Ireland, it is difficult to convict him of those accusations of wholesale debauchery and vile immorality. He was the most successful combination of soldier and statesman that England had produced up to that time. Ireland was no match for Oliver Cromwell, which is mainly why historically inaccurate judgements have been made about him. To put it another way, he is the subject of a colossal grudge held by one nation against its larger neighbour. With the massacre of the defenders of Wexford, Cromwell was well on his way to feeding that grudge by October 1649.

While the destruction of both the Wexford garrison and the town itself had not been planned by Cromwell, his reputation was now beginning to spread absolute horror throughout the country. Many loyalties that may formerly have been wavering quickly altered to side with the rampant Ironside army. The news of the double sacking spread to the nearby fortified towns, with the result that the respective governors realised that a visit from this army leader was not going to be a pleasant social occasion. Cromwell wasted no time. By the 15th he was

off again heading for Ross, having left a contingent of his army to protect the confiscated Wexford.[1] The same day he also detached Ireton to
capture the fort of Duncannon on the eastern side of the Waterford harbour. Ross, or New Ross, is situated on the River Barrow and controlled
the main passage over that river. The town was reached by the 17th. The
recently installed governor was Sir Lucas Taaffe, whose 1,500 men had
reinforced the already 1,000-strong garrison. On the opposite side of
the river to Cromwell's camp, Ormonde arrived and sat down in full
view of the enemy, but with the river in between, conveniently preventing an engagement. Cromwell's first act was to reach for his quill
and ink and write a note to the governor of the fort to advise him of his
intentions, should they have not been already apparent:

> For the Commander-in-Chief in Rosse, These;
> Before Rosse,
> 17th October, 1649

> Sir, Since my coming into Ireland, I have this witness for
> myself, that I have endeavoured to avoid effusion of blood;
> having been before no place to which such terms have not
> been first sent as might have turned to the good and preser-
> vation of those to whom they were offered, this being my
> principle, that the people and places where I come may not
> suffer, except through their own wilfulness.

> To the end I may observe the like course with this place and
> the people therein, I do hereby summon you to deliver the
> town of Ross into my hands, to the use of the Parliament of
> England. Expecting your speedy answer,

> I rest your servant, Oliver Cromwell.[2]

The letter was sent late on the evening of the 17th Cromwell's messenger was received at the gates but not allowed into the town. Despite
Cromwell's request for a speedy reply, the next day passed with no
word from behind the walls. Cromwell proceeded to erect his batteries
for the storm, no doubt puzzled by the silence from the town. On the
morning of the 19th, Taaffe despatched his trumpeter towards the
attacking army, who had by now started to fire at the walls. Taaffe, for
some peculiar reason, was no longer sure if Cromwell himself was still
in the area:

For General Cromwell, or, in his absence, for the Commander-in-Chief of the Army now encamped before Ross.

Ross, 19th October, 1649

Sir, I received a summons from you the first day you appeared before this place, which should have been answered ere now, had not other occasions interrupted me. And although I am now in far better condition to defend this place than I was at that time, yet am I, upon the considerations offered in your summons, content to entertain a treaty, and to receive from you those conditions that may be safe and honourable for me to accept of. Which if you listen to, I desire that pledges on both sides may be sent for performance of such Articles as shall be agreed upon; and that all acts of hostility may cease on both sides, and each party keep within their distance. To this your immediate resolution is expected by,

Sir, Your servant, Lucas Taaffe[3]

Taaffe appeared to have played a dangerous game by keeping the bloodthirsty Roundheads waiting in suspense for his answer, but Cromwell immediately replied upon receipt of his note, eager to acquire another Irish fort with the use of mere words:

For the Governor in Ross, These;
Before Ross, 19th October, 1649

Sir, If you like to march away with those under your command, with their arms, bag and baggage, and with drums and colours, and shall deliver up the town to me, I shall give caution to perform these conditions, expecting the like from you. As to the inhabitants, they shall be permitted to live peaceably, free from the injury and violence of the soldiers.

If you like hereof, you can tell how to let me know your mind, notwithstanding my refusal of a cessation. By these you will see the reality of my intentions to save blood and preserve the place from ruin,

I rest Your servant, Oliver Cromwell.[4]

Cromwell's terms to the defenders of Ross were more generous than those issued at Wexford. He required no prisoners to be taken and would permit the entire garrison to leave the town without recrimination. As for the inhabitants, they would not be ousted from their properties nor would their goods be plundered by the Parliamentarian soldiers. The massacre of Wexford was only eight days since, and the defenders of that town had included many townsmen. Cromwell had no real way of knowing the composition of the garrison at Ross. Even so, he was offering what could be described as charitable conditions. The offer to the inhabitants of the opportunity to 'live peaceably, free from the injury and violence of the soldiers', cannot but be compared to the alleged treatment of unarmed inhabitants of Drogheda or Wexford. If the military contingent of the town were allowed to leave without molestation, then obviously the civilians were to be afforded a compromise for surrendering their town to the Parliament of England. This concession was that they would retain their properties, and if unarmed, their lives were never in danger.

Irrespective of the ongoing rhetoric Cromwell had not agreed to a cessation and to improve his case he continued to batter the walls. There was soon a breach made near 'Bewly Gate' (since called 'Three Bullet Gate' since it was hit by three cannon balls that day),[5] and Cromwell ordered his men to assemble in line in preparation for an assault. This appears to have been an intimidatory measure by Cromwell, since he did not want another prolonged exchange of letters, yet with talks still active he did not order a storm. Taaffe soon realised his position and hastened to despatch his reply:

> For General Cromwell; These;
>
> Sir, There wants but little of what I would propose; which is, that such townsmen as have a desire to depart may have liberty within a convenient time to carry away themselves and their goods; and liberty of conscience to such as shall stay; and that I may carry away such artillery and ammunition as I have in my command. If you be inclined to do this, I will send, upon your honour a safe-conduct, an officer to conclude with you. To which your immediate answer is expected by,
>
> Sir, Your servant, Lucas Taaffe.[6]

Cromwell's reply was to emphasise the potency of his views regarding the religious inclinations of the majority of his adversaries in Ireland. Theological conformity was not the real issue in this war between the rebel Parliament government and the supporters of the monarchy. There were many Catholics and Protestants on the side of the Confederacy, who were a mixed bunch of Loyalists. Yet, the religious parameters were much clearer when it came to the mainly Puritan government, who had no Catholic affinities whatever. Catholic ceremonies were banned by Parliament and the latter now occupied the ultimate controlling position of authority, both militarily and executively. The outlawing of the mass, which in today's Catholic Ireland seems dreadful, was a very common practice in contemporary Ireland. Well before Cromwell's time, notably at the suppression of the monasteries by Henry VIII, the Roman faith had been periodically forbidden outward displays of veneration with the result that there were many hidden chapels throughout the mainly Protestant areas of the country. Cromwell was no different from either his predecessors or his peers. Taaffe's three small words 'liberty of conscience' were like a red rag to a bull for Cromwell, and he was about to advise the governor of *his* interpretation of those three words. He was also somewhat irritated with the governor's request to take with them their artillery and ammunition, which he had never mentioned in his correspondence:

For the governor of Ross; These;
Before Ross, 19th October 1649

Sir, To what I formerly offered I shall make good. As for your carrying away any artillery or ammunition that you brought not with you, or hath not come to you since you had the command of that place; I must deny you that, expecting you to leave it as you found it.

For that which you mention concerning liberty of conscience, I meddle not with any man's conscience. But if by liberty of conscience you mean the liberty to exercise the Mass, I judge it best to use plain dealing, and to let you know where the Parliament of England have power, that you will not be allowed of. As for such of the townsmen who desire to depart and carry away themselves and goods, as you express, I engage myself, they shall have three months time to do; and in the meantime shall be protected

from violence in their persons and goods, as others under
the obedience of the Parliament.

If you accept this offer, I engage my honour for a punctual
performance thereof.

I rest Your servant, Oliver Cromwell.[7]

And so in this letter to Taaffe, the English Puritan commander
revealed his own personal position with regard to spiritual matters and,
in particular, the right of private judgement. 'I meddle not with any
man's conscience': by this phrase, Cromwell acknowledged the prerogative of any person to choose his own direction to the Almighty.
That was something that he could not, and would not, interfere with.
Private individuals had every right to their intimate beliefs, and even
the doctrinal differences between most non-Puritan faiths and themselves were acceptable to Parliament. As Puritans, they were convinced
that *they* were the chosen ones, but they also recognised the existence
of those who were not chosen. It was the pernicious Roman religion
that the Puritans hated and feared. The performance of their mass was
objectionable, and now that Cromwell was deep in the cauldron of
Confederate Ireland, he was fully alert to the possibility of altercation
concerning the point. The mere mention of 'liberty of conscience' by
Taaffe activated his effervescent sensitivity to the subject, and he told
the governor of the constraints under which he must operate.

From this letter it is also possible to discern that Cromwell makes
the distinction between those 'townsmen who desire to depart' and
those that obviously wished to stay. This can be easily interpreted as
those in arms, as opposed to those not. Even the ones in arms, as well
as those pacifists who were in opposition to the Parliamentarian administration, were to be given plenty of time to vacate the town.

Taaffe was now ready to surrender:

For General Cromwell; These;

I am content to yield up this place upon the terms offered
in your first and last letters. And if you please to send your
safe-conduct to such as I shall appoint to perfect these conditions, I shall on receipt thereof, send them to you. In the
interval, to cease all acts of hostility, and that all parties
keep their own ground, until matters receive a full end.

And so remains, Sir, Your servant, Lucas Taaffe[8]

At Wexford, while negotiations were ongoing, the storm took place out of Cromwell's control, and he was not content with the manner in which the town had been taken. Since he was now so close to a peaceful resolution at Ross, he warned Taaffe not to trifle with the might of the Roundhead army who were poised and ready to punish any carelessness that might suddenly develop:

For the governor of Ross; These;
October 19th, 1649.

Sir, You have my hand and honour engaged to perform what I offered in my first and last letters; which I shall inviolably observe. I expect you to send me immediately four persons of such quality as may be hostages for your performance, for whom you have this safe-conduct enclosed, into which you may insert their names. Without which I shall not cease acts of hostility. If anything happens by your delay to your prejudice, it will not be my fault. Those you send may see the conditions perfected. Whilst I forbear all acts of hostility, I expect you forbear all actings within.

I rest, Your servant, Oliver Cromwell.[9]

The Irish Royalists had learned a great deal from both Drogheda and Wexford. The ridiculous conditions that the garrison and townspeople of Wexford had sought were not repeated at Ross. They knew it was futile to push their luck and so they capitulated. Taaffe did not continue with his appeal for 'liberty of conscience' and there the matter ended. Ross was delivered up to Cromwell under these conditions, and no doubt both sides were relieved that there was no unnecessary loss of life at that town. That day the following agreement was drawn up between both parties and signed by Cromwell and Taaffe:

Articles concluded and agreed upon, by and between the Right Honourable, the Lord Lieut. Of Ireland of the one part and the governor of Ross of the other part, this 19 Octob. 1649.

1. It is concluded and agreed, That the governor of Ross with all under his command, may march into Kilkenny or Loughlen Bridge, with their arms, bag and baggage, drums beating, colours flying, bullet in mouth, bandeliers full of

powder, and match lighted at both ends, provided they march thither in three days, and that no acts of hostility be committed during the said time.

2. It is concluded and agreed, That such townsmen as desire to depart, and to carry away themselves and their goods, shall have three months time so to do, and in the meantime shall be preserved from violence in their persons and goods, as others under the obedience of the Parliament; and that a convoy be sent with them to secure them in their journeys.

3. It is concluded and agreed, that the inhabitants shall be permitted to live peaceably, and enjoy their goods and estates free from injury and the violence of the soldiers.

4. In consideration whereof, the governor of Ross is to surrender into my hands the town of Ross, artillery, arms, ammunition and other utensils of war that are therein by three of the clock this present day, except such as were brought in by the said governor, or such as came in since he had the command thereof, and by two of the clock, to permit the Lord Lieutenant to put three hundred men into the blockhouse, gatehouse near the breach, and the white tower near the same.

5. For the performance of the Articles on the said governor's part, he is to deliver four such hostages as I shall approve.

Signed by; O. Cromwell.

Commissioners; James Crarford, Math Lynell, Thomas Gaynan, Math Dormer, Governor, Lucas Taaffe.[10]

Over a month later there was an extension to the terms that Cromwell would sign also, concerning the continued 'obedience' of those anti-Cromwellian inhabitants who seemed to have accepted their fate:

I do hereby grant and desire that the promises of protection and all other benefits granted to the inhabitants of the town of Ross in the third article concluded upon the surrender of the said town, shall be extended and concluded to the said inhabitants, as well after the three months mentioned in the second of the said articles as during that space, they behaving themselves peaceably and faithfully as becometh persons under protection submitting to the authority of the Parliament of England.

Given at Ross the thirteenth day of November, 1649. Oliver Cromwell.[11]

The Parliamentarian grip on the country was strengthening almost by the week. Most of Ulster, Leinster and now significant parts of Munster were gradually being absorbed by Cromwell and his followers. When the Royalists chose to fight, their efforts were steamrolled by both the overwhelming muscle and advantageous number of the invaders. When they decided to surrender their fortresses, the resultant confiscation was the same, but without the fatalities. Ormonde would still not consider a field battle since he knew he could not count on his disjointed army, especially now that the reputation of the attackers was so fierce. He had fled to Kilkenny when the guns had begun to batter the walls of Ross. Ironically, the proportion of numbers was slowly swinging towards him, now that the invading army shrank as men were left behind to man captured garrisons and the 'country sickness' pervaded its ranks.

It was during his time in Ross that Cromwell would first see an image of James Butler, the Earl of Ormonde. While Cromwell was lodging in the house of a Francis Dormer, there hung on the wall a portrait of the aristocrat, and it was this painting that allegedly prompted Cromwell to remark that 'the man whom the picture concerned was more like a huntsman than any way a soldier'.[12]

Cromwell would not move from the town of Ross for over a month as he supervised the activity in the southern province, which would yield mixed fortunes for Parliament, with its army now somewhat fragmented and depleted.[13] He would probably have been able to field about 5,000 men,[14] while Ormonde was in command of almost double that figure, with more reinforcements due from O'Neill in Ulster.[15] On 20 October Ormonde had despatched a delegation to meet with Eoghan Ruadh's party at Finnea in Longford, and an agreement was finally signed between the two. Ormonde had agreed to invalidate land confiscation from the O'Neill clan at the Ulster plantation and that which they had also lost since the rebellion started in 1641. The

Catholic religion was also to retain all churches and buildings held by them in Ulster. Eoghan Ruadh, although still the commander of 6,000 foot and 800 horse, was now virtually incapable of movement due to his infected limbs. His warranty with Ormonde was, therefore, quite an achievement, and while he would not live to reap the benefits, he ensured that his successors certainly had that opportunity.[16]

The bridge over the Barrow at Ross had been destroyed before Cromwell's arrival, and it was decided that it would be rebuilt before moving the army further westwards. Duncannon was not yet won, and so he sent Jones to Ireton's aid. On 25 October he took some parchment and sat down to advise the Council of State of the acquisition of Ross. (see Appendix No. 6.1)

The epidemic of 'the plague', which was probably severe dysentery, that was prevalent in the town of Ross, also ran through the Parliamentarian forces and would now reach its foremost member as Cromwell himself fell victim to its germ. For this reason, plus the fact that Duncannon, as well as his next target, Waterford, had yet to be reduced, he decided not to move his army anywhere until both the medical and the military situations had improved. In the meantime, an astute move that the resourceful Puritan leader had made in London earlier in the year was now about to pay off. Roger Boyle, otherwise Lord Broghill, who was the brother of the Earl of Cork, had been in exile in England having taken the side of the King earlier in the war. As a powerful Protestant landowner in the south of Ireland, he had sufficient stature to be sent a letter by the young Prince who requested his assistance in the defence of Ireland. At that stage Charles was lying low in Holland, and Broghill intended to travel there via London and receive a commission to raise troops in Munster for the Royal cause. Cromwell, who was still engaging in his preparations for the Irish war, got wind of Broghill's plan and cunningly sent him a letter asking to see him. Broghill was stunned that Cromwell even knew of his existence and arrived at the appointed place full of both curiosity and amazement. When he discovered that Cromwell knew of his intentions, he was sure that he would be arrested. Instead, the Lord Lieutenant of Ireland had a different plan. While this war was not between Catholics and Protestants, he would exploit the dividing line between those religions wherever he could. In a prime example of how defections could simply be procured, the Protestant Cromwell asked the Protestant Broghill to forsake the Protestant Charles and to take up arms in opposition to the mainly

Catholic Irish army. Such was the inconsistency of this complicated war that Broghill easily departed the Royal call and declared his support for Parliament. He would eventually become a close friend of Cromwell.[17] On 16 October 1649, Cromwell heard the news that the English military contingent of the garrison in Cork, allied by the English inhabitants, had caused that city to revolt for the cause of the Commonwealth. They had overpowered the Irish troops and governor placed there by Ormonde and driven them from the city walls. Inchiquin lost all but 200 of his foot soldiers as a result of this action, and Ormonde was berated by the Confederacy for trusting in the allegiance of the Protestant English.[18] Broghill had done well. Duncannon, however, was not reduced, and the siege would eventually be lifted on 5 November when the besiegers would decide to divert their attention to Waterford. Broghill was greatly assisted in his efforts in the south by Colonel Richard Townsend, who would eventually give his name to the beautifully picturesque town of Castletownsend on the rugged Cork coast.[19] Cromwell also ordered Colonels Blake and Phayre to assist Broghill in stirring the Munster garrisons into revolt.

The day that Ross surrendered was the same day that the Council of State received confirmation that 5,000 troops were now fully prepared to depart for the Irish war.[20] On 26 October, Cromwell wrote to that body to remind them of the necessity for reinforcements:

> To the Council of State.
>
> Sir, Since my last to you, it hath pleased God to give us in Ross, a port much more considerable for shipping than Wexford, and we can be able by ships and boats to make a bridge over. We are in a fair way to enter into the bowels of Munster, this town is in the circuit of the wall, I believe every whit as big if not bigger than Wexford, and therefore you may easily imagine what this and some other places in this country and up the Barrow will take us up. Our army lies in the field, and we could not satisfy our consciences to keep the field as we do were it not that we hope we save blood by it, and indeed do follow Providence in prosecuting the enemy whiles the fear of God is upon them; how be it if our successes in taking garrisons should continue unless we be furnished with fresh supplies of foot, we shall quickly be at an end with our field army. Therefore I cannot but again

importune you that as you have ordered us 5,000 foot, so you would also speed some good proportions of them unto us. Yet we think we ought to love England and our friends there so well that what you cannot safely spare we hope God will make us willing to want.

We think it is our duty to let you know that all the Popish party in Ireland and the Septs and Ormondian are like to join as one man. Owen Roe O'Neale his son is come up to Kilkenny with a great party. We trust when they are gathered together it shall be that God may yet more manifest himself. How be it, we having those ways to spend our force, are not to be wanting to let our friends know their concernments.

Yours very affectionately, O. Cromwell.[21]

The undertaking of the rebuilding of the bridge over the junction of the Barrow with the Nore was the next move for part of the invading army. Ormonde, garrisoned at his ancestral domain of nearby Kilkenny, had more men than Cromwell but still did not dare to engage the attackers. He was also criticised by his Irish allies for making no effort to impede the bridge construction, since he had the obvious benefit of the treacherous currents of the Barrow between him and the Parliamentarian engineers.[22]

Cromwell in the above letter insisted that the administrational body assist in the subjugation of Ireland with the aid of much needed additional troops. He also repeats his desire to avoid bloodshed. Indeed, during his stay at Ross his ironlike grip of control over the invading army sometimes loosened, as some of his weather beaten soldiers got loose from his disciplinary clutches:

Proclamation.

By the Lord Lieutenant General of Ireland. Whereas there are divers complaints daily made by the inhabitants in and near the town of Ross that the soldiers under my command do daily take away their garrons and plough horses and their seed corn, and do hinder them from threshing their seed corn and from following their business of husbandry, whereby the land is unmanured and unsown, which doth manifestly tend to the prejudice of the public and may prove to be of very ill consequence if not timely prevented: these are strictly to charge and command all officers and soldiers under my command that they do not presume to take away any plough horses or garrons or any seed corn from any persons whatsoever residing and inhabiting within our quarters, nor in any wise to hinder them from threshing out their corn, ploughing their lands or following their business of husbandry, upon pain of the severest punishment that may be inflicted on them. And I do hereby require all officers under my command in their several places to endeavour the preventing of the said outrages and offences, and to bring all offenders of that kind to condign punishment.

And I do hereby require the Provost Marshall of the army to cause this my Proclamation to be published in the town of Ross and also to the several and respective regiments of the army. Given under my hand at Ross this 27th of October 1649.

O. Cromwell.[23]

The incident concerning the two hens that were stolen from the old woman outside the walls of Drogheda was being suspended over the felons as a threat by their commanding officer. He had signed and sealed an agreement with the town of Ross that their goods would not be plundered, and when he got news to the contrary, he immediately moved to thwart such impudence. There is no question that 'the severest punishment' he would inflict on apprehended offenders would be death. His compliance with civil as well as military laws would be a factor that would surround his Irish campaign.

Cork was now in Cromwell's hands without a single shot having been fired, nor had he himself yet ventured near to the city. He now became increasingly aware that other Munster garrisons might follow the same course as Cork. Cromwell had requested Blake and Phayre to seek the assistance of those insurgents to induce a province-wide rebellion. Ulster was virtually secure, Leinster was the same, and while Connaught was as yet untouched, the acquisition of Munster would certainly mean that Connaught would soon follow. Any individual garrisons that the Puritans could acquire without laying siege to them would be of huge benefit to the Parliamentarian cause. The inhabitants of Cork would first require some conditions before they would submit to Cromwell's request, and they were as follows:

The propositions sent in by the English Inhabitants of the city, suburbs, and liberties of Cork, to his Excellency General Cromwell:

1. The said inhabitants, out of a sense of a former good service and tender care of the Lord Inchiquin to and for them, they desire that an act of oblivion pass for any act committed which might redound to the prejudice of his lordship or his heirs, and that he might quietly enjoy his own estate, and that satisfaction be made for what arrears are due to him until the perfection of the last peace.

2. The said inhabitants for themselves desire that an act of indemnity be passed for any former actions which they or any of them have done or might be supposed to have committed, whereby they and every one of them may and shall as quietly pass and freely enjoy their liberty and estates which now they are possessed of, or shall be in the same freedom of any of the people of England now do or shall do; and that all prize goods that have been bought by the said inhabitants, they may and shall enjoy them from any that might claim them.

3. The said inhabitants desire that whereas the charter of the city of Cork hath been forfeited by reason of non 'nadge, that there be a charter granted to the now inhabitants in as large and ample manner as the former.

4. They can make appear by ticket they have in any way lent, disbursed, or delivered for the use of the army before the late peace, and likewise for what they or any of them have or shall disburse either in money or goods since the time of their present declaration, and that one of the city be chosen to audify the said account on what debentures to be issued for payment.

5. The said inhabitants desire that what they shall make appear is due unto them by speciality or otherwise from

any person or persons whatsoever before or since the wars, satisfaction be made as to justice appertaineth.

6. That all English garrisons and persons that will come in and submit to these propositions shall have the benefit of the same.

7. That all lands, messuages, and tenements within the said city and county thereof that was held in burage, to be totally confirmed on the now inhabitants of the said city, and that the inhabitants of the said city and suburbs be regulated unto a regiment under the command of Mr. John Hodder as colonel, to be in pay when they pass on duty, not else.[24]

Cromwell more or less acquiesced to the proposals of the men of Cork, with the notable exception of the clause which they had put on the top of their list regarding the local Lord Inchiquin. To their first article, he replied 'I shall forbear to make answer'. Inchiquin's reputation as a soldier of fortune who had deserted the Parliamentarian cause earlier in the year and who was now one of Cromwell's chief adversaries was enough to inspire Cromwell to totally ignore that particular proposal and get on with the business in hand. There was no love lost between these two essentially English noblemen, but it is obvious that Inchiquin was the one who was the less scrupulous of the two. (see Appendix No. 6.2).

As a consequence of the Cork mutiny the smaller garrisons of Kinsale, Bandon and Youghal along the south coast (who had revolted in the intervening period) soon rebelled against their Confederate leaders and proclaimed their support for Cromwell. Prince Rupert, who had been harboured in Kinsale awaiting his opportunity to enter the Irish war on the King's behalf, suddenly found himself with no cover and fled to Portugal with his fleet, much to the disappointment of the overthrowing Parliamentarians who were anxious to capture him. Munster gradually succumbed to the Parliamentarians as town after town rebelled against Ormonde's forces.

In a letter from Ross to his son Richard's father-in-law (his son 'Dick' had married Dorothy Mayor earlier that year and her father soon became a confidant of Cromwell), he tells him, 'I have been crazy in my health, but the Lord is pleased to sustain me'.[25] Cromwell's health problems paled into insignificance beside those of the nephew of the Earl of Tyrone, Eoghan Ruadh O'Neill. He was by now at Clough Uachtair (or Cloghouter) in Cavan, having been carried there from Ballyhaise, no longer able to ride or walk. On 6 November he lost his last battle – this time it was for his life. Tradition has it that he wore a priestly habit under his clothes 'as a sure buckler against the rigour of future judgement'.[26] In the context of Cromwell in Ireland, it is not surprising that O'Neill has emerged as a true Irish hero who has since come to represent Irish nationalism. Many subsequent writers saw the loss of this commander as a major tragedy for Ireland since he never got the opportunity to confront the British enemy in the field. The contemporary newsbook *Aphorismal Discovery* writes: 'He died in our Lord, the 6th of November, 1649, a true child of the Catholic religion in sense and memory, many of both secular and regular clergy assisting him in such a doubtful transit, behaving himself, most penitently.'[27] However gallant O'Neill was, what is manifestly obvious now is that the disunion between the Royalist forces for which he was a major contributor was a tremendous influence on the eventual outcome of the war. In a time when colonisation was a fundamental fact of life, O'Neill, like so many other Irish champions, hopelessly pledged his allegiance to the Crown. That Crown would never return the favour. It is doubtful that, had O'Neill lived, there would have been any other result, although the inevitable may have been put off for a period of time. Naturally, in the creative climate of 1640s Ireland, there is a tradition that O'Neill was murdered, having worn a pair of boots that had been laced (pun intended) with poison. The culprit allegedly was a Plunkett from Louth.[28] Ironically the famous Plunketts of Louth are now associated with Archbishop Oliver Plunkett, executed at Tyburn later that same century. The family name is today a byword for Catholicism, and the Archbishop's preserved head, as coincidence would have it, is on display today in the Roman Catholic parish church of Saint Peter's, Drogheda. The story, however, is most likely a contrived composition of the romantic and frightful world of seventeenth century Ireland.

In the last century, before the first publication of their nationalist newspaper *The Nation*, Thomas Davis along with his Young Irelander compatriots Dillon and Duffy agreed to attempt political ballads in order to stir anti-British feeling throughout Ireland. Their aggrandising the sacrifice of dying for Ireland and the glorification of past rebellions and oppressions was typical of their time. This was also the climate

in which Murphy would publish his *Cromwell in Ireland*, a time when
the Irish were promised that they would be 'A Nation Once Again'.
Davis had never attempted verse before, but, having analysed seventeenth century Ireland, he returned to his comrades with his 'Lament
for the Death of Eoghan Ruadh O'Neill', which had the desired effect.
It began:

> Did they dare, did they dare, to slay Owen Roe O'Neill?
> Yes, they slew with poison him they feared to meet with steel
> May God wither up their hearts! May their blood cease to flow!
> May they walk in living death who poisoned Owen Roe!
> Though it break my heart to hear, say again the bitter words!
> From Derry against Cromwell he marched, to measure swords;
> But the weapon of the Sasanach met him on his way,
> And he died at Clogh Uachtair, upon St. Leonard's Day.

The seventh verse reads:

> We thought you would not die – we were sure you would not go,
> And leave us in our inmost need to Cromwell's cruel blow,
> Sheep without a shepherd, when the snow shuts out the sky –
> Oh! Why did you leave us, Owen? Why did you die! [29]

Colonel Hunger and Major Sickness, as Ormonde had predicted,
would still play their part in this terrible war. The difficulty was that
both afflictions were indiscriminate, and as Cromwell lay in bed due to
the latter, the former was always a threat to his mobile army. On 25
November in a letter to Lenthall, he remarks, 'I tell you a considerable
part of your army is fitter for an hospital than the field; if the enemy
did not know it; I should have held it impolitic to have writ it. They
know it, yet they know not what to do'. [30] Had Ormonde not been aware
of this fact and had Cromwell's letter been intercepted, one would
imagine that he would have moved to exploit the news. The fact is, he
was aware that sickness prevailed through the Ironside forces and he
remained indecisive. His army would always appear as disjointed as
Cromwell's were united, and unable to wage an offensive campaign.
With O'Neill dead and no successor yet elected, the staunchly Protestant Ormonde faced the prospect of controlling the Catholic Ulster
squadrons sent to him. On 14 November Cromwell sent Ireton and
Jones towards Ormonde at Kilkenny in an attempt to force him to battle, but Ormonde took refuge at Thomastown and the Parliamentarian

troops returned to Ross. By that time Cromwell was fit again, and he marched in the direction of Waterford. New recruits had arrived to increase his forces to 7,000 men in the field.[31] On 20 November, Carrick-on-Suir was taken by the Roundheads. The townspeople of Waterford had been dedicated supporters of Rinuccini and were ardent Catholics. Upon the approach of the Roundheads, the municipal authorities wrote to Ormonde to request military assistance, but insisted that the only troops they would countenance were those of Ulster origin who were their religious brethren. They also requested a delay to hostilities of fifteen days from Cromwell, who agreed to five, and in that time he took the town of Passage (Passage East), which cut Waterford off. The weather then suddenly took a turn for the worse and prevented Cromwell's cannon, which were following the army, from reaching his camp. On 2 December Cromwell opted to raise the siege and march away. He remarked that the day they left Waterford behind was 'as terrible a day as ever I marched in my life'.[32] On his departure his decision seemed to be justified as he witnessed the arrival of the Ulster Irish under the command of Captain Ferrall on the opposite side of the River Suir.

Control of both the eastern and southern coasts from Belfast to Cork was interrupted only by the small fort of Duncannon (the attempt to take it having been abandoned on 5 November) and the town of Waterford. Cromwell knew that it was not necessary to acquire every single garrison that they encountered. His objective was to reduce Munster in the most expedient fashion possible. The obduracy of Duncannon and Waterford was not going to tempt the English commander into wasting valuable time by deploying much needed troops to lay lengthly siege to these forts, not when towns like nearby Dungarvan suddenly revolted the day after he left Waterford and delivered themselves into his hands with no effort on his part. His retreat from those strongholds, however, was against the grain of his Irish mission and was not in keeping with his aggressive military strategy. His decision must have been based on the fact that his troops were both sodden and ill, and anyway, even if the guns had arrived, the wet ground would not have been conducive to heavy artillery fire. Waterford eventually surrendered to Ireton after Cromwell's departure from Ireland in August 1650 and Duncannon four days later.

The severe weather conditions that prevailed during Cromwell's retreat from Waterford to Dungarvan would strike down one of his most competent commanders, Colonel Michael Jones. The Parliamentary hero of the battle of Rathmines fell ill on the journey and would not progress any further than Dungarvan, where he died on 10 December. He was not the only Commonwealth victim of the Irish climate. Cromwell describes his losses to Lenthall in a letter written at Youghal nine days later:

> The noble Lieutenant-General (whose finger to our knowledge never ached in all these expeditions) fell sick (we doubt upon a cold taken upon our late wet march and ill accommodation) and went to Dungarvan, where (struggling for some four or five days with a pestilent and contagious fever) he died, having run his course with so much honour, courage and fidelity, as his actions speak better than my pen. What England hath lost is thereby above me to speak. I am sure I have lost a noble friend and companion in labours. Before that my poor kinsman Major Cromwell (if I may name him) died before Waterford of a fever; since that two persons eminently faithful, Godly and true to you, Lieut-Colonel Wolfe and Scout-Master-General Rowe are dead at Youghal. Thus you see how God mingles out his cup unto; indeed we are at this time a crazy company, yet we live in His sight, and shall work the time that is appointed to us and shall rest after that in peace.[33]

From Dungarvan Cromwell marched his army to Youghal and arrived there himself on 5 December. Winter had taken a grip of the country and he decided finally that this location would be his winter quarters. Resumption of the war would take place when the weather would improve. Too many casualties were the result of being abroad in the damp and hostile climate of southern Ireland. Ormonde, too, realised the need for deferment, and he dispersed his troops throughout the immediate countryside. Waterford and Limerick were the two most significant strongholds still under Royalist dominion, yet they would not receive Ormonde's soldiers even for the purposes of rest.

Cromwell's first recorded act three days after he entered the town of Youghal was to address the continual problem of plundering by a small disobedient portion of the soldiers under his command. These persistent declarations against pillaging could have been because the

'soldiers under his command' to whom these words were directed
were the recent revolters of various garrisons now on his side. There
is no reason to suspect that the original members of the New Model
needed constant reminder of his attitude to social injustices. On 8
December he issued the following proclamation to troops who had
been used to having a free reign in the countryside:

Proclamation

Whereas I am informed that the horse under my command
(since their being quartered within the Black-water) have
and do in their several quarters take away and waste wheat
and barley for their horses, and do behave themselves out-
rageously towards the inhabitants, not contenting themselves with such provisions as they are able to afford them,
but to kill their sheep and other cattle within and as often
as they please.

I do hereby straightly charge and command all soldiers to
forbear such like practices upon pain of death . . . And I do
farther will and require all officers and soldiery within the
limits aforesaid, that they do not break down any stacks of
barley or wheat in their respective quarters, to give the same
to their horses, but that they content themselves with peas,
oats, hay, and such other forrage, as the country affords,
paying or giving tickets at such reasonable rates for the
same, as they were usually sold for, before their coming into
the said quarters.

Given under my hand this 8 day of December 1649, O.
Cromwell[34]

It is worth noting that throughout Murphy's *Cromwell in Ireland* the
author practically refuses to acknowledge these empathetic resolutions
of the Lord Lieutenant of Ireland. They do, of course, portray a genuinely merciful individual, compared to the fiend that is depicted in
that publication.

Cromwell did not spend the winter passively. From Youghal he
busied himself visiting the various garrisons in Munster. On 17
December he was in Cork and from there he attended Kinsale and
Bandon. As the year drew to a close, the Parliamentary army was

sequestered in various garrisons around Munster recovering from the debility of their illnesses. In the middle of December, Enniscorthy Castle was regained by the Royalists. Despite this, the year that began with the execution of the King would now end with his supporters in Ireland inauspiciously defending the right of his son to succeed.[35] Cromwell spent Christmas, according to one of the many traditions applied to him, in Cork city as the guest of one Mr Coppinger, whose house was on South Main Street.[36]

On 19 December some of Cromwell's recent letters were read to the Council of State in London. The House then decided that they would recall Cromwell back from Ireland as their control in England was always under threat from Royalist sympathisers, of whom there was a majority. Their army was abroad under the control of the commander in whom they now began to place immense trust and belief. Charles II was having negotiations with the Scots and other foreign powers who were quite unsure of this 'civilian' government in control of a powerful European country.

The Confederacy also endeavoured to make optimum use of the winter recess and so the Irish prelates met on 4 December at Clonmacnoise. Their objective was to fuse into one body the divided parties in order to halt the relentless momentum of the Puritans. The result was a written plea to the various groups in Ireland in opposition to Parliament to ignore their past disagreements and to form an effective force.

The Clonmacnoise decrees were issued by the principal echelons of the Catholic faith in Ireland in two separate forms, the first on 4 December and the second on 13 December and were printed in pamphlet format to aid general circulation.

The first document is dated 4 December 1649 and immediately launches an attack on Cromwell's attempts at clemency towards the ordinary Irish people by declaring that 'many of our flock are misled with a vain opinion of hopes that the Commander-in-Chief of the rebel forces, commonly called Parliamentarians, would afford them good conditions . . . to undeceive them in this their ungrounded expectation, we do hereby declare as a most certain truth that the enemy's resolution is to extirpate the Catholic Religion out of all his Majesty's dominions . . .' These words were designed to incite the acrimony of their readers, and they highlight perfectly the reciprocal contempt that the bishops held for the Commander-in-Chief of the rebel forces. This seventeenth century smear campaign continues with audacious predictions of wholesale destruction at Cromwell's hand's by declaring, 'And in effect this banishment and other destructions of the common people must follow the resolution of extirpating the Catholic Religion, which is not to be effected without the massacring or banishment of the Catholic inhabitants.' The clergy then appeal to the people of Ireland to increase their resolve when they announce that they 'beseech the gentry and inhabitants, for God's glory and their own safety, to the uttermost of their power to contribute with patience to the support of the war against the enemy in hope that by the blessing of God they may be rescued by the threatened evils . . .'. The decrees that were issued on 13 December in a separate document emphasised the request for unity. The bishops directed all of the clergy countrywide to initiate public prayers, fasting, confessions and other works of piety and expressed their disdain at the segmented state of all the Royalist parties that prevailed, in no uncertain manner: 'And we do hereby manifest our detestation against all such divisions between either provinces or families, or between English and Old Irish, or any of the English or Scots adhering to his Majesty. And we decree and order, that all ecclesiastical persons fomenting such dissensions or unnatural divisions be punished by their respective prelates and superiors.' (see Appendix 6.3).

It was not until January that Cromwell would receive copies of the Declarations of the Prelates. As the war was at an inactive stage, he had ample time to draft a document of his own concerning the points that the clergy had raised. This following chronicle, he wrote in a fit of extreme passion, and as a display of his understanding of Ireland and its history its significance is vital. He discloses in remarkable detail his contempt for Catholicism and the practice of the mass. He leaves no holds barred as he strikes at the heart of that detestable Roman Church. Ecclesiastical authority was not part of his personal world. As a Puritan he believed that the power of the Catholic Church centred around their superior members. His treatment of priests in the two garrisons of Drogheda and Wexford is easily explained (but not excused) in his disclosure. His perception of Ireland, developed from contemporary news literature, was unfortunately quite wide of the mark. Yet his campaign was motivated entirely by the sentiments that are expressed in this publication. Today it seems both incredibly arrogant and patronising, and as an example of British attitudes to the Irish and their Catholicism in former days, it appears perfectly typical. By today's standards Cromwell's proclamation could be considered to be the words of a fanatic. However, there is no reason to doubt the sincerity of his beliefs. As an insight into the mind of the Puritan commander who was fighting a war with this precise agenda, the value of this letter is immeasurable. (See Appendix No. 6.4).

There is no need to look any further than this Declaration to see into the mind of Oliver Cromwell as he passed through Ireland 350 years ago. There is no need either to look further than this document to realise the essence of his tolerant attitude towards Irish civilians. Contained in these words is the fundamental basis of his campaign, his feelings towards the Catholic authorities, their (deluded) laity, his own religious beliefs, his thoughts concerning the mass etc. etc. He calls into question the credentials of the clergy to govern the 'Laity'. He alleges that the actual words 'clergy' and 'laity' were 'unknown to any save the anti-Christian Church and as such as derive themselves from Her'. He does not hold anything back when he tells them; 'You are part of Anti-Christ whose Kingdom so expressly speaks should be laid in blood; yea in the blood of the Saints. You have shed great store of it already, and ere it be long, you must, all of you, have blood to drink, even the dregs of the cup of the fury and the wrath of God, which will be poured out unto you.' But most of all, contained in this document is his humanitarian attitude to those people, *not in arms*, throughout the country. Time and time again he repeats that unarmed civilians are to be continuously excluded from all acts of violence. Concerning the Act of Subscription which entitled the Adventurers to reparation for their investments, he emphasises that those to suffer loss of estates in Ireland as a consequence would be 'that only reaching to them who have been in arms, for further it goes not . . . for such of the nobility, gentry and commons of Ireland as have not been actors in this rebellion, that they shall and may expect the protection in their goods, liberties and lives which the law gives them, and in their husbandry, merchandising, manufactures and other trading whatsoever'. In response to the Declaration of the Prelates from Clonmacnoise, he even goes so far as to ask them to 'give us an instance, since my coming into Ireland, of one man, not in arms, massacred, destroyed or banished' – and this coming after the events at Drogheda and Wexford. He could still hold his head high with justification and ask such a question. It is at this stage that the ridiculous fables of Mr Thomas Wood are impeached beyond reproach. *Not one unarmed civilian had been deliberately killed by him or his men since his Irish campaign had begun!*

Samuel Gardiner has asserted the following about this outburst of Cromwell's: 'As a contribution to Irish history, nothing could be more ludicrously beside the mark than these burning words . . . nevertheless as an explanation of Cromwell's own conduct in Ireland, this Declaration is of supreme importance.'[37] While the Parliamentarian commander's ideals are sometimes totally misplaced, there can be absolutely no doubt that he had sincere intentions. There is nothing but ostensible decency contained in this letter. To the modern Irish Republican the following words are offensive and threatening: 'We are come, to hold forth and maintain the lustre and glory of English liberty in a nation where we have an undoubted right to do it.' Irrespective, however, of the political implications that are conjured up today from such statements, Cromwell's sense of justice and propriety can not be ignored.

Cromwell's antipathy towards the Catholic Church was also due to the abuses of that body in the forms of nepotism, pluralism and absenteeism. That organisation had been rife with corrupt practices, such as positions of authority being 'purchased' by some of its most affluent members, and friends and relations of members were drafted in to powerful 'jobs' within that body. The clergy were frequently away from their parishes for years. Luther's reformed Church was the consequence of these abuses. As a Puritan, Cromwell was a prime adversary of Catholicism, a corrupt body that had the audacity to vie for the attention of *his* God. As a Protestant he would have had much more of a personal and intimate relationship with his God. It was his opinion that the laity, most of whom he perceived as 'poor and ignorant', were the ones who suffered most. He says:

> As for the people, what thoughts they have in matters of religion in their own breasts I cannot reach . . . But how dare you assume to call these men your flocks, who you have plunged into so horrid a rebellion, by which you have made both them and the country almost a ruinous heap, and whom you have fleeced and polled and peeled hitherto, and make it your business to do so still . . . You poison them with your false abominable and antichristian doctrine and practices . . . Thus are your flocks fed; and such credit have you of them. But they must take heed of losing their religion. Alas poor creatures, what have they to lose?

His reply to the prelates regarding their wild allegation of his extirpating the Catholic religion was that he would simply endeavour to
'convert' the flocks that they were misleading. He writes:

> . . . you have chiefly made use of fire and sword, in all the
> changes of religion that you have made in the world. If it be
> change of your Catholic Religion so-called, it will not follow,
> because there may be found another means than massacring,
> destruction and banishment, to wit the Word of God, which
> is able to convert (a means that you as little know as practise,
> which indeed you deprive the people of) . . .

The idea that he could forcibly eradicate that faith was, in his view,
a nonsensical claim from a debased and coercive organisation. He also
makes the point that Catholicism would probably cease to exist without the support of that laity. The very structure of their establishment
was contrary to his religious beliefs, it was certainly not a framework
on which to develop a pious existence. Cromwell had no human figure of religious authority to whom he reported in this life. Parliament
was his taskmaster in his present employment and God his superior,
always.

He emphasises the point that the subjugation of Ireland could cost
the treasury £6,000,000, compared to the quarter of a million invested
by the Adventurers. The vindication for such otherwise apparently
hopeless economics he suggests is that:

> England hath had experience of the blessing of God of
> prosecuting just and righteous causes, whatever the cost
> and hazard be. And if ever men were engaged in a right-
> eous cause in the world, this will be scarce a second to it.
> We are come to ask account of the innocent blood that hath
> been shed; and to endeavour to bring them to an account
> . . . We are come to break the power of a company of law-
> less rebels, who having cast off the authority of England,
> live as enemies to human society, whose principles (the
> world hath experience of) are, to destroy and subjugate all
> men not complying with them.

However nauseous this may sound today, it was very much part of
Cromwell's world, and he cannot be personally blamed for such an
attitude.

He also exposes the tenuous attachment of the Irish Catholics to the English monarchy, in particular the executed Charles I and his son the Prince of Wales:

> We know you love great Majesties. Or is it because he has not fully come over to you in point of religion? . . . His father who complied with you too much, you rejected, and now would make the world believe you would make the Son's interest a great part of the state of your quarrel. How can we but think there is some reserve in this or that the Son is agreed to do somewhat more for you than ever his Father did.

Predictably, Cromwell lays the blame of the 1641 rebellion firmly at the door of the ecclesiastics:

> Remember ye hypocrites, Ireland was once united to England. Englishmen had good inheritances which many of them purchased with their money . . . They lived peaceably and honestly amongst you . . . You broke this union, You, unprovoked, put the English to the most unheard of and most barbarous massacre (without respect of sex or age) that ever the sun beheld. And at a time when Ireland was in perfect peace.

It is in this letter that he discloses his famously inaccurate perception of Saxon and Celt living in perfect harmony until the clergy stepped in and persuaded the Celts to revolt. This has enormous ramifications when it comes to his hatred of priests. The victims were the 'commons', those ordinary civilians who were so easily led by a contemptible administration. His compassion for the average people of Ireland, a people whom he felt were totally misguided, while undoubtedly fallible, is nonetheless obvious from this disclosure. These are not the words of the butcher of defenceless men, women and children at Drogheda or Wexford. These are the words of a character in Irish history who has been fallaciously painted as such.

Futile as it seems now, Cromwell, in this declaration, also offered those still in arms the opportunity to 'come over' and disavow their allegiance to the Confederacy. He insisted that they would receive mercy from the English authorities, and there was no reason to doubt his intentions. In the light of the details contained in the above Declaration, the

motivation behind his campaign from *his* standpoint is perfectly under-
standable, even from this remote distance.

The news that Parliament now desired his presence back in London
had not yet officially reached him. It had, however, been printed by the
correspondent of *Severall Proceedings* at Cork on 18 January.[38]
Cromwell ignored the rumours and began planning for an early
resumption of the conflict since the winter was one of the mildest in
living memory. Immediately prior to the winter break his own military
operations had lost some momentum, and had it not been for the revolt
of some of the Munster garrisons, his position might not have been so
strong.

On 29 January 1650, the mission was renewed. He despatched
Reynolds and Ireton towards the Confederate bulwark of Kilkenny, and
he himself made his first foray inland and marched towards Fethard,
crossing the Suir three miles south of Cahir. His army was now replenished with reinforcements from England, and the majority of the
dysentery victims had quite recovered and were ready once more for
battle. Arriving before the walls of Fethard at the late hour of nine on
a stormy February evening, he sent a summons to Pierce Butler, the
governor of the town. Butler unbelievably scolded the Puritan commander for his summons at such a late hour:

> For Oliver Cromwell, General of the Parliament forces now
> in Ireland;
>
> May it please Your Lordship, I have received your letter
> about nine of the clock this night, which hour I conceive
> unreasonable for me to treat with you. Yet if your Lordship
> pleases to sent sufficient hostages in for such as I will
> employ to treat with you, I will be ready to entrust some in
> that business. Having no more at present. I remain,
>
> Your honour's friend and servant,
>
> Pierce Butler.
>
> From the garrison of Fethard, Feb. 2nd 1650, half an hour
> of nine o clock of the night.[39]

The generous terms that were offered to the garrison, incredibly,
included any priests that were ensconced within its walls. Cromwell's

mood must have been upbeat during his negotiations with Butler as he allowed occupants of the town of Fethard to evade transplantation in the subsequent settlement of the country by the agreement made that night. The conditions were discussed through the night, and the New Model marched through the gates before eight the following morning:

Articles of Agreement made and concluded on the 3rd day of February, 1650 between the Most Hon. Oliver Cromwell, Lord Lieutenant General of Ireland, and Lieutenant Colonel Pierce Butler, Governor of the town of Fethard, concerning the surrender of the said town as follows:

1. That all the officers and soldiers shall march freely with their horses and arms and all other goods, bag and baggage, colours flying, matches lighted, ball in bouche, into any place within his Majesty's quarters or garrisons except such as are now besieged, safely convoyed thither free from violence from any of the Parliament's party.

2. That all the country families and inhabitants, as also any of the officers, may freely live and enjoy their goods either in the town or abroad; if they or any of them be disposed to betake themselves to their former habitations in the country, they may have respite of time for that, and admittance to enjoy their holdings, paying contribution, as others in the country do, and carry with them safely such goods as they have within the garrison.

3. That all clergymen and chaplains both of the soldiers, town and country, now in this garrison, may freely march, bag and baggage, without any annoyance or prejudice in body or goods.

4. That all and every the inhabitants of the said town, and their wives, children and servants, with all their goods and chattels, both within the town and abroad in the country, shall be protected from time to time, and at all times, and shall quietly and peaceably enjoy their estates, real and personal, in as free and as good condition as any English or Irish shall hold his or their estates in this Kingdom, they

and every of them paying such contribution as the rest of
the inhabitants of the county of Tipperary pay proportionably to their estates and no more.

In consideration whereof the said Governor doth hereby
engage himself that he will deliver up the said town with
all things therein, except such things as are before agreed
upon, to be taken away with them by eight of the clock this
morming.

Pierce Butler

Oliver Cromwell[40]

The town of Cashel also surrendered to Cromwell in an attempt to
cash in on the clemency which marked the opening of his spring campaign. From Fethard he focused northwards towards Callan and the
nearby city of Kilkenny. Tradition tells us that as Cromwell stood on a
hill, somewhere between Fethard and Callan and beheld the striking
Irish landscape, he declared, 'This, indeed, is a country worth fighting
for.'[41] Having initially experienced some resistance from the garrison
of Callan, the town was soon taken on conditions. Since Kilkenny was
rumoured to be engulfed with 'the plague', Cromwell drew back
southwards to Cashel and then to Fethard. On 24 February the Puritans then arrived before the walls of Cahir, and after some resistance
the town was delivered up to Cromwell by its governor, Captain
George Matthews, who was Ormonde's half brother.[42]

There were now only five major towns remaining in Ireland for
Cromwell to take: Waterford, Clonmel, Galway, Limerick and Kilkenny. In order to attempt a successful assault on the place that housed
the headquarters of the Catholic Supreme Council and Ormonde's
own castle, Cromwell requested Hewson (who had been left in charge
of Dublin) to join him. While Hewson picked off various smaller garrisons on his way southwards, Cromwell busied himself overthrowing
the strongholds that surrounded Kilkenny, thereby cutting the city off
from outside assistance. Back at Youghal, Cromwell's son Henry
arrived on 5 March with reinforcements, making the position of the
Royalists particularly dire. Ormonde met with the prelates at Limerick on 9 March to discuss the acuteness of the position of the Royalist
allies. Instead of stepping up the momentum of the war, the irreconcilable divisions between the parties left Ormonde with less control

than he had previously had over the army.[43] Meanwhile in Ulster, Emer McMahon, the Bishop of Clogher, was elected as Eoghan Ruadh's successor, and was immediately curtailed in exercising control over the Ulster forces by his ecclesiastic occupation. A Catholic bishop was not an ideal replacement for that military genius O'Neill.

Cromwell had hoped that a Captain Tickell (or Tickle) would betray Kilkenny for a preorganised fee of £4,000, plus a command in the Parliamentarian army, but the deal was exposed and Tickell was hanged before he could act.[44] The city was still enveloped with the plague, and on 23 March, Cromwell summoned the garrison to surrender. Despite the fact that Kilkenny had represented the embodiment of Catholicism and was also Ormonde's own realm, no check was made to the Ironside's progress there. Between 23 and 28 March, negotiations between both the military and civilian representatives and Cromwell continued, while intermingled with unsuccessful assaults by his forces on the breached walls. Eventually, conditions were agreed upon and the Puritans were allowed possession of the city by the municipal authorities.[45] Ormonde was not present during the siege.

Meanwhile Broghill was actively engaged in covering Cromwell's rear in the south. As a result of his successful assailing of the town of Macroom, Boetius Egan, the Bishop of Ross, was captured. Broghill then took the bishop to the walls of the castle of Carrigadrohid, hoping that the sight of the distinguished captive would persuade the governer to surrender the fort, in return for the bishop's life. The officer refused to capitulate, and the bishop was hanged on Broghill's orders. It is alleged that in the bishop's pocket was a document in the handwriting of Lord Inchiquin declaring the peer's intent to submit to Cromwell.[46] The latter's regiments were by this time quite eager to do just that.

After the acquisition of Kilkenny, Cromwell returned southwards to Carrick (Carrick-on-Suir), where he again reported to Lenthall of his operations, this time advising Parliament that he was aware of the rumours for his recall to England:

> I have received divers private intimations of your pleasure
> to have me come in person to wait upon you in England,
> as also copies of the votes of Parliament to that purpose.
> But considering the way they came to me were but private
> intimations, and the votes did refer to a letter to be signed
> by the Speaker, I thought it would have been too much

forwardness in me to have left my charge here, until the said letter came.[47]

He suggests that having received a letter from the Council of State on 22 March, the day he arrived before Kilkenny, dated 8 January, Parliament obviously supposed him still to be at his winter quarters. Now that the campaign was renewed, he could not desert the Irish mission unless his presence in London was imperative. Although he had no way of knowing it, there was, in fact, a letter from Parliament at that very moment winging its way towards him declaring that, 'Affairs here are very urgent and we desire your presence and assistance.'[48]

Ormonde was now sequestered at Loughrea and in a letter to the Bishop of Derry he sums up his relationship with the Catholic clergy: 'Trust me, they will not, and trust them, I cannot.'[49] Inchiquin's English and Scottish troops now sent a delegation headed by Michael Boyle, Dean of Cloyne, to Cromwell to surrender in return for permission to leave the country. Cromwell negotiated terms with Inchiquin's soldiers and effectively prevented the latter from retaining an official command. During the exchange, Cromwell attempted to include both Inchiquin and Ormonde in the deal and drafted passes for them to depart for Europe unmolested. The latter returned the pass disdainfully, and the former, now relieved of his regiment, did the same. A pass for the Lady Inchiquin was, however, accepted.[50]

The plain facts were that Royalist resistance in Ireland was almost at an end. Most of the scattered outposts, as well as the major urban centres, were now under Cromwell's jurisdiction. His subjugation of Ireland that had begun at the walls of Drogheda in September of the previous year, following hard on Jones' victory at Rathmines, was nearly complete. His presence was urgently required in London. Ormonde had talked of deserting Ireland and leaving it to the Puritans.[51] Losses on the side of the invading army were paltry compared to those on the defender's. Five hundred Parliamentarian soldiers at most may have been killed in active service to date, compared to some 5,000 Royalists. The appalling facts are that in the ten year period between 1640–50, approximately 600,000 people had lost their lives in Ireland due to famine, pestilence and war. Cromwell's Irish expedition was almost over. Almost, but not quite . . .

Notes to Chapter Six

1   W.C. Abbott, *The Writings and Speeches of Oliver Cromwell*, reprint edition, 4 vols. (Oxford: Clarendon Press, 1988), vol. II, p. 143. On the town's main street today is Penny's Boutique, which was formerly Woolworths, and prior to that it was known as Kenny's Hall. It is traditionally believed that this is the site of Cromwell's quarters during his short stay in the town. Up to this century an oak-panelled room existed where he was supposed to have slept, with a concealed door opening into a shaft in the wall leading to depths unknown. I am grateful to Celestine Rafferty for the information on the recent occupiers of the building.

2   Rev. Denis Murphy, *Cromwell in Ireland, A History of Cromwell's Irish Campaign* (Dublin, M.H. Gill & Son, 1883), p. 180–81. Also, Abbott, *Writings and Speeches*, vol. II, p. 145.

3   Murphy, *Cromwell in Ireland*, p. 181.

4   Abbott, *Writings and Speeches*, vol. II, p. 146; Murphy, *Cromwell in Ireland*, p. 182.

5   Ibid.

6   Murphy, *Cromwell in Ireland*, p. 182.

7   Printed in *A Brief Relation of State Affairs; Severall Proceedings*, 16 November 1649; quoted from Abbott, *Writings and Speeches*, vol. II, p. 146; also reproduced in Murphy, *Cromwell in Ireland*, p. 186.

8   Murphy, *Cromwell in Ireland*, pp. 186–87.

9   Abbott, *Writings and Speeches*, vol. II, p. 147; Murphy, *Cromwell in Ireland*, p. 187.

10   From *Severall Proceedings*, 16 November 1649; quoted from Abbott, *Writings and Speeches*, vol. II, p. 147–48; Murphy, *Cromwell in Ireland*, p. 188.

11   Abbott, *Writings and Speeches*, vol. II, p. 148, who uses Murphy, *Cromwell in Ireland*, p. 189.

12   *Aphorismical Discovery*, vol. II, p. 55; in Murphy, *Cromwell in Ireland*, p. 189; also in Abbott, *Writings and Speeches*, vol. II, p. 152.

13   In J.T. Gilbert, *A Contemporary History of Affairs in Ireland from A.D. 1641–1652*, 3 vols. (Dublin: Irish Archaeological and Celtic Society, 1879), vol. II, pp. 312–13, there is a *Design For the Recovery of the Town of Ross*, by the Royalists, appended by a contemporary illustration of the plan, which was never actually attempted. Taken from The Carte Manuscripts' Collection, in the Bodleian Library, Oxford, vol. XXVI, p. 43.

14   S.R. Gardiner, *History of the Commonwealth and the Protectorate*, reprint edition (Stroud: The Windrush Press, 1988), p. 135; also Abbott, *Writings and Speeches*, vol. II, p. 148.

15   Ormonde to Jermyn, 30 November 1649, Carte, *Original Letters*, vol. II, p. 415; from Abbott, *Writings and Speeches*, vol. II, p. 155.

16   Gardiner, *History of the Commonwealth and the Protectorate*, p. 139.

17   The Broghill affair is recounted in Antonia Fraser, *Cromwell Our Chief of Men* (London, Mandarin edition, 1994), pp. 321–22; Abbott, *Writings and Speeches*, vol. II, pp. 83–84; Murphy, *Cromwell in Ireland*, pp. 192–95.

18   'Ormonde was assailed with Irish complaints of his folly in trusting English Protestants.' Gardiner, *History of the Commonwealth and the Protectorate*, p. 136. See also Abbott, who states, 'the Irish complained bitterly of Ormonde's favour to the English'. *Writings and Speeches*, vol. II, p. 151.

19   From Burke's *Landed Gentry*, p. 1507, in Murphy, *Cromwell in Ireland*, p. 197.

20   Abbott, *Writings and Speeches*, vol. II, p. 152.

21   Cromwell to a Member of State, *Severall Proceedings*, 16 November 1649 in Abbott, *Writings and Speeches*, vol. II, p. 154.

22   Abbott says, 'Ormonde was severely criticized for not offering resistance to this project.' He adds some details concerning the actual bridge, 'The length (742ft) is given in a petition from Derrick Curtis, a ships carpenter, employed in its construction, to the Admiralty Committee, Oct. 13, 1655.' *Writings and Speeches*, p. 155; quoted from *Aphorismical Discovery*, vol. III, p. 155 and *Calender of State Papers Domestic*, vol. CXV, p. 154. See also W. Dunn & MacRay (eds.), *Calender of the Clarendon State Papers*, 5 vols. (Oxford: Clarendon Press 1876), vol II, p. 29, where Clarendon quotes from a letter from Inchiquin to Ormonde: 'Cromwell's army are said to be exceedingly afraid; the prevention of the bridge which Cromwell is building in order to avoid fighting, would be the greatest service that could be done, except the beating him.'

23   Abbott, *Writings and Speeches*, vol. II, pp. 154–55.

24   MS in the Royal Irish Academy, Dublin, quoted in Murphy, *Cromwell in Ireland*, p. 204.

25   Oliver Cromwell to Richard Mayor, 13 November 1649; reproduced in full in Abbott, *Writings and Speeches*, vol. II, pp. 159–60.

26   *Aphorismical Discovery*, vol. II, p. 62; from Murphy, *Cromwell in Ireland*, p. 132. Murphy says that the author of *Aphorismical Discovery* was none other than O'Neill's secretary.

27   Ibid.

28   Murphy, *Cromwell in Ireland*, p. 130.

29   Reproduced in full in Murphy, *Cromwell in Ireland*, pp. 381–82. See also O'Neill's genealogy, pp. 376–80.

30   Original in *Tanner MSS*, *A Letter from the Right Honourable the Lord Lieutenant of Ireland*, printed in *Severall Proceedings*, 7–14 December 1649; also in Gilbert, *Contemporary History*, vol. II, p. 324; Abbott, *Writings and Speeches*, p. 173.

31   Cromwell to Lenthall, 14 November 1649; in Gardiner, *History of the Commonwealth and the Protectorate*, p. 141.

32   Cromwell to Lenthall, 19 December 1649, from *Severall Proceedings*, 4–11 January 1649, copy in the *House of Lords MSS*; also in Gilbert, *Contemporary History*, vol. II, p. 468; Abbott, *Writings and Speeches*, p. 176.

33   Cromwell to Lenthall, ibid. I have heard a story that Cromwell himself was actually buried near Waterford. This legend probably arose from the death and burial of his namesake, Major Oliver Cromwell, somewhere in the area.

34   In Abbott, *Writings and Speeches*, vol. II, p. 175.

35 The calender year in 1649 in England actually started on 25 March. The calender of Pope Gregory XIII, which came into force in 1582, was not adopted in England until 1743.

36 Murphy, *Cromwell in Ireland*, p. 245.

37 Gardiner, *History of the Commonwealth and the Protectorate*, pp. 147–48.

38 *Severall Proceedings*, 8 February 1650; Abbott, *Writings and Speeches*, vol. II, p. 207.

39 MS in the Royal Irish Academy; reproduced in Murphy, *Cromwell in Ireland*, p. 256.

40 Abbott, *Writings and Speeches*, vol. II, p. 209; Murphy, *Cromwell in Ireland*, pp. 256–57.

41 Murphy, *Cromwell in Ireland*, p. 261.

42 Ibid., p. 269. Ormonde's mother was married after her husband's death in 1619, to George Matthews. Abbott, *Writings and Speeches*, vol. II, p. 216.

43 Gardiner, *History of the Commonwealth and the Protectorate*, p. 153.

44 Captain Tickle to Cromwell in The Carte Manuscripts' Collection, XXVI, quoted in Murphy, *Cromwell in Ireland*, pp. 293–94. Tickle writes: 'If your Excellency will draw before this town, I shall send a messenger unto you upon your first approach, and shall give you an account of the weakest part of the town and the force within exactly, and what else I shall find, or you may direct me to be most necessary for you.'

45 The *Articles of Agreement* between the Commissioners of Kilkenny and Cromwell are reproduced in full in Abbott, *Writings and Speeches*, vol. II, p. 229; also in Murphy, *Cromwell in Ireland*, pp. 307–08.

46 Murphy, *Cromwell in Ireland*, p. 324. 'The brave Bishop was abandoned to the fury of the soldiers. His arms were first severed from his body, he was then dragged along the ground to a tree close by, and hanged from one of its branches with the reins of his own horse.'

47 Cromwell to Lenthall, 2 April 1650. This letter was read in the Commons on 13 April 1650, also printed in *Severall Proceedings*, 13 April 1650 and is reproduced in full in Abbott, *Writings and Speeches*, p. 234.

48 *Calender of State Papers* (1650), p. 62, from a letter sent by Jenkin Lloyd, Cromwell's chaplain; from Abbott, *Writings and Speeches*, vol. II, p. 237.

49 In Carte *Original Letters*, vol. II, p. 426; in Abbott, *Writings and Speeches*, vol. II, p. 239.

50 In Abbott, *Writings and Speeches*, vol. II, p. 249, the pass is reproduced in full. From Gilbert, *Contemporary History*, vol. II, p. 410, and from The Carte Manuscripts' Collection, vol. XXVII, p. 339.

51 Gardiner, *History of the Commonwealth and the Protectorate*, p. 154.

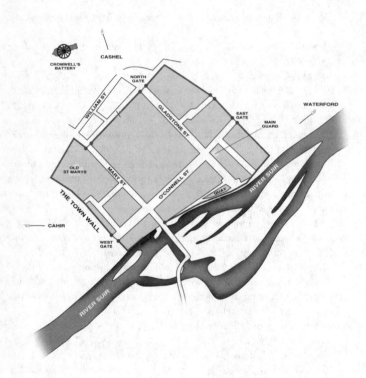

THE TOWN OF CLONMEL
AS IT WAS DURING
THE CROMWELLIAN OCCUPATION

CROMWELL'S BATTERY

CASHEL

NORTH GATE

WILLIAM ST

GLADSTONE ST

EAST GATE

MAIN GUARD

WATERFORD

OLD ST MARYS

MARY ST

O'CONNELL ST

QUAY

RIVER SUIR

THE TOWN WALL

CAHIR

WEST GATE

QUAY

RIVER SUIR

RIVER SUIR

N
W — E
S

Chapter Seven

CLONMEL

'the inhabitants of the said town shall be protected'
(Cromwell's pledge to the citizens of Clonmel)

RECENTLY AN ALTERCATION erupted in a pub in Clonmel between two locals. No doubt the subject was trivial and intoxicants were to blame. The two men squared up to each other across a congested and bemused assembly in a smoke-filled lounge and began to exchange insults. The confrontation ended when a bewildered expression came over the face of one of them. He could suddenly find no response to the most recent aspersion that had just been hurled at him: 'Ah sure you're only a Puller anyway.' A 'Puller' was a local term of derision in the area that had emanated from Cromwell's visit to Clonmel in May 1650. Local tradition has survived that tells stories of inhabitants in the region who had sided with Parliament helping to pull the big cannons from Fethard to Clonmel in preparation for the battle. Needless to say, if one were to be labelled a 'Puller' in Clonmel today, it would not be intended as a compliment.[1]

The story of Cromwell in Ireland has so far been painfully bereft of a Royalist hero. The concluding dispute for an Irish garrison would finally serve up a champion of the Irish Royalist cause, a man whose roots were deep in the heart of Celtic Ulster under that celebrated name of O'Neill. Hugh Dubh, who was a nephew of Eoghan Ruadh, was about fifty years of age at the time of the siege of Clonmel and had spent sixteen years under the command of his distinguished uncle in

European fields. During this time he was involved in one of the great examples of siege warfare of his day, the battle of Arras. Here he learned his trade well, and these Continental experiences would not go amiss when it came to the defending of Clonmel.

Situated on the north bank of the River Suir on the fringe of the Golden Vale, under the shadow of Slievenamon, is the picturesque Norman town of Clonmel. This urban district is also credited as having Viking beginnings. Unlike other towns such as Waterford, Wexford or even Dublin, where significant Viking settlements have been unearthed in excavations, to date the Clonmel earth has turned up no such finds.[2] Two explanations for the town's name have been suggested. Popular tradition ascribes its derivation to medieval Gaelic writers who adopted the term 'Cluain Meala' (the meadow of honey). The second origin for the appellation is deduced from Norman state papers of the thirteenth century which refer to 'Clumell' (1215), 'Clomele' (1243) and 'Clomeil' (1291).[3] The term 'Cliu' meaning property or territory, the area therefore being the property of Mel, which would lead to the conclusion that the name is personal in origin. Mal Lane (which existed up to this century and is now called Hopkins Lane) was a trace of Mel, who was purported to have been the wife of Crimthan, King of the Uí Cinnselagh of the Celtic tribe known as the 'Deisi'.[4]

The town today still retains much of its medieval fabric, in particular significant portions of the town wall including various well-preserved towers. The area surrounding St Mary's Church of Ireland in the north-western corner of the medieval enclosure is still encompassed by the original walls and towers. These remains are well maintained by an enlightened Corporation and are fully accessible to visitors, having recently being separated from the church grounds in the form of a charming public right-of-way. Recent excavations on the site of the old Franciscan Friary near the river have revealed significant remains of river walls to be still extant, albeit well below modern day ground level. Goubet's 1690 map of the town depicts an elegant walled fortress, situated north of the river, containing four gates: West Gate, North Gate, East Gate and the southern Bridge Gate.[5] The southern face was fortified by the natural rush of the Suir, over which there was a single bridge leading from the southern gate. The present West Gate, while being a marvellous feature of today's Main Street, is not medieval and dates back to the last century. Even so, its survival is primarily due to the active endeavours of the local historical society.[6] The walls rose to a height of twenty to thirty feet, and the area practically formed a parallelogram, its sides being approximately 500 by 400 yards in length. With regard to these Norman boundaries, earlier this century a local historian by the name of Lyons threw the locals into confusion by declaring his version of the actual line of the town walls.[7] The breach that was made by Cromwell on the north wall was so large that significant amounts disappeared without trace. (The position of the breach would appear to have been near the entrance to the present day Marian Court retirement home in Morton Street.) Lyons had the town walls running along the south side of William Street and the North Gate sited at the junction with Catherine Street.[8] In the intervening years and with the absence of any excavations ever having taken place there, the path of the fortifications became unclear. Leahy's map of 1832 can easily refute the allegations of Mr Lyons.[9] This means that a plaque commemorating the siege, currently situated at the junction of Upper Gladstone Street with Catherine Street, is erroneously placed. It cites that the North Gate was in the immediate vicinity, implying that the breach was therefore somewhere along William Street. The North Gate was actually located further south on Gladstone Street, below the junction with Morton Street.[10] The westerly line of the walls ran along the rear gardens of the houses in the latter street.[11] Gladstone Street, which was originally called Lough Street, was for many years after the siege called Breech Street.[12]

The distinguished 'Main Guard' which was erected about 1800 and designed by Sir Richard Morrison, occupies the focus of attention in the centre of this most appealing town.[13] This architectural gem, the former seat of the Palatinate government of Tipperary, is also known as the Tholsel and was in use as a courthouse for centuries. Many of Clonmel's older buildings are today refurbished and are tastefully incorporated into the modern streetscapes. As many of its streets are now pedestrianised and numerous curious lanes run down to the river, with the elevated Comeragh foothills in the background, Clonmel has a fascinating allure.

When the new planters of Ulster were in full flight for their lives from the out-of-control Celtic Irish in 1641, Clonmel, like Wexford, sided firmly with the Irish. With the development of the mechanism of government in the shape of the Catholic Confederacy, the town proclaimed its support for that body and the King and were rewarded with possession of the old churches to the local Catholic population, which were in the majority.[14] By April 1650, with the Roundheads having captured the smaller outposts surrounding the town, and the taking of the nearby towns of Kilkenny, Cahir, Cashel, Ardfinnan and Fethard, the siege of an isolated Clonmel was well under way before Cromwell even got there.

Hugh Dubh (Black Hugh) was so called since he was born in the Spanish Netherlands and was of sallow complexion. He was the son of Art Óg (Young Art) O'Neill, brother of Eoghan Ruadh (Red Owen). He followed his uncle to Ireland in 1642, was captured at the battle of Clones in 1643, but was released by exchange after the battle of Benburb in 1646.[15] He was then appointed Major General of the Ulster army by Eoghan Ruadh. He was an obvious choice to succeed his uncle as supreme commander of the Ulster forces, but the election of Bishop McMahon had put paid to his chances of achieving that position. He had arrived at Clonmel in December 1649 under Ormonde's instructions to garrison the location in anticipation of a siege by Cromwell. His troops were primarily Cavan and Tyrone men. Rinuccini described the resilient Northerners as being 'accustomed to suffering and hardened to the cold of the northern climate, having few wants and fewer wishes, living on milk and butter, and who were more careful of their swords and muskets than of their own bodies'.[16]

On 10 December, having settled into his new role as defender of Clonmel, O'Neill wrote to Ormonde asking to be appointed governor, thereby having total control over the town.[17] His request was granted. Insufficiently supplied with arms, particularly gunpowder, he began the ineffectual process of appealing to Ormonde for replenishment of his armoury, but his efforts were constantly in vain.[18] The Parliamentarian Axtell's dragoons were in the neighbourhood by February, and O'Neill made an urgent request to Ormonde for assistance. He was very aware that the menacing Ironsides were now close to besieging his bastion, since other fortresses were falling to them by the day. It was only a matter of time before the seemingly invincible Puritan commander would arrive himself before the walls of Clonmel:

> May it please your Excellencie.
>
> This day received your letter of the 25th of this instant. Since my last letter to your Excie. I have not to intymate more then that Cahir was yealded without shott or blowe, upon what condicons I know not, which I believe your

Excie. Knows ere nowe, likewise Kilteenan was beseedged eare yesternight and yealded yesterday morninge about nyne of the clocke. All their armye is within a myle to the towne and the rest are cominge to them, in great hast they have sent a number of horses and oxen for more cannons. Wee expect nothinge else but bee besieged every houre, they having no other place to ayme att but this. Your Excie. May know in what condicon wee are and the consequence of this place to the Kingdom which receives a speedye succour all which I humbly refer to your Lordshipp's grave consideracon I humbly take leave and remayne.

Your Excie's most humble servt. Hugo O'Neill

Clonmel ultimo February [19]

The grip that the 1649–50 winter had had on the country was loosening. It was that optimistic time of the year when plants and shrubbery were again returning to life. Daylight was stretching further into the evenings and the icy chill began to disappear from the air. O'Neill had no constructive reason to be optimistic, but his years of Continental seasoning in the art of siege warfare was the ace that he had up his sleeve. His garrison comprised of 1,500 of his own men and about 100 on horseback under a Major Fennell. The townsmen were also on his side and the mayor, John White, assisted O'Neill with the preparations for the defence of the town. On Saturday, 27 April, Cromwell himself appeared on the hill at the north side of the town, having made the short journey from Fethard. The text of his summons to the town to surrender can only be conjectured, since no copy has survived.[20] O'Neill's response was that unless he was reduced to a weaker position, then he had no intentions of delivering the town to his enemy, and so saying, he dared Cromwell to take his best shot.[21] The big guns were then planted on the prominent ground of Gallows Hill overlooking the town from the north side. Due to the height of the terrain it was actually possible for the attackers to see beyond the walls and into the town. There was no sense in making an assault from either the east or the west due to marshy ground, and the south side contained the current of the river as protection. Cromwell chose the north side since the topography was quite suitable for the work in which he would be engaged.

When Cromwell had first arrived in Ireland his plan was to waste no time in capturing whatever garrisons that he could with the least expense possible in terms of men and munitions. Siege warfare was not an inexpensive activity in financial terms, to say nothing of human losses. Drogheda was assailed after two days of battery, and it was only when he got to Ross in October that Cromwell's momentum had abated somewhat. In six weeks he had secured the entire eastern and southern coasts as far as Waterford. His campaign was now nearly at an end, and he knew it. Clonmel, while on the face of it not the most formidable garrison that he had ever encountered, was definitely the most opportunistic. Despite many Parliamentarian assaults on their walls, none was successful. O'Neill proved to be an expert military guardian. Aston had complained at Drogheda that the surrounding countryside was totally unsuitable for sallies from the town. O'Neill had no such complaints. With the aid of local guides and scouts, he soon introduced highly successful sally tactics in an area that was most conducive to such operations. When Cromwell was least expecting it, O'Neill's Ulstermen would regularly advance from the town to terrorise the weakest section of the Ironsides camp, instantly returning through the town gates with almost no losses. In this way he is alleged to have been successful to the tune of 200, 300, and some days even 500 of Cromwell's men.[22] Although he was inadequately supplied with provisions and ammunition, O'Neill made the best from a bad lot, but his best was assuredly still to come.

The Roundhead army was by now riddled with disease and they seemed much less polished then those forces that had travelled with their commander from England, in August the previous year. The author of the *Aphorismical Discovery* alleges that Cromwell had conspired a deal with Fennell so that he would betray the town to the Puritans.[23] However, O'Neill was suspicious of his subordinate and decided to visit the various posts of the garrison himself one night. When he arrived at a gate that was guarded entirely with Fennell's men, he smelled a rat and dismissed the troops. He replaced them with Ulstermen and proceeded with Fennell's treacherous act. Five hundred Parliamentarians were admitted into the town and immediately slaughtered by a waiting army as the attempted sabotage was quickly foiled by a reciprocal conspiracy. No other contemporary source confirms this story, however. Cromwell summoned Broghill and his company to meet him at Clonmel in order that the town could be taken with no further ado. The force that now sat down in front of the walls of Clonmel consisted of approximately 14,000 men. At length the breach was deemed assaultable again.

The actual date of the storming of Clonmel is not clear from contemporary records. Many secondary sources ascribe it as being 17 May.[24] Whatever the precise day was, O'Neill was ready. Having held out for months with the presence of the attacking army always evident in the surrounding countryside, O'Neill's ace was now to be played. He guessed (correctly) that an attempt would be made on the walls the following day after the breach was made large enough for a full scale assault. It was a case of 'All hands on deck' for the defenders as he employed all available men and women at the breached walls in order to execute his plan. Immediately inside the gaping walls and under the cover of darkness, the frantic occupants of the town fashioned an artificial cul-de-sac from mud, stones and timber: anything that they could find. He constructed a pound about eighty yards long on both sides up from the breach. At the end of the fabricated lane he had a large ditch dug and above it, he erected two cannons hidden from view, directly facing the hole in the wall. As morning drew closer, he assembled his men and instructed them well. They were lined alongside the makeshift barriers and armed with swords, scythes, pikes and muskets and instructed to maintain a steady barrage on all those who would enter the breach. The cannons at the end of the lane above the great hole were loaded with chain-shot which would impact at about waist height. The surrounding houses were also kitted out for battle as the strategic position of the windows overlooked the entire area.[25] The Royalists of Clonmel were ready.

Cromwell had no knowledge of the activity that had occurred during the night. His view into the town at that point was obstructed by the walls. At about eight o'clock in the morning, he gave the order to storm. The Roundheads poured into the lane with no riposte from the garrison. In they came, thick and fast, fully expecting hand-to-hand confrontation. It is traditionally said that when those in front could progress no further, they cried out to those behind to 'Halt! Halt!' Those behind, assuming that those at the front were calling after the retreating Royalists, enthusiastically shouted 'Advance! Advance!' Soon the lane was thronged with about 1,000 trapped Roundheads, with nowhere to run. Things began to happen very quickly, giving them no opportunity to alter their position. The breach was suddenly filled by O'Neill's men who had been waiting in the wings, thus repulsing those still entering. Those already inside were now cut off from both ends. Then it happened. O'Neill gave the order to open fire. The ensuing scene must have been mayhem. Pikes, scythes and swords suddenly appeared from nowhere and hacked at those packed bodies in the lane. The two guns at the end began cutting holes in the wall of human flesh that was in the line of fire. Bodies fell in their hundreds, most of them horribly mutilated. None of the attackers survived the assault. Cromwell had badly underestimated the capability of his Spanish-Irish counterpart. At this time he is alleged to have been outside the North Gate on horseback, waiting for the gates to open. Having realised that his men were beaten back, he returned to them and tried to rally them a second time.

O'Neill had made his mark. The awesome power of the New Model Army was finally beginning to waver. Cromwell's foot soldiers refused to advance a second time. He then implored the cavalry to attempt another attack. A Colonel Charles Langley immediately agreed to mobilise his regiment, as did Colonel Sankey. The daring Puritan horse soldiers dismounted and assembled on foot for an assault on the breach. Langley led the charge. At the breach they had more success than the first attempt as they were better prepared and knew where the Royalists were positioned. In his attempt to scale the broken defences, Langley's hand was cut off by the swift movement of a defender's scythe. (Langley afterwards settled at Coalbrook, Ballingarry, and had a steel hand fashioned in order for him to see out the rest of his days capably. The hand is reputed to have been preserved by his family up to the 1920s).[26] In an attempt to secure the town once and for all, Cromwell ordered hoards of troops to assail the walls. O'Neill's forces, however, were more than equal to the task. With the advantage of the ditch, the contrived lane and the hidden cannons, hundreds of Parliamentarians were ruthlessly cut down as they tried to enter. For hours the battle raged and eventually Cromwell realised that God had not blessed his attempt to take Clonmel. He ordered a retreat. O'Neill and his troops must have fought like men possessed. Finally the tables had turned. Death and destruction was now consuming the might and authority of the Puritan army. Never before had Cromwell or his men experienced such competent defiance. Never before had Cromwell been defeated in battle, never mind on such a scale. Cromwell ordered the trumpeter to sound the retreat.

There is a legend that Cromwell found a coarse silver bullet in the ground at this point, the implication being that he knew that O'Neill

was now reduced to smelting every available metal in the town for use
in their guns. This would mean that his ammunition must nearly have
been spent.[27] Whatever about the story, the truth is that O'Neill's
mammoth efforts had virtually exhausted the entire garrison. Provisions were practically wiped out, and many of the defenders were now
injured. The day was almost at an end. It was to be Cromwell's worst
day in battle in his entire career. He evacuated the area immediately
outside the walls and returned to the safe distance of the camp with the
remainder of his forces. Despite the disastrous attempt to take the town
by force, he resolved to remain in the area and maintain the siege. The
town was completely cut off from the arrival of any relief in the shape
of reinforcements or supplies, and it could only be a matter of time
before they would have to capitulate.

Night fell and the midnight hour had just passed when Cromwell
was advised that a delegation from the town was now seeking a parley.
John White, the mayor, was head of the group, and his plan was to
negotiate conditions of surrender for the town at all costs. Cromwell
jumped at the chance to acquire the town with no further bloodshed
and quickly agreed articles with the municipal authorities. The story
goes that before and during the negotiations Cromwell did not specif-
ically ask if O'Neill were aware of the mayor's decision to talk. His
impetuosity to gain the garrison obviously clouded his overall perception of the prevailing circumstances. The mayor had achieved his conditions and the surrender was signed and sealed by both parties. It was
only afterwards when Cromwell asked the mayor if O'Neill knew that
he had come out for discussions that he learned of the major deception
in which he had now been caught.[28] O'Neill and his army were by this
time some twelve miles away and heading south for Waterford. They
had sneaked out through the southern gate unnoticed, their work at
Clonmel now complete. They were in no position to fight on and so
they chose instead to fight another day. Cromwell is believed to have
been infuriated. He had just agreed conditions with a place that had
proved more than his military equal. Two thousand Roundheads had
been killed.[29] Defeat was something new for him and his troops. No
doubt they expected to exact full retribution on all officers of the
defending force when they would enter the town after agreeing terms.
In such a circumstance, it is a matter of some conjecture exactly what
Cromwell had intended to do with the armed defenders if we believe
that he had signed an agreement under the illusion that they were still

present in the town. We will never know, since O'Neill had absconded so cunningly under the cover of darkness. We certainly know that despite his alleged fury, he adhered to his bargain and fully respected the conditions that had been drawn up. This leniency towards a garrison that had been the most obstinate he had ever encountered is not something that would have been expected from the systematic killer of vast amounts of defenceless Irish civilians.

Once again and for the final time, Ormonde's inability to acquit himself militarily by assisting in the attack on Clonmel was made apparent. By this time he had scant power over his reduced forces, who were still as disjointed as they had ever been. O'Neill not long later found himself as the governor of Limerick, once again defending an Irish town against the forces of Parliament. This time it was Cromwell's successor and son-in-law Ireton who would be his chief opponent. He would keep the attackers at bay from June to October 1651. His defence of Limerick would have been comparable to that of Clonmel had not the plague-infested city been betrayed to Parliament. When he was captured his sentence was death. On 30 October in a letter to one of Ireton's officers he would declare that he had no apology to offer following the battle at Clonmel. He would insist that he had not been guilty of any 'base or dishonourable act, having only discharged the duty of a soldier as became a man subject to a superior power to which I must have been accountable'[30] In January 1652 he would be transported to London to be imprisoned in the Tower. One of his fellow passengers on the ship across the Irish sea would be Ireton, whose embalmed body would lie in a coffin in the hold. Ireton had fallen victim to the deadly disease and died at Limerick.[31] Incredibly, O'Neill would be released from the clutches of the Commonwealth in an effort by them to maintain friendly relations with Spain in 1653. Seven years later, around the time of the Restoration, his cousin, another Hugh O'Neill, grandson of the great Hugh, would die, leaving Hugh Dubh to inherit the acclaimed title of Earl of Tyrone.[32]

The conditions that were signed that night had definitely included the departed garrison as being involved in the agreement. However, they were signed and sealed by the Puritan commander and Mayor White. They are as follows:

> Articles between the Lord Lieutenant and the inhabitants of
> Clonmel touching the rendition thereof, May the 18th 1650

It is granted and agreed by and betwixt the Lord Lieutenant General Cromwell on the one part, and Mr.
Michael White[33] and Mr Nicholas Betts, commissioners
instructed in the behalf of the town and garrison of Clonmel on the other part as follows;

1st That the said town and garrison of Clonmel, with the
arms ammunition and other furniture of war that are now
therein shall be surrendered and delivered up into the
hands of his Excellency, the Lord Lieutenant by eight o
clock this morning.

2nd That in consideration thereof the inhabitants of the
said town shall be protected as to their lives and estates,
from all plunder and violence of the soldiery, and shall have
the same right, liberty and protection as other subjects
under the authority of the Parliament of England have, or
ought to have or enjoy within the dominion of Ireland.[34]

Most of the colourful stories relating to the battle of Clonmel are to
be found in *History of the Warr in Ireland from 1641 to 1653* written by
the unnamed officer in the regiment of Sir John Clotworthy. We can
say with some authority that the same writer is prone to substantial
exaggeration. We have already examined the authenticity of his contribution when discussing Drogheda. Clotworthy's regiment was not
employed at Clonmel, yet typically, the anonymous soldier's account of
the war, although he is seldom an actual eyewitness, is frequently used
to describe the events. The commentary must be cautiously treated for
the reasons mentioned earlier, even though it is particularly com-
pelling. The narrative, therefore, was written thirty-five years after the
actual events, its author being converted to the Royal cause by that
time. (see Appendix No. 7.1).

In the report the writer furnishes us with elaborate detail concerning the taking of Clonmel, including a conversation between the
mayor and Cromwell which has quite a charming ring to it. Cromwell
asks the mayor why he did not tell him that O'Neill had left the town
without his permission, to which the mayor replied that Cromwell did
not ask him. The writer, while not an eyewitness to the events, paints
quite a picture of O'Neill's successful deception, the essence of which
must be true. Bulstrode Whitelocke in his account of the Irish and

English military campaigns, posthumously published in 1682, records a letter that he had been sent from Clonmel dated 19 May 1650, describing the battle:

> This day [19th May] we entered Clonmel, which was quit by the enemy the last night, after a tedious storm which continued four hours. Our men kept close to the breach, which they had entered, all the time, save only one accidental retreat in the storm. We lost in this storm Colonel Cullum and some other officers with divers private soldiers, and others wounded.
>
> The enemy had made many great preparations within by a transverse or crosswork; and to beat our men off as they entered; but afterwards many of them stole out of the town, and left some few with the inhabitants, to make conditions. In the morning our forces pursued and killed all they could light upon. From Clonmel we heard that Colonel Reynolds is waiting upon the motions of [Lord] Castlehaven with 1,500 horse and dragoons.[35]

Whitelocke himself adds 'that they found in Clonmel the stoutest enemy that ever was found by the army in Ireland, and that there was never seen so hot a storm of so long continuance, and so gallantly defended, neither in England nor Ireland'.[36]

Dr George Bate also wrote an account of Clonmel that reads as follows:

> Next upon the stage of war succeeds Clonmel, a considerable well peopled town and walled round, lying upon the Suir four leagues from Waterford. This place was defended by Hugh Boy O'Neill with a garrison of two thousand foot and a hundred horse; whose reputation was much heightened by his pains and assiduity as having caused considerable works to be made for the security of the place. Hither does Cromwell now convert the stress of the war; and having encamped and strongly entrenched himself, he sends two thousand five hundred horse under the command of Colonel Reynolds and Theophilous Jones, the brother of the late Jones, to hinder the Lord

Lieutenant's levies and to reduce towns everywhere as occasions did present.

In the meantime the siege of Clonmel is carried on, and though the garrison bravely defended it, and had beat off the enemy in a fierce assault, with the loss of Colonel Culham, and many others; yet fearing that since there was no hope of relief, that they would at length fall as sacrifices, under the bloody hands of Cromwell, packing up bag and baggage, about midnight they desert the town and secure themselves by flight. The Mayor and townspeople, destitute of defence, without mentioning the departure of the garrison, desire a cessation and parley; and upon condition of saving their houses from being plundered and of liberty of living as they had formerly done, they very willingly open their gates.

But in the morning, discovering the trick, Cromwell was vexed and sent some troops to pursue the garrison in the rear. But they were before got out of reach, having in the night passed the hills and the most difficult ways; but the Cromwellians, overtaking many stragglers, who by reason of their wounds or hindrances, stayed behind, among them were not a few women, put them all without mercy to the sword.[37]

Bate, it seems, couldn't help himself and casually threw in the bit about defenceless women at the end, since at the time he was writing, it was fashionable to display antipathy towards 'that plague of England, the late Usurper Oliver Cromwell'. He was never at Clonmel, nor had he any reasons, other than those that are malicious, to include those otherwise incriminating words in his account.

An account in *Severall Proccedings* in Parliament, dated 23 May to 6 June, is asserted to be the words of Cromwell by some observers:

Yesterday we stormed Clonmel, to which work both officers and soldiers did as much and more than could be expected. We had with our guns made a breach in their works, where after a hot fight we gave back a while; but presently charged up to the same ground again. But the enemy had made themselves exceeding strong, by double works and transverse, which were worse to enter than the breach; when we came up to it they had cross-works, and were strongly flanked from the houses from within their works, the enemy defended themselves against us that day, until towards the evening our men all the while keeping up close to their breach; and many on both sides were slain. At night the enemy drew out the other side, and marched away undiscovered to us, and the inhabitants of Clonmel sent out for a parley. Upon which articles were agreed on before we knew the enemy was gone. After the signing of the conditions we discovered the enemy to be gone, and very early this morning pursued them, and fell upon their rear of stragglers, and killed above 200 besides those we slew in the storm. And of our party we had slain, Colonel Cullum, Capt. Jordan, Capt. Humphrys, and some others are wounded. We entered Clonmel this morning, and have kept our conditions with them; the place is considerable, and very advantageous to the reducing of these parts wholly to the Parliament of England.[38]

Ludlow in his *Memoirs* also gives a brief account of the siege:

Youghal, Cork and Kinsale were delivered to the forces of the Parliament by the contrivance and diligence of some officers and well affected persons in those places; and thereupon the Lieutenant General sent a detachment under the Lord Broghill to their assistance in case anything should be attempted by Inchiquin, or any other to their disturbance; whilst he with the rest of the army marched towards Clonmel. Being upon his march thither, he was met by the Corporation of Feather [Fethard] with a tender of their submission, wherewith the Lieutenant General was so satisfied, the army being far advanced into the enemy's quarters, and having no place of refreshment, that he promised to maintain them in the enjoyment of their privileges. Having left our sick men here, he marched and sat down before Clonmel, one side of which was secured by a river and the rest of the town encompassed with a wall, that was well furnished with men to defend it. Our guns having made a breach in the wall, a detachment of our men was ordered to storm, but the enemy, by the means of some houses that stood near, and earthworks cast up within the wall, made good their breach, till night parted their dispute, when the enemy perceiving ours resolved to reduce the place, beat a parley and sent out commissioners to treat. Articles were agreed and signed on both sides, whereby it was concluded that the town with all the arms and ammunition therein should be delivered up the next morning to such of our forces as should be appointed to receive the same. After this agreement was agreed and signed the General was informed that Colonel Hugh O'Neal governor of the place, with all the garrison, had marched out at the beginning of the night towards Waterford, before the commissioners came out to treat. It something troubled the commanders to be thus over reached; but conditions being granted, they thought it their duty to keep them with the town.[39]

Murphy, in his own inimitable style, tells us that while there is not a lot of documentation concerning the immediate aftermath of the taking of Clonmel, there are always the dissertations of later clerics.[40] In an extract from *Hibernia Dominicana*, he describes (with the absence of contemporary sources) what he calls 'the deaths of two holy priests of the order [Dominican] at this time':

Father James O'Reilly was a learned theologian, an eloquent preacher and a famous poet. He had been sent a short time from Waterford to Clonmel, to train the youth of the town in polite learning and in the Christian doctrine. When the garrison abandoned the town, he too sought safety in flight. Not knowing whither the road led, he wandered about and fell in with a troop of Puritan cavalry. They asked him who he was. He replied fearlessly: "I am a Priest and a religieux, albeit an unworthy one, of the order of St. Dominic. I have lost my way and while trying to escape you, I have fallen into your hands. I am a member of the Roman Catholic Apostolic Church. So have I lived, and so will I die. May God's will be done." The soldiers fell on him and covered him with wounds. For a whole hour he lay weltering in his blood; he did not cease to invoke the holy names of Jesus and Mary, and to beseech his patron saints to aid him in his last struggle. At length, exhausted by his numerous wounds, the holy martyr gave up his soul.

Father Myler Magrath was put to death after the capture of the town. He came to Clonmel to give the consolations of religion to those who should need them. He was seized while engaged in his holy work by the bedside of a sick man. The governor's satellites hurried him off to their master's presence. His trial was a brief one. He was condemned to death and hanged immediately after.[41]

Clonmel was now Cromwell's. O'Neill's actions did not prevent the inevitable; it merely postponed it. However, as an operation of defending a besieged town, it is easily the most successful that the Irish had yet attempted. The only other significant Irish victory of the period was the battle of Benburb (before Cromwell entered the country), which was also presided over by an O'Neill of Ulster. Cromwell ploughed his way through the Irish countryside with virtually little or no opposition. In order for the Irish Royalists to have stood a chance against him, it would have been necessary for him to have been confronted with other enterprising officers like O'Neill in this conflict. Alas, this was not to be the case. Ireland was both a divided and a poor country. England was neither impoverished nor was it disorganised. Cromwell had the full backing of his government in London and use of that body's opulent treasury. From time to time in Ireland he had complained of lack of supplies and the need for reinforcements, all of which he eventually acquired, never to be left without. On the other hand Ormonde's divided forces had no such competent governmental administrators, nor did they have access to the financial resources that would have been necessary for conducting a cohesive defence of the country. One of Ormonde's biggest problems was supplying his army, which was to have enormous implications, particularly during Cromwell's Munster campaign. When these two forces had entered into this conflict, there was always only going to be one outcome. The rebel English Parliament, who had chopped the head from their King and seized power, were clearly too strong for the disjointed Irish Royalists. One wonders what effect, if any, an Irish army under Ormonde would have had on English soil in defence of their King. Ormonde may have been in command of the Irish forces in name, but in reality, it was they that commanded him. The apprehension that

Parliament had previously entertained of an accomplished Irish force attempting an attack on England seems now to have been a very questionable proposition. That army was always going to be made up of men who professed a mixture of religions and who had only the unappreciative monarchy as their unconvincing common affinity. Religious jealousies and ethnic tensions would have pervaded its ranks particularly on foreign soil, as indeed happened on home ground. Its greatest potential leader, Eoghan Ruadh O'Neill, was always going to die, such was the inevitability of his fatal ailment. Ormonde, as the King's Viceroy in Ireland, who was far from being militarily gifted, would have been the supreme leader of such a force. The result would almost certainly have been a defeat for the Royal Irish.

During his nine months in Ireland Cromwell's health was generally bad. It had reached its worst point when at Ross he was confined to his bed. As he said himself, 'I have been crazy in my health but the Lord is pleased to sustain me.'.[42] It was not a period in which to fall ill casually, as hundreds of thousands of Irish citizens were dying across a countryside that was ruined with plague and war. His recovery, he no doubt saw as being the divine will, and this time, the remedial, intercession of God. He obviously determined that the Almighty had intervened to preserve his life in order for him to fulfill his mission. Cromwell was now fifty-one years of age and an individual who had been described as hypochondriacal in his youth; the rabid conditions of the hills and bogs of Ireland were no place for the frail or the emaciated. He had spent many nights and days exposed to the extreme Irish climate while travelling from one town to the next, many of which he had camped outside for some time. In a time when life expectancy was not a lot more than his present age, it has been suggested that the decline in his health, which would eventually lead to his death eight years later, began in Ireland.

Despite his personal health concerns, Cromwell's reputation had now assumed enormous proportions. His successes at Marston Moor and Naseby were now eclipsed by his conquest of Ireland. He nominated Ireton as his successor and made plans to leave immediately for England. Trouble was brewing in the highlands of Scotland, and there was talk that Charles, the Prince of Wales, was now attempting to raise a Scottish force against the London administration. Charles Stuart was after all one of their kinfolk and spoke with a distinct Scottish accent. Whitelocke reports that:

. . . the news of the King's coming to Scotland became more probable than formerly, and the Scots' proceedings in the raising of new forces gave an alarm to the Parliament; and some of their members who had discoursed with the Late General Fairfax on these matters and argued how requisite it would be to send an army into Scotland, found the General wholly averse to any such thing, and by the means of his lady, a strict Presbyterian, to be more of a friend to the Scots than they; that, therefore, they thought this a fitting time to send for the Lord Lieutenant of Ireland, and the rather, his army being now drawn into winter quarters.[43]

Parliament's initial request had expected to find Cromwell still resting at Youghal. But owing to a rather temperate January he was well into the second stage of his assignment before he received the summons to return. Things were obviously now at a critical stage in England. In Ireland, Limerick, Galway and Waterford were the only garrisons of substance that had yet to be captured. With the rest of the country now under Parliament's control, those three locations never stood a chance of success. They were cut completely off from all hope of relief and eventually they too came into the possession of Parliament, to complete the conquest.

Oliver Cromwell made his way back towards Youghal through a countryside that no longer posed any threat to him. All potential hostility was virtually extinguished. On 29 May 1650, he brought his own Irish quest to a conclusion. He boarded a frigate called the *President* and set sail on the return voyage to his beloved England. He would never see Ireland again. This had been his first trip abroad, and he would never again leave mainland Britain. He left behind him a country that was bleeding badly through the ravages of warfare and widespread fever. As he sailed away from the harbour at Youghal, little did he know that by his latest actions he would be immortalised as the epitome of evil through the writing of Irish folklore in the subsequent centuries. As he took his last look at Ireland's breathtaking southern shoreline, he could not have known that this Isle of Saints and Scholars would soon wield their pens in preference to their swords, against him. They would soon exploit his actions by deprecating his image to the degenerate level of Satan himself. Despite his achievement in excluding all of the unarmed laity of the Catholic religion from the war, the pens of Irish lyricists and poets would make him personally the ultimate target of intense loathing. This perception remains, even up to the present day. While his direct involvement with Ireland was now at an end, his influence over that country would become profound over the next few years.

Cromwell reached London by 31 April, and huge crowds turned out to meet him on Hounslow Heath just to catch a glimpse of the most successful soldier in England. The welcome he received was as great as if he had brought the young Prince of Wales back with him to surrender to Parliament.[44] When he got to Hyde Park the lord mayor was eagerly awaiting his arrival, complete with the flourish of a military salute.[45] There is a tradition that when passing Tyburn one of his subordinates declared, 'What a crowd has come out to see your Lordship's triumph!' The wily Cromwell sarcastically replied, smiling, 'Yes, but if it were to see me hanged, how many more would there come?'[46] From there he retired to St James' Palace where he received countless well-wishers, both Members of Parliament and officers of the army who had come to congratulate him on his great success in Ireland. In the documented proceedings of Parliament of 4 June, his homecoming is recorded thus: 'This day Cromwell, the Parliamentary victorious general and Lord lieutenant of Ireland, took his seat in the House, give thanks in an eloquent oration for his great and faithful services unto the Parliament and Commonwealth, setting forth the great providence of God in those great and strange works which God had wrought by him as the instrument.'[47] On 11 June Cromwell was still the main centre of attention of the government as he made his final report, this time in person, about the current state of affairs in Ireland. In the proceedings of Parliament for that day, the following entry is made:

> All the members of the House having been required to give
> their attendance this day by nine in the morning, General
> Cromwell, standing up in his place in the House made a nar-
> rative of the state of the garrisons and forces of the enemy in
> Ireland and their interest there, and likewise of the Parlia-
> ment's forces in garrison and in the field and their condition,
> in what employment they were, and under what commands,
> at the end of which it was resolved – that it be referred to the
> Council of State to take care of sending such speedy supplies
> of money for Ireland as shall be necessary for the carrying

out of that work, and to see what money there is in the present view that can be made effectual for that service, and how the obstructions against bringing it may be removed; also to consider by what means the reduction and settlement of Ireland may be perfected to the best advantage and the futureage of the charge of this Commonwealth.[48]

Immediately after his return, Parliament ordered a censure of all the Royalist newspaper publications. The Lord Lieutenant of Ireland had, during the past year, been described by some of them as 'Copper nose', 'Nose Almighty' and 'The town Bull of Ely'[49] Conversely, the official Parliamentarian newsbook *Mercurius Politicus* pointed out his 'famous services in Ireland; which being added to the garland of his English victories, have crowned him, in the opinion of all the world, for one of the wisest, most accomplished of leaders, among the present and past generation'.[50]

One of the first things that Cromwell did now that he was back in London was to visit his Commander-in-Chief, Lord Fairfax, at his home in Queen Street.[51] Fairfax was still, officially, the absolute leader of the English army. Cromwell's autonomy over the Irish expedition and his exemplary credentials had not yet earned him that position. Fairfax, who had fought with and felt some loyalty to the Scots, and whose wife was a Scot and a Presbyterian, would refuse to take command of an army that would invade Scotland, despite Cromwell's overtures to him to do just that. Eventually it was Cromwell who would take up the slack that Fairfax would refuse to deal with. In order not to antagonise his superior officer, Cromwell was bestowed with the conciliatory title of 'General of the forces of the Commonwealth of England', and the Commander-in-Chief of that army stood meekly aside and resigned. In hindsight, Cromwell was the only man to whom the Scottish campaign could ever have been given. He had surpassed both his military peers and superiors in terms of achievements. Furthermore, within the domain of the Puritan regime, it seemed that God Himself had chosen him to lead the army against the Scots, such was his stature at this time. Meanwhile Edmund Ludlow was appointed Lieutenant General of the horse and Commander-in-Chief of the forces in Ireland on 2 July. He did not seem completely satisfied with the position, and it was not until the following January that he would depart from England to take up his post.

After only a month's interval Cromwell was on the battle trail again. On 28 June he departed London for Scotland. The Prince of Wales had now only the potential support of the Scots to attempt to retrieve the throne. By 22 July, Cromwell had crossed the border into Scotland. By 2 September (almost one year exactly after he had arrived at the walls of Drogheda), he found himself in a vastly inferior position at Dunbar against the Highlanders under Charles' Scottish henchman, Leslie, who had 23,000 men compared to Cromwell's 12,000. To add to his dilemma, Cromwell occupied the lower level of a narrow coastal strip, while his adversary held the high ground and, therefore, the advantage. Due to their intimate knowledge of the unpredictable terrain, the Scots had the English army well and truly trapped. The day passed and the night became windy. Cromwell's position was perilous. Yet, he, along with his officers, decided that attack would be the best form of defence. While Scots seemed content to wait overnight and attack the following day, Cromwell did not wait until morning. Well before dawn, under the cover of the blustery night sky he positioned his army so that they could assail the Scots above. The latter were by now lying horizontal on the exposed hillside, attempting to avoid the weather and trying to sleep. Only small numbers of them were ordered not to extinguish their match. Cromwell's decision to take the offensive was justified. Only three hours after he gave the order for the surprise attack, the more numerous, but less disciplined Scots were routed. Four thousand were killed, and 10,000 taken as prisoners. The Battle of Dunbar, on 3 September, 1650, would now be Cromwell's greatest military triumph to date.[52]

The following year while still in Scotland, his health would fail again. This time his indisposition would result in rumours circulating the country, and even the Continent beyond, that he was dead. Indeed this illness was more detrimental than that which he had contracted in Ireland. He became shaky through sheer weakness and it was thought that he was suffering with a gall-stone condition as well as the fluctuating debility of a fever. When he had finally recovered he would declare that God 'hath plucked me out of the grave!'[53]

The final battle between the Cavaliers and the Roundheads would be fought at Worcester the following year. The intervening year had not yielded a victory for Parliament, and the threat of the Royalists was still formidable. With Cromwell apparently striving further northwards towards Perth, the young King and Leslie saw their chance and headed southwards for an attack on England, hoping to get to London before they were challenged. With the Parliamentarian army preoccupied deep in the Scottish Highlands, the road appeared open for the Royalists to mobilise southwards. But Cromwell had purposely enticed his enemies into such a move. He wrote: 'I do apprehend that if he [Leslie] does go for England, being some few days march from us, it will trouble some men's thoughts. We have done to the best of our judgements knowing that if some issue were not put to this business, it would occasion another winter's war to the ruin of your soldiery.'[54] Cromwell immediately turned his army around and began to follow Charles as soon as he had received the intelligence of the latter's movements. Suddenly the situation escalated. The Puritans had nearly caught up with the King's army. A detachment was sent out from London to prevent Charles' progress thereto, and Cromwell sent an advance party to catch up on the Royalists as they headed southwards. Cromwell's army were now marching in the summer sunshine in their shirt sleeves (their heavy clothing and arms being carried by horses and mules that had been commandeered on the march). In this way they averaged the incredibly high mileage of twenty miles a day in pursuit of the future King. By 22 August, the latter had reached Worcester, close to the Welsh borders, now with 13,000 men. On 27 August, Cromwell was only about twenty miles away. He had reached Stratford-on-Avon, the birthplace of the great Bard (who had died only thirty-five years earlier). His army, which had now been joined by all of the Parliamentarian forces in the area as well as those from London, numbered some 28,000 men. The stage was set. On 29 August the Parliamentarians held a council of war and proposed to flush the Royalists out of the town of Worcester. It seems that since it was almost 3 September again, Cromwell delayed the start of the battle until his lucky day dawned. So it was on that very day that the Roundheads finally crushed the resistance of the Royalists. No quarter was given to the retreating Royalist army as the sheer numbers of the Parliamentarians cut down the King's men. Two thousand Royalists were killed outright, compared to only 200 Roundheads.[55] Cromwell was once again victorious and by now must have seemed invincible. He would never take to the field again.

There is a wonderful myth that surrounds Cromwell's lucky day, 3 September, and its significance with regard to the battle of Worcester. The following story, however, is a typical piece of contemporary propaganda. Before the battle he is alleged to have gone into a wooded area near the town with one of his own soldiers, a Colonel Lindsay. There they both met 'a grave elderly man with a roll of parchment in his hand'. The old man offered Cromwell a bargain with the devil, whereby he could 'have his will then, and in all things else for seven years'. Following this, Satan would then take complete control over Cromwell's soul and body. Cromwell protested that seven years was too short and that he wanted twenty-one. He pleaded for at least fourteen, but anxious as he was to reduce the Royalist threat, he agreed in the end to the term offered. He left the woods knowing that the battle was already won and he declared, 'Now Lindsay, the battle is our own, I long to be engaged.' This quaint anecdote was no doubt concocted on the basis that not long following the reduction of the Royalists at Worcester, Cromwell would become Protector and would die exactly seven years later to the day on 3 September 1658. The devil would keep his part of the deal. The story is curiously embellished by the fact that a couple of days before Cromwell died, there was a tremendous storm across England, the like of which had not been seen in years. This, in many people's eyes would be the heralding of Satan's arrival for Cromwell's soul.[56]

The war was finally over and England entered into a period of peace. The Prince of Wales, who by now was twenty-one years old, had fled to Paris and would remain in exile on the Continent for some time. Ireland, meanwhile, entered into a period of ruthless colonisation. Those English Adventurers who had invested money ten years earlier in the army for the subjugation of Ireland were now reaping the rewards of their speculation. Soldiers of the army whose pay was in arrears were being paid in kind by way of property in Ireland. All landowners in Ireland who had taken the King's side in the war were now to be relieved of their properties. That same King who would eventually regain the throne for the Stuarts would always appear to have more interest in things carnal than things Irish. Those who had taken the Royal side and did not own property had nothing to lose. The Catholic clergy would be hunted down and killed or banished and their ceremonies banned. The dislocated gentry were to be given land in the barren province of Connaught. The coastline of that area, however, was to remain under English dominion, since attacks from the sea could always have been attempted if the area were occupied with Irish right up to the western shores. European foes were to have no gateway into England from the west by this move.

By April 1653, the harmony that Cromwell had fought for by eliminating the monarchy and substituting it with the Parliamentarian government was not yet achieved. Instead of a tyrannical King, the country had to contend with a body of men who seemed more resolved to maintain their position in government than to implement the policies that would settle the nation. This Parliament would become known as the 'Rump Parliament' since it was now only made up of a small portion (or Rump) of its original membership. It had begun in November 1640 and still clung on tenaciously to its power. Cromwell was primarily an advocate of legitimacy in constitutional matters, and he pressed them on numerous occasions to call new elections. He believed that it was fundamental that Parliament must not make themselves perpetual. However, the government assembly to whom Cromwell had once displayed the utmost reverence in his letters from Ireland were gradually showing their true colours. With no King to dissolve them, they simply thought that they would pass a bill to prolong their sitting. This they thought they could do without admonition. Cromwell did not adhere to this unsavoury political Utopia, particularly when the despotic government was now highly questionable in his view. On 19 April 1653 the debate over the Bill of Elections was rescheduled for a later date since it was controversial in its substance. While the exact purpose of the bill is unclear today, historians have often interpreted the essence of the bill as essentially approving the continuation of those Parliamentary members then holding seats. Modern historians have suggested that it called for open, free and unrestricted elections. There were many implications in such a bill that had undercurrents of Royalism. Irrespective of its objectives, Cromwell's opposition to the bill is certainly apparent. In the case of unconditional elections being called, he feared that such an elected body might be antagonistic towards the Parliamentary army. He left the house content in the knowledge that the essence of the bill was to be deferred. The next day he got a message at his lodgings at Whitehall that the Chamber of the House of Commons was full and that the bill was now under debate. Parliament had broken their word and were now trying to adopt the concept contained in the act without the knowledge of Cromwell and his associates. He suddenly ran out of his house upon hearing about the assembly and flew to the Council Chambers, arriving there in casual dress and no doubt out of breath. He quickly took his seat to the astonishment of the other members. He then listened to the debate and eventually rose to his feet to speak. He gradually became more and more agitated with the men whom he had held in such high regard when they fought the war against the King. The dishevelled Cromwell strode around the Chamber calling some of them 'Whoremasters' and others 'Drunkards'. He declared, 'Perhaps you think this is not Parliamentary language. I confess it is not, neither are you to expect any such from me . . . it is not fit that you should sit as a Parliament any longer. You have sat long enough unless you had done more good.'[57] This verbal attack on men to whom he had pledged his undying loyalty and affection while in Ireland is a strange position for the Puritan commander to find himself in. He must have been exasperated in the extreme to have taken this course of action.

His next act, however, would elevate him to a position that would dominate the final years of his life. He was still in total control of the army. This was where the real power lay in seventeenth century England. Parliament's mistake had been to give him absolute authority over the forces of the Commonwealth. The army was loyal to the one man in whom they trusted implicitly. It was easy for them to detest the operations of Parliament as their leader also did the same. They were just as anxious to bring about the dissolution of Parliament yet, without total anarchy, there was no obvious resolution for them. That resolution was about to reveal itself. That day, the 20 April 1653, Oliver Cromwell stood in the hallowed chamber of the House of Commons, dressed in only a plain black overcoat and plain grey stockings, turned his head towards the door and bellowed, 'Call them in.' At this point, five or six files of musketeers from Cromwell's own regiment of foot marched menacingly into the sacred Council Chamber and took control of the proceedings. Cromwell pointed to the Speaker and shouted, 'Fetch him down.' This same Speaker was William Lenthall to whom Cromwell had addressed the bulk of his correspondence as he reported to Parliament on his Irish operations. Now he was casting him from the House in a fit of rage. Parliament had failed England, and as usual, Cromwell was the one who would put an end to a corrupt administration. He then stood at the Speaker's table and scoffed at the mace that lay there as a symbol of the Speaker's authority. 'What shall we do with this bauble?' he asked. The mace along with the paper containing the Bill of Election were then both taken by the soldiers. 'It is you that have forced me to do this,' he shouted, in response to the bewildered faces of the members, 'for I have sought the Lord night and day, that he would rather slay me than put me upon the doing of this work.' The journal of the House of Commons for 20 April 1653 has no official entry. Henry Scobell, the clerk of the House, unofficially put in his own handwriting the following words: 'This day his Excellency the Lord General dissolved this Parliament. Which was done without consent of Parliament.' A poster soon put up outside by a local wit read, 'This House is to be lett; now unfurnished.'[58] Had that particular Parliament continued to reign, England might well have been plunged into another period of turmoil.

England's difficulties did not end there. The successor of the dissolved Parliament also ended abruptly. In July Cromwell had formed this new Parliament, the members of which had been personally selected and were described as 'divers persons fearing God, and of approved fidelity and honesty'.[59] This was a Parliament that had been nominated, not elected. By December that body of men who had effectively been given the power to dictate by Cromwell failed to bond and they dissolved themselves. Although they believed in the same cause, they found themselves consistently divided. It was the farmer from Huntingdon who was now politically superior to the English government, although he held no official title in that regard. Cromwell's initial optimism upon their forming that they would effect a stabilised government was unfounded.

It was clear that England could not achieve a cohesive government since Parliamentary rule had failed again. Parliament did not enjoy the support of the majority of the electorate, so they did not dare go to the country for a government. Approximately 75 per cent of those able to vote were against them. The answer would seem to lie in the appointment of some supreme figurehead. There was too much support within their ranks for a civilian sovereignty at this point to have even considered a return of the King. Rumours had been rife in London for some time that Cromwell should have been offered that position of monarch. The army balked at the prospect. Cromwell himself was far too aware of his affiliation to the army and how much he owed his present position to their prowess. He would never have accepted that regal title. Eventually, on 16 December 1653, Oliver Cromwell was reluctantly installed as Lord Protector of England, Ireland and Scotland. A Bishop Burnet later recounted a portrayal of Cromwell's attitude to this bizarre twist in his whirlwind career in English politics:

He used to say with many tears, that he would rather have taken a shepherd's staff than the Protectorship, since nothing was more contrary to his genius than a show of greatness; but he saw that it was necessary at that time to keep the nation from falling into extreme disorder and from becoming open to the common enemy; and therefore he only stepped in between the living and the dead, as he phrased it, in that interval, till God should direct them on what bottom they ought to settle.[60]

There are many reasons for believing that Cromwell had only expected the appointment to be temporary, but he would die five years later during the second term of his Protectorate, still occupying the position of His Highness the Lord Protector. By accepting this appointment, he did not become a military dictator. He never again used the army to enforce his power, nor did he use his power to influence the army. He had found himself in a unique position of unprecedented authority. The commitments made during his administration were consistently supplemented with the advice of others in whom he had placed enormous reliance. He governed with a Council of twenty-one advisors. As he grew older he became less and less of a military man and more and more like a king. During the second period of his Protectorate, he was again offered the monarchy. This time he considered it in more detail, but eventually after having talks with the army, he declined the proposal. On two occasions he could have handed over some of his powers to an elected Parliament, in 1654 and 1656 – the first and second Protectorate Parliaments – but on both occasions Parliament refused the opportunity to acquire these Protectoral powers which they would have had a constitutional right to accept, had they chosen to do so.[61]

An analysis of the performance of the Protectorate government of 1653–58 is beyond the confines of this book. This period in England's history has been scrutinised in minute detail, and there is an abundance of written material available concerning the Puritan revolution.[62] Suffice it to say, Cromwell's ability to rule was supplemented by his logical and decisive mind. He enjoyed a successful foreign policy and he stabilised the economy. He became a great champion of religious freedom, in contrast to previous English kings. Those who could not accept the religion of the state were permitted their own religious beliefs. His policies of generous religious tolerance saw the return of the Jews to England from where they had been officially expelled as long ago as 1290. He developed the navy into a powerful international force. He reformed education and made third-level instruction available to the 'ordinaries'. He created an exciting age where scientific knowledge was encouraged and the mechanical aspects to education flourished. He systematically strove to improve the lives of the ordinary people of England through his programmes for government. He incessantly intervened to save convicted agitators of the government from the death sentence. In final recognition of his cause, it was his revolution that would eventually be the catalyst for future royal dictators to endure subordination to their Parliament.

Cromwell's place in history should never be underestimated. It was his personal involvement in the wars of the three kingdoms of England, Scotland and Ireland that ensured the continuum of Parliamentary control. The grip that the revolution had on the reins of power was always tenuous and always depended largely on military approval. That approval in turn depended on Cromwell's relationship with the army as he progressively grew in stature. When he ran to the breach in the walls of Drogheda, it was his sublime confidence that was seen by his soldiers to have won the day. It is a remarkable fact that his performances at Wexford, Marston Moor, Naseby, Dunbar and Worcester all resulted in the same outcome – wins for Parliament by an invincible commander. All of these victories contributed in no small way to the English Republic becoming a stable reality. While the name Oliver Cromwell will still conjure up obscure images of evil to anyone who has experienced the Irish educational system, his lifetime contribution to seventeenth century politics on these islands is monumental.

By the beginning of August 1658, Cromwell's health had seriously declined. In June of that year, his favourite daughter Elizabeth's son, named Oliver after his grandfather, died at the age of one year. Worse was to follow when Bettie herself died from cancer on 6 August, at the age of twenty-nine. Cromwell was devastated. He immediately collapsed and was not able to attend her funeral. He would never recover from his daughter's death. He went rapidly downhill from that time onwards. Now lodged at Hampton Court Palace, he began to take on the appearance of death to all who saw him.

By the end of August he had started to fall into fits and sweats, some of which would last for some time. The malaria that he had contracted either in Ireland or the Fens of Ely earlier in his life began to take control of his destiny. The 30 August was the night of the storm, the ferocity of which had not been seen in England for hundreds of years. On his death-bed he slipped in and out of consciousness. He is reported to have said, 'Truly God is good indeed he is, he will not leave me.' His last prayer is recounted thus:

> Lord, though I am but a miserable and wretched creature, I am in covenant with thee through grace . . . my work is done but God will be with his people. Thou hast made me, though very unworthy, a mean instrument to do them some good, and Thee service; and many of them have set too high a value on me, though others wish and would be glad of my death; Lord, however Thou do dispose of me, continue to do good for them.[63]

During the night of 2 September when offered a drink he murmured, 'It is not my design to drink or to sleep, but my design is to make what haste I can to be gone.'[64] On Friday, 3 September, he told his doctors around his bedside, who looked distressed at the prospect of his death, 'You physicians think I shall die, I tell you I shall not die this hour.'[65] He was wrong. Oliver Cromwell died later that day at three o'clock in the afternoon, at the age of fifty-nine. It was the anniversary of his two greatest battles at Dunbar and Worcester.

It is not accurate to say that the inhabitants of Drogheda and Wexford delighted at the news of Cromwell's death. The citizens of the town of Drogheda, whose allegiance was now totally to the Commonwealth, acted as though they had just lost a king. Those inhabitants were the ones that had witnessed the Protector's capture of their town from Royalist hands nine years earlier. The occupants of Wexford were little affected by Cromwell's death. They were mainly new English planters from the recent settlement. The previous citizens had either fled or were by now well transplanted. That planting policy would always endure, no matter who was at the helm in England.

While those around Cromwell had been aware of his failing health, the outside world was taken completely by surprise at the news of his death. The Royalists were stunned and did nothing for some days until they got used to the idea that he was really no more. The written constitution, otherwise known as the Humble Petition and Advice, allowed and required an existing Lord Protector to nominate his successor.

Cromwell had apparently nominated his son Richard to take over from him. This nomination was shrouded in controversy since it was during his final moments, when he was almost incoherent, that he allegedly chose Richard in preference to the more suitable Henry. Richard would prove to be a poor replacement for his father and would last only seven months and twenty-eight days as Protector. Cromwell's effigy lay in state from 18 October to 10 November at Somerset House, his body having been quickly buried at Westminster Abbey. The funeral took place on 23 November. It was an extremely elaborate affair with dignitaries and ambassadors from all over the world attending. The cortège took seven hours to wind its way through the streets of London. The route from Somerset House to Westminster was cleared of traffic throughout the day in preparation for the procession. The wax effigy was in an open chariot and was followed by thousands of mourners who wore special mourning gowns. The army lined the streets, forming a final line of inspection as the image of their great leader passed by. Their red coats were lined with black. When the funeral procession finally arrived at the Abbey on that chilly November evening, there was no ceremony. The hearse was simply installed inside above the vault that contained the real body of the dead Protector.

By 1660, Charles II was restored as King of England. The Royalists were exultant at his return. Soon those regicides and usurpers would be hunted down and put on trial for their part in the rebellion. Many members of Parliament had to flee the country to live in exile. On 29 January 1660, the Royalists decided that they wanted to display their hatred for the former Protector, and so they had his body exhumed. They also dug up the body of Cromwell's son-in-law Henry Ireton who had died at Limerick in 1652 and another Member of Parliament and regicide called John Bradshaw who had died in 1659. That night they stored the bodies in the Red Lion Inn at Holborn and the next day they hung the dead corpses on gallows at Tyburn. From ten o'clock in the morning they dangled there in public view, to be pelted with stones and mud by the populace. At four in the afternoon they were then cut loose and their heads were hacked from their bodies. Because Cromwell was embalmed, it took eight blows to sever the head from the body. The bodies then appear to have been cast into a deep pit at Tyburn and the heads taken to the railings of Westminster Hall upon which they were firmly stuck.[66] There they remained until 1684. The final destiny of Cromwell's head would tell a curious tale. It is traditionally said that the head was blown down from Westminster Hall during a storm and that a sentry on duty picked it up and took it home under his coat. His daughter sold it to a Cambridgeshire family, who in turn sold it to a vagrant actor by the name of Samuel Russell. By the 1790s it had been bought for £230 and put on display. It finally came into the possession of the Wilkinson family, who donated it to Sydney Sussex College, Cambridge, which was Cromwell's own college. In the 1930s, Messrs Morant and Pearson carried out scientific experiments on the head and concluded that it was in fact the head of the Protector. It was finally buried in 1960 at Sydney Sussex College, Cambridge, but its exact location remains a closely guarded secret. A plaque placed in the corner of the entrance hall of the chapel reads: 'Near to this place was buried on 25 March 1960 the head of Oliver Cromwell, Lord Protector of the Commonwealth of England, Scotland and Ireland.'[67]

Cromwell was merely one in a long line of English oppressors. He became prominent during, and was a consequence of, a war-torn century. He should have emerged with an intact reputation that was both distinguished and honest in what were dreadful times in which to live. To the Irish, he sums up all that is evil in sectarianism, since in their opinion he was in league with the devil. To Cromwell his Irish mission was a laudable cause and one that involved no ambivalence. Both the King's party and the Papist party were to be suppressed. After the complicated conflicts with the various factions of Parliament who had trouble opposing the King, as well as the quarrels with the Levellers, the task was abundantly clear in Ireland. It was Cromwell's opinion that the Irish had appealed to the judgement of Heaven, but God had declared against them. He was convinced that he was on God's side and therefore he had concluded that God was on his. The plantation that would follow would cement his memory as Ireland's greatest enemy in the ensuing centuries. He knew that he was living in a time of extraordinary events. Even as he lived, he was aware that he was being misunderstood. If his career is viewed objectively, he seems genuine to us today, but it did not appear so to many of his contemporaries. There is therefore a magnetism to his personality that fascinates the historian. Every modern generation tries to evaluate his life. His Irish campaign is usually misconstrued and, therefore, is frequently apologised for by the English. It now appears that there has been an acute misunderstanding of his nine months in Ireland. He did not implement a flagrant violation

of the fundamental rights of the Irish to exist, contrary to popular opinion. He actively encouraged the dispersion of what he considered the
despotic Church regime that had deluded them, in order that they
might seek the correct path to God. The power of Royalist propaganda
combined with misinterpretations of his own words have to date concealed the facts. It is usually estimated that he lost complete control of
his moral standards on Irish soil, indiscriminately slaughtering the
Catholic population, simply returning to his former self when he again
set foot in England. This perception has always been *apparently* backed
up by the contemporary documentation. Today, eminent historians will
declare that Cromwell himself and even his own soldiers have testified
to the deaths of thousands of innocents in Ireland – not so! The truth
is that Cromwell did not change his spots when he landed at Ringsend
in August 1649. He did not temporarily become the murdering religious tyrant that history depicts. While his judgement may have been
erratic in some areas of political life, when it came to both religious matters and military combat he was relentlessly consistent. He was the same
person, employing the same principles in Ireland as he had always done
in England. Yet, there was a demon that lurked deep within his psyche
that would manifest when he would dissolve the Rump Parliament in
such a rage. That fury had also emerged at Drogheda but not at Wexford. Both events he saw as grave injustices and he believed that it was
up to him to put things right. The two weak spots in defence of
Cromwell's Irish campaign are why quarter was promised and broken
in Drogheda and why the killings in Wexford occurred when the town
was close to falling. No acceptable explanations will suffice for these
fiendish acts except to place them firmly in context. It is quite practica-
ble to suggest that a combination of numerous valid factors was the
cause of these massacres, not the least of which was an attempt to speed
up the expedition by eliminating potential resistance. Nine months was
too long for him to be away from England. The Irish war had to be quick
to be effective. The slaughter of the garrisons at Drogheda and Wexford, to prevent further bloodshed, were the only times that he surprised the world. His scrupulous reputation in battle up to that point
meant that there was no warning sign for the poor defenders of
Drogheda or Wexford.

And so a sad and complex chapter in Ireland's history came to a
close. Those who proclaim that it is naive to think that unarmed civilians did not die at either location during the volatile warfare conditions

of the times will need to offer more than bland generalities as an argument. Indeed, it is the opinion of this writer that it would be naive to believe the opposite. The respective partisan nationalist elements of the population of today's towns of Drogheda and Wexford have immense difficulty with a rehabilitated version of Oliver Cromwell. To them a reformed Cromwell is a most distasteful modification of a hate figure that for years has characterised English despotism. Many will not agree with the essence of this narrative. But history is not a matter of opinion, although sometimes historians surmise and discuss the inconclusive facts surrounding a particular event. But history should always be understood, never abused. Drogheda and Wexford have been the victims of the most serious historical abuse. There is a proverb that suffices as an appropriate closing point: 'A person convinced against their will, is of the same opinion still.' In other words, generalities that promote the wholesale slaughter theory will be enough for some people. Those whose vehement views of the period is the traditional perception may not be converted by this book. However, if this revision of the period serves to encourage an evenhanded view of the subject, then perhaps those who have yet to form an opinion will embrace the concepts of this submission. They will conclude that there must now be reasonable doubt regarding Cromwell's involvement in the deaths of the ordinary unarmed people of Ireland.

Notes to Chapter Seven

1   I am grateful to Bob Withers of the Clonmel Museum for this anecdote and also for copies of documentation concerning the siege of Clonmel.

2   The archeology of Clonmel has been closely studied under the auspices of Mary Henry M.A. I am indebted to Mary for this information.

3   Phillip O'Connell, 'Cluain Meala or Cliu Mel', *Tercentenary of the Siege of Clonmel* (Clonmel: Clonmel Tercentenary Committee, 1950), p. 82.

4   Ibid.

5   *Plan de La Ville de Clomelle, Goubet Fecit*, 1690. I am grateful to Mrs Margaret Rossiter for a copy of this map.

6   I am told by Mrs Rossiter that a certain local councillor had once urged the removal of this fine feature only to be foiled by the diligent work of the local preservationists.

7   Patrick Lyons, 'The Cromwellian Assault On Clonmel', *Tercentenary of the Siege of Clonmel*, p. 17.

8   Ibid.

9   Leahy's map of Clonmel, 1832, in Clonmel Museum.

10   Recent excavations carried out in the area by Mary Henry uncovered what are believed to be the foundations of the North Gate.

11   See Leahy's map of Clonmel, 1832.

12   'Clonmel Street Names', *Tercentenary of the Siege of Clonmel*, p. 50.

13   'Items of Clonmel History', *Tercentenary of the Siege of Clonmel*, p. 37.

14   The Very Rev. William P Burke (Canon), *History of Clonmel*, with an introduction by Thomas Wall (Waterford: Clonmel Library Committee, 1907), p. 62.

15   Rev. Denis Murphy, *Cromwell in Ireland, A History of Cromwell's Irish Campaign* (Dublin: M.H. Gill & Son, 1883), appendix IV, p. 383.

16   Burke, *History of Clonmel*, p. 72.

17   Ibid., p. 69.

18   Ibid.

19   Ibid., p. 71.

20   W.C. Abbott, *The Writings and Speeches of Oliver Cromwell*, reprint edition, 4 vols. (Oxford: Clarendon Press, 1988), vol. II, p. 245.

21   Murphy, *Cromwell in Ireland*, p. 329.

22   *Aphorismical Discovery*, vol. II, p. 77; partly quoted in Burke, *History of Clonmel*, p. 73; Murphy, *Cromwell in Ireland*, pp. 329–30. 'Many valiant sallies and martiall stratagems did loose some daies, 200, other daies 300, other 400, other 500 men, this losse was so often and common that he [Cromwell] was wearie of the place and raise the siedge.'

23   *Aphorismical Discovery;* in J.T. Gilbert, *A Contemporary History of Affairs in Ireland from A.D. 1641–1652*, 3 vols. (Dublin: Irish Archaeological and Celtic Association, 1879), vol II, p. 77–78; Murphy, *Cromwell in Ireland*, pp. 330–31; Abbott, *Writings and Speeches*, vol. II, p. 246.

24   Abbott, *Writings and Speeches*, pp. 250–60: 'Only two contemporary sources have been found which assign a definite date to the siege of Clonmel. One is Dr. Jones' Diary, who says "the 17 [of May] Clonmel was taken where and when colonel Arthur Culme was slain, being shott at the Breach". The other is a letter in *Severall Proceedings*, May 23–30, which is there dated May 10 and describes the siege. This letter, received with letters dated Dublin May 17 and May 19, the first silent about Clonmel, the second mentioning it, was reprinted in Cromwelliana and also by Gilbert who, assuming the date was printed correctly, inserted May 9 and May 10 in brackets in all the other accounts which gave a definite date, making the basis for them all a letter printed in a newspaper whose accuracy is by no means infallible and is definitely open to question in this case because other news sent after the 10th from Ireland appeared in print in London earlier than the news of Clonmel. Moreover, besides Dr. Jones' Diary, we have the articles of surrender whose date of May 18 is not questioned even by Gilbert who printed them. Murphy, whose careful scholarship is at all times reliable, sidesteps the question of the date of Clonmel. Carte who had access to much manuscript material for his Life of Ormonde, gives May 18 as the date of surrender. A careful search for activities of any of the chief officers in the siege during the

week between May 10 and May 17 yields nothing, which would seem to add weight to the theory that they were before Clonmel.'

25   The details offered here are primarily from Edmund Hogan (ed.), *History of the Warr in Ireland from 1641 to 1653 by an Officer in the Regiment of Sir John Clotworthy* (Dublin: McGlashan & Gill, 1873). We know that this individual was not present during the siege, but most of the other accounts agree with the idea that some sort of earthwork had been fashioned in preparation for the assault. Quoted in Murphy, *Cromwell in Ireland*, p. 334, the full account is repeated here later and is taken from *Tercentenary of the Siege of Clonmel*, pp. 30–31, which also reproduces most of the other contemporary accounts.

26   See Murphy, *Cromwell in Ireland*, p. 336, who calls him 'Langley of the Iron Hand'. Also Colonel Patrick F. Dineen, 'The Siege of Clonmel', *Tercentenary of the Siege of Clonmel*, p. 14.

27   Dineen, 'The Siege of Clonmel', *Tercentenary of the Siege of Clonmel*, p. 13; also in Abbott, *Writings and Speeches*, vol. II, p. 251.

28   Hogan, *History of the Warr in Ireland from 1641 to 1653 by an Officer in the Regiment of Sir John Clotworthy*, pp. 105–12, describes this officer's version of events; also quoted in *Tercentenary of the Siege of Clonmel*, pp. 30–32.

29   Abbott, *Writings and Speeches*, vol. II, p. 251, says that Cromwell 'poured men into this desperate attack, until his losses were reckoned – again, no doubt, with exaggeration – at fifteen hundred to twenty-five hundred men'.

30   O'Connell, 'The Defenders of Clonmel – Major General Hugh O'Neill', *Tercentenary of the Siege of Clonmel*, p. 22.

31   Ibid.

32   Murphy, *Cromwell in Ireland*, appendix VI, p. 385.

33   Burke, *History of Clonmel*, p. 78, refers to the mayor's first name as being John and quotes a letter from him to Ormonde dated 10 November 1649, p. 65. However in the articles which he also reproduces, his name is given as Michael.

34   Abbott, *Writings and Speeches*, vol. II, p. 252; Gilbert, *Contemporary History*, vol. II, pp. 411–12; Murphy, *Cromwell in Ireland*, p. 341.

35   O'Connell, 'Contemporary Accounts of the Siege', *Tercentenary of the Siege of Clonmel*, p. 26.

36   Ibid.

37   Ibid., pp. 27–28.

38   Ibid., p. 26. Phillip O'Connell has asserted in 'Contemporary Accounts of the Siege', *Tercentenary of the Siege of Clonmel*, p. 26, that this account is Cromwell's own. Abbott does not submit a letter of Cromwell's relating to Clonmel at all. This account appears in *Severall Proceedings*, 23 May to 6 June 1650. The style could not be described as being Cromwell's.

39   Edmund Ludlow, *Memoirs of Edmund Ludlow, Esq., Lieutenant General of the Horse, Commander-in-Chief of the Forces in Ireland, One of the Council of State and a Member of the Parliament which began on Nov. 3rd 1640*, 2 vols. (Canton of Berne: 1698; reissued Oxford: C.H Firth, 1894), pp. 307–08.

Also reproduced in O'Connell, 'Contemporary accounts of the Siege', *Tercentenary of the Siege of Clonmel*, p. 28.

40   Murphy, *Cromwell in Ireland*, p. 341.

41   Ibid., p. 342.

42   Cromwell to Richard Mayor, 13 November 1649; in Abbott, *Writings and Speeches*, vol. II, p. 160.

43   Bulstrode Whitelocke, *Memorials of the English Affairs from the beginning of the Reign of King Charles the First to the Happy Restoration of King Charles II* (London: 1682; reissued, Oxford: 1842), p. 422; quoted in Murphy, *Cromwell in Ireland*, pp. 345–46.

44   Abbott, *Writings and Speeches*, vol. II, p. 261, quoting from Whitelocke, tells us that 'he was welcomed at Bristol with a triple salute from the great guns'; from Whitelocke, *Memorials*, p. 457.

45   *A Speech or Declaration of the Declared King of Scots . . . Also some excellent Passages concerning the Lord Generall Cromwell, his Entertainment at Windsor Castle, and the manner of his coming thence to London, the first of June, 1650*, p. 5; from Abbott, *Writings and Speeches*, vol. II, p. 261: '[H]e was entertained with many vollies of shot, his lady also met him here, and many persons of eminency, Members of Parliament, and of the Councel of State, and chief officers of the Army; after much time in expressing civil respects one to another, and in congratulating his welcome tither, they had some discourse on the affaires of Ireland, and of the prosperous success wherewith it had pleased God to crown his undertakings. From Bristol to Windsor he came with a small retinue of his own servants, and some few Gentlemen and Officers of the Army, he shews himself very affable, and courteous unto all, and as time will afford, admitteth any man that hath business, to speak with him. This evening came some part of Colonel Riche's Regiment of Horse, and most of the Innes in town are full of guests, which come from London on purpose to attend him in his way tomorrow. They tell us that a great number will also meet him by the way, in his passage to London; but his Lordship expresseth much humility, and when any Victory obtained is spoken of, he acknowledgeth God to be in all, and saith, that that which is of God shall stand, but if it be not of God, t'will come to naught. He also declareth that it is not suitable to his desire, to come up to London in great Pomp and Glory, yet because men would not be thought guilty of that abominable vice of ingratitude, and for that Worthy deeds are not to be requited with neglect, it may be decent and seemly, for such as are well-wishers to the common good, to testifie their affections this way, which may be done without ostentation in the one, and ascribing more than is due by the other.'

46   Murphy, *Cromwell in Ireland*, p. 348. Antonia Fraser, *Cromwell, Our Chief of Men* (London: Mandarin edition, 1994), p. 362, recounts the same story but under different circumstances. She says that on Cromwell's trip north to Scotland, 'Turning towards Northampton, it was here that the great crowds inspired in him the bluff aside to Lambert and Ingoldsby: those very persons would shout as much if you and I were going to be hanged.'

47 From Tonson's *Debates*, vol XIX, p. 263; quoted in Murphy, *Cromwell in Ireland*, p. 349.

48 Ibid.

49 Abbott, *Writings and Speeches*, vol. II, p. 262.

50 *Mercurius Politicus*, 3 June 1650; quoted in Fraser, *Cromwell, Our Chief of Men*, p. 356.

51 Abbott, *Writings and Speeches*, vol. II, p. 262, quotes from *Mercurius Politicus* describing the meeting 'where they passed many remarkable expressions of mutuall love and Courtesie, sufficient to check the false tounges'.

52 For the Battle of Dunbar, see Fraser, *Cromwell, Our Chief of Men*, pp. 366–72; Abbott, *Writings and Speeches*, vol. II, pp. 297–332, where more detail is given.

53 Fraser, *Cromwell, Our Chief of Men*, p. 381.

54 Ibid. p. 383. Cromwell to Lenthall, 4 August 1651; also in Abbott, *Writings and Speeches*, vol. II, p. 444.

55 For the Battle of Worcester, see Fraser, *Cromwell, Our Chief of Men*, pp. 384–90; Abbott, *Writings and Speeches*, vol. II, pp. 451–68 in more detail.

56 Fraser, *Cromwell, Our Chief of Men*, p. 387.

57 Ibid., p. 420.

58 Ibid., pp. 420–21.

59 Ibid.; also in Abbott, *Writings and Speeches*, vol. III, p. 649.

60 Fraser, *Cromwell, Our Chief of Men*, p. 449.

61 See John Broome, *Cromwell, A Vindication* (Leicester: The Gospel Standards Baptist Trust, 1969), p. 4.

62 Antonia Fraser, *Cromwell, Our Chief of Men*; also Christopher Hill, *God's Englishman: Oliver Cromwell and the English Revolution* (London: Penguin Books, 1972); S.R. Gardiner, *History of the Commonwealth and the Protectorate*, 4 vols. (1903; reissued Stroud: The Windrush Press, 1988); John Buchan, *Oliver Cromwell* (London: 1934); John Morrill (ed.), *Oliver Cromwell and the English Revolution* (London: Longman, 1990); Toby Barnard, *The English Republic, 1649–1660* (London: Longman, 1982); Barry Coward, *Profiles in Power – Oliver Cromwell* (London: Longman, 1992); Roger Howell Jr., *Images of Oliver Cromwell*; R.C. Richardson (ed.), *Essays for and by Roger Howell Jr.* (Manchester: University Press, 1993); Peter Gaunt, *Oliver Cromwell* (Oxford: Blackwell, 1996); C.H. Firth, *Oliver Cromwell and the Rule of the Puritans* (London: 1900); Ivan Roots, *Cromwell – A Profile* (London: 1973).

63 Fraser, *Cromwell, Our Chief of Men*, p. 676.

64 Ibid.

65 Ibid.

66 Tyburn is today buried under Marble Arch in Connaught Square, London. It could be said that Cromwell eventually went to Hell *and* to Connaught!

67 See Fraser, *Cromwell, Our Chief of Men*, p. 697. See also Karl Pearson and G.M. Morant, *The Portraiture of Oliver Cromwell with Special Reference to the Wilkinson Head*, issued by the Biometrika Office, University College London (Cambridge: University Press, 1935), for full account.

APPENDICES

Appendix No. 1

Whereas we, the Roman Catholics of this Kingdom of Ireland, have been continual and loving faithful subjects to his sacred Majesty and notwithstanding the general and heavy oppressions suffered by subordinate governors to the ruin of our lives, honours and estates, yet having some liberty of religion from his Majesty, out of the affluence of his princely love to us, we weighing not corporal loss in respect of the great immunity of the soul are invioably resolved to infix ourselves in an immutable and pure allegiance for ever to his Royal Majesty and his successors. Now it is that the Parliament of England, maligning and envying any graces received from his majesty by our nation and knowing none so desired of us that of religion, and likewise of perceiving his Majesty to be inclined to give us the liberty of the same, drew his Majesty's prerogative out of his hands, thereby largely pretending the general good of his Majesty's Kingdoms. But we the said Catholics and loyal subjects to his Majesty do probably find, as well by some Acts passed by them the said Parliament, touching our religion, in which the Catholics of England and Scotland did suffer, as also by threats to send over the Scottish army with the sword and Bible against us, that their whole and studied plot was, and is, not only to extinguish our religion (by which only we live happily), but also likewise to supplant us, and rase the name of Catholics and Irish out of the whole Kingdom; and seeing this surprise so dangerous, tending absolutely to the overthrow of the liberty of our consciences and country, and also our gracious King's power forced from him, in which and whose prudent care of us our sole quiet and comfort consisted, and without which the fear of our present ruin did prescribe opinion and premonish us to save ourselves. We, therefore as well to regain his Majesty's said prerogative, being only due to him and his successors, and being the essence and life of monarchy, hoping thereby to continue a strong and invincible unity between his Royal and ever happy love to us, and our faithful duty and loyalty to his incomparable majesty, have taken arms and possessed ourselves of the best and strongest forts in the Kingdom, to enable us to serve his Majesty, and preserve us from the tyrannous resolution of our enemies. This in our consciences, as we wish the peace of the same to ourselves and our posterity, is the pretence of our true cause of our present rising in arms, by which we are resolved to perfect the advancement of truth and safety of our King and country. This much we thought fit in general to publish to the world to set forth our innocent and just cause, the particulars whereof shall be speedily declared. God save the King.[1]

Note to Appendix 1

1 "Declaration of the objects of resistance of Sir Phelim O'Neill" dated 23 October 1641, is quoted in John D'Alton, *History of Drogheda* (Dublin: M.H. Gill, 1844; re-issued: Drogheda: Buvinda, 1997), pp. 222–23.

Appendix No. 2.1

This declaration is appointed to be printed and published throughout all Ireland: by special direction from – Oliver Cromwell.

Whereas I am informed that, upon the marching out of the Armies heretofore, or of parties from Garrisons, a liberty hath been taken by the Soldiery to abuse, rob and pillage, and too often to execute cruelties upon the Country People: being resolved, by the grace of God, diligently and strictly to restrain such wickedness for the future.

I do hereby warn and require all Officers, Soldiers and others under my command, henceforth to forebear all such evil practices as aforesaid; and not to do any wrong or violence toward Country People, or persons whatsoever, unless they be actually in arms or office with the Enemy; and not to meddle with the goods of such, without special order.

And I do further declare, That it shall be free and lawful to and for all manner of persons dwelling in the country, as well as gentlemen and soldiers, as farmers and other people (such as are in arms or office with or for the Enemy only excepted), to make their repair, and bring any provisions unto the Army (while in march or camp), or unto any Garrison under my command: Hereby assuring all such, that they shall not be troubled or molested in their persons or goods; but shall have the benefit of a free market, and receive ready money for goods or commodities they shall so bring and sell: and that they, behaving themselves peaceably and quietly; and paying such Contributions, proportionably with their neighbours, as have been, are, or shall be duly and orderly imposed upon them, for maintenance of the Parliaments forces and other public uses, shall have free leave and liberty to live at home with their families and goods; and shall be protected in their persons and estates by virtue thereof, until the 1st day of January next: by or before which time, all such of them as are minded to reside, and plough and sow, in the quarters, are to make their addresses, for now and further protections, to the Attorney-General, residing at Dublin, and to such other persons as shall be authorised for that purpose.

And hereof I require all Soldiers, and others under my command, diligently to take notice and observe the same: as they shall answer to the contrary at their utmost perils. Strictly charging and commanding all Officers and others, in their several places, carefully to see to it that no wrong or violence be done to any such person as aforesaid, contrary to the effect of the premises. Being resolved, through the grace of God to punish all that shall offend contrary hereunto, very severely, according to Law or Articles of War; to displace and otherwise punish, all such Officers as shall be found negligent in their places, and not see the due observance hereof, or not to punish the offenders under their respective commands.

Given at Dublin, the 24th of August 1649. Oliver Cromwell.[1]

Appendix No. 2.2

'To the honourable John Bradshaw, President of the Council of State.

Sir,

It hath pleased God the bless our endeavours at Tredah. After battery we stormed it. The enemy were about 3,000 strong in the town. They made a stout resistance, and near 1,000 of our men being entered, the enemy forced them out again. But God giving a new courage to our men, they attempted again, and entered, beating the enemy from their defences.

The enemy had made three entrenchments, both to the right and left, where we entered; all of which they were forced to quit. Being thus entered, we refused them quarter; having the day before summoned the town. I believe we put to the sword the whole number of the defendants. I do not think thirty of the whole number escaped with their lives. Those that did are in safe custody for Barbadoes. Since that time the enemy quitted to us Trim and Dundalk. In Trim they were in such a haste they left their guns behind them.

This hath been a marvellous great mercy. The enemy, being not willing to put an issue upon a field-battle, had put into this garrison almost all their prime soldiers, being about 3,000 horse and foot under the command of their best officers; Sir Arthur Aston being made governor. There were some seven or eight regiments, Ormonde's being one, under the command of Sir Edmund Verney. I do not believe neither do I hear that any officer escaped with his life, save only one lieutenant, who, I hear, going to the enemy said, that he was the only man that escaped of all the garrison. The enemy were filled upon this with much terror. And truly I believe this bitterness will save much effusion of blood, through the goodness of God.

I wish that all honest hearts may give the glory of this to God alone, to whom indeed the praise of this mercy belongs. For instruments, they were very inconsiderable the work throughout.

We are marching the army to Dublin, which we hope will be here tomorrow night, where we desire to recruit with victual, and shall then, God willing, advance towards the southern design – you know what – only we think Wexford will be our first undertaking in order to the other.
Captain Brandley did with forty or fifty of his men very gallantly storm the tenalia; for which he deserves the thanks of the State.

September 16th 1649

O. Cromwell.[2]

For the honourable William Lenthall, Esquire, Speaker of the Parliament of England; These:

Sir,

Your Army being safely arrived at Dublin; and the enemy endeavouring to draw all his forces together about Trim and Tecroghan (as my intelligence gave me); from whence endeavours were used by the Marquis of Ormond to draw Owen Roe O'Neill with his forces to his assistance, but with what success I cannot yet learn, I resolved, after some refreshment taken for our weather beaten men and horses, and accommodations for a march, to take the field. And accordingly upon Friday 30th August last, rendezvoused with eight regiments of foot and six of horse and some troops of dragoons, three miles on the north side of Dublin. The design was, to endeavour the regaining of Tredah; or tempting the enemy upon his hazard upon the loss of that place, to fight.

Your Army came before the town upon the Monday following, where having pitched, as speedy course was taken as could be to frame our batteries, which took up the more time because divers of the battering guns were on shipboard. Upon Monday the 9th of this instant, the batteries began to play. Whereupon I sent Sir Arthur Aston, the then Governor a summons to deliver the town to the use of the Parliament of England. To the which I received no satisfactory answer, but proceeded that day to beat down the steeple of the church on the south side of the town, and to beat down a tower not far from the same place, which you will discern from the chart enclosed.

Our guns not being able to do much that day, it was resolved to endeavour to do our utmost the next day to make breaches assaultable, and by the help of God to storm them. The places pitched upon were that part of the town wall next a church called St. Marys, which was the rather chosen because we did hope that if we did enter and possess that church we should be the better able to keep it against their horse and foot until we could make way for the entrance of our horse, which we did not conceive that any part of the town would afford the like advantage for that purpose with this. The batteries planted were two; one was for that part of the wall against the east end of the said church, the other against the wall on the south side. Being somewhat long in battering, the enemy made six retrenchments, three of them from the said church to Duleek gate and three from the east end of the church to the town wall and so backward. The guns, after some two or three hundred shot, beat down the corner tower and opened two reasonably good breaches in the east and south wall.

Upon Tuesday the 10th of this instant, [*Monday was the tenth. Cromwell continues the error as to the day of the month throughout the letter.*] about five o'clock in the evening, we began the storm, after some hot dispute we entered about seven or eight hundred men, the enemy disputing it very stiffly with us. And indeed, through the advantages of the place, and the courage God was pleased to give the defenders, our men were forced to retreat quite out of the breach, not without some considerable loss; Colonel Cassell, being there shot in the head where he presently died, and divers officers and soldiers, doing their duty, killed and wounded. There was a tenalia to flanker the south wall of the town between Duleek Gate and the corner tower before mentioned, which our men entered, wherein they found some forty or fifty of the enemy, which they put to the sword. And this [*tenalia*] they held, but it being without the wall, and the sally-port through the wall into that tenalia being choked up with some of the enemy which were killed in it, it proved of no use for our entrance into the town that way.

Although our men that stormed the breaches were forced to recoil, as before is expressed, yet, being encouraged to recover their loss, they made a second attempt, wherein God was pleased [so] to animate them that they got ground of the enemy, and by the goodness of God, forced him to quit his entrenchments. And after a very hot dispute, the enemy having both horse and foot and we only foot, within the wall, they gave ground and our men became masters both of their retrenchments and the church, which indeed, although they made our entrance the more difficult, yet they proved of excellent use to us so that the enemy could not annoy us with their horse, but thereby we had advantage to make good the ground, that so we might let in our own horse, which accordingly was done, though with much difficulty.

The enemy retreated, divers of them into the Mill-Mount: a place very strong and of difficult access, being exceedingly high, having good graft and strongly palisadoed. The Governor, Sir Arthur Aston, and divers considerable officers being there, our men getting up to them were ordered by me to put them all to the sword. And indeed, being in the heat of action, I forbade them to spare any that were in arms in the town, and I think that night, they put to the sword about 2,000 men, divers of the officers and soldiers being fled over the bridge into the other part of the town, where about one hundred of them possessed St. Peter's church steeple, some the West gate and others a strong round tower next the gate called St. Sundays. These being summoned to yield to mercy, refused, whereupon I ordered the steeple of St. Peters church to be fired, where one of them was heard to say in the midst of the flames 'God damn me, God confound me; I burn I burn'.

The next day the other two towers were summoned, in one of which was about six or seven score; but they refused to yield themselves, and we knowing that hunger must compel them, set only good guards to secure them from running away until their stomachs were come down. From one of the said towers, notwithstanding their condition, they killed and wounded some of our men. When they submitted, their officers were knocked on the head, and every tenth man of the soldiers killed, and the rest shipped for the Barbadoes. The soldiers in the other tower were all spared, as to their lives only, and shipped likewise for the Barbadoes.

I am persuaded that this is a righteous judgement of God upon these barbarous wretches, who have imbrued their hands in so much innocent blood and that it will tend to prevent the effusion of blood for the future, which are the satisfactory grounds for such actions, which otherwise cannot but work remorse and regret. The officers and soldiers of this garrison were the flower of all their army, and their great expectation was, that our attempting the place would put fair ruin to us, they being confident of the resolution of their men, and the advantage of the place. If we had divided our force into two quarters to have besieged the north town and the south town, we could not have such a correspondency between the two parts of our army, but that they might have chosen to have brought their army, and have fought with which part they pleased, and, at the same time have made a sally with 2,000 men upon us, and have left their walls manned, they having in the town the number specified in this enclosed, but some say near four thousand.

Since this great mercy vouchsafed to us, I sent a party of horse and dragoons to Dundalk, which the enemy quitted and we are possessed of, as also another castle they deserted between Trim and Tredah, upon the Boyne. I sent a party of horse and dragoons to a house within five miles of Trim, there being then in Trim some Scots companies, which the Lord of Ardes brought to assist the Lord of Ormonde. But upon news of the Tredah, they ran away, leaving their great guns behind them, which we also have possessed.

And now give me leave to say how it comes to pass that this work is wrought. It was set upon some of our hearts, that a great thing should be done, not by power or might, but by the Spirit of God. That which caused your men to storm so courageously, it was the Spirit of God, who gave your men courage, and took it away again; and gave the enemy courage, and took it away again; and gave your men courage again, and therewith this happy success. And therefore it is good that God alone have all the glory.

It is remarkable that these people, at the first, set up the mass in some places of the town that had been monasteries; but afterwards grew so insolent that, the last Lord's day before the storm, the Protestants were thrust out of the great church called St. Peters, and they had public mass there: and in this very place near one thousand of them were put to the sword, fleeing thither for safety. I believe all their friars were knocked on the head promiscuously but two; the one of which was Father Peter Taaff (brother to the Lord Taaff), whom the soldiers took, the next day and made an end of; the other was taken in a round tower, under the repute of lieutenant, and when he understood that the officers in that tower had no quarter, he confessed that he was a friar; but that did not save him.

A great deal of loss in this business fell upon Colonel Hewson, Colonel Cassell, and Colonel Ewers' regiments; Colonel Ewers having two field officers in his regiment shot; Colonel Cassell and a captain of his regiment slain; Colonel Hewson's captain-lieutenant slain. I do not think we lost one hundred men upon the place, though many be wounded.

I most humbly pray the Parliament will be pleased [that] this army may be maintained; and that a consideration may be had of them, and of the carrying on of affairs here, as may give a speedy issue to this work, to which there seems to be a marvellous fair opportunity offered by God. And although it may seem very chargeable to the State of England to maintain so great a force, yet surely to stretch a little for the present, in following God's providence, in hope the charge will not be long, I trust it will not be thought by any (that have not irreconcilable or malicious principles) unfit for me to move for a constant supply, which in human probability as to outward means, is most likely to hasten and perfect this work. And indeed if God please to finish it here as he hath done in England, the war is likely to pay itself.

We keep the field much, our tents sheltering us from the wet and cold, but yet the country sickness overtakes many, and therefore we desire recruits, and some fresh regiments of foot, may be sent us. For its easily conceived, by what the garrisons already drink up, what our field army will come to, if God shall give more garrisons into our hands. Craving pardon for this great trouble, I rest,

Your most humble servant

Oliver Cromwell.

Dublin Sept 17 1649.

P.S. Since the writing of my letter, a major who brought off forty-three horse from the enemy told me that it's reported in their camp that Owen Roe and they are agreed.

A list of the defendants in Tredah: The Lord of Ormonde's regiment (Sir Edmund Verney Lieutenant Colonel), 400; Colonel Byrn, Colonel Warren, and Colonel Wall, 2,100; the Lord of Westmeath, 200; Sir James Dillon, 200, and 200 horses.[3]

Appendix 2.3

Aston to Ormonde 29 August:

Me Lord, may it pleas your Excellency, Notwithstanding that I have formerly importuned your Excellency concerninge divers defects in this garnison, yet the pressing nesessety inforseth me againe to sende this bearor, captain Garner, to solisset in our behalfes. The charge of this garnison, horse, foote, traine of artillery, and payment of artifissers and workmen, amounts weekly to neer £700. The weekly asignement for contribution to bee asigned mee out of ye countrey I have not received, but only for the Barrony of Duleeke, which is but £80 weekly, and that Barroney hath before my cooming heether paide 6 weekes controbution before hand. The beeves and meale which Collonell Warrin toulde me was promised mee is not yet coome. The offisers have not received any payment from mee heer this last weeke and those of the foote say they are 5 weeks in ariers. Round shot and match I desier your Excellency to be mindfull to give order for, as also the materialls which Me Lord of Ardes promised, I wish I had them. I beseech your Excellency be pleased to be mindfull of the redgiment of foote; heer is in this garnison Sir Robbert Byrons company and Captin Smiths company, who are not alotted to any redgiment as yet. Collonell Warrin doth earnestly desire to have his Lutennant-collonell sent him from Trim, or else that your Excellency would be pleased to give him leave to place an other, and indeed hee were very usefull heere.

I have heer a yonge captin of horse, named Fitzgarrot; I wish he had been made a souldier when hee was stampt a captin, for hee knows so little of his profession, and is so troublesoom in a toune, that I have made boulde to sende him back to your excellency. His cornet hath so abused the countray that I have him heer in areste untill the business be triede. I beseetch your Excellency to pardon me for trubling you so often, and withall to returne this berer speedely with a suplye, or wee are all broke. The foe it is said will martch in too armeys, won towards your Excellency and the other this way; if I were but redy with provissions and other nesessaries I would hope to welkoom him heether with shutch entertainment as shutch gest deserve from the handes of, Me Lord, Your Excelleny's moste humble servant while life lasts. Arth. Aston.

Tredagh, this 29th at night, August 1649. For his Excellency the Lorde-Lutennant: Theas humbly. Endorsed: Sir Arthur Astons [Dated] 29 Rec. 31 Aug., 1649 Concerning ye charge of ye garrison, amounting to £700 a weeke, etc.

Ormonde to Aston 31 August:

After our hearty comendacons: Wee receaved yours of the 29th this instant, to which wee return you that ye contribucons appointed for maintenance of that guarrison is made certaine, as you will finde by orders of yesterdayes date sent you, and for what hath beene formerly taken upp before hand, must be owing untill wee are in better condicon to forbear the present cominge in of money.

The beaves and meale wee are certaine are before this tyme with you, and to the regiment of foote shall bee made upp for you as soon as possibly wee can. As for round shot, we have none heere of lesse then 12lbs ball. As for the materialls of the Lord of Ards, he hathe sent a second order in all haste to have it conveyed unto you, though he thinks they are before this tyme with you, and Collonell Warrens Lt-Collonell shalbe sent him very soone.

Capt. Fz-Gerrald I sent you back to be taught his duety. For his Cornet, let him receave his punishment according to his fault. If the Boyne rise it willbe necessary to put 15 or 20 men into the castle on the bridge of Slane, which castle stood in the middle of the bridge, and cannot be taken but with cannon.

The inclosed order will furnish you with match, but you must send for it. Wee expect moneyes this night and you shall have your share of it, which wee doubt will not bee much.

We send you here inclosed the copy of the advertisment which wee nowe receaved of the enemyes motions and strength, with an order for demolishing certaine castles twixt you and Dublin, in case you have tyme to do it, or that busines of greater conserment divert not. And so we bid you heartily farewell, from Tecroghan, the last day of August 1649. Your affectionate friend, Ormonde.

Sir Arthur Aston. Endorsed: Coppie of a lettre to Sir Arthur Aston.

Aston to Ormonde 1 September:

May it pleas your Excellency, yesternight, late, I receved your Excellency's letter and humbly that [sic] your Excellency for your favours to mee theerin expresed. The Bishop of Dromore writ unto Collonell Warren the which hee showed mee, that theare was coom unto this towne too fryers who intended no good. It may bee my fortune to light uppon them, which if I doe, uppon my credit wee shall have a rubbers worse then I have had with my grandmother, who with mutch adoe hath yelded yesternight to leave this place and to go to Mellefant, but sore against her will, and highly offended with mee, who am very glad to be rid of her uppon anye tearmes, with her deer sun Francke. Yesternight I had intelligence that the rebbels have put sum greate cannon a ship borde to bring alonge with them heether. Thay bring 8 ships a longe with them, and other cannon and morter peeses thay intende to bring by lande; thay have provided sckaling lathers to bring with them. In the meane I am providing, as well as the time will give leave for theer entertainment. I beseetch your Excellency be pleased to sende a speedy supply of mony. I meete with sum assignements, passes, and protections signed by your Excellency I beleeve not rightly made use of. Won was given unto the Scotch Sherrif heere, who under the culler of free tradinge, without eather my knowledge or the Mayors hath carried away a great part of his goods and himselfe lefte the toune. Another thing I thought good to informe your Excellency of, heer are in the Offis for Exsise 5 Commissioners eitch at 15 shillings weekly paye, tooe masters of imposte eitch of them weekly, at 13s-4d, besides a clarke at 6s, and 4 waiters at eitch 3s weekly, and the whole sum that the Exsises amounts unto weekly is but between twenty and £30, and a good part of that asigned unto severall persons for pensions. I intended to have sent your Excellency Captin Ffitz-garrets troope back againe, but hee beeing a yonge man and now becoming senseible how great a disparredgment it will bee unto him to be sent for misdemenors out of the garrison, hath faithfully promised an amendment and humbly craves your Excellency's favoure. I yesterday dispatched a Captin from hence with an information of our condission heere. I am very sory to bee so often trublesoom unto your Excellency and with all that the charge thereof is soe greate which is at least weekly. There came yesternight unto mee 36 barrells of corne, 9 caske of meale, and 4 caske of biscute. I would willingly send sum horse to doe mischeefe but for hay.

Your Exlence most faithfull and most humble servant. Arth. Aston. Trogodaghe, this ferst of September, 1649. For his Exlns. Me Lord-Lutennant: Theas with my humble servis. Endorsed: Sir Arthur Aston's. Dated 1. Rec. Sept., 1649. Concerning some fryers which the Bishop of Dromore writt to Collonell Warren were gone to Drogheda to doe mischeefe, etc.

Aston to Ormonde 2 September:

May it pleas your Excellency, I receved your orders for the demollishing of divers castles in theas partes. This day, according to your commaundes, I have sent out to destroy Ballegarde (*Ballygarth*),

Ackarne (*Athcairne*), Dardistoune (*Dardistown*), and Bedlistoune (*Bellewstown*). The rest which wee find considerable shale, God willing, so far as I am able, bee destroyed. But in my opinion, amongst all that are named Gorminstone is the most considerable, and from whens wee shall receave the greatest disadvantage; but in the ferst place, it is your Excellency's expres orders that Me Lady Lukas shall receave favoure, and that Gorminstone shall bee the laste that shall bee destroyed, which shall bee a compas that I will steer by beyonde all other conciderations; and againe, if I shoulde sende to destroy it I shoulde finde sum difficulty theerin; espetially now the demollishing of strong places are begoon, for she hath 40 armed soilders therin, and it is conceaved woulde strive to defend it; but for that I refer it unto your Excellency's concideration and further order. Plantin Castle (*Platin*) I heare is a stronge place, but no water in it. I have this day receved five hundred pound the which is very welcoom. I will doe my best to get in sum contribution hereafter. I have been forced to give beoves in part of a weeks pay to the foote before this came. The river of Boyne is rissen, but if the rebbels coom, no doubte but they will bring cannon with them, and then to man the castell uppon the bridge of slaine will but bee to haserde the los of them, but I shall if your Excellency houlde it fitt observe your commaundes in all thinges, and so therin. I am glad that your Excellency returned a negative answer unto Toby Butlers demaunde concerning the asiginge of him any particuleer quarters, for that woulde have sum thing deminuse the authorrety which your Excellency hath favoured mee with all, besides the Barrony of Dulike (*Duleek*) is the neerest unto this plase, and if need bee the horse may fetch theer controbution further of. Thus with my humble servis unto your Excellency remembred, and desiring your Excellency's resolution on this and in my yesterdays letter,

I rest forever, Your Excellency's most faithfull and most obleedged humble servant, Arth. Aston. Drogodaghe, the 2nd of September, 1649. I feare I mistooke the date of my letter yesterday. For his Exlins: Theas with my humble servis. Endorsed: Sir Ar. Aston. Dated 2 Rec. 3 Sept., 1649. Concerning £500 which he received and the destruction of castles etc.

Aston to Ormonde 3 September, morning:

May it pleas you Excellency, According as my letters of yesterday mention I sent (with as mutch speed as coulde bee) a party for the demolishing or burning of Ballingart, Duddingstone, Bedlestone and Athkarne, and intended according to your Exlns' orders to have doon so with the reste; but before my party came theether, the enemy had possessed sum of them, and secured by theer advansing with a greate boddy of horse of the rest of them. Lutennant-collonell Fingles promised to have given mee more timely intelligens of the enemies advanse, and to that ende leftt his Cornet with a party to wait uppon theer motion; whot the faulte was I know not, but the Cornet is not yet returned, and the Lif-Collonell feares hee is loste. This last night the said boddy of horse of the enemy incamped aboute too miles from this toune. The foote are not as yet coom up to them, but I beleeve this daye thay will advanse neerer. I was this morninge my selfe out with the horse very early abrawde, but findinge them to stronge for me to deale withall I returned, and have lefte Fingles in the feelde with order not to engadge but uppon an advantadge, but only with smale parties to discover theer motions. I could wish I had receved your Excellency's orders concerning thoes castalls a daye sooner, for thay will now, as I am toulde, be very disadvantagious to us. Just now I have nuse sent mee that theer are aboute 500 horse of the rebbells drawing towards the forde at Ouldbridge, which will compell our cattle into a narrow compas. As I formerly sertifyed your Excellency heere is but small store of salt in the toune. But if our soildiers will but doe whot I am shure thay may doe I hope the ennemy will finde sum good resistance. But yesterday theer ran foure away. I have not had time since my cooming heether to Munster eather the horse or foote, wherefore if your Excellency be cussoned (as I mutch doubt it) it is not my faulte, and provided that they will but doe theer duties as thay aught it is the les matter. I will asshure your Excellency it shall not bee longe of mee if thay doe not. But a litle quickning admonission in a letter from your Excellency unto them all (espetially unto the horse) would doe well. May it pleas your Excellency, this bearer, Sir Thomas Dakers, a gentleman of good quallety, desiered to recommend him unto your favour. Hee hath ben driven out of his estate by the rebels of England, as many honest men hath been. So soone as I know more of the ennemies motions I will, if messingers may pas, adverties your Excellency therof; if not, then I recommend things unto Godes mersy and your Excellency's favour unto.

Your most faithfull humble servant, Arth. Aston. Drogeda, this 3rd of September, about 9 in the morning. For his Exlins. The Lord Lutennant- generall. Endorsed: Sir Arthur Aston, Dated 3. Rec. 4 Sept., 1649. Concerning ye advance of the enemy and Sir Thomas Dacres, etc.

Aston to Ormonde 3 September, afternoon:

Me Lord, Since the writing of my former letter, this day sent by Sir Tho. Dakers, the enemys armey, or the greatest part of them, apears; theer foote, being convoyed by an over awing power of horse, hath takin all the advantaaegous plases without the walles, insomutch that I am very confident this night thay will make theer batteries, the which (all plases beeing so servisable unto them) wee can hardly prevente; in sum I doe beleeve thay will suddenly use theer utmost violence and forse, and with Gods helpe wee will doe our endevours to resiste them; the rest I leave to God and your Excellency's provident care. I have lost won Captin of Collonell Warrins redgiment who was slaine with a musket shot. Maior Butler hath lost too horses, the won of them shot under him self, the other a troopers, a soilder or too wounded and this is alle heethertoe that I can informe your Excellency of, but only that, both in life and death, I am, Me lord,

Your Excellency's most faithfull and moste humble servant. Arth. Aston. Drogodaghe, this 3rd of September, about 2 in the afternoone. I pray God my horse doe not jade it. Thay seemed sumthing out of countenance; it may bee within the walles that will renue thear curradges. For his Exlns. The Lord Lutennant. Endorsed: Sir Arthur Aston's dated the 3rd of Sept., 1649.

Aston to Ormonde 5 September:

Me Lorde, may it pleas your Exxxlens, Uppon Sunday laste [I] writ unto your Excellency giving you notis of the ennemies apeering before this toune, and that day (beeing only horse) thay possessed them selves of divers petty castles heerabouts. Uppon Munday theer foote came up, sum with smale feeld peases. All that day and yesterday thay only plaide uppon our men, and thay at them with muskets. Yesterday at a low water they pased over sum horse and foote at the forde, neere the toune. Our horse and sum foote sallied out to prevent them, and so pressed them, that before the flud towards evening thay retired againe over the water. As yet thay have not had any considerable forese uppon the other side of the water. But yesternight I, having intelligens that sum of theer officers were at Melifont. I intended to have surprised them, but sending by my Lady Moores means to theether I had sertain notis that theer weare forty foote allredy theer who Franck Moore fetched theether. This last night they have made batterys ready but I do verrely beleeve their greate peeces are not yet com, but are to come by sea and the wind is contrary, and when thay come thay will put hard to us. In the meane time our provisions waste and beeing that I got not any contribution out of the counties I was forced to parte with halfe of my corne and a good parte of the last mony imediately. My Collonells and other offisers are very dilligent, the souldiers very laborious; Finglas is very active and so are sum other few of the horse, but for the greater part of them they are not worth the keepeing officers nor troopers. I am credibly informed and have intelligence that the rebells intend this day to pass forces over the river and to besseege both sides. Thus with my humble duty unto your Excellency remembred, and hoping shortly to understande of your martch with a gallent armey, I rest Me Lorde,

Your most humble and for ever faithfull servant, Arth. Aston. Drododaghe, this 5th of September, about 7 of the clock in ye morninge, 1649. Eather the enemy hath mor forses, as yet not coom upp, or els, in my opinion, thay are mutch mistaken in the number which thay report them selves to be of. I am toulde the ennemy say thay will not summon mee, the which I am glad of; it will spare mee so mutch time, as I must have had to answer them. For his Excellns the Lord Luten-genrel of Irland: Thes, with my humble servis. Endorsed: Sir. Ar. Aston, Dated 5. Rec. 6 Sept., 1649.

Ormonde to Aston 7 September:

Sir, I receivd yours of the 5 of this month last night after 11 of the clock. All dilligence shall bee used to put provision into you. Coll. Trevor goes to Atterdy (Ardee) with a party of 500 hors, as well to distract ye rebells as to meet with Owin O'Neill whoe with his army will be near Dundalke on Tewsday next. Let mee have as frequent intelligence as you can, of your particular wants, and what is like to presse you soonest. God send you good successe and us in your succor.

Endorsed: A coppy of the letter to Sir Ar. Aston.

Aston to Ormonde 8 September:

Me Lord, Yesterday in the after noone after the dispatch of my last letters unto your Excellency (wherin I gave an account of the former nights sally) I made annother stronge sally both with horse and foote uppon that parte of the ennemies campe which lodgeth uppon St. Johns hill. My hors was commaunded and led by Captin Plunket, who behaved him selfe gallently, and fell uppon theer mayne garde (and I am informed this day by a Captin, who formerly served his Majesty and is coom over to mee) of the enemy theer was slaine a Lutennant-collonell, a Lutennant and a Sargent: thay will not owne above 9 or 10 other souldiers to bee slaine, but they confes aboundans wounded. I have never lost a man, only Captin Plunket, his legg broke with a musket shot, a Reformadow Cornet, and an other man ill wounded. The ennemy receave (since our sallies) allarums very lightly, and our men are mutch incurredged by them, but indeed I have not been in a place wors situated for sallyes then this toune is. But nevertheles if I had but amunition they should have little rest but my amunition spends very fast. I have spent above fower barrells eaich day ever since Sunday and now I must against my will bee quiet. I beseetch your Excellency to send me some more amunition the which I conceave may come safe to mee. Provisions growes short and after this day I have not a penny of mony. Sum gallant men have lost horses and are now on foote. I beseetch your Excellency to bee mindefull of them. If you could speedily assault the greater campe and that I may have notices, I will, God willing beate up these uppon Saint Johns hill. Me Lorde, I am afearede I have been to tedious in trubling your Excellency with so long a sipher,* but I hope your Excellency will pardon all the errours of Me Lord,

Your Exlens most humble servant, Arth. Aston. Drogodagh, this 8th, about 4 in the afternoon. For his Exlns. The Lord Lutennant-generall of Irelande: Thes with my most humble servis. Endorsed: Sir Ar. Aston, Dated 8 Rec. 9 Sept., 1649.

*Much of this letter is written in code with the use of Ciphers (in this case they used predesignated numbers). There would be an original decoding list of ciphers in the possession of both men which would enable them to decipher them.

Aston to Ormonde 9 September:

Me Lorde, yesternight aboute 10 of the clock, your Excellency's supply of foote came saef to mee. The horse returned back before I coulde get to the gate to speake with them, I beeing at theer aryvall uppon the other side of the river. I perceave by the Lutennant-collonell that your Exlns. writ unto mee the daye before, but I did nether receave that nor any other since won of ye 4th of this munthe. I sent an expres yesterday unto your Exlns who I hope by this time is arived in saefty, as also won the day before, wherin I gave your Exlns notis of too sallies which I made uppon the enemy, which proved both sucsesfull and advantagious; as also I informed your Exlns that my amunition was far spent each day haveing cost mee since Sunday last foure barrells by keeping ye ennemy from working and with sallyes. My provisions growe short and not a penny of mony. More over I informed your Exlns that if speedely you could assault the bigger camp, I haveing notice would God willing beate up the lesser with the side of a few more horse. Good me Lorde some more amunition and money or provisions, as also bee pleased to informe mee wheather theas men that came last bee intended for the making up of my regiment or not, to the ende that I may know how to dispose of the comand over them. Me Lorde, I beseetch your Exlns to continue your favours and good opinnion towards of, me Lorde,

Your Exlns most humble and most faithfull servant for ever, Arth. Aston. Drogodaghe, this 9th in the fore noone, 1649.

Since the writinge of this letter I have thought good, for the more asshurance (seeing messingers doe miscarry), to send this berer, Captin Gaynor, to informe your Exlny more particularly of all thinges. This day the foe dischardged 3 greate peeses towards the towne, wheruppon I conceved a summons woulde follow, but as yet none is come. I am notwithstanding, creddably informed that Crumwell intends to set his reste uppon it, and if my men will but fight it out, I hope hee will get his reste. 'Tis only the remembrance of what I sawe before Dublin that makes me mis-doubte theer performance, and to prevent that your Exlns speedy aprotch will bee a certain cure. In my former letters I writ your Exlns word of the desire of Collonell Warrin, which is that your Exlns would be pleased to conferme what I have doon in placing Ignatius Burnell, Captin in the place of his Captin-Lutennant, and his former Captin-lutennant in the place of the deseased Captin, the which beeing both good men, I desire your Exlns to bee pleased withall.

Your most humble A.A. For his Exlenes the Lord Lutennant-general of Irelande: Theas, with my humble servis Endorsed: Sir Ar. Aston. Dat. 9 Rec. 10 Sept., 1649.

Aston to Ormonde 10 September:

Me Lorde, This morning about 8 of the clock, I receaved the inclosed summons. My answer is by it, as also a letter from the apostite Harding. Since this summons I heard no answer but by the mouth of cannon, the which hath ever since without intermission plaide upon our walles and works. Theay have aight peases of battery, the leaste therof shute 12lb won of 30lb bullet. Thay have made a very greate breach neere the church and I am confident theer resolutions are to gaine it immedi-atly by an assaulte. The souldiers say well, pray God doe well. I will asshure your Exlns that theare shall be no want in mee but your Exlns speedy help is much desired. I refer all thinges unto your Exlns provident care. Living I am, and dying I will end, Me Lorde,

Your Exlns most faithfull and most obleedged humble servant, Arth. Aston. Drogodaghe, this 10th of September, about 7 of the clock at nighte. Just now cooms a messenger who brought mee letter of the 7th of this monthe, but I heare nothing, nor have not dun of Coll. Trevor. My amuni-tion decayes apace and I can not help it. For his Exlns the Lorde Lutennant: Theas, with my hum-ble servis. Endorsed: Sir Ar. Aston. Dated 10. Rec. 11 sept., 1649.

Ormonde to Aston 10 September:

Sir I have received your letter of the 8th giveing an accoumpt of fryday nights sally, but doe miss that advertiseing that on Thursday night. I think fitt to dispatch your messenger with an assurance of my undelayed endeavours to see all your wants seasonably supplyed. Coll Trevor is gone with a strong party of horse, who has direccon to furnish you with powder, match and bullett, and such other provisions for your garrissons as those partes afford. He has a coppy of your cypher, so as you may write your mind safely to him to Laggan Castle Water, where you shall be sure to heare of him. Soe I rest,

Your very affectionate frend, Ormonde. 10 of Sept., 6 in ye morning. Endorsed: A coppy of My Lords to Sr Ar. Aston.

The Lady Wilmot affair

This affair is related in the letters that passed between Aston and Ormonde during the last days of August from the Carte *papers reproduced in Gilbert,* Contemporary History, *pp. 233–236, Sir Arthur Aston to Ormonde 25 August 1649:*

My Lorde, Your Excellency was no sooner out of towne, but I meete with sum people whome I beleeve know not well my constitution; your Excellency will by theas smale inclosed coppies perceave whot inclination Me Lady wilmut hath, to doe mischiefe if it lay in her powre. By her commaunde thees papers weare to have been sent to Dublin, her owne boye was the berer of them, whio, I feare is of to smale a sise to bee hanged. The Lord Blanyes daughters writ too of the papers, and Me Lady Wilmot her selfe the therde, I have put my wi[f]es unckle Frank More in a reste, for I cannot well disieste shutch knavish foolinge. As for the ladies, I say nothing to them untill I have your Excellency's positive orders how to proseede againste them; as for the other too named, to wit Kerkham and Owins, I will examin the busines and with your Excellency's permission proseed with them accordingly. This Kerkham is Me Lord Moore's shurgin. Sum halfe an howre before I sawe the boye (but hee was allredy taken), Me Lady Wilmot sent unto mee to desire leave to sende a messenger to Dublin. I answered I had no commission to doe itt, but it seems she had nottis that the boy was then bringing to mee which occationed this motion of herrs, I beseetch your Excel-lency's expres commaundes to turne her and her malignant famely out of the towne, for though she bee my grandmother, I shall make pouther of her, else she play mee shutch foule playe. I humbly crave your Excellency's speedy commaundes heerin, for thay are very dangerous company, as the case standes with mee, who is for ever Me Lord,

Your Excilence faithfull and most humble servant, Arth. Aston.

Trogodaghe, this 25th August in the evening.

My Lord, if they shoulde now keepe my wife, I have femalles inoughe to release her. May it please your Excellency, since the sealing of this letter, I receved won from your Excilence, and will God willing early in the morninge sende out for may bee gotten, and in all thinges strive to approve my selfe your Excellency's most humble servant, Sir Arth. Aston.

For his Excellency, theas with my humble servis. Endorsed. Sir Ar. Astons, dated and rec. 25 Aug., 1649. Concerning the Lady Wilmot, Frank Moore, etc.

Aston had enclosed the three papers of the female spy faction to Ormonde and they are as follows:

The 1st *paper is signed A. B. and is presumably written by one of the daughters of Lord Blayney, it reads:*

Sir, I must beg one favour from your Excellencie, which is to send me a protection from Mr. Cercome (Kirkham), who I will confidently ingage myselfe woold have beene at Dublin longe since, had not his goodnesse taken great pitie on me in this sadd condicon that I am now in, which you will see when you see me. I must beg the same favour for my poore cozen Owens, who on my word is as much a servant to that cause as anye one can be. And had not his great charge hindered him he woold have beene their, for on my credit his heart is their. And I hope you will consider him. And it shall alwayes owne as a speciall favore to hir, who is most really your faithfull servant, A.B. *My service to all, Col. Coots and Capt. Edmons. Endorsed: Mrs Blayney to Lieut - Col. Foulks, etc.*

The 2nd *paper is written by Lady Wilmot to the same Lieut. - Col. Foulkes:*

Sir, I am now to crave your advice and Coll. Johnes (Jones), and what I shall doe, ffor I am in a very great strate and sad condition. Their fore let me here from you speedilie. I am your faithful friend. Poore Frank and I are in one condition. M. Wilmot. La[dy] Wilmotts to Lt.-Collonell Foulks, etc.

The 3rd *and final enclosure of Aston's uncovered conspiracy of the civilian occupants of Drogheda to Ormonde is also signed A.B:*

Sir, The hearing of your comming this way is a great joy to me, but it has driven all the Lords away. And My Ladie Moore. I have more to wryte, but I leave you to the boy to learne more news. Sir, I here their is one Captain Kitely who intends to come to this partie, with manye more of his comrades; and my unckle is desireous you should knoe it. Sir I must now give you thanks for your token I received by Mr. Blackster, and desire you to be assured I am the same you left me; and will be. I am your faithfull servant, A. B.

My service to captain Edmores. Endorsed by Ormonde: Mrs Blayny to Liet.-Col. Foulkes.

Aston wrote again to Ormonde concerning the conspirators on 27 August:

May it please your Excellency, This morning Sir Edmund Varney is arived, as also Collonell Fleminge. The money Collonell Warrin brought mee which was very welcoom, I wish it had been more. I am extreamly trubled with complaints about cattle which I have caused to bee doven, this waye espetially me Lady Lucas taketh it haynously, but she hath a protection from Coll. Jones and none from you. I heare thay are drawne out with theer cannon at Dublin and reddy for a martch. Thus with my humble duty to your Excennency remembbred I rest, your Excellency's most humble servant, Arth. Aston. Trogodaghe, this 27 August 1649.

I would have taken it for a very great favour, if your Excellency would have been pleased to have sent your possitive answer, what I should have doon with my femall traytors, and so have taken mee of the business, by reson my neere relation unto sum of them, but thay shall not fare the better for that; if the begun unusiall coors by Jones, for the exchange of woomen may bee observed, I would not doubt, but to get honester and better subjects for them. I have niether case shot, nor rounde shot for the cannon, the which I beseetch your Excellency I may have. Collonell Warrin is coom, but his Lieutennant Collonell is stayed at Trim. I beseetch your Excellency not to deprive me of so good a helpe, nor indeed I never saw any offiser taken from his redgiment to commaunde another menes souldiers, unless your Excellency will permit the Collonell to make a chois of an other.

For his Excellency: Theas humbly. Endorsed: Sir Ar. Aston Dated 27. Rec. 28 Aug., 1649. Collonell Warren arrived with mone - Lady Lucas and Lady Willmott, etc.

To which Ormonde replied:
Sir, I received yours of ye 27 this morning. The mony was to a peny all I had, more I expect, and will send it in if it bee possible, as also a settled contribution for that garrison. The bearer goes upon a good pretence, yet take heed he keeps himself to his proper function. Warren is absolutely his, and they are both General Preston's, who aimed at that government. Women is given much to make little factions: I doe not much apprehend this, but it is fit you know all I doe. If you cannot better imploy some of your men, it were not amis partys were sent to interrupt the Dublin market and destroy corne a nd hay, I rest, your affectionate servant.
Endorsed 28 Aug. 1649. A coppy of ye letter to sir Ar. Aston.[4]

Gilbert, vol. ii, preface, p. xix, says that 'Aston was much embarrassed by the movements of Lady Wilmot, Lord Blayney's daughters, and other ladies, his near relatives, then in Drogheda, whom he discovered to be in communication with Colonel Michael Jones and officers of the Parliamentary Army at Dublin'. *Gilbert proceeds to give a family background to Aston's grandmother:* 'Lady Mary Wilmot, daughter of Sir Henry Colley of Castle Carberry, Co. Kildare. Her first husband was Sir Garret Moore of Mellifont, Co. Louth, who died in 1627, leaving, by her seven sons and five daughters. She re-married with sir Charles Wilmot, Viscount Wilmot of Athlone and died in 1654. Francis Moore referred to by Aston, was her sixth son. Her second son, Sir James Moore of Ardee, married Lord Blayney's daughter, Jane. One of the above mentioned Henry Wilmot, the second Viscount of Athlone, was the father of John Wilmot, the noted Earl of Rochester who died in 1680.

Notes to Appendix 2

1   Printed in *Perfect Diurnall*, 14 September 1649, A Declaration by the Lord Lieutenant of Ireland (Dublin 1649) quoted in W. C. Abbott, *The Writings and Speeches of Oliver Cromwell*, Reprint edition, 4 vols. (Oxford: Clarendon Press, 1988), pp. 111–12.
2   Cromwell to Bradshaw, 16 September 1649, Abbott, *Writings and Speeches*, vol. II, p. 124.
3   Cromwell to Lenthall, 17 September 1649, Abbott, *Writings and Speeches*, vol. II, p. 126.
4   John T. Gilbert, *A Contemporary History of Affairs in Ireland from A.D. 1641 to 1652*, 3 vols., (Dublin: Irish Archaeological and Celtic Society, 1879), pp. 233–261.

Appendix No. 3

Gardiner in his History of the Commonwealth and the Protectorate, *quotes at length from Bernard's contemporary tract, unaware of its title. Bernard was a Royalist and was therefore a potential target for Cromwellian troops in this complicated war. Gardiner says* 'Not only does Bernard say nothing of Wood's horrors, but he implicitly denies their existence when he writes that "when the town was stormed and all that bare arms in it put to the sword". Bernard was a strong Royalist having taken a prominent part in proclaiming Charles II at Drogheda. He had been threatened by death by Cromwell and he had no reason to spare him, especially after his tract was published after the Restoration'. *The following extract is from the* Thomason *tracts and gives more details of the taking of Drogheda; The writer refers to Bernard in the second person and calls him the 'Doctor', its title is as follows: A Brief Relation of that Bloody Storm at Drogheda in Ireland and the Doctors Sufferings by Oliver Cromwell in it, and after it, with his Preservation.*

The 3rd of September 1649 was the first day Oliver Cromwell came before it, in making any attempt to that and he had 11,000 Horse and Foot completely provided, the Town had 3,500. Two days he battered. Upon the second day about five of the clock in the afternoon, he assaulted it, but received a repulse; yet returning again, took it: the word was given throughout his army, 'no Quarter'; the Millmount, where the governor Sir Arthur Aston was with about 300 men was yielded upon promise of quarter but as soon as it was possessed by them, all were put to the sword. When the town was fully taken, the Doctor's house was one of the first the soldiers fell upon, but by the strength of it could not enter; The Mayor of the town and divers other of the principal men that were Protestants to the number of about 30 came in to it for refuge.

There came five or six who were sent from a principal officer – the Doctor's former acquaintance – under pretence of a guard for his house, but had a command from him, as soon as they were entered, to kill him, which an ear witness hath since assured him of. The Doctor denying to open the door to them, one of them discharged a musket bullet at him, it passed through the door and only fired the skin of one of his fingers, leaving a spot upon it, which burned four or five days after, and did him no more hurt. Then a cornet of troop of horse came to his relief and pretending he had an order from the General to take care of that house, the soldiers withdrew, and so at the back door he brought in his quartermaster, whom he left to secure him. About a quarter of an hour after, another troop of horse came to the window, and demanded the opening of the door. The quartermaster and himself, with an old servant, left him (for he had sent his wife and children out of the town) stood close together, and told them it was the minister's house and all therein were Protestants. As soon as they heard the Doctor named and his voice, one of them discharged his pistol at him, wherein being a brace of bullets, with the one the quartermaster was shot quite through the body, and dyed in the place, and the other shot his servant through the throat, but recovered; the Doctor only was untouched. After this he made a stand at another place, and seeing the soldiers breaking in at a low window, he went up to his study, where his said friends were making great lamentation expecting present death, they all kneeled down and commended their souls to God, No sooner had the Doctor begun, but in comes the soldiers and interrupts them with bullets, but it pleased God they were so mollified that they only took all they had about them and fell upon the Spoyle of the house. In the midst of these confusions comes one Colonel Ewres (whom the Doctor had not seen in 16 years before, and knew not of his being there) and took up his house for his quarters, turned the soldiers out and made the doors fast for himself. Not long after came Colonel Hewson and told the Doctor he had orders to blow up the steeple (which stood between the quier and the body of the church) where about threescore men were run up for refuge, but the three Barrells of Powder which he caused to be put under it for that end, blew up onely the body of the church and the next night *(should read the next thing)* Hewson caused the seats of the church to be broken up, and made a great pile of them under the steeple, which firing it took the lofts wherein five great Bells hung, and from thence it flamed up to the top and so at once men, and bells and roof came all down together, the most hideous sight and terrible cry, that ever he was a witness of at once. The next day the Colonel that had saved the Doctor's life comes to him and tells him that he was very sharply checked for it, by the Generall and many of the officers, and that he must yet expect to dye, that no protection could be had for him; which was confirmed unto him by others also, whereupon divers that came to see him, took their leaves as never to see him again and the number of the dead bodies (with the churchyard and streets were already filled) daily encreasing, even in coole blood to the number of 3,500 gave him little hope of the contrary; that which at present reprieved him, was Colonel Ewres sending two of this officers which were wounded to lie there.

Then was the proclaiming of his majesty inciting and encouraging of the army, and what else might favour ill with the soldiers, mustered up against him. The next day Oliver Cromwell with many of his officers came to the Doctor's house, began with aspersing his ordination as Popish, then the late Archbishop of Armagh, from when he had received it, then his Majesties title, and the Doctor's praying for him came into discourse, the disputes of which, with divers other subjects which lasted about three quarters of an hower, would be impertinent to be related here, but when he found the Doctor to be of that judgement he had heard, he left him without any assurance of life, only gave order to the governor to have him sent up to Dublin as a prisoner. When he came there it so fell out that he met Cromwell himself with his officers in the streets, where after great menaces that he would make him an example, and expressly threatening him as he was carried away, beside the votes of all the officers against him, Hugh Peters fell most upon him who (as was affirmed then) had blamed Cromwell for saving of his life so long. Seventeen days he was close prisoner and afterwards upon bonds confined six months within the city, and after that sent up to the army at Clonmel, permitted to come then with Cromwell in to England, where to himself he never varied in any discourse in the said subjects from what he had said to him at the first sight of him. Thus far his sufferings in that storm and his Deliverance.

There were many reasons why Bernard was an enemy of Parliament and why he was subjected to such abuse. Appended to this account are the charges against him; Some Articles Objected Against the Doctor while he was a Prisoner in Dublyn:

I. That he had refused to obey Colonel Michael Jones, his order for the forbearing the use of Common Prayer, in his church at Drogheda.

II. That he had preached a thanksgiving sermon for the taking of the Town of Drogheda by the Lord of Inchiquin under the command of the Lord Marquesse of Ormond.

III. That he saluted one Colonel Trenchard, with great joy the town was taken, accordingly for the King.

IV. That he moved the Mayor of the town to come in his Scarlet to the proclaimimg of the King, and that he attended at it himself, and went immediately to the church and observed the Book of Common Prayer & in special those prayers for him.

V. His praying for the Lord Marquesse of Ormond, as Lord Lieutenant of Ireland, then besieging of Dublyn.

VI. His praying for a Confusion of Oliver Cromwell's army while he was besieging Drogheda.

VII. His withdrawing of some Commanders and Souldiers from the service of Parliament and in special the speeches of one of their captains upon his death bed produced, in complaining of the Doctor for that purpose.

VIII. That he was with the Lord Marquesse of Ormond at his camp before Dublyn.

IX. That he refused to go with the Parliament Army out of the said town of Drogheda, but staid with the Lord Of Inchiquin and his party in it, attended the Lord Marquesse of Ormond, when he came back to it and preaching before him and praying accordingly for a good success upon his designs.

X. That he had employed his parts (to use the very words as it was written to him) against the Saints and that interest which the Lord Jesus is now bringing forth in the world'.

Quoted in F. Madan, Thomason Collection, *British Museum, notes on the Thomason Collection of Civil War tracts (London: 1897). Also partly quoted in Gardiner,* History of Commonwealth and Protectorate, *p. 123. Also partly quoted in Murray, "Cromwell at Drogheda, The Nineteenth Century", p. 1234. Bernard was a fierce antagonist of Cromwell's, yet throughout the above account, he does not endorse the tradition of a civilian massacre. The death of the quartermaster and the wounding of his servant seems not to have been deliberate, since he himself was the target of the soldiers as a well known tenacious Royalist. What is very obvious is that when the soldiers entered the house, they were solely intent on plunder and not murder.*

Appendix No. 4.1

The propositions of Colonel David Sinnott, Governor of the town and castle of Wexford, and on behalf of the officers, soldiers and inhabitants in the said town and castle, to General Cromwell:

1. That all and every the inhabitants of the said town from time to time and at all times hereafter, shall have free and uninterrupted liberty, publicly to use, exercise, and profess the Roman Catholic religion, without restriction, mulct, or penalty, any law or statute to the contrary notwithstanding.

2. That the regular and secular Roman Catholic clergy now possessed of the churches, church livings, monasteries, religious houses, and chapels in the said town and in the suburbs and franchises thereof, and their successors, shall have, hold and enjoy to them and their successors for ever, the said churches &c., and shall teach and preach in them publicly, without any molestation, any law or statute to the contrary notwithstanding.

3. That Nicholas, now Lord Bishop of Ferns, and his successors shall use and exercise such juristiction over the Catholics of his diocese as since his consecration hitherto he used.

4. That all the officers and soldiers of whatever quality and degree soever in the town and castle, and such of the inhabitants as are so pleased, shall march with flying colours and be conveyed safe with their lives, artillery ordnance, ammunition, arms, goods of all sorts, horses, moneys, and whatever else belongs to them, to the town of Ross and there to be left safe with their own party; allowing each musketeer towards their march, a pound of powder, four yards of match, and twelve brace

of bullets; and a strong convoy to be sent with the said soldiers, within twenty-four hours after the yielding up of the said town.

5. That such of the inhabitants of the said town as will desire to leave the same at any time hereafter, shall have free liberty to carry away out of the said town all their frigates, artillery, arms, powder, corn, malt, and other provisions which they have for their defence and sustenance, and all their goods and chatttels, of what quality or condition soever, without any manner of disturbance whatsoever, and have passes and safe conducts and convoys for their lives and said goods to Ross, or where else they shall think fit.

6. That the Mayor, bailiffs, free burgesses and commons of the said town may have, hold and enjoy the said town and suburbs, their commons, their franchises, liberties and immunities which hitherto they enjoyed; and that the Mayor, bailiffs and free burgesses may have the government of the said town, as hitherto they enjoyed the same from the realm of England, and that they have no other government, they adhering to the State of England and observing their orders and the orders of their governors in this realm for the time being.

7. That all the burgesses and inhabitants, either native or strangers, of the said town, who shall continue their abode therein, or come to live there within three months, and their heirs shall have, hold and enjoy their several castles, houses, lands, tenements and hereditaments within the land of Ireland, and all their goods and chattels, to them and their heirs to their own several uses for ever without molestation.

8. That such burgess or burgesses or other inhabitants of the said towns as shall at any time hereafter be desirous to leave the said town, shall have free leave to dispose of their real and personal estates respectively to their best advantage; and further, have full liberty and a safe conduct respectively to go into England or elsewhere, according to their several pleasures who shall desire to depart the same.

9. That all and singular the inhabitants of the said town, either native or strangers, from time to time, and at all times hereafter, shall have, reap, and enjoy the full liberty of free born English subjects, without the least incapacity or restriction therein; and that all the freemen of the said town shall be as free in all the seaports, cities, and towns in England as the freemen of all and every of the said cities and towns and all and every the said freemen of the said cities and towns to be as free in their said town of Wexford as the freemen thereof for their greater encouragement to trade and commerce together on all hands.

10. That no memory remain of any hostility or distance, which was hitherto between the said town and castle on the one part, and the Parliament or State of England on the other part; but that all acts, transgressions, offences, depredations and other crimes, of what nature and quality whatsoever, be they ever so transcendent, attempted or done, or supposed to be attempted or done by the inhabitants of the said town or any other, heretofore or at present adhering to the said town, either native or stranger, and every of them shall pass in oblivion, without chastisement, challenge, recompense, demand, or questioning for them or any of them, now or at any time hereafter.

Appendix No. 4.2

For the Honourable William Lenthall, Esquire, Speaker of the House of Parliament of England: These

Sir, The army marched from Dublin, about 23rd of September, into the county of Wicklow, where the enemy had a garrison about fourteen miles from Dublin called Killingkerick; which they quitting, a company of the army was put therein. From thence the army marched through almost a desolated country, until it came to a passage over the river Doro, about a mile above the castle of Arklow, which was the first seat and honour of the Marquis of Ormonde's family which he had strongly fortified, but was, upon the approach of the army, quitted; wherein we left another company of Foot.

From thence the army marched towards Wexford, where in the way was a strong and large castle at a town called Limerick, the ancient seat of the Esmonds; where the enemy had a strong garrison, which they burnt and quitted, the day before our coming thither. From thence we marched towards Ferns, an episcopal seat, where was a castle, to which I sent Colonel Reynolds with a party to summon it; which accordingly he did, and it was surrendered to him; where we having put a company, advanced the army to a passage over the river Slane, which runs down to Wexford; and that night marched into the fields of a village called Eniscorfy belonging to Mr Robert Wallop where a strong castle was very well manned and provided for by the enemy, and, close under it, a very fair house belonging to the same worthy person, a monastery of Franciscan friars, the considerablest in all Ireland: they ran away the night before we came. We summoned the castle and they refused to yield at the first, but upon better consideration, they were willing to deliver the place to us; which accordingly they did, leaving their great guns, arms, ammunition and provisions behind them.

Upon Monday the first of October, we came before Wexford, into which the enemy had put a garrison, consisting of [part of] their army; this town having until then, been so confident of their own strength as that they would not, at any time, suffer a garrison to be imposed upon them. The commander that brought in those forces was Colonel David Synnott, who took upon him the command of the place, to whom I sent a summons, a copy whereof is this enclosed; between whom and me there passed answers and replies, copies whereof these also are.

While these papers were passing between us, I sent the Lieutenant General with a party of dragoons, horse and foot, to endeavour to reduce their fort, which lay at the mouth of their harbour, about ten miles distance from us, to which he sent a troop of dragoons, but the enemy quitted their fort, leaving behind them about seven great guns; betook themselves by the help of their boat, to a frigate of twelve guns lying in the harbour, within cannon shot of the fort. The dragoons possessed the fort and some seamen belonging to your fleet coming happily in at the same time, they bent their guns at the frigate, and she immediately yielded to mercy bothe herself, the soldiers that had been in the fort, and the seamen that manned her. And whilst our men were in her, the town, not knowing what had happened, sent another small vessel to her which we also took.

The governor of the town having obtained from me a safe-conduct for the four persons mentioned in one of the papers, to come and treat with me about the surrender of the town, I expected they should have done so, but instead thereof, the Earl of Castlehaven brought to their relief, on the north side of the river, about five hundred foot, which occasioned their refusal to send out any to treat, and caused me to revoke my safe-conduct, not thinking it fit to leave it for them to make use of it when they pleased.

Our cannon being landed, and we having removed all our quarters to the south-east of the town, next the castle, it was generally agreed that we should bend the whole strength of our artillery upon the castle, being persuaded that if we got the castle, the town would easily follow.

Upon Thursday the 11th instant (our batteries being finished the night before) we began to play betimes in the morning, and having spent near a hundred shot, the Governor's stomach came down, and he sent to me to give leave for four persons intrusted by him to come unto me, and offer terms of surrender, which I condescending to, two field officers, with an Alderman of the town and a captain of the castle, brought out the propositions enclosed, which for their abominableness, manifesting also the impudency of the men, I though fit to present to your view, together with my answer, which indeed had no effect. For whilst I was preparing of it, studying to preserve the town from plunder, that it might be of the more use to you and your army, the captain, being one of the commissioners, being fairly treated, yielded up the castle to us, upon the top of which our men no sooner appeared, but the enemy quitted the walls of the town, which our men perceiving, ran violently upon the town with their ladders and stormed it. And when they were come into the market-place, the enemy making a stiff resistance, our forces brake them and then put all to the sword that came their way. Two boatfuls of the enemy attempting to escape, being overprest with numbers, sank, whereby were drowned near three hundred of them. I believe in all, there was lost of the enemy not many less than two thousand; and I believe not twenty of yours killed from first to last of the siege.

And indeed it hath not without cause been deeply set upon our hearts, that, we intending better to this place than so great a ruin, hoping the town might be more use to you and your army, yet God would not have it so; but, by an unexpected providence, in His righteous justice, brought a just judgement upon them to become a prey to the soldier, who in their piracies had made preys of so many families, and made with their bloods to answer the cruelties which they had exercised upon the lives of divers poor Protestants; two of which I have been lately been acquainted with. About seven or eight score poor Protestants were put by them into an old vessel, which being, as some say, bulged by them, the vessel sank, and they were all presently drowned in the harbour. The other [instance] was thus: they put divers Protestants into a chapel (which since they have used for a Mass-house and in which one or more of their Priests were now killed), where they were famished to death.

The soldiers got a very good booty in this place, and had they not had opportunity to carry their goods over the river, whilst we besieged it, it would have been much more. I could have wished for their own good, and the good of the garrison, they had been more moderate. Some things which were not easily portable, we hope we shall make use of to your behoof. There are great quantities of iron, hides, tallow, salt, and barrel-staves, which are under commissioners hands, to be secured. We believe there are near a hundred cannon in the fort, and elsewhere in and about the town. Here is likewise some very good shipping: here are three vessels, one of them of thirty-four guns, which a week's time would fit to sea, there is another of about twenty guns, very near ready likewise, and one other frigate of twenty guns, upon the stocks, made for sailing, which is built up to the uppermost deck. For her handsomeness' sake, I have appointed the workmen to finish her, here being materials to do it, if you or the Council of State should approve thereof. The frigate, also, taken by the fort, is a most excellent vessel for sailing. Besides divers other ships and vessels in the harbour.

This town is now so in your power, that [of] the former inhabitants, I believe scarce one in twenty can challenge any property in their houses. Most of them are run away, and many of them killed in this service. And it were to be wished that an honest people would come and plant here, where are very good houses, and other accommodations fitted to their hands, and may by your favour be made of encouragement to them, as also a seat of good trade, both inward and outward, and of marvellous great advantage in the point of herring and other fishing. This town is pleasantly seated and strong, having a rampart of earth within the wall, near fifteen foot thick.

Thus it hath pleased God to give into your hands this other mercy, for which, as for all, we pray God may have all the glory. Indeed your instruments are poor and weak, and can do nothing but through believing, and that is the gift of God also.

I humbly take leave, and rest, your most humble servant

O. Cromwell.

Wexford, October 14th, 1649

[P.S.] A day or two before our battery was planted, Ormonde, the Earl of Castlehaven, the Lord of Ardes and Clanneboyes were on the other side of the water with about 1,800 horse, 1,500 foot, and offered to put in four or five hundred foot more into the town, which the town refusing, he marched away in all haste. I sent the Lieutenant General after him with about 1,400 horse, but the enemy made haste from him.[1]

Note to Appendix 4

1 Summarised in Abbott, *Writings and Speeches*, vol. II, pp. 138–38; reproduced in full in Murphy, *Cromwell in Ireland*, pp. 152–54; also in Hore, *History of the Town and County of Wexford*, pp. 300–02.

Appendix No. 5.1

Wexford, 15 October, 1649.

We having removed our Campe to the south end by the castle for more safety and convenience sake, first played with eight great pieces and two mortyr-pieces upon the Castle, and finding the same batterable, courage began wonderfully to increase in us and to quaile in the besieged. The Towne within had 2,000 men, most mariners, and before our coming they had taken in from Ormond 800 Auxiliaries, and since our sitting downe they had received in twenty colours more from the other shore (not having been by us impeached) and they had gabled all their streets and had plenty of Artillery, Armes and all manner of provisions, and till the tryal of our cannon they appeared very daring, but now on a sudden, all spirit, councell and manhood causelesly forsook them.

The people within could not be restrained from boating away by water, this made the Magistrates seek a parly which granted, my Lord proffered onely to the Souldier to depart home, renouncing bearing arms against the Parliament of England for the future; and for the towne, their persons were to be secured from violence, and their goods from plunder. This was accepted and by my Lord's hand signed, but before delivery, the Captaine of the Castle having some Trunks of value, belonging to Sir Ralph Aston, it seems out of hope to save the same, agrees by himseffle for his owne souldiery and immediately receives in a garrison of ours. The towne therefore seeing their commissioners not returned, but our flag advanced upon the Castle, and our Gunns (for they were to play all the time of the treaty) traversed from the Castle and bent against them, dispaired presently, and some of the souldiers threw themselves over the wall amongst our Horse, but with the greatest part made escape by water. This being seen by us made us fall on, and storme with ladders and without resistance, or losse of a man, the towne was entered, won and sackt.

The spoyling of the Towne was extremely incommodious to ourselves, and we all desired to reserve it for our winter accomodation, both parties were agreed about it, and the agreement was drawne up and signed, but God hath otherwise determined upon it.

Indeed the Towne, though of old English extraction, and retaining the old English dialect, still without any Irish [ad] mixture and being composed of such as had not been very obstinate from the beginning from letting us in upon termes, had not Ormonde's military Faction overruled, yet were guilty of much Piracy, having been the receptacle of all the Prince's roving Frigots for diverse years past, and so we may conceive God had further quarrel with them than we had, and by Him the issue was otherwise ordered, than we or the Irish had designed.

Upon entering the Towne about [?] men were put to the sword, and about [?] more drowned by overcharging vessels in the flight, and a great spoyle and havock was made of many rich commodities, so that now we are inforced to seek further for a winter retirement, and want that refreshment which else the place might have afforded in the declining of the yeare; but for my part I am strong in my confidence that this is so directed by God for our good; and that though our army now be very sick and impaired, and likely to be further weakened by accesse of winter and more gusty weather, yet God crosses us here that we may be onely better provided for and entertained elsewhere. My Lord accordingly is now advancing to Rosse, the most invincible Refuge and Rendezvous of the Irish.

All our disadvantage is that we fight not with men armed with steele, but with walls lined with men, and that our Enemies doe not onely lye in ambuscadoe behind walls, but (as I may say) behind diseases, tempests, wants and difficult ways; for nothing is more obvious to sense than this, that a Lyon-like heart is inspired into our men, whilst all that is man-like is taken from our enemy[1].

Appendix No. 5.2

We lay before this citty eight days, and the ninth day, which was the 11th of this month, God delivered it and the strong castle thereof into our hands, having got the fort, six miles off upon the mouth of the Haven, the next day after we came, the enemy that kept it (their hearts being taken away) run out of the Fort upon the first appearance of our men, and betook themselves to a Pyrat Frigot, belonging to this Towne, which road within the mouth of the Haven within shot of the Fort and our men playing upon them but three or four shots with their own guns (which they left in the Fort) they presently sent a shoare and surrendered both themselves prisoners and also the Frigot with 16 or 18 pieces of Ordnance in her. This gave us opportunities for our ships and vessells that attended us along the coast from Dublin with provisions, Ordnance and ammunition, to be brought into the Haven, and so up to the Campe near the Tomne where the army lay, within 4 or 5 dayes, so soon as the winds and Spring Tide served. But in this time our men endured great extremity for want of bread and other necessaries. Wee had a strong enemy within the Towne and [a] Field Army greater than ours hovering about us (for most parte a days march), but keeping themselves upon the advantage of Rivers, Hills and Woods, and not having confidence to come out to fight us. On Wednesday last [i.e., October 10th] having made our approaches and prepared our Batteries, we made two breaches in the Castle. They had upon our first summons (when we came before the town) seemed willing to treat, and upon good tearmes to surrender. But making some trifling delays for 3 or 4 dayes, till they had got more strength into the Towne from the other side of the river (which we could not prevent) they then slightly broke off, and we heard no more from them till we had made the breaches in the Castle, and then they sent out againe desireing to treat. We received their Propositions which contayned large demands and rejected them with disdaine, and without answer. But being desirous, if it had appeared [to be] the Will of God to save blood [shed] and prevent the spoyling of so Rich a Towne, which we thought might be a place of receipt for many honest families out of England, we offered them in short, if they would immediately surrender to let the common souldiers goe to their homes. But though thus we (then not knowing otherwise the mind of God towards them) were mercifully inclined, God showed that he had a further controversy against such a place and people, who had inricht themselves with the spoyle of the Innocent (by robbing and pillaging at sea) all English merchants they could light on since the Warr began, and making a Trade of that Pyracy) and where (as we better understand since) there hath been so great cruelties exercised towards English Protestants that were many in these Parts at the beginning of the Warre, and now none left, but [are] either killed or driven away.

And therefore God so ordered it as to make them vomit up again their stolen riches in one hour, and pay dearly for the innocent blood here spilt, for when we had set downe our aforesaid offer, and delivered it to their commissioners to convey to the Towne, our men being ready to assault the breaches of the castle; the Governor thereof for feare and haste accepted our termes for himself and his, and admitted our men into the castle (and thereupon though it stood cleare without the walls of the Towne) yet so soone as ever the Garrison within the Towne saw our colours upon the Castle, they had not confidence to stand to their armes, or maintaine their walls so long as to receive their Commissioners back with our offer. When wee (although wee would grant no Cessation of Arms for a minute yet) had no thoughts of attempting any more at that time than the Castle; But they ran away from their walls on that side that was towards the Castle, quitted their guards, and betooke themselves towards their boats (whereof they had abundance belonging to their ships at their Keys within their Haven) which many of our souldiers from the Castle and some higher ground perceiving, they fell on their owne accords, first without ladders, lifting and helping one another with their Pikes or any other way over the walls, and after with ladders, till they were got in a good number into the Towne, and then the enemy made head and got heart againe and attempting to have returned to their guards and walls we soon beat and disperst them, and possessed the Towne (their Commissioners this while, not having hearts to put themselves into the Towne againe with our offer): Seeing thus the Righteous hand of God upon such a Towne and People, we thought [it] not good nor just to restraine off our souldiers from their right of Pillage, nor from doing of execution upon the enemy, where the entrance was by force and a resistance endeavoured though too late. There was more sparing of lives (of the Souldiery part of the enemy here) than at Drogheda, yet of their Souldiery and Townsmen here were about 1, 500 slaine (or drowned in boats sunk by the multitude and weight of the people pressing into them). It was a place settled the most deepe in superstition and darknesse that I have seen or heard of and a people zealous against anything of better light.

God visited both the deceivers and the deceived together. Of their Priests (which deceived and led them) were many slaine. Some (I heard of) came holding forth Crucifixes before them and conjuring our Souldiers (for his sake that saved us all) to save their lives; yet our Souldiers would not own their dead images for our living Saviour, but struck them dead with their idols. Many of their Priests being got together in a Church of the Towne (where 'tis sayd, many poore Protestantas were kept and killed together in the beginning of the Rebellion) were slaine together by our Souldiers about their Altar.

The riches of this Towne (wherein as to Household Furniture, merchandise, and Trading commodities, it did abound) being so ill gained, as I have said, was (for the most part) taken, or rent and torne a pieces, or wasted and spoyled by the Souldiery in one hower or two. The grosser sorts and stores of Merchandise which our Souldiers minded not in the hour of plunder, as Hides, Tallow, Salt, Pipe Staves, Iron, &c., with all their Ships and Boats fall into the State hands, and we have appoynted Commissioners to collect and improve them for the Publique, as also to preserve and buy back from the Souldiery, as they may for small prices, all Household Furniture to be kept for such honest Families as shall hereafter come out of England to inhabit this Towne, we being desirous by any such encouragements to draw over a generation and seed of good People (if God see it good) to possesse such places and to plant the Countreyes.[2]

Appendix No. 5.3

TO THE KING'S MOST EXCELLENT MAJESTY

The humble petition of the Ancient natives, inhabitants of the town of Wexford, and of the heires, orphanes and widowes of such of them as are dead.

Humbly Sheweth That the Petitioners in the beginning of the Rebellion in Ireland helde firme to their ancient loyalty, and never acted anything relating to the said troubles till they observed that some of his late Majestie's shipping revolted against him; and finding their trade was interrupted by those in England that stood in opposition to his late Majestie's authority, then and not sooner did the said inhabitants begin to stand upon their defence; and having fitted and armed some shipps for the support of their trade in the year 1643, the Earle of Castlehaven and the Lord Viscount Taffe being sent by advice of the Lord Marquess Ormonde then your majestie's Lord Lieutenant of Ireland to demand assistance of shipping from the petitioners for his late Majestie's Service, they having imparted the contents of their employment to the said inhabitants, they chearfully and freely agreed to supply the said Lieutenant with the number of tenne shipps, and to have them in readynes in 15 days, and had not failed so to doe but that the occasion was diverted; yet the petitioners zeal and readynesse did sufficiently appeare if there were cause. And as the said inhabitants have been always a people adhearing to the interest of the Crowne and ancient Collonies continued there since the reigne of King Henry the second, soe did they on all occasions expresse their chief loyalty in his Majestie's Service and particularly in embracing the peace concluded by your Majestie's authority 1648, as was manifested afterwards in the time of greatest danger; for the late Usurper Oliver Cromwell, arriveing with a powerful army in Ireland in the year 1649 and having upon the taking of Drogheda put all the inhabitants and soldiers to the sword, that the example thereof might strike a terror into the hearts of the inhabitants of other townes which hee was soone after to besiege, he writt to the petitioners of Wexford being his next designe, and courted them to submitt to his authority and to quitt the royal interest, and that they should injoy all their possessions and fortunes, and be used as well as any others under his power; whose proposall the petitioners did reject, and sent to the Lord Marquess of Ormond, then your Majestie's Lord Lieutenant, praying his Lordship to take care of that place of consequence, and to garrison it as hee should thinke fitt, and that they were ready to expose their lives and fortunes for the defence thereof against the said Usurper, the said Lord Lieutenant did garrison the said towne accordingly and sent thither an able and resolute Commander, Sir Edmund Butler, to whose government and care the inhabitants submitted the whole towne and fortifications, with their lives and fortunes. Yet soe it is, may it please your Majestie, that after all the resistance they could make, the said Usurper having a great Army by sea and land before the said towne, did, on the nynth of October 1649, soe powerfully assault them, that hee entered the towne, and put man, woman and child, to a very few, to the sword, where among the rest the said Governor lost his life and others of the souldiers and inhabitants to the number of 1500 persons; and besides the whole stock and fortune of the inhabitants, to an inestimable value, became pillage and booty to the said Usurper and his souldiers.

The petitioners therefore in the behalfe of themselves who escaped the sword of the said Usurper, and in the behalfe of the children, heires, and widowes of those who soe sacrificed their lives in your Majestie's Service, doe most humbly beseech your Majestie, to be graciously pleased to looke on them as deserved objects of your favour and justice, soe farr as to give order for their restitution to their former habitations, possessions, and interests in the said towne and country; and that the rather, that such of them as were capable to serve your Majestie went first to Silly and Jerzey then in your Majestie's hands and afterwards followed your fortune into forraigne parts, still acting by your Commission in all occasions untill that after your Majestie's happy restauration their Commissions were called in. To which they readily submitted; and now to the number of 30 Captains of them are expecting your Majestie's favour and justice for restoring their former possessions aforesaid, having noe other livlyhood or subsistance at present: which being granted they will ever pray.[3]

Notes to Appendix 5

1   Philip Herbert Hore, *History of the Town and County of Wexford*, pp. 286–87; also quoted in Williams, 'Cromwell's Massacre at Wexford', pp. 561–78.

2   Hore, *History of the Town and County of Wexford*, pp. 295–96; also quoted in Williams, 'Cromwell's Massacre at Wexford', pp. 561–78.

3   Hore, *History of the Town and County of Wexford*, pp. 330–31.

Appendix No. 6.1

For William Lenthall, Speaker of the Parliament of England,

Sir, Since my last from Wexford, we marched to Ross, a walled town, situated upon the Barrow, a port town up to which a ship of seven or eight hundred tons may come.

We came before it upon Wednesday the 17th instant, with three pieces of cannon. That evening I sent a summons; Major General Taaff, being Governor, refused to admit my trumpet into the town, but took the summons in, returning me no answer. I did hear that near 1,000 foot had been put into this place some few days before my coming to it. The next day was spent in making preparations for our battery, and in our view there were boated over from the other side of the river of English, Scots, and Irish, 1,500 more, Ormond, Castlehaven, and the Lord of Ardes, being on the other side of the water to cause it to be done.

That night we planted our battery, which began to play very early the next morning. The governor immediately sent forth an answer to my summons, copies of all which I make bold herewith to trouble you, the rather because you may see how God pulls down proud stomachs. He desired Commissioners might treat, and that in the mean time there might be a ceasing of acts of hostility on both sides which I refused; sending in word that if he would march away with arms, bag and baggage, and give me hostages for performance, he should. Indeed he might have done it without my leave, by the advantage of the river. He insisted upon having the cannon with him, which I would not yield unto, but required the leaving of the artillery and the ammunition, which he was content to do, and marched away leaving the great artillery and the ammunition in the stores to me. When they marched away at least 500 English, many of them the Munster forces, came to us.

Ormond is at Kilkenny, Inchiquin in Munster, Henry O'Neill, Owen Roe's son is come up to Kilkenny, with near two thousand horse and foot, with whom and Ormond there is now a perfect conjunction. So that now, I trust, some angry friends will think it high time to take off their jealousy from those to whom they ought to exercise more charity.

The rendition of this garrison was a seasonable mercy, as giving us an opportunity towards Munster, and is for the present a very good refreshment for our men. We are able to say nothing as to all this, but that the Lord is still pleased to own a company of poor worthless creatures, for which we desire His name to be magnified, and the hearts of all concerned may be provoked to walk worthy of such continued favours. This is the earnest desire of,

Your most humble servant, Oliver Cromwell

Ross, October 25th 1649.[1]

Appendix No. 6.2

Answer to the several desires of the inhabitants of Cork sent by their Commissioners and received 12 November 1649 by the Lord Lieutenant of Ireland.

1st I shall forbear to make answer.

2nd The inhabitants of the city of Cork, that have joined in the late declaring for Parliament, shall be fully indemnified for anything that's past, as is desired, so as to restore them to the same condition of freedom, privilege and safety, that they were in before the lord Inchiquin's defection. And as is the same, or anything that had issued thereupon had never been, and particularly shall enjoy the benefit of any prize goods they have bought, without being troubled or damnified by any for the same.

3rd That the charter of the city of Cork shall be renewed as is desired and no advantage taken of the forfeiture mentioned.

4th For what they have lent, disbursed, or delivered for public service, since the Declaration, or hereafter shall sent or advance. It shall be satisfied with all speed, out of any revenue or income, in those parts out of which it may best and surest be done, which I leave to themselves to think of and propose. And if anything so due to them from the public, before the Lord Inchiqiun's defection, they shall have the same right and be in the same capacity of satisfaction as before the said defection were, and I shall endeavour it for them equally, as for any other to whom such debt, from the public is due, by all ways and means in my power. But for anything so lent, disbursed or delivered (as to a public use) since the said defection, and before the said declaration. It cannot be otherwise considered, than as damages sustained by persons well effected, lying under the power of the enemy. And in that nature so far as anything shall appear to have been formerly taken from such persons, it shall be considered, examined and represented to the Parliament to be satisfied equally, as the damages of any other well effected persons in Ireland.

5th For debts due from private persons, they shall be left to their full legal rights.

6th As all that is granted to the soldiery and inhabitants of Cork, Youghal, and other neighbouring places that have already corresponded and joined with them, in their late declaration, is most freely and heartily granted, because not bargained for before their declaring, and because to men appearing (by the carriage of the business), to have done, what they have done therein, really, from a recovered sense, and affection to the English parliamentary and protestant interest in this nation so to any other places and persons that (having formerly been of the parliamentary party), shall so come in, as that it appear to be from the same sense and affection, and not from policy or necessity.. I shall bear the same mind and shall have the same readiness to do them good and no hurt.

7th Not fully understanding the nature of the extent of the things desired, I can give no present full resolution, but shall be ready, not only to do them full right in all things, but also to perform, any such good office of respect (within my power) unto the city of Cork, as may be a reward and memorial of their faithfulness and public affection, which in this late action, I really think they have deserved.

Lastly, as to the desire in the other paper, concerning the militia of the city of Cork, I am very willing that the inhabitants be formed into a regiment under Mr. John Hodder as Colonel, Mr. Maurice Cuffe to be Lieutenant-Colonel and Major Borman, major. And the regiment or any part thereof when called upon duty, to have the State's pay. For other officers of the regiment, I leave to the said field officers, or any two of them to nominate and I propound to the Lord Broghill, Sir Will. Fenton and Colonel Phayre for approbation.

O. Cromwell [2]

Appendix No. 6.3

Declaration of the Bishops and Clergy assembled at Clonmacnoise, 4th December 1649.
By the Ecclesiastical Congregation of the Kingdom of Ireland, we, the Archbishops, Bishops and other Ordinaries and Prelates of this Kingdom of Ireland, having met at Clonmacnoise [proprio motu] on the 4th day of December in the year of our Lord 1649, taking into our consideration among other the affairs then agitated and determined for the preservation of the Kingdom, that many of our flock are misled with a vain opinion of hopes that the Commander-in-Chief of the rebel forces, commonly called Parliamentarians, would afford them good conditions, and that relying thereon, they suffer utter destruction of religion, lives, and fortunes, if not prevented. To undeceive them in this their ungrounded expectation, we do hereby declare as a most certain truth that the enemy's resolution is to extirpate the Catholic religion out of all his Majesty's dominions, as by their several covenants doth appear, and the practise wherever their power doth extend, as is manifested by Cromwell's letter of the 19th of October, 1649 to the then Governor of Ross; his words were "for that which you mention concerning liberty of religion, I meddle not with any man's conscience; but if by liberty of conscience you mean a liberty to exercise the mass, I judge it best to use plain dealing and to let you know where the Parliament have power that will not be allowed of". This tyrannical resolution they have put in execution in Wexford, Drogheda, Ross and elsewhere; and it is notoriously known that by the acts of Parliament called the acts of subscription, the estates of the inhabitants of this kingdom are sold, so there remaineth now no more but to put the purchasers in possession by the power of forces drawn out of England. And for the common sort of people towards whom if they show any more moderate usage at the present, it is to no other end but for their private advantage and for the better support of their army, intending at the close of their conquest (if they can effect the same as God forbid) to root out the commons also, and plant this land with colonies to be brought hither out of England, as witness the number they have already sent hence for the Tobacco island and put enemies in their places.

And in effect this banishment and other destructions of the common people must follow the resolution of extirpating the Catholic religion, which is not to be effected without the massacring or banishment of the Catholic inhabitants.

We cannot therefore, in our duty to God and discharge of the care we are obliged to have for the preservation of our flocks, but admonish them not to delude and lose themselves with the vain expectation of conditions to be had from that merciless enemy. And consequently, we beseech the gentry and inhabitants, for God's glory and their own safety, to the uttermost of their power to contribute with patience to the support of the war against that enemy, in hope that by the blessing of God they may be rescued by the threatened evils, and in time be permitted to serve God in their native country and enjoy their estates and the fruits of their labours, free from such heavy levies or any other such taxes as they bear at present; admonishing also those that are enlisted of the army to prosecute constantly, according to each man's charge, the trust reposed in them, the opposition of the common enemy in so just a war as is that they have undertaken for their religion, King and country, as they expect the blessing of God to fall on their actions. And that to avoid God's heavy judgement and the indignation of their native country, they neither plunder nor oppress the people, nor suffer any under their charge to commit any extortion or oppression, so far as shall lie in their power to prevent.[3]

Declaration of the Bishops and others assembled at Clonmacnoise, 13th December, 1649.
Whereas heretofore many of the Clergy and Laity did in their actions and proceedings express much discontent and divisions of mind, grounding the same on the late difference of opinion which happened amongst the Prelates and the laity, by which the nation was not so well united as was necessary in this time of great danger, wherein all as with one heart and hand ought to oppose the common enemy. We, the Archbishops, Bishops and Prelates of this Kingdom, met [motu proprio] at Clonmacnoise, 4th December 1649 having removed all difference among us, not entering into the merits of diversities of former opinions, thought good for the removing of all jealousies from our own thoughts, hearts and resolutions, and from others who had relation or who were adherent to the former diversity of opinion, to manifest hereby to the world the said divisions and jealousies grounded thereupon are now forgotten and forgiven among us on all sides as aforesaid. And that all and every one of us, the above Archbishops, Bishops and prelates, are now by the blessing of God as one body united, and that we will, as becometh charity and our pastoral charge, stand all of us as one entire body, for the interest and immunities of the Church, and of every, the Prelates, and Bishops thereof, and for the honour and dignity, estate, right, and possession of all and every the said Archbishops, Bishops, and other Prelates. And we will as one entire and united body, forward by our council, action, and devices, the advancement of his Majesty's rights and the good of this nation in general and in particular occasions according to our power, and that none of us, in any occasion whatsoever concerning the Catholic religion or the good of this Kingdom of Ireland, will in any respect single himself, or be, or seem opposite to the rest of us, but will hold firm and entire in one sense, as aforesaid, hereby detesting the actions, thoughts, and discourses of any that shall renew the least memory of the differences past, or give any ground of future differences among us, and do in the name of Jesus Christ exhort all our flock to the like brotherly affection and union, and to the like detestation of all past differences or jealousies as aforesaid, arising hitherto among them. And we desire that this, our declaration be printed and published in each parish, by command of the respected Ordinaries-ut videant opera vestra bona et glorificent Patrem vestrum qui eoelis est.'

Decrees of the Bishops &c., assembled at Clonmacnoise, 13th December 1649.
We, the Archbishops, Bishops and other Ordinaries and Prelates of the Kingdom of Ireland, having met at Clonmacnoise [proprio motu] the 4th day of December, in the year of our Lord 1649 to consider the best means to unite our flocks for averting God's wrath fallen on this nation, now bleeding under the evils that famine, plague, and war bring after them, for effecting a present union, decreed the ensuing acts:
1. We order and decree as an Act of this Congregation, that all Archbishops and other Ordinaries within the respective dioceses shall enjoin public prayers, fasting, general confessions, and receiving, and other works of piety, to withdraw from this nation God's anger and to render them capable of His mercies.

2.   We order and decree as an Act of this Congregation, that a declaration be issued from us, letting the people know how vain it is for them to expect from the common enemy commanded by Cromwell, by authority from the rebels in England, any assurance of their religion, lives or fortunes.

3.   We order and decree as an Act of this Congregation, that all the pastors and preachers be enjoined to preach unity. And for inducing the people thereunto, to declare unto them the absolute necessity that is for the same, and as the chief means to preserve the nation against the extirpation and destruction of their religion and fortunes resolved on by the Enemy. And we hereby do manifest our detestation against all such divisions between either provinces or families, or between old English and old Irish, or any of the English or Scots adhering to his Majesty. And we decree and order, that all ecclesiastical persons fomenting such dissensions or unnatural divisions be punished by their respective prelates and superiors juxta gravitatem excessus, et (si opus furrit) suspendantur beneficiati et pastores a beneficio et officio ad certum tempus, religiosi autem a divinis juxta circumstantias delicti. Leaving the laity offending in this kind to be corrected by the civil Magistrate by imprisonment, fine, banishment, or otherwise as to them shall seem best for plucking by the roots so odious a crime; the execution whereof we most earnestly recommend to all those having power and that are concerned therein, as they will answer to God for the evils that thereout may ensue.

4.   We decree and declare excommunicated those highway robbers commonly called the Idle Boys, that take away the goods of honest men or force men to pay them contribution; and we likewise declare excommunicated all such as succour or harbour them, or bestow or sell any victualling, or buy cattle or any other thing wittingly from them; likewise all ecclesiastical persons ministering sacraments to such robbers or Idle Boys, or burying them in holy grave, to be suspended ab officio et beneficio si quod habent, by their respective superiors. This our decree is to oblige within fifteen days after the publication thereof in the respective dioceses.'[4]

Appendix No. 6.4

A declaration of the Lord Lieutenant of Ireland, for the Undeceiving of Deluded and Seduced People: which may be satisfactory to all who do not shut willfully their eyes against the light: In answer to certain late Declarations and Acts framed by the Irish Popish Prelates and Clergy in a Conventicle at Clonmacnoise.

Having lately perused a book printed at Kilkenny in the year 1649, containing divers Declarations and Acts of the Popish Prelates and Clergy framed in a late Conventicle at Clonmacnoise the 4th day of December, in the year aforesaid, I thought fit to give a brief answer unto the same.

And first to the first; which is a Declaration wherein (having premised the reconciliation of some differences among themselves), they come to state their War, upon the interest of their Church, of his Majesty and the Nation, and their resolution to prosecute the same with unity. All which will deserve a particular survey.

The meeting of the Archbishops, Bishops and other Prelates at Clonmacnoise is by them said to be 'proprio motu.' By which term they would have the world believe that the secular power hath nothing to do to appoint or superintend their spiritual conventions (as they call them) although in the said meetings they take upon them to intermeddle in all secular affairs; as by the sequel appears.

And first for their union they so much boast of. If any wise man should seriously consider what they pretend the grounds of the differences to have been, and the way and course they have taken to reconcile the same; and their expressions thereabout, and the ends for which, and their resolutions how to carry on their great design declared for; he must needs think slightly of it. And also for this, that they resolve all other men's consents into their own, without consulting them at all.

The subject of this reconciliation was (as they say) the Clergy and Laity. The discontent and the division itself was grounded on the late difference of opinion, happening amongst the prelates and laity, I wonder not at differences in opinion, discontents and divisions, where so Antichristian and dividing a term as Clergy and Laity is given and received; a term unknown to any save the Antichristian Church, and such as derive themselves from her, 'ab initio non fuit sic'. The most pure and primitive times, as they best knew what true Union was, so in all addresses to the several Churches they wrote unto, not one word of this. The members of the Churches are styled Brethren and Saints of the same household of Faith, although they had orders and distinctions amongst them for the administration of ordinances (of a far different use and character with yours), yet it nowhere occasioned them to say, 'contemptim', and by way of lessening in contra distinguishing Laity to Clergy. It was your pride that begat this expression, and it is for filthy lucre's sake that you keep it up, that by making the people believe that they are not so holy as yourselves, they might for the penny purchase some sanctity from you and that you might bridle, saddle and ride them at your pleasure; and do (which is most true of you) as the Scribes and Pharisees of old did (by their Laity), keep the knowledge of the Law from them, and then be able in their pride to say 'this people that know not the Law are cursed'.

And no wonder (to speak more nearly to your differences and union) if it lie in the Prelate power to make the Clergy and the Laity go together by the ears when they please, but that they may as easily make a simple and senseless reconciliation which will last until the next Nuncio comes from Rome with supermandatory advices; and then this Gordian knot must be cut, and the poor Laity forced to dance a new tune. I say not this as being troubled at it; much good may do you with it, By the grace of God, we fear not we care not for your union. Your covenant is with death and Hell, your union is like that of Simeon and Levi. Associate yourselves, and you shall be broken in pieces; take council together, and it shall come to naught. For thought it becomes us to be humble in respect of ourselves, yet we can say to you, God is not with you. You say your union is against a common enemy; and to this, if you will be talking of union, I will give you some wormwood to bite on, by which it will appear God is not with you.

Who is it that created the common enemy? I suppose you mean Englishmen. The English! Remember ye hypocrites, Ireland was once united to England. Englishmen had good inheritances which many of them purchased with their money; they or their ancestors, from many of you and your ancestors. They had good leases from Irishmen for a long time to come; great stocks thereupon; houses and plantations erected and their cost and charge. They lived peaceably and honestly amongst you. You had generally equal benefit of the protection of England with them, and equal justice from the laws, saving what was necessary for the State (out of reasons of State) to put upon some few people apt to rebel upon the instigation of such as you. You broke this union. You, unprovoked, put the English to the most unheard-of and most barbarous massacre (without respect of sex or age) that ever the sun beheld. And at a time when Ireland was in perfect peace, and when through the example of the English industry, through commerce and traffic, that which was in the natives' hands was better to them than if all Ireland had been in their possession and not an Englishman in it. And yet, then I say, was this unheard-of villainy perpetrated by your instigation, who boast of peacemaking and union against this common enemy. What think you by this time, is not my assertion true? Is God, will God be with you? I am confident He will not!

And though you would comprehend old English, new English, Scotch, or who else you will, in the bosom of your Catholic charity, yet shall not this save you from breaking. I tell you and them, you will fare the worse for their sakes, because I cannot but believe some of them go against, some stifle their consciences. And it is not the figleaf of pretence that they fight for their King, will serve their turn, when really they fight in protection of men of so much prodigious blood; and with men who have declared the ground of their union and fighting (as you have stated in your Declaration) to be 'Bellum Prelaticum et Religiosum', in the first and primary intention of it; especially when they shall consider your principles: That, except what fear makes you comply with – viz. That alone without their concurrence you are not able to carry on your work-you are ready, whenever you shall get the power into your hands, to kick them off too, as some late experiences have sufficiently manifested. And, thus we come to the design, you being thus wholesomely united intended to be prosecuted by you.

Your words are these: 'That all and every of us, the above Archbishops, Bishops and Prelates, are now by the blessing of God, as one body united. And that we will as becometh charity and our pastoral charge, stand all of us as one entire body for the interests and immunities of the Church, and of every the Prelates and Bishops thereof; and for the honour, dignity, estate, right and possessions of all and every of the said Archbishops, Bishops and other Prelates. And we will as one entire and united body, forward by our councils, actions, and devices, the advancements of his Majesty's rights, and the good of this nation in general, and in particular occasions to our power. And that none of us, in any occasion whatsoever concerning the Catholic religion, or the good of this Kingdom of Ireland, will in any respect single himself, or be or seem opposite to the rest of us, but will hold firm and entire in one sense, as aforesaid &c'.

And if there were no other quarrel against you but this, which you make to be the principle and the first ground of your quarrel:- to wit, as so standing for the rights of your Church (falsely so called) and for the rights of your Archbishops, Bishops and Prelates, as to engage people and nations into blood therefor. This alone would be your confusion. I ask you, is it for the Lay-fee (as you call it), or revenue belonging to your Church, that you will after this manner contend? Or is it your jurisdiction, or the exercise of your ecclesiastical authority? Or is it the Faith of your Church? Let me tell you, not for all or any of these is it lawful for the ministers of Christ, as you would be thought to be, thus to contend. And therefore we will consider them apart.

For the first, if it were St. Peter's Patrimony, as you term it that is somewhat that you lawfully came by, although I must tell you, your predecessors cheated poor seduced men in their weakness on their deathbeds; or otherwise unlawfully came by most of this you pretend to. Yet Peter, Though he was somewhat too forward to draw the sword in a better cause, if that weapon, not being proper to the business in hand, was to be put up in that case, he must not, nor would he, have drawn it in this. And that blessed Apostle Paul, who said the labourer was worthy of his hire, chose rather to make tents than be burdensome to the Churches. I would you had either of those men's spirits on the conditions your revenues were doubled to what the best times ever made them to your predecessors.

The same answer may be given to that of your power and jurisdiction, and to that preeminency of prelacy you so dearly love. Only consider what the Master of the same Apostles said to them; 'So it shall not be amongst you. Whoever will be chief will be servant of all!'.For he himself came not to be ministered unto, but to minister. And by this he that runs may read of what tribe you are. And surely, if these, that are outward things, may not thus be contended for: how much less may the doctrines of Faith (which are the works of Grace and the Spirit) be endeavoured by unsuitable means! He that bids us contend for the Faith once delivered to the Saints tells us that we should do it by avoiding the spirit of Cain, Corah, and Balaam; and by building up ourselves on the most holy Faith, not pinning it upon other men's sleeves, praying in the holy Ghost, not mumbling over Matins; keeping ourselves in the love of God, not destroying men because they will not be of our Faith; waiting for the mercy of Jesus Christ; not cruel, but merciful! But, alas, why is this said? Why are these pearls cast before you? You are resolved not to be changed from using the instrument of a foolish shepherd! *You are a part of Anti-Christ, whose Kingdom the Scripture so expressly speaks should be laid in blood; yea in the blood of the Saints. You have shed great store of it already, and ere it be long, you must, all of you have blood to drink; even the dregs of the cup of the fury and the wrath of God, which will be poured out unto you!*

In the next place, you state the interest of his Majesty, as you say. And this you hope will draw some English and Scots to your party. But what Majesty is it you mean? Is it France or Spain or Scotland? Speak plainly! You have, some of you lately been harping (or else we are misinformed) upon his Majesty of Spain to be your Protector. Was it because his Majesty of Scotland is too little a Majesty for your purpose? We know you love great Majesties. Or is it because he is not fully come over to you in point of religion? If he be short in that, you will quickly find out upon that score, another Majesty. His Father who complied with you too much, you rejected; and now would make the world believe you would make the Son's interest a great part of the state of your quarrel. How can we but think there is some reserve in this, and that the son is agreed to do somewhat more for you than ever his Father did. Or else tell us whence this new zeal is? That the Father did too much for you, in all Protestant's judgements instead of many instances let be considered what one of your own doctors, Dr. Enos of Dublin, who (writing against the agreement made between the Lord of Ormond and the Irish Catholics) finds fault with it, and says that it was nothing so good as the Earl of Glamorgan had warrant from the King to make; But exceeding far short of what the Lord George Digby had warrant to agree with the Pope himself at Rome in favour of the Irish Catholics.

I intend not this to you; but to such Protestants as may incline to you, and join with you upon this single account, which is the only appearing inducement to them, seeing there is no such probability of ill in this abstracted; and so much certainty of ill in fighting for the Romish religion against the Protestant; and fighting with men under the guilt of so horrid a massacre. From participating in which guilt, whilst they take part with them they will never be able to assoil themselves, either before God or good men.

In the last place you are pleased, having after your usual manner remembered yourselves first, and his Majesty (as you call him), next; like a man of your tribe with his 'Ego et Rex meus', you are pleased to take the people into consideration, lest they should seem to be forgotten; or rather you might make me believe they are much in your thoughts. Indeed I think they are! *Alas poor Laity! That you and your King might ride them, and jade them, as your Church hath done, and as your King hath done by your means, almost all ages.* But it would not be hard to prophesy, that the beasts being stung and kicking, this world will not last always. Arbitrary power men begin to weary of, in Kings and Churchmen; their juggle between them mutually to uphold civil and ecclesiastical tyranny begins to be transparent. Some have cast off both and hope by the grace of God to keep so. Others are at it! Many thoughts are laid up about it, which will have their issue and vent. This principle, that people are for Kings and Churches, and Saints for the Pope and Churchmen (as you call them) , begins to be exploded; and therefore I wonder not to see the fraternity to be so much enraged. I wish the people wiser than to be troubled at you, or solicitous for what you say or do.

But it seems, notwithstanding all this, you would feign have them believe it is their good you seek. And to cozen them, in deed and in truth, is the scope of your whole Declaration, and of your acts and decrees, in your aforesaid printed book. Therefore to discover and unveil those falsities, and to let them know what they are to trust from me, is the principle end of this my Declaration. That if I be not able to do good upon them, which I most desire (and yet in that I shall not seek to gain them by flattery; but tell them the worst, in plainness, and that which I am sure will not be acceptable to you; and if I cannot gain them), I shall have comfort in this, that I have freed my own soul from the guilt of the evil that shall ensue. And upon this subject I hope to leave nothing unanswered in all your said Declarations and Decrees at Clonmacnoise.

And because you carry on your matter somewhat confusedly, I shall therefore bring all that you have said into some order, that so we may the better discern what everything signifies, and give some answer thereunto.

You forewarn the people of their danger; which you make to consist; First, in the extirpation of the Catholic religion; secondly in the destruction of their lives; Thirdly in the ruin of their fortunes. To avoid all which evils you forewarn them: First that they be not deceived by the Commander-in-Chief of the Parliament Forces: and in the next place (having stated [the ground of] your war as aforesaid), you give them your positive advice and councel to engage in blood; and lastly bestow on them a small collation in four ecclesiastical Decrees or Orders, which will signify as little, being performed by your spirit, as if you had said nothing. And the obligation to all this you make to be your pastoral relation to them, over your flocks.

To which last a word or two. I wonder how this relation was brought about? If they be flocks, and you ambitious of the relative term, you are pastors: but it is by an antiphrasis – 'a minime pascendo!' You either teach them not at all, or else you do it, as some of you came to this conventicle who were sent by others, 'tanguam Procuratores', or as your manner is, by sending a company of silly ignorant priests who can but say the mass, and scarcely that intelligibly ; or with such stuff as these your senseless Declarations and edicts! – But how dare you assume to call these men your flocks, who you have plunged into so horrid a rebellion, by which you have made both them and the country almost a ruinous heap, and whom you have fleeced and polled and peeled hitherto, and make it your business to do so still. You cannot feed them! You poison them with your false abominable and antichristian doctrine and practices. You keep the word of God from them and instead thereof give them your senseless orders and traditions. You teach them implicit belief; he that goes amongst them may find many that do not understand anything in the matters of religion. I have had few better answers from any since I came into Ireland, that are of your flocks than this, that indeed they did not trouble themselves about matters of religion but left that to the Church. Thus are your flocks fed; and such credit have you of them. But they must take heed of losing their religion. Alas poor creatures, what have they to lose?

Concerning this, is your grand caveat; and to back this, you tell them of Resolutions and Covenants to extirpate the Catholic Religion out of all his Majesty's dominions. And you instance in Cromwell's letter of the 19 of October 1649, to the then Governor of Ross, repeating his words which are as followeth, viz- 'For that which you mention concerning liberty of religion, I meddle not with any man's conscience. But if by liberty of conscience you mean, a liberty to exercise the Mass, I judge it best to use plain dealing, and to let you know where the Parliament of England have power, that will not be allowed of'. And this you call a tyrannical resolution; which you say hath been put in execution in Wexford, Ross and Drogheda.

Now let us consider. First you say that the design is to extirpate the Catholic Religion. Let us see your honesty herein. Your word extirpate is as ill collected from these grounds, and as senseless as the word Catholic, ordinarily used by you when you mention Catholic Roman Church. The word extirpate supposes a thing to be already rooted and established which word made good by the proof of Covenants, your letter which expressed the non-toleration of the Mass wherein, it seems you place all the Catholic Religion (and therein you show some ingenuity) and [by] your instance of what was practised in the three towns aforementioned. Do these prove either considered apart or all together, the extirpation of the Catholic Religion?

By what law was the mass exercised in these places, or in any dominions of England or Ireland, or Kingdom of Scotland? You were intruders, you were herein open violators of the known laws! And yet you will call the Covenant, that in the letter, and these practices, extirpations of the Catholic Religion, thus again set on foot by you, by the advantage of your rebellion, and shaking-off the just authority of the State of England over you. Whereas I dare be confident to say, you durst not own the saying of one mass above these eighty years in Ireland. And through the troubles you made, and the miseries you brought on this nation and the poor people thereof (your numbers which is very ominous, increasing with the wolves through the desolations you made in the Country); you recovered again the public exercises of your mass! And for the maintenance of this, thus gained, you would make the poor people believe that it is ghostly counsel, and given in love to them as your flocks, that they should run into war, and venture lives, and all upon such a ground as this! But if God be pleased to unveil you of your sheep's clothing, that they may see how they have been deluded and by whom I shall exceedingly rejoice; and indeed for their sakes only have I given you these competent characters (if God shall so bless it) for their good.

And now for them, I do particularly declare what they may expect at my hands in this point; wherein you may easily perceive that, as I neither have nor shall flatter you, so shall I neither go about to delude them with specious prentences as you have ever done.

First, therefore, I shall not, where I have the power and the Lord is pleased to bless me, suffer the exercise of the Mass where I can take notice of it, nor suffer you that are Papists, where I can find you seducing the People, or by an overt act violating the Laws established; but if you come into my hands, I shall cause to be inflicted the punishments appointed by the laws (to use your own terms) 'secundum gravitatem delicti', upon you; and to reduce things to their former state on this behalf. *As for the people, what thoughts they have in matters of religion in their own breasts I cannot reach; but think it my duty, if they walk honestly and peaceably not to cause them in the least to suffer for the same, but shall endeavour to walk patiently and in love towards them, to see if at any time it shall please God to give them another or a better mind.* And all men under the power of England, within this dominion, are hereby required and enjoined strictly and religiously to do the same.

To the second, which is the destruction of the lives of the Inhabitants of this Nation to make it good that this is designed, they give not one reason. Which is either that they have none to give, or else for that they believe the People will receive everything for truth they say, which they have too well taught them, and God knows the people are too apt, to do. But I will a little help them. They speak indeed of rooting out the Commons; and also by way of consequent, that the extirpating the Catholic Religion is not to be effected without the massacring, destroying or banishing the Catholic Inhabitants. Which how an illogical argument this is, I shall easily make appear by and by.

Alas the generality of the Inhabitants are poor Laity (as you call them) and ignorant of the grounds of the Catholic Religion. Are these then so interwoven with your Church Interest as that the absence of them makes your Catholic Religion fall to the ground? We know you think not so. You reckon yourselves (and yourselves only) the pillars and supporters thereof; and these as far as they have the exercise of club-law, and, like the ass you ride on, obey your commands. But concerning these [in?]relation of your Religion, enough has been spoken in another place, only you love to mix things for your advantage.

But to your logic, here is your argument. The design is to extirpate the Catholic religion. But this is not to be done by the massacring, banishing or otherwise destroying the Catholic inhabitants; ergo it is designed to massacre, banish and destroy the Catholic inhabitants. To prove this no-concluding argument, (but yet well enough agreeing with your learning), I give you this dilemma, by which it will appear That ,whether your religion be true or false, this will not follow:

If your religion be the true religion, yet if a nation may degenerate from the true religion, and apostatise (as too many have done) through the seducements of your Roman Church, then it will not follow that men must be massacred, banished or otherwise destroyed, necessarily, no, not as to the change of the true religion in a nation or country! Only, this argument doth wonderfully well agree with your principles and practice; *you have chiefly made use of fire and sword, in all the changes of religion that you have made in the world.* If it be change of your Catholic religion so-called, it will not follow: because there may be found another means than massacring, destruction and banishment; to wit the Word of God, which is able to convert (a means that you as little know as practise, which indeed you deprive the people of) together with humanity, good life, equal and honest dealing with men of different opinion, which we desire to exercise towards this poor people, (if you by your wicked counsel, make them not incapable to receive it, by putting them into blood).

And therefore by this also your false and twisted dealing may be a little discovered. *But well; your words are, 'massacre, destroy and banish'. Good now: give us an instance of one man, since my coming into Ireland, not in arms, massacred, destroyed or banished, concerning the two first of which justice hath not been done, or endeavoured to be done.* But for the other of banishment, I must speak unto the People whom you would delude, and whom this most concerns that they may know in this also what to expect at my hands.

The question is of the destruction of life, or of that which is but little inferior to it, to wit, banishment. *I shall not willingly take or suffer to be taken away, the life of any man not in arms,* but by the trial to which the people of this nation are subject by law, for offences against the same. *And for the banishment, it hath not hitherto been inflicted on any but such who, being in arms, upon the terms they were taken might justly have been put to death* – as those instanced in their Declaration to be sent to the Tobacco Islands. And therefore I do declare, that if the people be ready to run to arms by the instigation of their clergy or otherwise, such as God by his providence shall give into my hands may expect that or worst measure, from me, but not otherwise.

Thirdly, to that of the ruin of their fortune. You instance in the Act of Subscription, whereby the estates of the inhabitants of this nation are sold, so as there remaineth now no more but to put the purchasers in possession, and that for this cause are the forces drawn out of England. And that you might carry the interest far, to engage the common sort of people with you, you further say to them, that the moderate usage exercised to them, is to no other end but to our private advantage, and for the better support of our army, intending at the close of our conquest (as you term it) to root out the commons also, and to plant the land with colonies to be brought hither out of England. This consisting of divers parts will ask distinct answers.

And first, to the act of Subscription. It's true there is such an Act, and it was a just one. For when by your execrable massacre and rebellion, you had not only raised a bloody war to justify the same, and thereby occasioned the exhausting of the treasure of England in the prosecution of so just a war against you – was it not a wise and just Act in the State to raise money by escheating the lands of those who had a hand in the rebellion? Was it not fit to make their estates to defray the charge, who had caused the trouble? The best therefore that lies in this argument is this *(and that only reaching to them who have been in arms, for further it goes not);* you have forfeited your estate, and it is likely that they will be escheated to make satisfaction, and therefore you had better fight it out than repent, or give off now, or see what mercy you might find from the State of England. And seeing Holy Church is engaged in it, we will, by one means or another, hook-in the commons, and make them sensible that they are as much concerned as you, though they were never in arms, or came quickly off. And for this cause doubtless are these two coupled together, by which your honest dealing is manifest enough.

But what? Was the English army brought over for this purpose, as you allege? Do you think that the State of England will be at five or six millions charge merely to procure purchasers to be invested in that for which they did disburse little above a quarter of a million? Although there be a justice in that also, which ought, and I trust will be seasonably performed to them. – *No I can give you a better reason for the army's coming over than this. England hath had experience of the blessing of God in prosecuting just and righteous causes, whatever the cost and hazard be. And if ever men were engaged in a righteous cause in the world, this will be scarce a second to it. We are come to ask an account of the innocent blood that hath been shed; and to endeavour to bring them to an account (by the blessing and presence of the Almighty, in whom alone is our hope and strength), who by appearing in arms seek to justify the same. We are come to break the power of a company of lawless rebels, who having cast off the authority of England, live as enemies to human society, whose principles (the world hath experience of) are, to destroy and subjugate all men not complying with them. We come (by the assistance of God) to hold forth and maintain the lustre and glory of English liberty in a nation where we have an undoubted right to it; – wherein the people of Ireland (if they listen not to such seducers as you are) may equally participate in all benefits, to use liberty and fortune equally with Englishmen if they keep out of arms.*

And therefore, having said this to you, I have a word to them, that in this point, which concerns them in their estates and fortunes, they may know what to trust to. Such as have been formerly and are not now in arms, may (submitting themselves) have their cases presented to the State of England, where no doubt the State will be ready to take into consideration the nature and quality of their actings, and deal mercifully with them. For those that are now in arms, and shall come in, and submit, and give engagements for their future quiet and honest carriage, and submission to the State of England, I doubt not but that they will find like merciful consideration; – excepting only the leading persons and principle contrivers of this rebellion, whom I am confident they will reserve to make examples of justice, whatsoever hazards they incur thereby. – And for such private soldiers as lay down their arms, and shall live peaceably and honestly at their several homes, they shall be permitted so to do. – And for the first two sorts, I shall humbly and effectually represent their cases to the Parliament, as far as becomes the duty and place I bear. But as for those who, notwithstanding all this, persist and continue in arms, they must expect what the providence of God (in that which is falsely called the chance of war) will cast upon them.

For such of the nobility, gentry and commons of Ireland as have not been actors in this rebellion, that they shall and may expect the protection in their goods, liberties and lives which the law gives them; and in their husbandry, merchandising, manufactures and other trading whatsoever, the same. They behaving themselves as becomes honest and peaceable men, testifying their good affections, upon all occasions, to the service of the State of England, equal justice shall be done them with the English. They shall bear proportionably with them in taxes. And if the soldiery be insolent upon them, upon complaint and proof, it shall be punished with utmost severity, and they protected equally with Englishmen.

And having said this and purposing honestly to perform it, if this people shall headily run on after the counsels of their Prelates and Clergy and other leaders, I hope to be free from the misery and desolation, blood and ruin, that shall befall them, and shall rejoice to exercise utmost severity against them.

O. Cromwell.[5]

[Author's emphasis]

Notes to Appendix 6

1   From *Calender of State Papers Domestic*, (1649-50), p. 390, quoted in Abbott, *Writings and Speeches*, p. 152; also in Murphy, *Cromwell in Ireland*, p. 190.

2   In Gilbert, *Contemporary History*, vol. II, p. 238; also in Abbott, *Writings and Speeches*, vol. II, pp. 158–59; also Murphy, *Cromwell in Ireland*, pp. 205–06.

3   Ibid. Appendix viii, pp. 406–407.

4   Ibid. Appendix viii, pp 409–410.

5   *Declaration &c. Licensed by the Secretary of the Army, Printed at Cork; and now reprinted at London, by E. Griffin, and are to be sold in the Old Baily*, 21 March 1650; reproduced from Abbott, *Writings and Speeches*, vol, II, pp. 196–205. Also in Murphy, *Cromwell in Ireland*, appendix IX, pp. 411–23.

Appendix No. 7

Seeing now that all is calm in Ulster and gone to their quarters and that the Ulster is returned from the Lord-Lieutenant from Leinster let us see what is doing there and in Munster. As for the latter it seems that most of them of the English is revolted from the Lord-Lieutenant and the Lord Inchiquin, and joined with Cromwell's party, and headed by the Lord Broghill (afterwards made Earl of Orrery by the King at his restoration), and surrendered their garrisons to Cromwell's disposing. On which the Lord-Lieutenant commanded Major-General Hugh Duff O'Neill with an Ulster regiment, of which one Tirlagh Oge O'Neill Mac Henry of the Fews was Colonel, and about one hundred horse under the command of Colonel Fennell to go and garrison in Clonmell, a considerable place then as affairs stood, and it was much feared that Cromwell had a design upon it – which commands were accomplished by Hugh Duff O'Neill. Then Cromwell hearing that the Lord-Lieutenant's forces were dispersed, took his opportunity of taking towns and castles without any great opposition, and sent two or three regiments of horse and foot before him to block up Clonmel at a distance which was done a month before he himself appeared before it, who, as soon as he came, drew close to it and then sent his summons to Hugh Duff to surrender it on good quarters and conditions.

To which answer was made, that he was of another resolution than to give up the town on quarters or conditions, till he was reduced to a lower station, and so wished him to do his best. On which Cromwell fell to his work and planted his cannons at which time and before several resolute sallies were made out, and sometimes with good success and sometimes not. At this play they were like sons of Mars, till along breach was made near one of the gates but proved not level enough till night fell.

Within two hours after the Major-General O'Neill sent out two hundred chosen men and officers, with a good guide, through byways from a place of the wall next the river that was neglected by the besiegers, and fell on the backs of those in a fort not fully finished, behind them and cut them all off before any relief came; on which immediately the next gate was opened for them and they got in safe with the loss of half a dozen. The number killed in the fort was about sixty, being one of their companies.

After this Hugh Duff did set all men and maids to work, townsmen and soldiers, only those on duty attending the breach and the walls – to draw dunghills, mortar, stones and timber, and made a long lane a man's height and about eighty yards length on both sides up from the breach, with afoot bank at the back of it; and caused to be placed engines on both of the same, and two guns at the end of it, invisible opposite to the breach, and so ordered all things against a storm.

Which storm was about eight o clock in the morning in the month of May and the English entered without any opposition; and but few were to be seen in the town till they so entered, and the lane was crammed full of horsemen armed with helmets, back breast swords, musquetoons and pistols. On which those in the front seeing themselves in a pound, and could not make their way further, cried out, 'Halt! Halt!' On which those entering behind at the breach thought by those words that they were all running away, and cried out 'Advance! Advance!' as fast as those before them, till that pound or lane was full and could hold no more.

Then suddenly rushes a resolute party of pike men and musqueteers to the breach, and scoured off and knocked back those entering. At which instance Hugh Duff's men within fell on those in the pound with shots, pikes, scythes, stones, and casting off great long pieces of timber with the engines amongst them, and then two guns firing at them from the end of the pound, slaughtering them by the middle or knees, with chained bullets, that in less than an hour's time about a thousand men were killed in that pound, being a top one another.

At this time Cromwell was on horseback at the gate, with his guard, expecting the gates to be opened by those who had entered, until he saw those in the breach beaten back and heard the cannons going off within. Then he fell off as much vexed as ever he was since he first put on a helmet against the King, for such a repulse he did not usually meet with.

The siege, at a distance and close, being about five or six weeks, and by the several sallies out and on the walls, several of those within were lost, but many wounded and sick, on which the Major-general consulted with his officers and seeing that their ammunition was gone, concluded to leave the town without Cromwell's leave, and so at nightfall he imported the same to the Mayor, one Whyte, and advised him after he was gone about half a dozen miles off as he might guess, to send privately out to Cromwell for licence to speak to him about conditions for the town; but not to make mention of himself on any account till he had done. After which advice to the Mayor he marched away with his men about two hours after nightfall and passed over the river undiscovered by a guard of horse that lay at the other side of the bridge, and he made no great halt till he reached to a town called Ballynasack, twelve miles from Clonmell, where he refreshed his men and then marched to Limerick [recte Waterford].

Then the Mayor according as he was advised about twelve o clock at night sent out to Cromwell very privately for a conduct to wait upon his Excellency; which forthwith was sent to him, and an officer to conduct him from the wall to Cromwell's tent, who after some coarse compliments was not long capitulating, when he got good conditions for the town, such in a manner as they desired.

After which Cromwell asked him if Hugh O'Neill knew of his coming out, to which he answered he did not, for that he was gone two hours after night fell with all his men, at which Cromwell stared and frowned at him and said 'You knave you have served me so and did not tell me so before'. To which the Mayor replied if his Excellency had demanded the question, he would tell him. Then he asked him what that Hugh Duff O Neill was; to which the Mayor answered that he was an oversea soldier, born in Spain; on which Cromwell said; 'God Damn you and your oversea!' and desired the Mayor to give the paper back again. To which the other answered that he hoped his Excellency would not break his conditions, or take them from him, which was not the repute his Excellency had, but to perform whatsoever he had promised. On which Cromwell was somewhat calm, but said in a fury 'By God above he would follow that Hugh Duff O'Neill wheresoever he went'.

Then the Mayor delivered the keys of the gates to Cromwell who immediately commanded guards on them and next morning himself entered where he saw his men who had been killed in the pound, notwithstanding which and his fury that Hugh Duff went off as he did, he kept his conditions with the town.

This relation I had not only from some officers and soldiers of the besiegers, but also from the besieged, and that certainly Cromwell lost at the siege and the storm about fifteen hundred men, being more than he lost by all the towns he stormed and took over before and since he came to Ireland.

At this siege Cromwell was sent for by the Parliament of England to repair to them with all haste, to be General of an army to be raised to go into Scotland, hearing that the King was come, or to come thither, and so he stayed no longer than to get Clonmell.[1]

Notes to Appendix 7

1   Quoted in full in Abbott, *Writings and Speeches*, vol. II, pp. 140–43; and in part in Hore, *History of the Town and County of Wexford*, pp. 294–95.

BIBLIOGRAPHY

Abbott, Wilbur Cortez. *The Writings and Speeches of Oliver Cromwell*, 4 vols. Oxford: Clarendon Press, 1988 edn.

Abbott, Wilbur, Cortez. *A Bibliography of Oliver Cromwell*, Cambridge Mass: 1929.

Adair, John. *By the Sword Divided, Eyewitness Accounts of the English Civil War*. Stroud: Sutton Publishing, 1998.

Ashley, Maurice. *The Greatness of Oliver Cromwell*, London: Hodder & Stoughton, 1957.

Ashley, Maurice. *Oliver Cromwell and his World*, London: Hodder & Stoughton, 1972.

Bagwell, R. *Ireland under the Stuarts*, 3 vols. London: The Holland Press, 1909.

Barnard, Toby. *The English Republic, 1649–1660. Seminar Studies in History*, 2nd edition. London: Longman, 1997.

Beckett, J.C. *The Making of Modern Ireland, 1603–1923*. London: Faber & Faber Ltd., 1967.

Beckett, J.C. *The Cavalier Duke, A Life of James Butler — 1st Duke of Ormonde*, Belfast: Pretani Press, 1990.

Belloc, Hilaire. *Cromwell*, London: Cassell & Co, 1934.

Berrisford-Ellis, Peter. *Hell or Connaught, The Cromwellian Colonisation of Ireland 1652–1660*. Belfast: The Blackstaff Press, 1975.

Bradley, John. *Drogheda, Its Topography and Medieval Layout*. Drogheda: The Old Drogheda Society Publications Committee, 1997.

Black, Jeremy. *History of the British Isles*. Basingstoke: MacMillan, 1996.

Blackmore, David. *Arms and Armour of the English Civil Wars*. London: The Trustees of the Royal Armouries, 1990.

Broderick, David. *An Early Toll Road, The Dublin-Dunleer Turnpike, 1731–1855*. Dublin: Irish Academic Press, 1996.

Broome, John. *Cromwell — A Vindication*. Leicester: The Gospel Standard Baptist Trust, 1969.

Browne, Kathleen A. *Was Cromwell betrayed to Wexford?* Rathronan Castle: K. Browne, 1940.

Buckley, Victor, and Sweetman P.D. *Archaeological Survey of County Louth*. Dublin: Stationery Office, 1991.

Burke, James. 'The New Model Army and the Problems of Siege Warfare 1648–1651'. *Irish Historical Studies*, vol. XXXVII, no. 105, May 1990.

Burke, The Very Rev. William P. *History of Clonmel*. Waterford: Clonmel Library Committee, 1907.

Butler, W.F. 'Some Episodes of the Civil War', County Louth Archeological and Historical Journal, vol. IV, no. 4. 1919.

Byrd, Michael. 'Oliver Cromwell: A Personal Biography', *Cromwelliana*, Journal of the Cromwell Association. 1997.

Carlyle, Thomas. *The Letters and Speeches of Oliver Cromwell With Elucidations*. Edited by S.C. Lomas, Vol. I, London: Methuen & Co, London, 1904.

Carty, James. *Ireland From the Flight of the Earls to Grattan's Parliament (1607–1782)*. Dublin: Fallon, 1949.

Clarendon, Edward Earl of. *Clarendon's History of the Rebellion in Seven Volumes, The History of the Rebellion and Civil Wars in England Together With an Historical View of the Affairs in Ireland by Edward Earl of Clarendon. To which are subjoined The notes of Bishop Warburton*. Oxford: Clarendon Press, 1849.

Clonmel Tercentenary Committee. *Tercentenary of The Siege of Clonmel*. Clonmel: Clonmel Tercentenary Committee, 1950.

Colfer, Billy. 'Medieval Wexford', *Journal of The Wexford Historical Society, 1990–1991*. Wexford: The Wexford Historical Society, 1990–91.

Collins, M.E. *Conquest and Colonisation, A History of Ireland*. Edited by Margaret Mac-Curtain. Dublin: Gill and MacMillan, 1969.

Cogan, Rev. Anthony. *The Diocese of Meath-Ancient and Modern*. Dublin: Joseph Dollard, 1867.

Conlon, Patrick, OFM. *The Franciscans in Drogheda*. Drogheda: The Franciscan Friary, 1987.

Corcoran, Moira. 'The Streets and Lanes of Drogheda — Part 2'. *Journal of the Old Drogheda Society*, no. 3. 1978–79.

Coward, Barry. *Profiles in Power – Oliver Cromwell*. London: Longman Group, 1992.

Cusack, Mary Frances. *An Illustrated History of Ireland*. London: Bracken Books, 1997.

Cromwell, Thomas. *Oliver Cromwell and His Times*. 2nd edn., London: Sherwood, Neely & Jones, 1822.

D'Alton, John. *History of Drogheda*, vols. I & II. Dublin: M.H. Gill & Son, 1844; re-issued Drogheda: Buvinda, 1997.

Daniell, David Scott. *Battles and Battlefields*. London: Hamlym Publishing Group, 1961.

Davidson, Dr. C.H. 'The Diagnosis of Oliver Cromwell's Fatal Illness', *Cromwelliana*, Journal of The Cromwell Association. 1993.

Esson, D.M.R. *The Curse of Cromwell, A History of the Ironside Conquest of Ireland 1649–1653*. London: Leo Cooper, Ltd., 1971.

Firth, C.H. *Cromwell's Army*, London: Methuen & Co., 1967.

Foster, Roy. *Modern Ireland 1600–1972*, London: Penguin, 1989.

Fraser, Antonia. *Cromwell, Our Chief of Men*. London: Weidenfeld & Nicholson, 1973; London: Mandarin: 1994.

Gardiner, Samuel Rawson. *History of the Commonwealth and Protectorate*, vol. I 1649–1650. Reprint Stroud: The Windrush Press, 1988.

Gardiner, Samuel Rawson. *Oliver Cromwell*. Reprint London: Collier Books, 1962.

Gardiner, Samuel Rawson. *Cromwell's Place in History*, Followed on Six Lectures Delivered in the University of Oxford. London: Longmans, Green & Co., 1897.

Garry, James. *The Streets and Lanes of Drogheda*. Drogheda: The Old Drogheda Society, 1996.

Gaunt, Peter. *Oliver Cromwell*. Historical Association Studies, Oxford: Blackwell, 1996.

Gilbert, John T. *A Contemporary History of Affairs in Ireland from A.D. 1641 to 1652*. 3 vols., Dublin: Irish Archaeological and Celtic Society, 1879.

Gogarty, The Rev. Thomas. Council Book of The Drogheda Corporation 1649–1734, vol. I. Dundalk: County Louth Archaeological and Historical Society, 1988.

Gregg, Pauline. *Oliver Cromwell*. London: J.M. Dent & Sons, 1988.

Guizot, M. *Life of Oliver Cromwell*. London: Richard Bentley & Sons, 1877.

Hayward, F.H. *The Unknown Cromwell*. London: George Allen and Unwin Ltd., 1934.

Hewitt, James. *Eyewitness to Ireland in Revolt*. Reading: Osprey Publishing, 1974.

Hibbert, Christopher. *Cavaliers and Roundheads, The English at War 1642–49*. London: Harpur Collins, 1993.

Hill, Christopher. *God's Englishman, Oliver Cromwell and the English Revolution*. London: Penguin Books, 1972.

Hogan, Edmund (ed.). *History of the Warr in Ireland from 1641–1653 by a British Officer in the Regiment of Sir John Clotworthy*. Dublin: McGlashan & Gill, 1873.

Holmes, Reg. *Cromwell's Ely, 1975*. Ely: The Ely Local History Publications Board, 1975.

Hore, Phillip Herbert. *History of the Town and County of Wexford*. London: Elliot Stock, 1906.

Howell, Roger Jr. *Images of Oliver Cromwell*. Essays for and by Roger Howell, Jr. Edited by R.C. Richardson. Manchester: University Press, 1993.

Hughes, Anne. *The History of Drogheda Up to Date*, Drogheda: A. Hughes, 1893.

Johnston, L.C. *History of Drogheda From the Earliest Period to the Present Time*. Drogheda: Kelly Printers. 1826.

Lamont, William. 'Oliver Cromwell and English Calvinism'. *Cromwelliana*, Journal of the Cromwell Association, 1994.

Ludlow, Edmund Esq. *Memoirs of Edmund Ludlow, Esq. Lieutenant General of the Horse, Commander-in-Chief of the Forces in Ireland, One of the Council of State and a Member of the Parliament which began on Nov. 3rd 1640*, 2 vols. Canton of Bern: 1698; also Oxford: C.H. Firth, 1894.

Macken, Walter. *Seek the Fair Land*. London: Pan Books, 1988.

McCullen, John. 'The Elcocks of Drogheda', Journal of the Old Drogheda Society, no. 4, 1983.

McCullen, John. *The Call of St. Mary's*. Drogheda: J. McCullen, 1984.

McElligott, Jason. *Cromwell, Our Chief of Enemies*. Dundalk: Dun Dealgan Press, 1994.

Moody, J.W.; Martin, F.X.; and Byrne, F.J. *A New History of Ireland*. Oxford: Clarendon Press, 1976.

Moody, J.W.; Martin, F.X.; and Byrne, F.J. *A New History of Ireland, A Chronology of Irish History to 1976, A Companion to Irish History, Part I*, vol. VIII. Oxford: Clarendon Press, 1982.

Morrill, John (ed.). *Oliver Cromwell and the English Revolution*. London: Longman, 1990.

Murphy, Rev. Denis S.J., *Cromwell in Ireland, A History of Cromwell's Irish campaign*. Dublin: M.H. Gill & Son, 1883.

Murray, R.H. 'Cromwell At Drogheda — A Reply to J.B. Williams', The Nineteenth Century, vol. LXXII, December 1912.

O'Brien, Marie and Conor Cruise, *A Concise History of Ireland*. London: Thames & Hudson, 1972.

O'Connor, Susan. 'Tudor Drogheda 1504–1603'. Journal of the Old Drogheda Society, no. 10, 1996.

O Duinn, Tomas. 'How Hugh Dubh Stalled Cromwell's Advance'. *The Irish Times*. 26 August, 1982.

Ohlmeyer, Jane H. 'The Dunkirk of Ireland — Wexford Privateers During the 1640s', Journal of The Wexford Historical Society, 1988–89.

O'Sullivan, Harold. *The English Commonwealth Re-Visited-Revision or Revisionism*, Unpublished.

O'Sullivan, Harold. 'Military operations in County Louth in the Run-Up to Cromwell's Storming of Drogheda', County Louth Archaeological and Historical Society Journal, vol. XXII, no. 2. 1990.

O'Sullivan, Harold. 'Women in County Louth in the Seventeenth Century', County Louth Archaeological and Historical Society Journal, vol. XXIII, no. 3. 1995.

O'Sullivan, Harold. 'Cromwell in Drogheda — Cromwell, No Evidence of Drogheda Massacre', *Drogheda Independent*, 1 October 1993.

Pearson, Karl, and Morant G.M. *The Portraiture of Oliver Cromwell With Special Reference to the Wilkinson Head*. Issued by the Biometrika Office, University College London. Cambridge: University Press, 1935.

Perceval-Maxwell, M. *The Outbreak of the Irish Rebellion of 1641*. Dublin: Gill & MacMillan, 1994.

Prendergast, John P. The Cromwellian Settlement of Ireland. London: Constable & Co., 1996.

Reilly, Tom. *Cromwell at Drogheda*. Drogheda: Broin Print Ltd, 1993.

Reilly, Tom. *Tracing Drogheda's Medieval Walls*. Drogheda: Drogheda Monuments Preservation Committee, 1995.

Rice, Rev. Gerard. 'The Five Martyrs of Drogheda', Records of Meath Archaeological and Historical Society, vol. IX, no. 3, 1997.

Rice, Rev. Gerard, 'Cromwell — Was there really a Massacre?' *Drogheda Independent* Supplement *Drogheda 800*, 31 January 1984.

Roots, Ivan (ed.). *Speeches of Oliver Cromwell*. London: J.M. Dent and Sons, 1989.

Russell, C.W., and Prendergast J.P. *The Carte Manuscripts in the Bodleian Library Oxford*. London: H.M.S.O., 1871.

Sherwood, Roy. *The Court of Oliver Cromwell*. Cambridge: Willingham Press 1989.

Sherwood, Roy *Oliver Cromwell — King In All But Name*. Oxford: Clarendon Press, 1997.

Simms, J.G. 'Cromwell at Drogheda 1649'. *The Irish Sword*. 1974.

Smiles, Samuel M.D. *History of Ireland and The Irish People*. London: Wm. Strange, 1844.

Smith, David, L. *Oliver Cromwell — Politics and Religion in the English Revolution, 1640–1658*. Cambridge: University Press, 1991.

Tangye, Sir Richard. *The Two Protectors, Oliver and Richard Cromwell*. London: S.W. Partridge, 1899.

Tong, Raymond. 'The Saga of Cromwell's Head'. *Cromwelliana*, Journal of the Cromwell Association, 1996.

Watson, D.R. *The Life and Times of Charles I*. Introduction by Antonia Fraser. London: Weidenfeld and Nicolson, 1972.

Williams, J.B. 'Fresh Light on Cromwell at Drogheda'. *The Nineteenth Century*, vol. LXXII, September 1912.

Williams, J.B. 'Cromwell's Massacre at Wexford' *Irish Ecclesiastical Record*, series 5, vol. I, June 1913.

Williams, J.B., 'The Truth Concerning the Massacre at Drogheda', *Dublin Review*, vol. CXLVI.

Miscellaneous Publications

Cromwelliana, A Chronological Detail of Events in Which Oliver Cromwell was Engaged from the Year 1642 to his Death 1658, With a Continuation of Other Transactions to the Restoration. Printed for Michael Stace, Middle Scotland Yard, Whitehall, by George Smeeton, St. Martin's Lane, Charing Cross, 1810.

South Tipp Today. 19 July 1995, 2 August 1995, 16 August 1995, 30 August 1995.

The Drogheda Independent. 24 February 1906.

The Drogheda Argus. 21 December 1912.

The Dublin Penny Journal, vol. I, no. 36. March 2, 1833.

Dublin. National Library. *Two Great Fights in Ireland, on Sunday, Monday, Tuesday and Wednesday last [9–12 Sept.] between the Marq. of Ormond's Forces and the Lord Lt. Cromwel's at Tredah and Dundalk.* Manuscript.

The Civil War 1642–51, A Pitkin Guide, 1992.

Guide to the Cromwell Museum Huntingdon. 2nd edition, 1981.

Wexford People Saturday June 21, 1913, Saturday June 14, 1913, November 3 1934, 20 September 1902, 27 September 1902.

B.B.C. Timewatch series. *Faces of Cromwell,* June 1997.

A Seventeenth Century Description of Drogheda. *Journal of The Old Drogheda Society,* no. 3, 1978–79.

McCarthy, Jerimiah F. 'The Evolution of the County of Tipperary', Thesis, date unavailable.

O'Neill, Eoghan. The Siege of Clonmel. Lecture delivered to the Clonmel Historical Society, 1964.

R.G. *A Copy of a letter of an Officer in the Army of Ireland to His Highness, The Lord Protector, Concerning His Changing of the Government,* Contemporary pamphlet, Cromwell Association Library

INDEX